SOMME

LYN MACDONALD

MACMILLAN LONDON

First published in Great Britain 1983 by Michael Joseph Limited

First published in Great Britain in paperback 1984 by
PAPERMAC
a division of Macmillan Publishers Limited
4 Little Essex Street London WC2R 3LF
and Basingstoke

Associated companies in Auckland, Dallas, Delhi,
Dublin, Hong Kong, Johannesburg, Lagos, Manzini,
Melbourne, Nairobi, New York, Singapore, Tokyo,
Washington and Zaria

ISBN 0 333 36648 4

Printed in Hong Kong

This book is dedicated to a single soldier of Kitchener's Army. His name is Legion.

And he asked him, What is thy name? And he answered, saying My name is Legion: for we are many.

St Mark v, 9

Contents

List of illustrations   x

Author's Foreword and Acknowledgments   xiii

Part 1
Lads, You're Wanted!   1

Part 2
The Big Push   53

Part 3
'High Wood to Waterlot Farm . . .'   129

Part 4
The Mouth of Hell   253

Part 5
Friends Are Good on the Day of Battle   339

Bibliography   345

Author's Note   351

Index   359

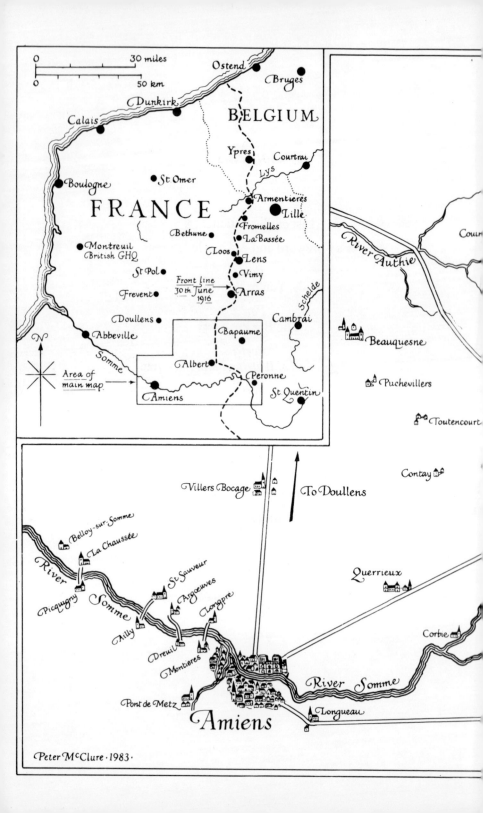

PICARDY · 1914 ·

The scene of the Battle of the Somme

To Arras

To Cambrai

Monchy-au-Bois

Bienvillers

Hannescamps

Fonquevillers

Gommecourt

Bucquoy

Achiet le Petit

Achiet le Grand

Gommecourt Wood

Hébuterne

Sailly au-Bois

Puisieux

Iles

Warlencourt

Bapaume

Serre

Miraumont

Pys

Thilloy

Tigny

Beaumont Hamel

Beaucourt

Le Sars

Butte

Beaulencourt

Auchonvillers

Eaucourt L'Abbaye

Guedaucourt

Le Transloy

y-Maillet

Mesnil Ridge

Mesnil

Thiepval Wood

Grandcourt

Courcelette

Mouquet Farm

Martinpuich

High Wood

Flers

Lesbœufs

Transloy Ridges

Aveluy Wood

Authuille

Thiepval Ridge

Pozières

Longueval

Delville Wood

Morval

Sailly~ Saillisel

ille

Bouzincourt

Aveluy

Nab Wood

Thiepval

Ovillers

Batentin le Petit

Irones Wood

Ginchy

Bouleaux Wood

Combles

loy

encourt

La Boisselle

Contalmaison

Mametz Wood

Maison

Leuze Wood

Rancourt

Fricourt

Mametz

Montauban

Bernafay Wood

Guillemont

Albert

Carnoy

Maricourt

Hardecourt

Maurepas

Bouchavesnes

Buire

Curlu

Clery sur Somme

River Ancre

Suzanne

Morlancourt

Bray-sur-Somme

Frise

Péronne

River Somme

River Somme

Estrees

rs Bretonneaux

To St. Quentin

List of Illustrations

Between pages 46–47

Valley in front of Beaumont Hamel from which British troops attacked on
 the First of July
German line on the Thiepval plateau
Fields between Hébuterne village and Gommecourt where the
 Territorials of the 56th Division were decimated
British jumping-off line where the boys of the Pals Battalions waited to
 attack the German line
Beaumont Hamel Valley from the Hawthorn Redoubt
British and German front-line trenches in front of Thiepval village
British and German lines seen from the German trench line in front of
 Thiepval chateau
The present-day view to the right of old Thiepval village shot from the
 Thiepval Memorial
Rose Vaquette pointing to the spot where her father was shot on 27th
 September 1914
The old well of Thiepval still looks out across No Man's Land
Ruins of Thiepval Chateau in 1915
Heap of stones which today is all that remains of the Thiepval Chateau
Present-day Thiepval village
German trench in the Ovillers defences
Albert-Bapaume Road showing magnitude of German defences
German line to the left of la Boisselle

Between pages 110–111, and 126–127

Grave of Boromée Vaquette in Authuille village cemetery
Grave of Clem Cunnington in Ovillers Military Cemetery
Reg Parker with two comrades of the Sheffield Pals
Reg Parker's brother, Willie
Still-visible trench-lines to the left of Contalmaison attacked alone by the
 13th Rifle Brigade on the evening of 10th July
Road from la Boisselle to Contalmaison
Traces of the line that formed the Fricourt Salient
Contalmaison Château in 1917
Entrance to a dugout near Contalmaison
Reserve trenches on the Somme

Between pages 150–151

The ground attacked on 14th and 15th July, with the two stumbling blocks of High Wood and Delville Wood
German communication trench to the right of Crucifix Corner where Fred Beadle lost his way
Remains of the windmill which concealed a deep dugout
From the windmill above Crucifix Corner, Bazentin, looking across to Longueval and Delville Wood
Part of letter from Ethel Bath
Reginald Bath
Bill Turner and Maggie Gaffney
Jack Beament of the Church Lads Brigade
Some of the Church Lads of the 16th Battalion, Kings Royal Rifle Corps

Between pages 214–215

Death Valley and Caterpillar Wood and valley
Looking across to Longueval and Delville Wood from the corner of Trones Wood on the road to Guillemont
German dugout and gallery at Guillemont
Remains of a machine-gun post in the Triangle
Panorama of the Ancre valley and the Thiepval Ridge
First message transmitted by the 1st Anzac Wireless section
Statue of Sir Douglas Haig at Montreuil-sur-Mer
View of the land beyond Ginchy and Guillemont, the scene of the September fighting

Between pages 230–231

Formidable defences of the German Second Line at Ginchy
Ginchy, Autumn 1982, still yielding its annual harvest of shells
Where the Switch Line ran
The site of the Triangle and the Quadrilateral from the Guards Memorial on Ginchy Ridge
Christchurch Boys' High School Cricket team in 1908; four of the eleven were killed fighting with the New Zealanders
The menacing Quadrilateral which blocked the advance from Guillemont
The invitation to Arthur Agius's wedding

Between pages 302–303

The Butte de Warlencourt and the land beyond le Sars where the fighting came to a standstill at the end of the Battle of the Somme in November 1916
The valley behind Beaumont Hamel and the slopes to the right above it where the boys of the Glasgow Tramways Battalion were cut off
The British and German lines on either side of the present-day Newfoundland Park
The valley behind Beaumont Hamel with the Thiepval Ridge to the east

The 'fortress' village of Beaumont Hamel sheltered in the cleft of its valley
Station Road, running from Beaumont Hamel village to Beaucourt
  station, which was the 'Green Line' captured by the Royal Naval
  Division
The Order issued from G.H.Q. on the eve of the First of July
A single pane of stained glass depicting the head of the Virgin Mary, all
  that remains of the old Beaumont Hamel village
Photograph found on a dead German soldier
The letter Captain Agius received from Harold Scarlett's widow,
  Florence
Popular postcard, 'Fond Love to my Dear Boy'
Joe Hoyles, Fred Lyons and Sid Birkett on the day they joined up
Len Lovell
George Roy Bealing, MM
Tom Easton in 1914

Maps

The Line from Gommecourt to Thiepval   46
The Line from Thiepval to Montauban   47
The Attack at Contalmaison on 10th July   117
The Ground Attacked on 14th/15th July   150
The Battle of Guillemont and Ginchy   214
The General Attack on 15th September   215
The October Fighting   302
The Line at the End of the Fighting in November   320

Author's Foreword
and Acknowledgments

If this book had a sub-title it might appropriately be *Whatever happened to Kitchener's Army?* The Somme happened to it. When the Battle of the Somme finished Kitchener's Army was all but finished, too. It seemed at the time that the country would never get over it – and it never has.

In one sense Kitchener's Army was hardly an army at all. Before it was formed in August 1914, the British Army had been a small, tight-knit force of highly-trained professionals (as it is again today) equally skilled in dealing with the impertinent skirmishes in foreign parts which, since the death of Napoleon, had passed as wars, and with the rebellions and insurrections in various parts of the Empire it garrisoned and policed. To the domestic population of Great Britain in those days before instant communication and responsible journalism unrolled international events before the daily judgement of the domestic scene, wars and disturbances alike were remote affairs. Most people were complacent, confident, proud enough of their disciplined and structured society to be content to leave power to the politicians, morality to the churchmen, administration to the Establishment and fighting to the Army.

Nineteen-sixteen was to change all that, although the murmur of the first tentative questioning was drowned by the clamour of the War itself, and the first tremor in the rock-like foundations of British society was masked by the monstrous vibrations of the fighting. A decade was to pass before the murmur grew to a growl and half a century before the tremor was perceived as the first wave of a full-sized earthquake.

From the turbulent present it is seductive to look back on those days before the Great War as on a halcyon age. With the benefit of hindsight and the cultivation of the habit of criticism, it is tempting to condemn those whose duty it was to conduct the war and even to marvel at the attitude of those who saw it as their duty to fight it. The very horror of their experience has given birth to a widely held emotional view of the war in which every Tommy wears a halo and every officer above the rank of captain a pair of horns.

Perhaps it is logical, in the spirit of our times, that some of us should think like that. But it is equally logical that, in every echelon of their society, the Great War generation should have been impelled to act as they did. They were not endowed with the gift of foreseeing the future. It is doubtful, even if they had been, if they would have acted differently, for they were as much the children of their time as we are of ours.

I am constantly amazed by the passion of controversy and argument which discussion of the War can still arouse after the passage of seventy years. It is not my intention to enter the lists. This book does not set out to draw political conclusions and, although it is the story of a battle, it is more concerned with the experience of war than with the war itself. The whole nation experienced that war just as, three generations on, the nation is still experiencing its repercussions.

There was hardly a household in the land, there was no trade, occupation, profession or community, which was not represented in the thousands of innocent enthusiasts who made up the ranks of Kitchener's Army before the Battle of the Somme. By the end of the War there was hardly a family in the land which, in its inner or outer circle, had not suffered bereavement and hardly a young man who was lucky enough to return who would not be affected to the end of his life by his experience of that War to end Wars, and who would not see the world through new eyes because of it.

Most of them survived long enough to see ideals they had nurtured at its outset turn sour in its aftermath. Some survive still, but the voices, like the old soldiers themselves, are rapidly fading away. Soon all that will be left to tell us something of what it was all like in 1914 will be their sepia images in old photographs, grinning in self-conscious khaki, as the mouthless crowds cheer and the silent bands play and the flags fly frozen in the air. When the last of them has gone, a great silence will fall. I hope that these histories of their war will at least continue to transmit the echo.

My first thanks must go to the many old soldiers who with courtesy, patience, kindness and infinite enthusiasm have spent hours talking about the War, who have generously lent me precious souvenirs, books, letters, diaries, photographs, and who (often handicapped by ill-health or disability) have gone to the trouble of writing lengthy accounts of their experiences. Those who have contributed directly to this particular book are listed at the back with my special thanks, but in ten years of research and writing about the Great War I have 'on my books', so to speak, almost 3,000 men and women who served in it. Although it would be impossible to quote them all I owe all of them a debt of gratitude for a plethora of stories, of viewpoints, of first-hand details which have added to my own knowledge and have helped me to learn, to understand and to 'tell it like it was' for them, within a broader context than perhaps these very young people understood themselves at the time. They have done more than that. They have enabled me to build up a considerable collection of oral and written history, documents and ephemera. From a practical point of view a mere fraction can be utilised in the books I write, but, in its natural home in the care of the Imperial War Museum, the collection will, I know, be of value and importance long after we have all 'faded away'.

Ironically, the larger such a mass of material becomes the more difficult it becomes to make use of it unless one is gifted with a computer-like memory. Few working authors (and none whose field is military history!) can rise to the dizzy heights of owning a computer, but my life has been eased and my efficiency increased a hundredfold through the hard work and enthusiasm of members of the (1981) Sixth Form of the Harvey Grammar School, Folkestone, who, with zeal and breath-taking attention to detail, undertook the mammoth task of cataloguing, collating, indexing and cross-indexing some four million words of written and recorded material and then claimed to have enjoyed doing it! I hope they did, and I am very grateful to them, and, in particular, to John Botting and Bill Westall, the two schoolmasters who not only organised the project, guided the boys through it and made themselves responsible for much irreplaceable material, but through their teaching imbued the boys with the enthusiasm and interest which led them to undertake the task in the first place.

I first heard of the Harvey Grammar School one soggy morning on the Somme through a chance meeting with Neill Page, Paul Iverson and Simon Marshall who had just finished A-levels and, inspired by school trips organised by Messrs. Botting and Westall, were making the most of their spare time on a camping holiday exploring the Somme for themselves. Since then Neill and Paul, in particular, have become valuable lieutenants on research trips to the battlefields and in return for sleeping space on the floor, a few beers and a square meal or two, have enthusiastically undertaken all the difficult jobs from patiently teaching me how to read a compass properly to identifying obscure trenches, plotting gun-positions, crawling through tunnels (which they had found in the first place) and digging the car out when it got bogged down on rough tracks where no car should reasonably be expected to go.

I never cease to be amazed at the generosity and willingness of people who volunteer to help. It is obvious that I could never undertake such a mammoth task of research unaided and equally obvious that, so far as the collection of first-hand information is concerned, it is not so much the eleventh hour as two minutes to midnight. Since the publication of *They Called it Passchendaele*, the first of my books on the Great War, I have had amazing luck to acquire a corps of helpers who, between them, have enabled me to enlarge the scope of my work to a degree which would otherwise have been impossible for one person to cover. Some have come through chance meetings in France; many are readers, quite unknown to me, who have volunteered information or introductions to old soldiers; others I have met on the Battlefield Tours I occasionally accompany as guest-lecturer. A good number of them have proved to be first-rate interviewers. Some have made a hobby (valuable to me) of scouring the yellowed files of their local newspapers in search of information about local battalions. Others, like Mollie Jewsbury and Helen McClure, have undertaken the tedious but infinitely worthwhile chore of transforming long and often indecipherable diaries and journals into clean typescript. I am immensely grateful to these ladies, as well as to the people throughout the country who have given much of their time to tracing and talking to old soldiers who would otherwise be out of my reach. Frank Hobson in the North-east, Robert Trafford in the West-country, Alastair McNeilage in East Anglia, Barbara Taylor in Nottingham, Albert Texeira de Mattos and Yves de Kok in Belgium, Elizabeth Ogilvie in New Zealand, Vivien Riches in Australia, and Don Dean, Chris Sheeran, Stan Taylor, Ken Handley, Graham Winton, Hugh Williams, Ken Smallwood and Graham Maddocks.

Of the 'old firm' – the original team who have been helping since the beginning of this project ten years ago – my thanks are yet again due to Guy Francis, to John Woodroff, who checked units, dates and actions against official records with his customary meticulous care, and to my BBC colleague, Ritchie Cogan, for his support and interest both in this country and on forays to the battlefields and particularly for his expert assistance with the illustrations, competently photographed by John Daniel who, like me, will not forget the hair-raising experience of getting the aeriel shots from a one-engined aircraft flown by a co-operative but insouciant pilot! It was the way he kept smiling when the engine cut out that made us glad to regain terra firma!

Richard Dunning (who purchased the mine-crater at la Boisselle rather than see it filled in and built on) has given help which I much appreciate, as has Tom Gudmestad in the U.S.A.

The Commonwealth War Graves Commission has, as always, dealt with enquiries in Britain and in France with unfailing courtesy and efficiency and I am particularly grateful to Stuart Campbell at its Headquarters at Maidenhead and to Steve Grady and his staff in Arras.

I must also record my thanks to Eyre Methuen Limited for allowing me to use extracts from *The Private Papers of Douglas Haig.*

Colin Butler deserves a paragraph to himself. I met him in Ypres three years ago and since then he has travelled more miles, conducted more interviews and done more work than anyone else, with the possible exception of myself – although I wouldn't be too sure! His energy is boundless, his enthusiasm inexhaustible and his contribution has been immense. In trying to thank him, words fail me. All I can say is that *he* never does. He even co-opted the services of his long-suffering wife, Wendy, who collated the information on the 13th Service Battalion, The Rifle Brigade, from a multitude of disparate sources and she combined this time-consuming job with having a baby at the same time!

Of my friends 'on location' in France, where most of this book has been researched and written, I must thank Serge and Jeannine Mills, who have not only provided a roof over my head, cosseted, fed, watered and warmed me over two Somme winters and inclement springs, regardless of muddy boots, dripping anoraks and trench maps spread out across half their premises, but have introduced me to many valuable contacts on the Somme and have also indulged me with many hours of relaxing conviviality, hospitality, conversation and friendship. Neither they, nor my other friends in Authuille who have made me feel 'one of the family' (Monsieur Oscar, Mario, Danielle, Roger, Madame Rose, to name but a few) will ever know how much that meant at the end of a long day's slog at the typewriter or out on the ground.

But my unfailing support has been my assistant Alma Woodroff, who has had less than most of us of the interest involved in tramping the Somme or of meeting old soldiers. But, in a sense, she knows them better than any of us, for it is she who transcribes the hundreds of hours of recordings, organises the research, keeps tabs on everything and keeps everyone in order. Somehow she also managed, uncomplainingly, to fit in the typing of the draft and the manuscript of this book, deciphering the indecipherable, making sense of the unintelligible and, best of all, still came up laughing at the jokes. After three books on the War, if anyone has earned a campaign medal, she has.

My husband, Ian Ross, loathes publicity but I hope he will indulge my feeling that, after ten years of re-fighting the Great War, I owe him my formal thanks for allowing a third of his house to be taken over as an archive-cum-office, for putting up with my frequent absences, for his disinterested advice and invaluable judgement, and for only very occasionally complaining of shell-shock.

Lyn Macdonald.
London and Authuille. January 1983.

Part 1

Lads, You're Wanted!

'Lads, you're wanted! Over there,'
Shiver in the morning dew,
More poor devils like yourselves
Waiting to be killed by you.

E. A. Mackintosh

Chapter 1

It was the Romans who first built the long straight road thrusting out from Amiens through Albert to Bapaume, swinging north to Arras and westward to the coast. Now the autoroute speeds down from Calais, swirls into a tangle of highways round Loos and Lens, swoops past the Vimy Ridge and round Arras, vibrating under the wheels of fast cars and Euro-lorries streaming south to Paris and beyond.

In summer, when the stream of traffic swells to a river, the Euro-driver, keeping an ill-humoured eye on his wing-mirror, is moved a dozen times an hour to curse certain motor cars, half-blinded by their right-hand drives, in their wavering attempts to overtake his juggernaut, and shrugs with Gallic resignation as the British registration plates squeeze by.

Past Arras, for the first time since leaving Calais, a driver can relax. The confusion of signboards disappears; the road runs straight; the landscape opens out into a sweep of downs and valleys and, on rising ground to the west, a scattering of copses and villages with the distant spires of country churches, half-hidden by clumps of trees. Curious, map-reading passengers can easily identify them – Gueudecourt, Flers, Lesboeufs, Morval, Combles – and may observe, with idle interest, that the river, soon to be bridged, is the River Somme. But they would have to be quick with the Michelin.

At motorway speed it takes, at most, twelve minutes to cover the twenty-five kilometres from the exit at Bapaume to the exit at Estrées. Between them, the highway, with singular precision, swings across the eastern limits of the battlefield of the Somme. The village of Estrées, at the end of the line attacked by the French Army, was the first and most southerly objective on the first day of the Battle. The British objective was the small town of Bapaume. In five months of almost continuous fighting, they struggled towards it through the summer and autumn of 1916. A hundred and fifty thousand men died. In the end, when the Battle itself died out in the November chill and the slough in front of Gueudecourt, Flers, Lesboeufs, Morval, Combles, they had not quite managed to get there.

Later, when it was long over, everyone remembered the bird-song. Doves, cooing beneath the eaves of a shell-wracked barn; the faint chirrup of a lark that still, astoundingly, wheeled in the clear sky, far beyond the reach of shot or shrapnel; the song of a nightingale when the guns fell briefly silent and, in the beginning, the endless cawing of rooks in the high trees along the springtime roads of Picardy as the soldiers marched along them in an endless khaki tide.

They were marching towards the Battle of the Somme. But that name, with its tragic connotations destined to ring hollow down the years, had not yet been coined. The soldiers preparing for the fight called it the Big Push. Very few of them were soldiers at all. They were shop assistants, clerks, artisans, aristocrats, butchers, errand boys, farmers, schoolmasters, miners, grocers, sheep-shearers, bankers – but they were united by a simple resolve to put the Germans in their place once and for all. That place, in the universal opinion of the British Tommies, was well below the salt in a world where few would have disputed the right of Great Britain, attended by her Empire, to occupy the head of the table.

Pouring into the Somme, marching to and from the training grounds, moving wholesale from billets in one indistinguishable French village only to tramp in apparently aimless circles to another, the infantry were glad, on the whole, to be on the move. They had been at the front for many months; they had held the trenches, graduating from quiet to 'lively' stretches of the line; they had become hardened to discomfort and cautiously blasé under shellfire. A few of the earlier arrivals had taken part in the Battles of Loos and Festubert, and lively spirits, handy with a knobkerry, had developed a penchant for prowling round No Man's Land and paying rowdy surprise visits to the enemy's trenches, but not one man in five hundred had ever been 'over the top' in a major battle. Until now, by exercising a reasonable degree of caution, the majority of Kitchener's Army had run a slightly greater risk of dying from boredom in the trenches than from the attentions of the enemy. Their philosophy was summed up by the phrase that had become a universal motto, *If you can't take a joke you shouldn't have joined!* They were half a million strong, volunteers to a man and, although there was a leavening of professional soldiers in their ranks, hardly anyone among them had been in khaki for more than twenty-three months. By the early summer of 1916, on the eve of the biggest battle of the war, they were, at best, half trained, and this unpleasant but inescapable truth was at the forefront of the minds of the professional army commanders throughout the long months of planning the battle. It was in their disquiet that the first seeds of the tragedy took root.

The Army had undeniably done its best, but the tide of patriotic enthusiasm which had swept a hundred thousand would-be soldiers into its ranks in the first ten days of the war had completely swamped its resources. At the beginning of August 1914, it had been a small, tight-knit professional force. By the end of the same month it had swelled, willy-nilly, into a vast amorphous mass of men and boys, united only by boundless enthusiasm at the prospect of being turned into soldiers. The problem was how to set about it. The Regular Army was occupied elsewhere and, by the beginning of September, Commanding Officers of Regimental Depots in Britain were turning grey under the strain of handling a strength that had catapulted from a disciplined body of one or, at most, two reserve battalions, to ten, eleven, twelve, thirteen 'Service' battalions of raw recruits, enlisted for the duration of the war, and whose only resemblance to 'battalions' as the Army knew them, was that they consisted of a thousand or so men apiece – all of them devoid of the slightest military skill, but asking nothing more than to be sent to France without delay. In desperation they closed recruiting lists, canvassed the ragged ranks of would-be soldiers for any who had at least seen service in the Boys' Brigade or as Boy Scouts, slapped corporals' stripes on the sleeves of their civilian suits, handed them over to bemused drill-sergeants and turned to the War Office with imperative demands for advice, for ration money, for equipment and, above all, for instructors. The replies, when they came, generally consisted of little more than terse orders to 'Carry On'.

The War Office had problems of its own. It was being besieged from all quarters, not only from the hard-pressed commands of its ballooning Army, wobbling under the weight of its unwieldy expansion, but from a hundred other directions where private enterprise had raised what amounted to a series of private armies.

In the first enthusiastic weeks of war it seemed that every county, town and borough all over the British Isles, each anxious to have at least one battalion of its own, had set itself up as a recruiting agency. As fast as young men poured into Town Halls to enlist, money poured in from the local citizenry to maintain them. Within days, and in numbers that those concerned with the administration of the Army preferred not to contemplate, they were happily encamped on Wimbledon Common, in Bellevue Park, on the Ayrshire coast and on private estates, village greens and local parks across the length and breadth of the country. There was no hope of Khaki as yet but, tweed-capped and flannel-trousered though they were, the new recruits basked in the glow of local admiration, and drilled as enthusiastically as though their broom handles were rifles in response to the tentative suggestions of young officers whose commissions, at present, emanated from the local Mayor, rather than from the King, and whose superior knowledge was cribbed shakily from some well-thumbed army manual dating from the Boer War.

> *Where are our uniforms?*
> *Far far away*
> *When will our rifles come?*
> *P'raps p'raps some day. . . .*

It was the first parody of a war whose parodies were to become immortal.

All officers of the Reserve, many of them verging on the antediluvian, had been called up and, unless actually confined to wheelchairs, had answered the call. An appeal had gone out for 'old sweats' who had served in the Boer War or even in the Sudan to come forward to help with the training. It was necessarily sketchy and not entirely relevant to the circumstances of modern warfare. In the summer and autumn of 1915, when certain battalions of the New Army started arriving at the front, it was not unknown for Divisional Headquarters to receive reports that were couched in terminology strangely inappropriate to the European landscape. The old soldiers, who had initiated the New Army into the military arts, and whose last experience of soldiering had been a dozen years earlier in South Africa, were accustomed to referring to 'plains' and '*kopjes*' and their pupils, assuming this to be standard military practice, had naturally followed suit. A year later, their error having been pointed out by a score of apoplectic brigadiers, they now knew better.

There was small resemblance between the arid veldt of South Africa and the dulcet countryside of Picardy. The River Somme ambled towards Amiens, coiling in long, lazy loops through a marshy valley, joined by a score of minor tributaries that turned it, here and there, into a waterscape of straggling streams and islands. Just behind Corbie it met the Ancre, flowing down through Albert from the north-east, where the British Army stood astride the river, on the edge of high chalk downs where the German Army was entrenched.

On 1 July the British had been in position for a bare ten months. But the enemy had been there for almost two years. The Germans had come to the Somme early on an autumn morning. It was 27 September 1914, and, in the tiny hamlet of Authuille, tucked under the high bluff of the Thiepval Ridge, not a man, woman or child would ever forget the date.

Swelling out of the valley carved by the River Ancre more than a hundred feet below, the crest of the Thiepval Ridge was deceptively gentle. A plateau rather than a summit, with broad shoulders that breasted the horizon as they ran down to Grandcourt, away on the left and reached towards Aveluy, away on the right. Both villages stood on the banks of the River Ancre and its gentle course, its wooded valleys, the high hills above, had made it a favourite place with holiday-makers who preferred green tranquillity to the elegant bustle of seaside resorts. In the summers before the war they came from as far away as Paris, to swim or fish in the river, to walk and ride in the hills, to climb the winding road to Thiepval village on the summit of the ridge, to admire the view and to take afternoon tea, in the English-style, enjoying the delicious cakes for which the pâtisserie in Thiepval was justly renowned.

Thiepval was a seigniorial village, not much changed from feudal times. It had a few shops, a café or two, a sizeable church and sixty odd houses occupied by the farmworkers who worked the fertile lands around. But what caught the eye from miles away was the Château. Large and imposing, it had stood for three centuries in front of the village, dominating the ridge on the foremost edge of the plateau, a landscape of formal gardens stretching from its elegant stone terrace to the verge of its private wood that ran down the lower slopes to the river valley. It commanded a magnificent view.

Strolling on the terrace of an evening, the old Count, Monsieur de Bréda, could almost have exchanged a nod with his neighbour, who owned a château nearly as grand diagonally across the way on the Mesnil Ridge above the dark mass of Aveluy Wood. Ahead, half concealed by the trees of the Count's own valley, Hamel village straggled up the opposite slope and, away on his right, where the long saddle of the Mesnil Ridge ran into the cleft of a narrow valley, the spire of Beaumont Church could just be seen above it. By strolling no more than a hundred yards from his domain, past the village and up the gradual rise of the hilltop, he could survey miles of lush farmland rolling up towards Pozières; away on the low ground to the right, if he could not actually see the town of Albert, set low in the fold of the valley four miles away, he might easily have caught a glimpse of its famous landmark, when a ray of the setting sun lingered briefly on the gilded Virgin towering above the roof of its cathedral. In structure, in outlook, in situation, the Château of Thiepval occupied a position that was second to none.

The de Brédas owned the Thiepval Ridge, with all its farms and villages, and the only thing that had disturbed the satisfaction of the Count, as he surveyed the rolling hectares of his property, was that there was no heir to succeed to it.

The de Brédas were old and childless. Earlier in the year the

Count had died and been laid to rest in the vault of the family sepulchre among his more prolific ancestors whose ancient coffins, it was rumoured by the villagers, contained not merely their earthly remains but all their costly jewels. Now the Comtesse de Bréda had gone too. The local servants had been paid off and Madame de Bréda, with her chauffeur and her maid, had swept through Authuille in the new motor car that had been her husband's pride and joy, making for Amiens and the safety of her sister's house. The château was empty and its long windows, accustomed to throw back the rays of the evening sun as it drifted down behind the Mesnil Ridge, stood blank and shuttered. The villagers, who had seen the Comtesse depart, deduced that the war was approaching too close for comfort.

It was just thirty-five days since the first shots had been fired and fired far to the north, over the Belgian frontier at Mons. It was almost beyond belief that in one short month the Germans could have swept through France, pushing the French and their British ally in front of them, to the very gates of Paris, that three great battles could have been fought and that, even now, the enemy was pouring apparently limitless forces across the captured plains of the north, as he raced towards the sea. In the past few days, rumour had moved faster than events, in a situation so fluid that the newspapers could hardly keep up with it. The *Voix du Nord* was printing little more than ringing calls to arms and patriotic rhetoric, but word of mouth had it that, three days ago, shooting had been heard at Chaulnes and that, only yesterday, the Germans were in Maricourt, not seven kilometres away from the village of Authuille.

On the morning of the 27th the village and the ridge above were wrapped in a thick September mist. Boromée Vaquette milked his six cows as usual and, as usual by seven o'clock, he was driving them out of his farmyard and up the steep path to their pasture on the ridge above. It was not much of a pasture – less than half a hectare and, each day, Vaquette set the cows to graze in a different corner and put up a moveable fence of chains and pickets to prevent them from wandering. It took him twenty minutes to move the stakes, to hammer them into the ground with a heavy mallet, another five minutes to encourage the cows into the enclosure and ten more to walk back down the road to the farm and his morning bowl of coffee.

That morning he never returned. By seven the children were up and dressed. By half-past seven the younger ones had set off for school, the eldest Vaquette girl was skimming the cream from the milk pans, the coffee pot simmered on the kitchen stove, Madame Vaquette was feeding the hens. By eight o'clock she was mildly concerned; by nine she was anxious; by ten it was all round the village that Boromée Vaquette had disappeared; by lunchtime Madame Vaquette was frantic.

During the morning French soldiers had marched into the village, and a sentry posted on the outskirts, despite all Madame Vaquette's pleading, barred the way to the ridge above. Shots had been heard. Late in the afternoon a French sergeant came into the courtyard and knocked at the farmhouse door. He found it difficult to blurt out his story. They had come out of the wood, he said, early in the morning. They were looking for Germans, expecting to see them any minute; they heard the sound of hammering and, across the field, near the place where the four roads met, they could just distinguish through the mist the figure of a man in grey clothes erecting a barricade. They had taken him for a German, fired a volley and retreated into the wood. The soldier began to cry. It was only now that they understood that they had killed a Frenchman and by now it was too late. The advance guard of the Germans had already moved forward to take up a defensive position on the ridge. A few yards beyond the line they had chosen, the body of Boromée Vaquette lay hidden in the long grass. There was no sign of the cows.

The German had occupied Thiepval village and spread purposefully across the hills on either side. That night their senior officers slept in Thiepval Château and their troops were digging trenches on the crest of the Thiepval Ridge.

It was a week before they could bring back the body of my father because nobody dared to approach. Then one evening a French officer came to see my mother and he said, 'Madame Vaquette, we must do something for you.' The French soldiers were very upset. The officer said, 'We know the place. We can show it to you, and tonight we can bring him back.' It was a very quiet night and it was dark, with no moon. My mother went with my eldest sister and the soldiers showed them the place. They had to go on stockinged feet, to make no noise, right up almost to the German trench to find my father's body. The soldiers carried him back to the house and next day they carried him to the church and the priest said a mass. There were not many there, just the people from the village and a few of the soldiers. After the mass, we followed the coffin to the cemetery and buried my father in the family grave. It was nine days since he had been killed.[1]

Madame Rose Glavieux (née Vaquette).

---

[1]Boromée Vaquette, the first man of thousands to die on the Thiepval Ridge, is buried in the family plot (now with a modern headstone) to the right of the gate in the small communal cemetery of Authuille.

During that nine days the fighting had trickled to the north and
Germans, French and British had begun to dig themselves in.

When the British had taken over this sector of the line, at the urgent
request of the French in the late summer of 1915, it had been easy to
sneer at their Ally for 'lacking the offensive spirit'. No one, least of all
the French, denied that the Somme had been a 'cushy' front, that
laissez faire had been the order of the day. It was true that there had
been occasional duels between the guns, that the Château of
Thiepval was distinctly knocked about, and, with its eyeless windows
gazing gauntly westwards from the German front line, it had long
ceased to be regarded as a desirable billet for German officers. It was
true that there had been intermittent skirmishing, and that German
engineers and French alike had developed a predilection for bur-
rowing under the lines of their opposite numbers and springing
mines beneath their trenches. But these were mere token gestures
compared to the battles which all through 1915 had raged to the north
and to the east. On the Somme neither side had had any particular
reason to stir things up. There was no particular objective and, short
of a major offensive which neither side was in a position to undertake, nothing to be gained by local attacks. In the light of the
casualties which both sides had suffered elsewhere, the philosophy
of 'live and let live' seemed, on the Somme Front, to be very much to
the point.

The French Army was stretched to its limit. Four hundred and
seventy-five miles of trenchline stretched from the Belgian coast,
sweeping across the face of France to the very doorstep of Switzer-
land. Until the autumn of 1915, the French were grimly holding on to
four hundred miles of its length, while the British Expeditionary
Force faced the enemy along a mere seventy miles of the front.
Certainly the British had not been idle. They had held the Germans
at bay at Ypres, they had fought the enemy at Neuve Chapelle, they
had stood alongside the French on the Marne, on the Aisne, at Loos,
but it was not enough. It was not nearly enough. The British must
shoulder more of the burden – and, for a start, they must take over
more of the line. So the British Army came to the Somme, took over
the French Front where it faced the arc of the German line from
Hébuterne to Thiepval, on the Ancre, from Thiepval to the banks of
the River Somme itself.

Unlike the French, fighting on their native soil and pledged to give
up their lives rather than to concede a single centimetre to the
invader; unlike the British, equally committed to kicking the enemy
off the face of France, the Germans had positioned their line with
care. Here giving up a stretch of low-lying ground, there withdraw-

ing from a steep river valley, they had backed off to build a line that hugged the high spurs and contours of the chalky downland, so that every slope, every natural ravine, each natural declivity, every wood and hilltop could be turned to maximum advantage for observation, for concealment, for defence. Now a complex of trenches marched from horizon to horizon in two distinct, conspicuous lines, as if a giant chalky finger had zig-zagged across the landscape. As the Germans were well aware, the observers of the Royal Flying Corps, buzzing in inquisitive sorties up and down the front, had charted every twist and turn of the German front line and every undulating stretch of their second line, bristling no less distinctly two miles behind it. But the tell-tale chalk of the subsoil, that blazoned their position to the skies, held deeper secrets. It was easily worked and, with characteristic thoroughness and considerable engineering skill, the Germans had tunnelled beneath their trenches and carved out a network of galleries and shelters, so deep and so secure that nothing short of an earthquake could have dislodged them. By the summer of 1916, every hilltop was a redoubt, every wood an arsenal, every farm a stronghold, every village a fortress.

Chapter 2

If the German Command had been able to choose a single stretch of their five-hundred-mile front on which to beat off an Allied offensive, they would have chosen to meet it on the Somme where their line was virtually impregnable. Intelligence reports left them in no doubt that an offensive was in the offing, and it was perfectly evident that, from the Allied point of view, the British would be bound to attack somewhere along their front, in order to relieve the pressure on the hard-pressed French Army, whose strength was fast ebbing away in a river of blood at Verdun, where they had lost two hundred thousand men since the Germans had launched their own offensive in February. But, had it been suggested that the long-expected attack would take place here on the Somme Front where the two armies met, where, consequently, the Allies' line was at its most confused and vulnerable, had there been a hint that it would be a joint operation and that the undermanned demoralised French would attack alongside the British in a major offensive, there was hardly an officer on the German Staff who would not have vented his disbelief in a hearty belly-laugh at the very idea.

The British Staff did not contemplate the prospect with amusement. The battlefield was not of their choosing; it had been chosen by the French, but, for political reasons and the wish to demonstrate goodwill in practical terms, there had been no choice but to acquiesce. When the idea of a joint offensive had first been agreed on at the Chantilly Conference in January, it had been conceived largely as a French affair. If the French Army attacked on a grand scale south of the River Somme, then the British on their left would support them by mounting a series of local attacks north of the Somme and astride the Ancre. But that was before Verdun. As the French strength diminished, as they threw more and more men and guns and munitions eastwards into the white heat of the melting-pot of Verdun, so the strength of the British Army in France was increasing with every raw battalion of Kitchener's Army that crossed the Channel and with every troopship that sailed into Marseilles bearing the gallant survivors of the sad adventure at Gallipoli. As the balance of manpower gradually shifted, and the plans for the offensive evolved and took shape, it became more and more obvious that the weight of the joint offensive must shift too and that the burden of the attack must now fall on the British Army, with the support of a few French Divisions on its right on a much truncated front.[1] This would unavoidably force the main thrust of the push against the bastion of the German line on the uplands of the Somme.

The plan did not appeal to Sir Douglas Haig. He had already set in motion the preliminaries for an offensive in the north and had not entirely given up hope that he might be in a position to launch it later in the summer. Strategically, there was more to be gained. A purely British attack in the north would be equally effective in taking the heat off Verdun and, he believed, would stand a real chance of breaking through the German line.[2]

But on his appointment as Commander-in-Chief in December 1915, Haig had been categorically informed that 'the closest co-operation between the French and the British as a united Army must be the governing policy'. When the French had pressed their case for a joint campaign at the Chantilly Conference, it was just five weeks since Haig had been entrusted with the Command of the British Army in France, and, with the words of the Supreme War Council still ringing in his ears, he was in no position to disagree. Nevertheless, he had his doubts about what, if any, strategic advantage was to be gained by such a battle. More to the point, he had strong doubts about the ability of his Army to fight it.

Kitchener's Army did not share the pessimism of its Commander-in-Chief. Its members were rather more inclined to have a good opinion of themselves. They were mildly tolerant of the French whose ways they found strange but attractive, and not entirely intolerant of the Germans, referred to familiarly as Fritz, with whom, in the discomfort of their opposing trenches, they felt a certain fellow-feeling. Officially, fraternisation had been severely frowned upon since the spontaneous Christmas Truce of 1914 but, in between bouts of belligerence, there was nothing to prevent bored Tommies and the equally bored soldiers of the German infantry

---

[1] The original intention had been for the Allies to attack over a forty-five-mile front, the French with sixty divisions, across thirty miles. Now the French could spare only eleven divisions and their frontage was reduced to six miles, mostly south of the Somme.

[2] It was a three-stage plan involving firstly blowing up and capturing the Wytschaete Messines Ridge, then breaking out of the Ypres Salient and swinging round to capture the ports of Ostende and Zeebrugge in conjunction with an amphibious attack from the sea. It was eventually put into execution a year later and was to be known as the Third Battle of Ypres. It was doomed to failure, partly because of an unusually wet summer and autumn, but largely because of the magnitude of the German defences, which they had hardly begun building by the summer of 1916. Had 'Third Ypres' been launched that summer, instead of the Battle of the Somme, it would have had an excellent chance of succeeding; thus two disasters of almost equal magnitude might conceivably have been avoided.

across the way from entertaining each other with an exchange of badinage and, occasionally, with an impromptu concert. On the whole, the Germans were more musical than the British, although their taste tended towards the sentimental. In the damp darkness of quiet nights in the trenches, undisturbed by gunfire or the flash of Very lights, it was the soulful strains of *Die Wacht am Rhein* or *In der Heimat* . . . which were most often to be heard drifting across from the German side of No Man's Land.

Apart from the occasional outburst, the British Tommies were not much given to singing in the trenches. In their opinion there was not much to sing about. There was the drudgery of working parties, the long boredom of sentry duty and, week after week, month upon month, the tedious routine of living in muddy ditches, enlivened by the excitement of occasional raids and forays, but more often chastised by punishing shellfire and inevitable casualties. It all added up to something to be endured rather than to sing about, and the Tommies reserved their vocal efforts to while away the tedium of long miles on the march or, when they happened to be on rest, for jolly evenings in one of the *estaminets* that were to be found in every village behind the front. After several months of active service – albeit static warfare – the songs they sang had altered somewhat in character from the jolly ditties that had lightened the leaden hours of route-marching around the English countryside a year before. *Where are our uniforms? Far far away* . . . they had warbled then in their impatience to get to the front. Now that they had attained that ambition and the long-awaited uniforms had already turned shabby in the rigours of trench warfare, the same melody served very well for a more realistic chorus.[1]

> *There is a sausage gun*
> *Over the way.*
> *Fired by a bloody Hun*
> *Three times a day.*
> *You should see the Tommies run*
> *When they hear that sausage gun*
> *Fired by a bloody Hun*
> *Three times a day.*

The lyrics were a trifle inglorious, but very much to the point, for, if Kitchener's Army had not yet proved itself in a major battle, it had been well and truly 'blooded' in the trenches. There was hardly a

[1] It was a catchy non-conformist hymn tune sung usually to the words, 'There is a Happy Land, Far, Far away . . .'.

man in the ranks who did not consider himself to be a seasoned warrior and as good as the next man. Some battalions of the Regular Army were aghast at the cheek of it. Even the illustrious Guards were not exempt. One scruffy service battalion of the East Surreys, passing a contingent of the Grenadier Guards drawn up in a village square, had the temerity to bellow in unison the traditional army taunt that dated from 1743, 'Where were *You* at Dettingen?' It took all the discipline of the Guards' professional training to prevent them from breaking rank and sorting the East Surreys out.

'Service' battalions of the Worcestershire Regiment as a matter of course threw themselves into a fracas, military or otherwise, with full-throated yells of '*GHELUVELT*'. They themselves had still been mastering the art of shouldering broomsticks in October 1914 when the regular soldiers of their 'parent' battalion were holding off the Germans on the lawns of Gheluvelt Château in the First Battle of Ypres, but this minor circumstance did not abash them. They were 'Worcesters' and that was that. If anything, they considered it something of a distinction to be 'Worcesters' of Kitchener's Army.

This opinion was not infrequently shared by commanding officers of the various Kitchener's Battalions which, by this time, were wearing the insignia of every regiment in the British Army with the exception of those in the exclusive Division of Guards. Until the early part of 1916, many battalion commanders and most brigadiers were 'Dugouts' – Officers of the Reserve who had been winkled out of well-earned retirement to take command of the burgeoning force of assorted civilians who had answered Lord Kitchener's call to arms. In many cases, in the time that had elapsed since those elderly gentlemen had first looked with dismay on the disordered ranks of boyish enthusiasts placed so abruptly under their command, they had developed a strangely paternal attitude towards their men, quite foreign to the general benevolence they had previously entertained towards the troops they had commanded long years ago in peace-time. Indeed, in the necessarily limited Establishment of the small professional Army, very few officers among the Dugouts had ever commanded a battalion before. Senior officers who had earned their colonelcies in peacetime were promptly given brigades; others, who had gone into respectable retirement with the rank of major, were promoted to colonel and put in command of a battalion of the New Army.

For more than a year now, the sole concern of such a colonel had been for 'his' battalion. Day in, day out, and for the best part of every night, he had toiled over every detail of the Herculean task of transforming his force of assorted civilians into troops of the British Army. With assiduous vigilance, he had watched his men progress from their first flat-footed attempts at drill to their final inspection, often by the King himself. He had despaired, or exulted, over their performance on the rifle range, the sports field, the parade ground. He had pondered pleas for compassionate leave, he had promoted the worthy, delivered judgement on defaulters. He had worked out dozens of different training programmes, written scores of reports, preached discipline to the men and the responsibilities of command to young officers and NCO's. He had, almost single-handedly, turned his men into soldiers. Finally, he had brought them to France with a sense of pride which stemmed less from self-congratulation than from recognition of the calibre of the men themselves.

They looked good on the march. They were taller and stronger, on the whole, than the undernourished recruits who had been driven by unemployment or poverty into the ranks of the pre-war Army. The standard of education and intelligence in both officers and men was high. They were enthusiastic, they were cheerful, and they had buckled down admirably to learning the unfamiliar trade of soldiering. They were the pick of the bunch. No matter how much of a martinet their 'Old Man' was held to be in the opinion of a Kitchener's Battalion, there was hardly a colonel who was not secretly convinced that his battalion was second to none.

Trevor Ternan, who had retired as a brigadier-general seven years before the war, went further than that. In his opinion, all four battalions under his command combined to form the finest brigade in the whole of Kitchener's Army and, such was his conviction, that he was determined to bring it to the notice of Lord Kitchener himself.

The 102nd Brigade formed part of the 34th Division. It was better known as the Tyneside Scottish and the paragons who made up its ranks were mainly pitmen and 'Geordies' to a man. The four Battalions had been raised by the patriotic efforts of the Tyneside Scottish Committee who, until they had been taken over by the War Office and co-opted into the Army, had contributed every penny for their soldiers' keep, their equipment, their training and their comfort. The men of one battalion had started their military career by bivouacking in the ballroom of Tilley's Assembly Rooms, marching out every day to drill on the Town Moor and returning to hearty meals supplied by a local caterer, and the let-down of their subsequent passage through a succession of leaky tents and draughty huts had been eased by a flow of 'comforts' which had generously redoubled now that they were actually in France and fighting in the trenches.

Best of all the benefits of local munificence were the pipe-bands. Each battalion had its own, and the equipment, the pipes themselves and the pipers' outfits (which alone had cost more than thirty pounds apiece) had been generously paid for by the open-handed Tyne-siders at home. The pipers were the real thing, specially recruited on the basis of their musicianship, even although a blind eye had to be turned to certain army regulations which dealt with such niggling inconveniences as the army age limit. It was obvious to all that Pipe-Sergeant Barton must be well over forty, for the family had joined up en masse, and three of Barton's sons were also serving in the bands of the Tyneside Scottish Brigade. Nothing exceeded the delight of the French peasants and their children than when the Tyneside Scottish Brigade swung through a village with a pipe-band blowing lustily at the head of each battalion. Nothing exceeded the pride of their Brigadier as he watched them march past.

The Brigadier was considerably put out when it was announced, at the beginning of February, that Lord Kitchener was to inspect a part of the 34th Division on parade, and that the part selected for this honour was the 101st Brigade. As this Brigade was made up of Royal Scots, Suffolks and Lincolns, it was thought to be a tactful choice which, in view of the well-known rivalry between the two remaining Brigades of the division – the 102nd Tyneside Scottish and the 103rd Tyneside Irish – would avoid any ructions or accusations of parti-ality. Brigadier-General Ternan was having none of that! He was acquainted with Field-Marshal Lord Kitchener. He had served under him in two previous wars. They had even shared a billet together, thirty-two years earlier, in the Khedive's Palace at Alexan-dria. It was true that, as an officer on the Intelligence Staff, Major Kitchener had been lodged in silk and satin splendour in one of the elaborate state apartments, while Ternan, as a junior subaltern, had shared a scullery with the cockroaches, but time and promotion had put their acquaintanceship on a more intimate footing. The Briga-dier had no qualms at all about the propriety of waylaying the Field-Marshal's car en route to the inspection, and waving it to a halt. Lord Kitchener was delighted to see him, delighted to see his fine Brigade – which just happened to be lined up on either side of the road ahead – and delighted to accept the Brigadier's invitation to alight and inspect it.

He walked for almost a mile along its ranks and was cheered to the echo by each company as he passed. He complimented the Brigadier in the warmest terms and, when he finally stepped back into his staff car at the end of the line, the pipers skirled him on his way to the strains of *Hielan' Laddie*. All in all, the only people who were not entirely delighted with the events of such a satisfactory afternoon were the Corps and Divisional Commanders, who were left kick-ing their heels for a full hour in front of the drawn-up ranks of

the 101st Brigade, at the official inspection point two miles ahead.
Now, just four months later, Lord Kitchener was dead. He had
been drowned in HMS *Hampshire* on his way to perform a mission in
Russia and his death was to prove to be an irreparable loss to the Army
as a whole, particularly with regard to its relations with the French.
There was no doubt about the fact that, compared to the Germans,
the Allies suffered from their lack of overall command at the highest
level. The difficulties involved in working out a joint strategy, of
directing independent campaigns in such a way as to contribute
effectively to a co-ordinated military effort, and the problems of
unanimously deciding who should attack where and when, were
never fully resolved. There was too much internecine bickering,
both among the French politicians and among the British, and, on
both sides, there was too much jockeying for position between the
officers of the General Staffs and even between the Commanders of
the Armies in the field. In all the joint deliberations there was too
much talk, too much time wasted, too much thought given to mutual
support in the short-term interest and too little given to the planning
of long-term strategy.

By 1916 the situation cried out to be taken in hand by a man who
would have the respect of both sides and who, without self-interest
or national partiality, would be able to exercise an effective overall
command in the common interest of the Allies. Lord Kitchener had
been such a man. As Britain's Secretary of State for War, he
occupied an eminence which automatically claimed the respect of
politicians; as an illustrious soldier of the highest rank, he was
unquestioningly honoured by the military. There was no other man
who could have taken his place at the hub of the wheeling machi-
nations of a dozen different Franco–British interests, flying off at a
dozen different tangents, held them together and sent them bowling
smoothly towards a common objective. There was no other man who
would have been acceptable to both sides. Now, Kitchener was gone
and there was no one to replace him.

In France, and in his dealings with the French, Sir Douglas Haig
was left holding the baby. So far as the Somme campaign was
concerned, Lord Kitchener's support would have been neither here
nor there. Over the preceding months, the sequence of events which
had inexorably shifted the main burden of the attack on to the
shoulders of the British, had happened so gradually that there had
never been a single clear-cut opportunity which might have been
seized to re-think the practicalities of the British role in the offensive
or to reconsider if, indeed, it should be launched on the Somme
Front at all. Even as far back as April, with the plans well under way,
and with half the troops already en route to the Somme, it had been

far too late to launch into protracted re-negotiations with the French, even if political considerations had not deemed that to be highly inadvisable. The Army was committed to an offensive on the Somme. There was no going back and nothing to be done except to concentrate on training the infantry and to make all possible efforts to rectify their deficiencies before they went into battle.

It was easier said than done.

If midnight oil had been an essential ingredient of victory, the troops would have romped home, for the conferences, the discussion, the debate went on at Army Headquarters and at GHQ itself, long into the night. If the troops could have been swept into Bapaume on a tidal-wave of paper work, they would have been swirling through its streets in no time, for the various Headquarters were pouring out orders, commands, suggestions, memoranda, operational plans and instructions faster than a legion of clerks and printers could keep up with them. If a battle could have been won by planning, then the result would have been a foregone conclusion, for never, in the history of warfare, had a campaign been more meticulously planned down to the last infinitesimal detail. It was self-evident that the New Army – officers and men alike – was rich in morale and the will to win, but it was woefully lacking in knowledge, skill and experience. It was up to the Staff to fill the gaps, to envisage every possible contingency, to anticipate every move, to lay down the plans for every individual unit, and to lay them down within such a rigid framework that they could not fail to be clearly understood. So long as the men of the New Army adhered strictly to the instructions of the professionals, together they would carry the day.

Adhering to instructions was not a characteristic for which the independent spirits of Kitchener's Army were renowned. They had no objection to fighting, which, after all, was what they were here for. Since they had picked up the old soldiers' trick of rubbing candle-grease inside their socks, they had no great objection to marching. They could put up with the trenches and even with the labour involved in fatigues and working parties, for which there seemed to be some reasonable necessity and, on the whole, to a certain philosophic degree, they were willing to acquiesce with the less immediately comprehensible whims of the Army.

Many of the Army's 'whims' sprang from the conviction that, in the final analysis, battles were won by discipline, by the unquestioning, automatic response of all ranks to orders. Such traditional discipline, inculcated over long years in the time-serving hierarchy of the peacetime Army, was not so easy to impose on a heterogeneous mass of well-meaning civilians who regarded themselves as very temporary and very private soldiers, with what they considered to be a healthy disrespect for 'bull'. The Army understood this but, in the months of training for the Big Push, it seemed to certain officers, whose brains were whirling in the effort of trying to assimilate the contents of the reams of orders and instructions that were piling up into mountains on their desks, that certain molehills were receiving undue attention.

> *Things which may appear trivial matters to those who have only lately joined the Army are really of great importance, such as saluting, cleanliness, tidiness in dress, manner when speaking to their superiors, strict observance of orders.*

> *The strictest attention must continue to be paid to the cultivation of the power of command in young officers, also to discipline, dress, saluting, cleanliness and care of billets.*

> *Men must learn to obey by instinct without thinking*

> *Too great stress cannot be laid on developing good morale, a soldierly spirit, and a determination in all ranks to achieve success at all costs.* [1]

In order after order, in tones that varied from the hectoring to the plaintive, the Staff never missed an opportunity of pressing the message home.

The practicalities involved in training some two hundred thousand men to play an effective part in a full-scale battle, was even more of a problem. Brigadiers and Battalion Commanders of long-serving divisions became sick of complying with insistent demands which reached them almost daily from GHQ, that they should supply immediately: *six men fully qualified to act as instructors in signalling . . . bombing . . . Lewis-guns . . . Stokes mortar . . . bayonet drill . . . musketry. . . .* The demands were never ending. They groaned, grumbled, and, in most cases, seized the opportunity of getting rid of the duds.

With more than one hundred and fifty thousand men to be trained for the great attack, the Army could have done with a thousand specialist instructors, and they simply did not exist.

The best that could be done with the few who were available, was to appoint 'specialist' officers and NCOs in each of several hundred battalions and send them, by contingents, on intensive training courses at one of the various Army Schools some distance behind the line. Then to depend on them, assisted by voluminous notes and instructions, to pass on their knowledge to junior officers and to train the troops under their command. All the enthusiasm of Kitchener's Army could not prevent the outlines from becoming blurred as they travelled down the chain of command.

[1] Army Order SS 109. Issued by General Kiggell, 8 May 1915.

Chapter 3

Had it not been for the fact that the Army Schools needed soldiers to 'practise on', the 13th Battalion of The Rifle Brigade would not have received the unexpected bonus of what amounted to a month's holiday. You had to be good to be a demonstration battalion, and Colonel Pretor-Pinney had seen to it that his Battalion *was* good and, as he constantly dinned into them, not so much a Kitchener's Battalion as a Battalion of the Rifle Brigade. He had been an officer of the Regiment for more than thirty years – long enough to have retired twice and twice returned to the Active List to serve in two wars. It was a stroke of luck that he had soldiered in South Africa with Colonel Edward Gordon, for Colonel Gordon was now Assistant Adjutant General of the 37th Division and he regarded the battalion commanded by his old friend with a benevolent eye. He was impressed by its performance and he had chosen it, out of all the battalions in his division, to go to the Army School of Instruction at Auxi-le-Château to show them how things ought to be done. It was a signal honour and a blessed change from a succession of miserable stints in the trenches at le Gastineau.

But Auxi-le-Château, in the spring of 1916, was pure and simple bliss, only slightly mitigated by the fact that it was also hard work. At Auxi perfection was the order of the day, and nothing short of perfection would do. The turn-out of the demonstration squads had to be so immaculate that even the handles of entrenching tools were required to glisten in the early sunshine of morning parades. Their drilling had to be carried out with the precision of a regular battalion on the Regimental Parade Ground at Winchester. Squad by squad, company by company, they were drilled twenty times a day by a succession of self-conscious young subalterns, who squeaked their commands in nervous falsetto under the critical eye of a drill-sergeant to whom mere second-lieutenants were objects of ill-concealed scorn, rather than 'objects of respect'. The appellation 'object of respect' had been a favourite phrase of Corporal Lucas, whose unhappy task it had been to impart to B Company something of the requirements of the Army when they had first joined it nineteen months before, and Corporal Lucas, who was still pursuing the same thankless vocation at Regimental Headquarters, would have been amazed – if not gratified – had he known how often his words were remembered and quoted. Certain of his expressions had become catch-phrases in the Battalion.

Sergeant Howard
Rowlands, Coy.,B
13th (S) Btn., The
Rifle Brigade.

We often remembered old Corporal Lucas during the time we were at Auxi, particularly when it came to company drill and saluting. This was all for the education of the officers in training, and we had to do this saluting over and over and over again, until the lads were weary and sick and tired of it. But it just needed one fellow to say, 'About this serluting . . .' and everybody smiled and saw the joke. Old Lucas used to say, 'About this serluting, what I says is yer don't take it serious enough. Look at me, for example. I always chucks one up every time I meets an object of respect. Don't matter if it's a pretty girl, a Solomon in all his glory – meaning a ruddy general! – or a glass of beer!' We referred to officers as 'Objects of Respect' for a long time. He was a real Cockney. He took us for rifle drill too and, in explaining the aperture of a rifle, he always asked us, 'What is a naperture?' At first he used to give the answer himself. 'Why, a naperture's a nole!' After a while, we decided to convince him that we really understood so, whenever he enquired, 'What is a naperture?' the whole squad would yell back in delight, 'A naperture's a nole.' What agonies we went through trying to hide our amusement, for it was a serious crime to be insolent to a superior officer. But we caught on to these expressions of his and they went right round the Battalion.

The only members of B Company who never saw the point of the joke were the men of No. 5 Platoon who all hailed from Bermondsey.
    Drilling on the barrack-square at Winchester, garbed in every form of civilian attire from city suits to boating blazers, shod in civilian shoes, whose thin soles were rapidly giving way under the strain, adorned with headgear that represented every facet of the hatter's trade from bowlers to straw boaters, the infant battalion had looked a motley crew. Behind the uniform khaki front they now presented to the world, they still were. There was The Welsh Mob, of No. 6 Platoon, B Company, actually a group of civil servants from Cardiff who had joined up together. There was the Boys Brigade, who made up all of No. 13 Platoon and half of No. 14. There were the gamekeepers, eight of them, who had left the pheasants on the Wynyard Park Estate to look after themselves for the duration of the war. The Brewery Boys had all worked together at Bass Rutley. There were twelve pairs of brothers in the battalion. Jack Knotman had been an acrobat on the music halls. Jack Cross, now a sergeant in

C Company, had been a footman and valet to Sir Eric Barrington and kept his platoon comfortably supplied with the gloves, socks, scarves and balaclava helmets that must have been knitted non-stop below stairs at 62 Cadogan Place, so regularly did they arrive by every other post. Riflemam Adams, on the other hand, prevailed upon his comrades to carry his rifle on long marches and in return regaled them with the quails in aspic, tinned pineapple, ham galantine and, occasionally, caviare, contained in his parcels from Fortnum and Mason. There was Rifleman Arthur Wright, one of the Bermondsey Boys, who made no bones about having been a professional burglar and who had seen service in one of His Majesty's Prisons before joining His Majesty's Forces. There was Duggie Jones, the baby of the Battalion, burly enough to have got away with enlisting at the age of fifteen and who, in a post-war incarnation, was to become Aubrey Dexter, a successful actor. Rifleman Phipps, known as Old Chelsea, was the oldest member and admitted to having a son in the trenches. Partial to kippers, which his wife despatched to France with faithful regularity, he was still living down the episode when he had caused the entire battalion to 'Stand to' for a gas attack as a result of frying a little supper for himself in the trenches.

The Battalion was proud of its 'characters', but most of all it was proud of its sportsmen. It had The Golfers, seventeen professionals and assistants who had joined up as a body. There were the Stockton Boys, all semi-professional footballers, now, to the fury of the rest of the Brigade, forming a team that made the result of every inter-battalion match a foregone conclusion. There was the youthful Captain Arnold Strode Jackson, a formidable runner, who, as an undergraduate, had won a gold medal at Stockholm in the 1912 Olympic Games. There was Ernie Lowe, the Battalion's boxing champion and, since the South Africans had joined them in October, the 13th Rifle Brigade had been well-nigh invincible on the rugby field.

The 'South African Mob' had banded together and sailed from Port Elizabeth under their own steam and at their own expense, under the aegis of Captain Bill Nothard. It had been his idea. It would have been perfectly possible to join up in South Africa and a South African Brigade was already serving in France. But there were other theatres of war and there was no guarantee that locally recruited troops might not be sent to the Middle East or to fight in German West Africa. The only way to avoid this, to get a sniff at the 'real' war, was to take passage for London and join up on the spot.

We all paid our own passages, and we could afford it because none of us were badly off and sea passages were cheap in those days.

Rifleman Percy Eaton, No. 13873, 13th (S) Btn., The Rifle Brigade.

There were still passenger ships running and we had a very
pleasant voyage. We were quite the heroes on board! There was
myself and George Murrell and about twenty others 'recruited' by
Nothard. We docked at Southampton, after about three weeks,
took the boat train to Waterloo and went straight from the station
to the recruiting office in Whitehall. I have a half idea they were
expecting us. Nothard had got to know Colonel Gordon when he
had been a soldier in South Africa and he must have been in touch
with him. Anyway, we were attested, had very sketchy medicals
and within half an hour we were given railway warrants for
Winchester. So back we went to the station and it really was
priceless, because, as we left the recruiting office, there happened
to be a Guards' band coming out of Horseguards' Parade and
marching down Whitehall, so we joined on behind and we
marched behind them all the way to Westminster Bridge. We had
no idea of marching and it was very difficult trying to keep time
and carrying suitcases and all our gear, but we were as pleased as
Punch! We did some very basic training at Winchester and we
were soon on our way to France. We joined the 13th at Gommecourt in October 1915 and we were told that this was on the
recommendation of Colonel Gordon and that they were the best
battalion in the 37th Division. Perhaps because a good few of us
had had experience of shooting in South Africa we nearly all
became Lewis-Gunners.

Now the South African Mob were appreciating the break at Auxi
more than any others in the battalion. The weather was fine, the
spring sun shone and, after the unaccustomed rigours of a European
winter spent almost entirely in the open in the trenches, or, when out
of them, billeted in draughty barns which were not much better, for
the first time since arriving in France they felt actually warm. After
the intricacies of command on the parade ground had been mastered by the young officers in training, and the perfection of
'serluting' was deemed to have been adequately demonstrated, they
had moved on to the real thing – command of troops in battle. That
was a lot more fun, at least for the guinea pigs. They mounted mock
attack after mock attack. They sniped, they machine-gunned, they
mopped up, they consolidated, they signalled, they advanced and
they vanquished the Kaiser's imaginary Army a thousand times over.

But the battles and the manoeuvering across the springtime
meadows stopped promptly at five o'clock. There was time for a kip
and a clean-up, before 'Men's Supper', which in itself was a
heartening improvement on the meagre fare that reached the troops
at the front, and, afterwards, for those intent on pleasure, an

embarrassment of riches to choose from. Auxi-le-Château itself was a real town, with streets where civilians and, in particular, pretty girls, could be seen, just as if there were no war on; there were buildings undamaged by shellfire, cafés and *estaminets*, concerts in the Hôtel de Ville and, best of all, a British Expeditionary Force Canteen which even the most impecunious could afford to patronise. In the 'Officers Only' cafés, earnest young subalterns fought table-top skirmishes and, assisted by Messrs Bryant and May, disposed platoons of matchsticks to illustrate the finer points of the tactical theories they were obliged to master in order to return to their battalions with satisfactory reports. As the spring evenings lengthened, the sportsmen of the battalion preferred to eschew the pleasures of Auxi. Even after the exertions of the day there was pleasure in a scratched up football match. To the golfers, most of whom had found some devious means of bringing a club or two to France, or having them sent on afterwards, the gentle slopes around the green valley of Auxi were natural reminders of Gleneagles, of Turnberry, of Deal or Lytham St Annes. They spent happy competitive evenings, putting and driving, joined occasionally by some officers who shared their passion and were only too happy to pick up a few professional hints.

The rugger players, like the footballers, never tired of training and practising. Since the Rifle Brigade had gone into wartime khaki, they were the only people who were privileged to sport its traditional colours of green and black, admittedly only in the stripes of their team jerseys, but the colours of the Regiment, nevertheless. It was a sore point with some of the non-sporting riflemen who, like Joe Hoyles, had been dazzled by pre-war glamour.

There were five of us joined up together, Archie Nicholson, Fred Lyons, Frank Bell, Sid Birkett and myself. We all worked at W. H. Smith's in Nottingham. I'd absolutely made up my mind and, when we went up to the barracks to join up, I said, 'We're going into the finest regiment in the British Army.' And they said, 'What's that?' And I said, 'The Rifle Brigade. Left of the Line and pride of the British Army.' I was only seventeen, but it was a unique regiment to me. In my own little town of Oakham, there were two officers of the Rifle Brigade who used to come home on leave and they looked so smartly dressed in the green and black and always with a black sash around their shoulders. It caught my eye. I thought it was wonderful. And there was another fellow in the town who also struck me when I was a boy. He'd been a private, they called him Scotchie Waterfield, and he must have been quite old then. But he'd been in the Rifle Brigade and when

Rifleman Joe Hoyles, MM, No. 3237, 13th (S) Btn., The Rifle Brigade you saw him walking down the main street he looked marvellous. It was his quick step. I found out afterwards it was a hundred and forty steps to the minute. From just a young boy I'd thought what a wonderful champion regiment this must be.

The practical wartime khaki which had succeeded green jackets and red coats alike was a poor substitute for the peacock traditions of peacetime, but at least the riflemen sported black buttons on their khaki and they had learned, as generations of riflemen had learned before them, to march at one hundred and forty steps to the minute. It was when the glorious month at Auxi was over and they were marching back to the trenches that this particular aptitude got them into trouble, for, by then, most of the Fourth Army was on the move and fanning out across the face of Picardy.

The sheer logistics of assembling the troops on the Somme in time to familiarise them with their sectors of the trenchline, and to move them back and forwards to rehearse the battle, was a monumental headache that had spread from the apex of GHQ down through the chain of command to furrow the brows of several thousand quartermasters and transport officers at battalion level. A single brigade on the move with its transport occupied at least three miles of road. With the tail of the column an hour's march behind the vanguard and the obligatory ten minutes' rest in every hour, it took two hours and a half, marching easy, to cover that distance. If one such procession met another at a crossroads proceeding in the opposite direction, the subsequent contretemps could hold up ten thousand men in a chain reaction that stretched for miles and hours behind and could throw out the carefully planned arrangements of a dozen hapless billeting officers, who had earmarked three or four adjacent villages for the accommodation of their brigades that night.

Working out the permutations by which the mass migration could be smoothly achieved, was a task so tortuous that the compilation of *Cook's International Time-table* would have been child's play by comparison. It took long laborious calculations, endless consultations with the scattered commands of a dozen other units and the careful working out of routes over a countryside whose roads could hardly be described as arterial, and where the main access roads must be left clear, so far as possible, for the endless columns of lorries carrying supplies and munitions to the forward areas. Marching along what was little more than a country track, the last thing a battalion of the Royal Warwicks had needed was a quick-stepping battalion of the Rifle Brigade marching up on its heels and creating mayhem in its rear ranks. The ensuing discussion between the two battalions turned the air blue and it was popularly supposed that it was about the time of the move to the Somme that Rifle Regiments earned the epithet 'Black Buttoned Bastards'.

If the 'Black Buttoned Bastards' returning to the trenches in the Third Army area were a touch despondent that their halcyon month was over, the troops of the Fourth Army arriving from the north, although they had no illusions about what was ahead of them, were revelling in the change of scene.

We thought it was lovely country when we got there, because we'd been up in the north before where it was very flat and uninteresting. Here it was all hillier and there were little cottages with gardens and spring flowers coming out. There was a lovely stream nearby and the lads used to bathe in it. It was cold when we first got there but the water gradually got warmer and warmer. What I liked especially was the delight of lying in the grass among the apple trees bursting into blossom and listening to the birds singing, instead of the whistling of the shells. Some lads got fishing rods and gear and were fishing in the stream, and there were plenty of sports and football matches. It was so peaceful you just couldn't believe it. Later on it got more strenuous.

Private Tom Easton, No. 1000, 21st Btn., Northumberland Fusiliers (2nd Tyneside Scottish).

Early in May we marched off again from the lovely peace and quiet and went to la Houssaye, where we joined up with the Third Corps and started training with the 8th and the 21st Divisions for the Battle of the Somme. The ground was supposed to correspond to the ground on the Somme and we were hard at it training; first in platoon and company movement under orders and then even on battalion movement on a wider basis, so that we could practise our art of offensive soldiering. Then we took over our sector of the front but there was always one or two brigades out of the line occupied with training.

They practised moving in the open by platoons, they practised manoeuvring in companies, then moving in waves as a battalion. Then came a whole week when all four battalions trained as a brigade, carrying out the complicated procedures of consolidation, reinforcement, 'leap-frogging' a second line of troops through the first and passing on to the second and third lines of enemy 'trenches' and even beyond. The bombers 'bombed', the snipers 'sniped'. The moppers up went through the motions of bombing 'dugouts', represented by flags inside the shallow 'trenches'. They were mere lines, scratched with spade or plough across the field and they did it all over and over again, until every man from a battalion's colonel downwards knew precisely what to do and when to do it.

It was in the brigade and divisional exercises that signallers like

Tom Easton truly came into their own, for the Royal Flying Corps took part, flying up and down the divisional front, swooping down towards the troops and climbing away with a cheerful waggle of wings when the troops signalled back their position in response to a loud klaxon horn sounded by the pilot. They signalled by spreading out white ground-sheets bearing an outsize divisional sign which transmitted the categorical statement, *We are here and so far as we know are the leading infantry and within fifty yards of the firing line.* Some signallers were taught to operate an even more sophisticated piece of equipment.

Private Tom Easton, No. 1000, 21st Btn., Northumberland Fusiliers (2nd Tyneside Scottish).

I was on aircraft communications. All the time we were doing these movements over open countryside, the aeroplanes were going up and down the line all the time and we had to practise communicating with them with flare lamps and ground-sheet signals. We signallers had to carry out a giant shutter, six foot square, lay it on the ground, peg it down, go to one end, grasp the ropes and it pulled open like a venetian blind. The surface was all brown when it was closed but it was a pure white surface when we pulled it open and we had to make coded letters in Morse Code: series of Cs, series of Hs, and so on, which were all part of the code. In my experience as a battalion signaller these were never used. They might have been used by other battalions – though I doubt it – but later on in battle, our reception was so hot that there was no possibility of using it. In fact we never even carried it into the battle.

In the long weeks of conferring and drawing up the battle plans at GHQ, at Army HQ and at Corps Headquarters, the question of signals had an important place in every agenda. Once the troops went over the top, a fool-proof system of communications was the sole means by which the Staff could control the battle. Only on the basis of a constant flow of up-to-the-minute information from the thick of the fight itself, would they be able to send in, or withhold, reinforcements, assist the troops with artillery fire, help them out of difficulties and support them in exploiting success – and do all these things instantly.

The lifeline that would carry vital news of the situation at the front far and fast to command posts in the rear, was the network of telephone wires and cables. For every mile of front, five hundred miles of cable had been buried – and buried six feet deep in the forward areas. Behind Divisional Headquarters, no less than three thousand miles of wire linked the infantry to the artillery, the artillery to the Flying Corps, to balloon sections, to transport lines, to reserves, and to corps and Army HQ in a cat's cradle of circuits and connections that would carry the news from the front, with mercurial despatch, through every stage of liaison and command to the ear of Sir Douglas Haig himself. Thus far the army could make its arrangements, but all would depend, and well they knew it, on the troops sending back information equally fast, once they had gone over the top. Signallers, of course, would go over with them as part of the second wave, reeling out heavy rolls of cable as they went to link up with the communications behind, but, in the hazards of battle, it would be foolish to depend on either all of them or all the cable escaping unscathed. What was needed were fail-safes and in such profusion as to guarantee ten times over that communications could not possibly break down.

There were to be signalling lamps, power buzzers, black and white discs by which Morse messages could be signalled back visually and even the despised semaphore flags were to be carried. There would be heliographs, telephones and carrier pigeons, which even now were being taken daily into the trenches and trained to fly back, straight and fast, to the lofts behind the line. There were to be runners – and twice the usual number of them, travelling in pairs – to bring messages back from the forward troops to the old jumping-off line. There were to be marker-pennants, six feet high, carried by the leading man of each company. There were to be coloured flares, five hundred per battalion, to be fired on the instructions of an officer or senior NCO in a complicated series of coded patterns and sequences which they were studiously committing to memory.

Towards the end of the training period, when such instructions as were not marked 'SECRET' reached company level, some officers poring over the long lists of equipment that were to be carried into the attack, came gloomily to the conclusion that the only thing the Army had neglected to consider was the provision of extra pairs of arms for the men to carry them.[1] But, somehow it would have to be managed, for these long and slender lines of communication were the reins by which the Army would direct it fledgling infantry and drive it forward to success.

[1] In the first moments of the attack, one German officer, astounded by the sight of the long lines of heavily encumbered Tommies approaching at a slow walk and looking, to his astonished eyes, as if they were setting out on a day's outing, later wrote that, '. . . some were even carrying picnic baskets and others Kodaks as if to take photographs as a souvenir of their outing'. The 'picnic baskets' contains pigeons, the 'Kodaks' were power buzzers.

Chapter 4

Standing on either side of the German Salient at Gommecourt, beyond the northern limit of the planned offensive, the 56th and 46th Divisions did not take much part in extensive rehearsals for the Big Push. For one thing, although they had an important supporting role to play, like the 37th Division they were part of the Third Army; for another they were part of the Territorial Force and they had been part-time soldiers since 1910 when the Territorials were formed as an emergency arm of the Army. But most battalions had long since outgrown the peacetime soubriquet of 'Saturday Afternoon Soldiers'. They had been fighting in France since the early days of the war, and justifiably considered themselves to be as good as the Regulars.

As an officer of the 3rd Londons, Arthur Agius had fought at Neuve Chapelle, at Aubers Ridge, at Festubert and at Loos. In more than a year of heavy fighting, the Battalion had been sadly depleted by casualties and brought up to strength again by drafts of soldiers who were just as inexperienced as any in the ranks of Kitchener's Army, but who had had the foresight to join local Territorial Battalions in August 1914. Even from the start they had considered themselves to be one up on 'Kitchener's Mob'. As Territorials, they were issued with uniforms months before their less fortunate comrades had glimpsed so much as a khaki sock, and they had been equipped with rifles even before they knew how to fire them. They also had the advantage of serving on their own doorsteps. At first, some of the Kensingtons were even allowed to continue living at home and to endow their grateful mothers with the Army billeting allowance of seven and six a week, travelling daily by tram-car to the White City at Shepherd's Bush, where the Battalion was housed in the garish pavilions left over from the Empire Exhibition of 1913. Fortunately, not all of the temporary buildings had been demolished and the old pavilions made admirable orderly rooms, offices, gymnasiums and dining halls where the troops enjoyed meals supplied by courtesy of Messrs Lyons whose tea rooms adorned almost every corner in the West End of London. Lyons factory and head offices were conveniently situated nearby at 'Cadby Hall' in High Street, Kensington, where a large staff of girls never failed to rush to the windows to shout and wave to the Kensingtons, marching past on their way to drill in Hyde Park. The Kensingtons, in their turn, never failed to favour this admiring throng with a lusty rendering of their favourite marching song:

> *We are the Kensington Boys*
> *We are the Kensington Boys*
> *We spend our tanners*
> *We mind our manners,*
> *We are respected wherever we go,*
> *When we're marching down the High Street Ken,*
> *Doors and windows open wide.*
> *You can hear the sergeant shout,*
> *Put those blooming Woodbines out,*
> *We are the Kensington Boys.*

The complacency of some of the Kensington Boys was jolted when they were drafted to France and discovered that their seniors in the 56th London Division did not look kindly on such vociferous self-praise. They had adopted as their anthem and marching song a music-hall ditty which had enlivened their peacetime Saturday evenings at Joy's or Wilton's:

> *I'm 'Enery the Eighth I am.*
> *'Enery the Eighth I am, I am,*
> *I got married to the widow next door,*
> *She'd been married seven times before.*
> *AND every one was an 'Enery,*
> *She wouldn't have a Willie or a Sam.*
> *I'm 'er eighth Old Man called 'Enery,*
> *'ENERY THE EIGHTH I AM!*

They marched for miles and miles singing it, and neither its swing nor its charm ever palled. Early in May they had marched to the village of Hébuterne and taken over a trenchline beyond it, facing the Germans to the right of Gommecourt village. Almost their first job had been to dig a trench, which struck some of the troops as being slightly ironic in view of the fact that at Hébuterne there were more trenches than there were troops to fill them. Hébuterne itself consisted of a long village street with a half-ruined church, a few run-down farms whose tenants had long since decamped and which now served, like the tumbledown rows of cottages, as advanced headquarters and billets for signallers, orderlies, and regimental police whose duties kept them near the front line. The front line itself ran parallel to the village street, a few hundred yards ahead of it, and the lanes that ran through orchards to the vestiges of the old fields served as communication trenches to the line – or lines, for the French, during their occupancy, had dug a complete complex of trenches. The British, thinking them too wide, too shallow and 'not much good', had dug a whole new system when they had taken over, a fact which runners of the newly arrived 56th Division frequently cursed whenever their travels between the front and Battalion Headquarters were delayed by involuntary meanderings that terminated infuriatingly in a dead end.

On their left the 46th Division stood in front of the village of Fonquevillers whose tongue-twisting proper name was seldom used by any soldier below the rank of full general. From the Brigadier downwards it was universally known as 'Funky Villas'. Between the two villages and the two Divisions, the woodland of Gommecourt Park stuck its impertinent snout towards the British lines in a salient that formed the westernmost point of the whole of the German trenchline in France. The German trenches followed its angular outline and swept back along both sides of the country road that once led from Puisieux to the village of Gommecourt and on to Fonquevillers. Now the road itself was part of the formidable complex of trenches that stretched southwards and swung over the downs of the Somme facing the Fourth Army. The Gommecourt sector, on the Third Army Front, was immediately adjacent to the left flank of the Fourth.

In front of the 56th Division a shallow valley separated the British trenches from the German line. It was across this valley that the new trench had to be dug, so far out in No Man's Land that it would be within spitting distance of the German front line. It was to be dug by one brigade over only two nights and Arthur Agius, acting under the Brigade-Major, was in charge of the operation.

Captain A. J. Agius, MC, 3rd Btn., Royal Fusiliers, City of London Regiment, 56th Division.

Our lines were about eight hundred yards from the Germans. We didn't know we were going to be selected for an attack, but we were told we were to go out and build a complete new trench system, four hundred yards in front and four hundred yards nearer the Germans, which sounded absolute madness. So, I went out with our Brigade-Major one night from a forward sap and we went on for a quarter of a mile, just the two of us, with a soldier carrying a sandbag full of chalk. After taking various measurements and compass directions, we dumped all this chalk and made a cairn of it. (It was chalk country, so it wouldn't be noticed.) We covered the German side with grass so that they shouldn't see the cairn and then we had to work to our left until we came to a road that ran out of our lines. The landmark there was a hawthorn bush that was in full blossom (this was the middle of May) and that made a very convenient point for a marker. It took some doing to lay out a complete front line with traverses and so on. But, in the hours of darkness, we marked all this out with string and pegs and then the next night we set off to do the actual digging.

I went out, almost as soon as it got dark, with a small covering party, a subaltern and about ten men, to lie out in front in case we were rushed by a German patrol. We taped the whole of this thing out and, as soon as we'd finished running the white tape across it, marking all the traverses and every inch of the line, and every angle and turn, the troops filed in and started to dig like billy-o. We had more than five hundred men out there and we dug that whole length of trench in two nights. What a job that was! Of course the Germans knew that something was up. So the second night they pounded us like mad with shellfire and we lost quite a few men. But we got it finished.

It was the Army's intention that the enemy should see that 'something was up'. It was doing its best to convince the Germans that 'something was up' along the whole of the Third Army Front from Gommecourt to Arras. If the Germans could be seduced into the belief that the Big Push was to take place here rather than on the Fourth Army Front on the Somme, then the troops there might be attacking with an element of surprise which could make all the difference. At the very least, the enemy might be misled into believing that the attack would take place on a wider front than was intended and would therefore maintain strong reserves of artillery and infantry opposite the Third Army, rather than sending them south to form part of the unpleasant welcome committee that all too clearly awaited the Fourth Army on the Somme.

The Third Army co-operated enthusiastically in the deception. Its artillery bombarded the enemy lines and cut the barbed wire in front of their trenches as effectively as if they really were about to storm across. Night after night, the infantry raided and patrolled and pushed its line forward as if preparing for a jump-off. They dug complexes of dummy assembly trenches behind the lines. They were only eighteen inches deep, but they looked authentic enough from the air, and some divisions even embellished the illusion by manning them with a phantom army represented by ragged sandbags fluttering on man-sized sticks. After dark, each night, all up and down the sector, convoys of army limbers, piled high with rattling cargoes of empty biscuit tins, clattered about in phantom convoys to simulate intense activity on the roads behind the lines.

At a meeting of corps commanders just two days before the battle, General Snow had the satisfaction of telling the Commander-in-Chief, 'They know we're coming all right!' And Sir Douglas Haig was able to reward him in return with the latest information, gleaned by Intelligence. The Germans had stiffened their Gommecourt front with a whole extra division and its artillery.

The bluff had worked. But, unlike the two divisions to the north of them, the 46th and 56th ranged in V-shaped formation in front of Gommecourt, were not entirely bluffing. So far as the Germans were concerned, they were indeed 'coming'. At the moment of the attack by the Fourth Army on their right, they too were to attack the Germans on either side of Gommecourt.

It had been Haig's own idea, and he had arrived at it after careful consideration. Any attack which would divert the attention of the Germans away from the Somme was desirable. But an attack at Gommecourt, just two miles north of the limit of the Big Push, would have one insuperable advantage. It would protect the 8th Corps. More particularly, it would protect the 31st Division on the extreme left flank not only of the 8th Corps but of the whole battle line. And, in Haig's opinion, the 31st Division badly needed some protection.

Most of the men in the 31st Division were hardly aware that they were in the Fourth Army, never mind the 8th Corps. It was doubtful if many of them could have reeled off the number of his brigade without hesitation. They seldom even referred to their battalions by their official titles. A man of the 13th or the 14th Battalion of the York and Lancaster Regiment preferred to think of himself as being one of the 1st or the 2nd Barnsley Pals. A man of the 12th Battalion regarded himself as one of the 'Sheffield Pals', while a soldier of any one of the four battalions which made up the 92nd Brigade would claim to belong to 'The Hull Mob'. Even within his own battalion a man's interest seldom extended beyond the limits of his own company. In many cases, it was pretty well confined to his own platoon of twenty or so, because, in the Pals Battalions, the real pals, often from a single village, a single street, a single factory or sports club, stuck together. In all of Kitchener's Army there was hardly a group of more happy-go-lucky amateur soldiers than the Pals and luck, so far, had been on their side. While the majority of the New Army had been enduring the chill and discomfort of winter on the Western Front, the Pals had been wintering in Egypt and had only been brought back to France late in the spring. Most of them had 'souvenirs', including 'lucky scarabs', acquired at swindling expense in some Alexandria bazaar, carried in hopeful optimism that their luck would continue.

The Commander-in-Chief was not quite so optimistic about the prospects of the men as the men were themselves. In the months before the offensive, like grand-masters hunched over an imaginary chessboard that stretched across the fields of France and Belgium, the High Command had moved and rearranged the component parts of divisions, of brigades, and even of battalions, so that almost every Regular division now contained an element of Kitchener's Army, and almost every division of the New Army contained a stiffening quota of experienced troops.

In the case of the 31st Division, a scant three months had not been long enough in which to switch them around. It had hardly been long enough to exchange their pith helmets and khaki drill for tin hats and warm clothing, to school them in the routine of the trenches and to take them through rehearsals of their part in the battle. But, with careful deliberation, the Army deployed its forces so that the Pals should not be overtaxed. Their task was simple. At the northern extremity of the line, all that the Pals were expected to do was to advance a thousand yards, capture Serre, and throw an encircling arm round the northern flank of the front that ran southwards over fifteen straggling miles. They would stand on this position so that, as the Army pursued its inevitable breakthrough, the whole glorious advance could pivot on this point and swing outwards from it towards the open country. The Pals were to oil the hinge that would open the door to Bapaume, to the French frontier, and, eventually, to Berlin itself.

It should be a piece of cake. On their left they would be protected by a smokescreen, rolling thick across two miles, and, beyond that, by the attack at Gommecourt.[1]

On the right the Regular 4th Division, as tried and tested as any troops could be, would carry the Pals forward by their very momentum. And, beyond them both, the 29th Division, which had proved itself at Gallipolli, could certainly be depended on. It was true that the 4th and 29th Divisions faced the strongpoint of Beaumont Hamel, but the Staff had made provision to trump that particular ace in the Germans' hand.

Beaumont Hamel lay at the foot of a dip in the cleft of a narrow valley, protected at its back by one arm of the deep Y-shaped ravine

---

[1] The instructions to the 56th and 46th Divisions were explicitly: *to assist in the operations of the Fourth Army by diverting against itself the fire of artillery and infantry, which might otherwise be directed against the left flank of the main attack near Serre.*

that ran towards the British line and then swung parallel to it. It was a natural feature, which provided shelter for men and guns alike. Immediately in front, the village was protected by rising ground which ran away to the north towards Serre and it was on this elevation, to the left of Beaumont Hamel and some two hundred yards in front of it, that the Germans had built the massive Hawthorn Redoubt, standing sentinel on the breast of the hill and pushing towards the British lines a mere two hundred yards away on the downward slope. Here, concealed by a sunken track, the British had driven long galleries through the chalky ridge and planted a mine, big enough and powerful enough to blow the Hawthorn Redoubt sky-high and breach the defences of Beaumont Hamel.

But Beaumont Hamel was not the only visible strongpoint on the German line. To the north there was Serre itself and, between it and Beaumont Hamel, another fort on the Redan Ridge. To the south, beyond the River Ancre, the ruins of Thiepval village stood high above the valley and the shoulders of the ridge on either side of it were armoured with defensive works. To the left, the labyrinths of the Schwaben Redoubt and Goat Redoubt were scribbled across the slope of the ridge, facing Beaumont Hamel and Beaucourt across the river. To the right of Thiepval, the complex of trenches they called the Wunderwerk dominated the summit of the ridge and beyond it, the maze of the Leipzig Redoubt thrust like an obstinate jaw towards the British line above Authuille. There it turned to swing over to the twin villages of Ovillers and la Boisselle across the valley beyond. And, around la Boisselle – like Ovillers, a strongpoint in itself – another network of complex defence systems glared, balefully protective, in full view of the British line. Then, to the right, was the great bulging salient where the fortified village of Fricourt was enclosed by the German line as it changed direction and swivelled briefly on an eastward route in front of Mametz and Montauban before turning southwards at the River Somme, where the British Army stood side by side with the French.

Even without positive knowledge of the extent of the German diggings and the concealed fortifications and defences, it was perfectly clear that there were some hard nuts to crack and that, if the advance was to go fast and far in the first vital hours, special attention would have to be given to the problems they presented.

Groaning under the weight of some million pounds of explosive, which had to be carried to the sap-heads over long weary miles by a thousand weary working parties, the infantry did not always bless the solicitous preparations which their Staff were making on their behalf.

Just how to tackle the strongpoints that spiked the German line

was a tactical headache, to which the Army had devoted considerable thought and the Fourth Army had issued its own thoughts on
the subject in mid-May. But, as they were very well aware and as
General Kiggell had stated quite categorically in his memorandum
from GHQ, *It must be remembered that officers and troops generally do
not now possess that military knowledge arising from a long and high state
of training, which enables them to act promptly on sound lines in unexpected
situations. They have become accustomed to deliberate action based on
precise and detailed orders. . . .*

Such 'precise and detailed orders' it was the business of the Army
to supply. It was unfortunate that there was not sufficient time to
plant mines under all or nearly all the most strongly defended
sections of the German Front but there was no help for it. The mine
at Beaumont Hamel was well under way and would be ready in good
time. A pair of mines on either side of la Boisselle would shake the
German garrison to bits along with its defensive outposts. Mines on
a smaller scale would give them a nasty surprise at Fricourt and,
although the troops would not be attacking the Fricourt Salient directly, would keep them on the *qui vive* while they swept past it on
either side and 'pinched it out', while two others, judiciously placed
under their line south of Montauban should assist the troops
forward in fine style. As for Thiepval, the effect of the explosions on
either side of its high fastness, at Beaumont Hamel and at la
Boisselle, should be sufficient to rattle the Germans – or, at least, so
it was hoped. And, in any event, the whole series of explosions were a
mere refinement, extra insurance, the final ounce of thrust that
would catapult the troops through and beyond the German line.

The citadels of intricate entrenchments, the battered villages they
defended, the deep palisades of barbed wire that lay in front of them,
would all long since have been shattered to atoms by the thundering
British bombardment, so heavy, so fierce and so continuous that not
a man nor a brick could hope to escape destruction.

The barrage opened up on 24 June. It was Midsummer's Day.

Chapter 5

From Frise on the French Front to Arras on the left of the Third Army, the guns opened on the forty-mile front in the full-throated knowledge that ammunition had been dumped in unprecedented quantities behind the batteries. That Sunday morning, 25 June, with a light easterly breeze blowing from the front, they could be heard quite plainly at Montreuil, set high on its fortress hill more than seventy miles away near the coast. At nine o'clock precisely, General Sir Douglas Haig and two ADCs stepped from the front door of the Château of Beaurepaire, mounted their perfectly groomed horses and turned their heads toward Montreuil four kilometres away. It was a pleasant ride along the narrow country road, through the lush greenery of early summer, to the foot of the steep cobbled hill and on up through the encircling ramparts into the town. Centuries earlier, the massive walls had been built to keep the marauding English at bay. From this vantage point, a hundred years before, Napoleon had looked covetously across the English Channel. Now the ramparts were guarding the security of the very people the French had gone to so much trouble to keep out and it was the French themselves who were the interlopers. The whole town had been taken over as the General Headquarters of the British Army and even the three thousand civilians who remained in Montreuil required the authority of the British to pass in or out of it. The civilians were outnumbered, two to one, by the military – almost all of them immaculate staff-officers, whose red hatbands had earned them the troops' nickname of 'geraniums'.

The nerve-centre of GHQ was in the Ecole Militaire in a narrow street a few yards away from the eastern ramparts. So many high-ranking officers passed so often through its exclusive archway, that the presentation of 'military compliments' had to be drastically revised. A mere colonel who, anywhere else, might have expected a full salute, was accorded no more than a token slap on a rifle butt, and generals were so thick on the ground that those who went regularly to and fro only expected to be greeted as befitted their rank once a day. Even the Commander-in-Chief, a stickler for military etiquette, issued orders that he should receive a full salute only on his first appearance – but woe betide the sentry who failed to turn out the guard to receive him. Although the guardroom was only a few yards down the passage leading to the inner courtyard, this was no easy task.

General Haig was in the habit of taking the longer but more pleasant route around the ramparts and, after the briefest of moments when he was just visible through a gap in the buildings, he appeared, only thirty yards away, already turning the head of his charger towards the École Militaire, expecting to be received by an immaculately turned-out guard and full military honours. Under these circumstances, the turning out of the guard was easier to expect than to achieve. After one unfortunate occurrence, when General Haig had caught them unawares, breathless, hastily buckling on belts and fastening buttons, and had insisted that they should do it all over again, the military mind had turned from consideration of weightier problems to contrive a solution which would satisfy both military etiquette and the Commander-in-Chief. It took the form of an electric bell, placed high on the wall at exactly the right height to be pressed by the tip of the sentry's rifle as he caught his first fleeting glimpse of General Haig's approach. There had been no further complaints.

Now, on the eve of the long-planned campaign, the Commander-in-Chief, with his Chiefs of Intelligence, was about to move to Advanced Headquarters for the duration of the battle. A château had been prepared for him at Beauquesne, fifteen miles behind the battle-line. Meanwhile, Sir Douglas Haig was on his way to church.

Some boys were kicking a ball around on the patch of grass in front of the bridge that crossed the moat to the massive citadel, where a pair of immaculate sentries stamped and strutted beneath the Union Jack, fluttering above the postern gate. They stopped to nudge each other and to admire as the small group of horsemen clattered by. Raymond Wable, thirteen years old and home for the weekend from his school at Berck Plage, noticed that they seemed to shine in the sunlight – polished buttons, polished belts, high-polished riding boots, glistening harness and burnished silver spurs against the glossy coats of the horses. ''Aig,' they whispered to each other, their eyes swivelling towards the sentries in delighted anticipation of the full 'Present Arms'.

But the destination of the Commander-in-Chief was not the citadel; it was a modest wooden barrack, twenty yards away on the ramparts, and the flag that fluttered above its modest entrance was the blue and white of the St Andrew's cross, announcing that this was the Church of Scotland Hut. Meticulously punctual, Sir Douglas Haig had arrived with just two minutes to spare before the start of the Sunday morning service. He was in need of a little quiet meditation.

The Reverend Mr Duncan had prepared his sermon with some care. He preached on a text from Chronicles, 'Yea, I will go in the power of the Almighty God,' and he drew from these words a simple theme. God is ever present. His plans rule the Universe. We are merely tools in His Hands, used for a special purpose. The Commander-in-Chief listened intently. Duncan's words struck a chord in his mind and, later that day, he carefully noted the details of the sermon. 'He quoted a saying of Abraham Lincoln's when asked if he was sure The Lord was with him. He replied that the important point was that "he should be on the side of The Lord". Mr Duncan also told the story of how, before the attack began, the Scots knelt down in prayer on the battlefields of Bannockburn in 1314. Altogether it was a most inspiring sermon.'

Sir Douglas Haig was a devout man. He was worried about the battle. He was uplifted, even reassured, by the re-statement of one of the tenets of his simple faith. At the door of the hut, shaking hands with the minister after the service, with one ear cocked towards the distant murmur of the bombardment seventy miles away on the Somme, the Commander-in-Chief was struck by a happy thought. Would Mr Duncan care to accompany him when he moved to Advanced Headquarters for the forthcoming battle? Mr Duncan was 'very pleased at the idea'. He would have forty-eight hours to make his arrangements. On Tuesday, the Commander-in-Chief would be moving to Beauquesne.

All across the seventy miles that separated GHQ at Montreuil from the front, in fields and meadows beyond the tumbledown barns and cottages of some hundreds of villages where the troops were encamped, the routine church parades took on a special significance on this last Sunday before the men went into battle. Just as the Church of Scotland Minister at Montreuil had sought to inspire the Commander-in-Chief, padres of all denominations had cast round for themes that would encourage and sustain the men through the ordeal ahead. Most of them automatically struck on the same choice of hymns. *Fight the Good Fight* and *Onward Christian Soldiers* were usually selected as being the most appropriate note to wind up the service before the men marched off. The 6th Battalion of the West Yorkshire Regiment sang them both at their service in the orchard at Puchevillers before marching off to dismiss for dinners and an afternoon of comparative leisure.

There had been no parades for several days. 'Enjoy yourselves,' Colonel Wade had said and, after months of heavy training, the implication of this benevolence was not lost on the troops. There was a wholesale exodus to Beauquesne and, on the philosophical principle that there was no point in going into battle with money in your pocket, champagne corks popped merrily in its cafés all afternoon. The less affluent played cricket or simply indulged in horseplay in the orchard. The favourite pastime which, even after two months ragging and rough and tumble, still amused a few, was 'testing' the efficiency of the new tin helmets by assaulting hard-headed volunteers with whatever implements were to hand – entrenching tools, knobkerries, or even spades. After 'casualties' amounting to one fractured skull and several cases of concussion the Colonel had forbidden this pastime, but the risk of retribution merely added spice to the proceedings and, if some amateur bookie was willing to give odds, the amusement of a mild flutter. Serious gamblers huddled round the forbidden Crown and Anchor board, set up in a discreetly distant corner of the orchard, and soldiers, at a loose end, strolled through the village, up the country road and gathered in curious groups outside the empty tents of the newly erected casualty clearing station, to indulge in the time-honoured holiday entertainment of watching other people at work. A little distance from the big marquees, the orderlies were hard at it. They were digging graves. The wags of the battalion, with heavy witticism aimed at the new recruits, speculated ghoulishly on who was destined to occupy them.

Forty-eight hours before the march-off there were a thousand details to be seen to and Colonel Wade had called a meeting of his officers to discuss them and to detail those who were to be left behind. Six officers and extra detachments of bombers, Lewis-gunners, signallers and scouts were to march off with the battalion but would stay behind at Bouzincourt ready to move forward to replace casualties. The main body was ordered to Thiepval – not to attack it but, timing their arrival for Zero plus two hours, to pass through the triumphant ranks of the 36th Ulsters of the first wave and to stride on to consolidate the third objective and wait there for the next move.

Now that the maps were actually being distributed, the next move looked interesting. The first was a mere leaflet, a sketchy affair covering three miles at most and showing the area behind and in front of the first three familiar objectives. The officers glanced at it with passing interest and turned their attention to the more beguiling attractions of the maps which only the senior officers would carry into action. They were large maps and, on the scale of one inch to a thousand yards, they illustrated the fifty miles of country between Douai and St Quentin and the thirty miles that lay between it and Bapaume.

There was no Sunday rest for the Gunners. The field guns, ranged in batteries a thousand yards behind the front, and the line of heavy siege guns a mile or so to the rear, were pounding the German defences – sending over 150,000 shells non-stop every twenty-four hours. They went on firing until the recoil buffers of some field guns snapped under the strain. They fired until the breeches were so red hot that they had to be broken open with an axe. And they were firing precisely to programme, for the barrage tables issued to each battery were as finely delineated as the detailed orders to which every battalion of the infantry was expected to adhere.

The 'heavies' in the rear were entrusted with the main task of pulverising the German trenches and dugouts with shells so numerous and so huge that, if you watched carefully, you could see them in flight on the lowest part of their trajectory as they left the muzzles of the guns. The infantry and the gunners of the field artillery within sight of the Germans, watching the awesome effect of the bombardment, were moved to feel pity for the men caught up in it.

Sheltering in a deep dugout in the Wunderwerk, passing the terrible hours of waiting by scribbling in his diary, young Freiwilliger Eversmann of the 143rd Regiment of Infantry, found that it was not quite deep enough to protect his nerves.[1]

> They went at it left and right with heavy calibre guns and hammered us with shrapnel and light calibre pieces. Only with difficulty and distress have we obtained rations today. Two of my comrades got fatal hits while fetching dinner. One of them was Drummer Ollersch, of Gelschenkirchen, a dear chap – three days back from leave and there he's gone. . . .
>
> *25 June, 7 o'clock:* The barrage has now lasted thirty-six hours. How long will it go on?
>
> *9 o'clock:* A short pause of which we avail ourselves to bring up coffee. Each man got a portion of bread.
>
> *10 o'clock:* Veritable *Trommelfeuer*. In twelve hours shelling they estimate that 60,000 shells have fallen on our battalion sector. . . . When will they attack? Tomorrow or the day after? Who knows?
>
> *27 June, 4 a.m.:* Ran to the cookhouse and fetched coffee, some having been brought up. There was also some bread to be had. By 6 o'clock the fire had increased and soon we had a headache. But, sit tight, it cannot last much longer. They say their munitions will soon be done. . . . There must be an end sometime to this horrible bombardment. . . .

---

[1] *'Freiwilliger'* was a rank equivalent to private (*gemeiner*) but meaning, literally, 'volunteer'.

But the British gunners were not having it all their own way. On the other side of the line, a little distance to the south, Sergeant Frank Spencer was also keeping a diary and recording remarkably similar experiences:

25 June: Lovely morning. Once again still heavy bombardments being carried out on either side. We were shelled for three and a half hours and had to cease our own firing and taking sights to seek refuge in tunnels. One gunner was slightly hit and the adjoining battery on our left was shelled very heavily (several casualties). Myself and four gunners now venture to fetch dinner and we have to dodge the shells which are falling down like rain upon us. We all had to jump into a cable trench. Although the soup is not absolutely spoilt, it is filled with chalk from bursting shells which are again chiefly directed towards C Battery.

Sergeant Frank Spencer, No. 1113, C Bty., 152nd Brigade, Royal Field Artillery.

26 June, Monday: Bombardments all night.

27 June: Bombardment continues no more than was expected. We still have further trouble due to springs going again, so two more guns are exchanged with ordnance. One was badly damaged as well as having springs broken due to the extraordinary strain from incessant firing. We bombarded all night.

28 June 1916: Bombardment continued. The coming attack is practised on German front lines with heavy curtain fire and 'lifts' at a pre-arranged moment. The infantry raid the enemy lines to report the damage done and bring back with them prisoners from whom we hope to gain some valuable news. . . . Our wire was well cut, but the left division had not cut theirs very well.

The field artillery had been schooled and trained in its role with the same scrupulous attention to detail as the infantry had been trained in theirs, for it was the artillery which would orchestrate the battle and the success or failure of the infantry would depend on its playing its part to the full. This had been made very clear to the infantry:

CO-OPERATION OF ARTILLERY WITH INFANTRY
The ideal is for the artillery to keep their fire immediately in front of the infantry as the latter advances, battering down all opposition with a hurricane of projectiles. The difficulties of observation, especially in view of dust and smoke ... the probable interruption of telephone communications between infantry and artillery ... renders this idea very difficult to obtain.

Experience has shown that the only safe method of artillery support during an advance, is a fixed timetable of lifts to which both the infantry and artillery must rigidly conform.

This timetable must be regulated by the rate at which it is calculated the infantry can reach their successive objectives:[1]

The calculations had been made with meticulous care. The shallow scratchings on the practice grounds that simulated German trenches had been laid out on the same scale as the known trench system of the enemy.

Stop watches in hand, Staff Officers had watched the Tommies blundering in full battle gear across the carefully measured ground, had timed them and, making allowance for the actual conditions of battle, had made their provisions accordingly.

The guns would operate in a series of carefully planned 'lifts'. For the last hour before the attack, the bombardment would fall with redoubled intensity on the enemy's front line – lifting at Zero to rake forward to his second line and to shell it for precisely as long as it would take the infantry to subdue the first defences and start off for the second. Travelling ahead of the infantry in a series of flea-hops, raining shells on successive lines of German positions, the guns would so prepare the way that all the infantry would have to do would be to take possession of what remained of the trenches and capture such of their defenders as had miraculously survived.

It worked superbly on paper. It would only work on the battlefield if both troops and gunners worked so rigorously hand in hand and adhered so exactly to the timetable that there was no room for error, no room for manoeuvre and no question of failure. The Army thundered instructions accordingly:

No changes must be made in the timetables by subordinate formations without reference to Corps Headquarters or confusion is sure to ensue.

The warning was reasonable enough. Having completed its part in the massed preliminary bombardment, when the attack started the artillery of each division was to pass back to the 'command' of its Divisional General. But he would not be in a position to know what was happening to his neighbours on either side and, if he adjusted his own fire-power to suit the position of his own men, the 'overs' might fall, with disastrous results, on other troops who were further ahead or less advanced than those in his own battle-line. It was no secret that the guns were getting 'tired' with incessant firing, that they were unreliable and that the gunners were still, for the most part, inexperienced. No matter how carefully they calculated ranges, their firing could not always be described as accurate.

[1] *Tactical Notes* issued from Fourth Army HQ, May 1916, for the guidance of divisional commanders.

Charlie Burrows who belonged to the 7th Divisional Artillery and had been firing guns in France and Belgium since October 1914, was firing, for the first time, with sufficient ammunition.

Fritz spots our position and shells us heavily. One gunner blown to pieces, one sergeant and one gunner wounded. One gunpit wrecked by a direct hit and the gun is out of action. They shell us continually for three hours. They get a few hits on our gunpit and smother us with shell-holes. We have a few anxious moments as we have about a thousand rounds of shells in our pits, high explosives. If they had hit us we would all have blown to pieces. They stopped suddenly. We are very relieved and very lucky. We afterwards heard that our heavies had got on to that battery and finished them. There is a quiet time for a short period, and we tidy the position and send the wrecked gun away, and get a new one the same night. Our heavies very busy. I was nearly wounded in the morning from the 25th Battery on our left rear by a premature shell. Something struck me on the left arm but glanced off quickly. Our section fire all night. Heavy artillery fire on both sides the whole night.

26 June: Battery fire all day. All our artillery keep up the bombardment. We have had no sleep for nights. Heard the infantry made another series of raids last night. They were after information.

28 June: Heavy rain last night and tonight towards evening. Bombardment still on. Our section fire all night on the 28th. No sleep for two nights. Still wire cutting.

> Gunner Charles E. Burrows, 104th Bty., 22nd Brigade, RFA, 7th Division. (His diary.)

The week which had started off with a fine Sunday and Monday, gradually deteriorated to chilly, showery weather, unseasonable for late June, hampering the work of the gunners ranging on distant targets and misting the eyes of the Royal Flying Corps as they tried to assess the effects of the bombardment. Because of the weather, the attack was postponed for forty-eight hours.

Whatever the feelings of the infantry, officers of the artillery were glad of this postponement. There was no doubt that they would have to be more sparing with ammunition, that the bombardment would have to be lightened, if they were not to be short of shells in the battle itself; on the other hand there were now two more days to devote to the all important task of wire-cutting.

The infantry had in front of them a triple line of German defences which went back from the front line for six or eight kilometres –

> Major J. Marshall-Cornwall,

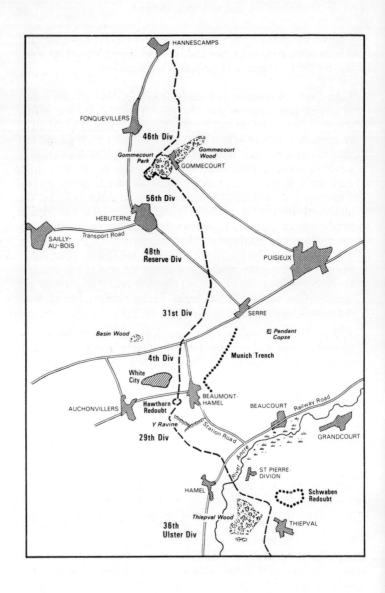

The Line from Gommecourt to Thiepval

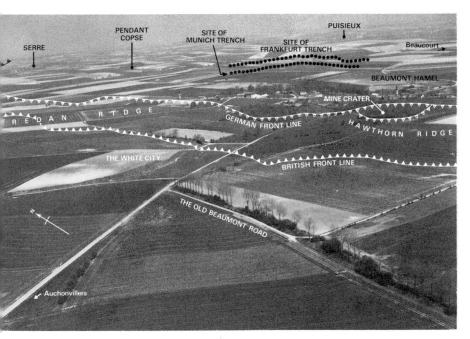

The valley in front of Beaumont Hamel from which British troops attacked on the First of July.

The old trench-lines can still be seen as chalk-marks on the ground. Here on the Thiepval plateau the German line took a sharp turn to run down to the valley of the Ancre and up beyond it to stand guard in front of Beaumont Hamel.

In the fields between Hébuterne village and Gommecourt Territorials of the 56th Division were decimated by shell-fire as they struggled to cross the land to the right of the village to reach the remnants of their first waves, cut off on the high ground beyond. The scars of the intense shelling can still be seen in the foreground. The tip of the wood was the westernmost point of the Germans' trench-line in France. It was known as the Kaiser's Oak.

In front of the British jumping-off line which can still be discerned running across the top corner of the ploughed field on the right and continuing to the edge of the copse on the left, the boys of the Pals Battalions, unprotected by the British barrage for ten minutes before the assault, waited to attack the German line on top of the hill in front of Serre village.

A German's eye view, shot from the lip of the Hawthorn mine crater, of the ground from which the British attacked their line at Beaumont Hamel. Saps were dug right through the sunken lane to the right of the monument and on the low escarpment of the White City there are many traces of the old tunnels and dugouts. Geoffrey Malins filmed the First of July attack from a position constructed for him by Royal Engineers. Its remains can still be seen where the escarpment runs down to the bend of the track to the left of the memorial to the Scots who eventually captured Beaumont Hamel in November, four and a half months later.

Fortress Thiepval. The complex of German and British front-line trenches in front of Thiepval village, now a small hamlet. The farm buildings to the right of the church are on the site of the old château. The rectangle which encloses them is the line of the original foundations. On the right is the vast Thiepval Memorial to the Missing which records the names of more than 72,000 men who died on the Somme and who have no known graves.

Looking from the German trench-line in front of the old château. The British line followed the edge of Thiepval Wood in the foreground, and ran in front of Hamel village up the slopes on the other side of the valley, facing the German line in front of Beaumont Hamel. On the extreme right of centre is the Ulster Tower, on the site of the 'Pope's Nose', which commemorates the 36th Ulster Division who attacked this sector on the First of July.

The present-day view to the right of old Thiepval village (shot from the Thiepval Memorial). The large mass of woodland on the opposite slope is Aveluy Wood; in the near centre is the village of Authuille. The British trenches ran across the slopes of Thiepval Ridge above the village and swung round along the edge of Nab Wood (*left centre*). The isolated clump of trees on the left surrounds the small quarry which was the nub of the German defence in the Leipzig Redoubt.

Rose Vaquette (Madame Glavieux) pointing to the spot where her father, Boromée, was shot on 27th September, 1914, coincidentally on the site where the Germans later constructed their Leipzig Redoubt. The swell in the ground, running from the indentation on the nearside verge of the track marks the front-line trench in its 'snout'. In the background the Thiepval Memorial to the Missing stands on the crest of the ridge.

The old well of Thiepval village still looks out across No Man's Land to the old British line round Thiepval Wood.

As this German photograph shows, the walls of Thiepval Château still stood, although ruined and battered, in 1915. It was snapped from the window of the church, which was likewise fairly intact, and the walled village pond in the left foreground still contains water.

A heap of stone in a farmyard – all that remains of the noble Thiepval Château above Thiepval Wood. Beyond it is the Mesnil Ridge and, on the left, the edge of Aveluy Wood.

Above: Thiepval village rebuilt, but a mere hamlet now. The farm in the foreground stands on the site of the old Thiepval Château and the foundations can still be traced. Opposite, in front of the new church, the rough uncultivated corner of what is now a field is the site of the village pond. As it was communal property no one, presumably, has the right to use it.

Left: By the summer of 1915 the Germans had built a formidable network of well-constructed trenches like this one which was part of the Ovillers defences.

The Albert-Bapaume road separates the twin villages of Ovillers and la Boisselle where the ground still bears witness to the magnitude of the German defences.

The formidable German line still reaches across the fields to the left of la Boisselle to the massive crater of the mine that breached it. Rising from the village the road runs over the Tara and Usna hills on its way to Albert. The village in the distance is Aveluy.

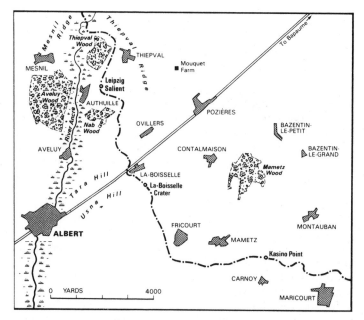

The Line from Thiepval to Montauban

three lines of defence, each defended by a chain of concrete pillboxes, which were machine-gun posts, surrounded by acres of barbed-wire entanglements. The whole thing depended on our artillery being able first of all to locate and then smash up the concrete machine-gun posts and then with the field guns to sweep away the wire entanglements. This was the primary essential. Well, bombardments started with 1,500 British guns – 450 of them were heavies – but, unfortunately, the weather broke. For five days out of the six of the bombardment there was low cloud and drizzle. Air observation was impossible and artillery observation was very hampered. The fact was that neither did they pinpoint the machine-gun posts opposite them, they also failed to cut the wire and the failure of the cutting of the wire was most disastrous.

GSO 2 (Intelligence Officer), GHQ Staff. (Now General Sir James Marshall-Cornwall, KCB, CBE, DSO, MC.)

Our procedure at that time was to use a shrapnel shell which burst about twenty feet above the ground and the hail of bullets going forward when the shell burst in the air swept away the wire entanglements. But it all depended on the accurate setting of the time fuze which ignited the shrapnel shells and our munition factories were only just getting into full swing. There were a lot of manufacturing faults in the fuzes. They didn't all burn the right length and, I'm afraid, a lot of the half-trained gunners of the New

Army Divisions didn't set the fuzes exactly accurate. The fact was that many of the shells burst too high and the bullets dropped into the ground, and the fuze didn't work and it buried itself into the ground so the wire was left.[1]

2nd Lieutenant
Kenneth Page, MC,
40 Brigade,
Royal Field
Artillery.

I was in charge of a section of an 18-pounder battery and we were given the job of cutting lanes through the German wire. It wasn't an easy thing to do. You had to do it very slowly and very deliberately. You would go on plugging away at one short stretch of wire, you see, and, bearing in mind that there was wire all the way along the front, the tendency was for a gap to get cut here and then a gap got cut a little way along there and the infantry had obviously got to get through this wire, so they tended to get in the gaps and, if the Germans knew the gaps were there – after all they'd watched them being cut – they could line their machine-guns up to cover them.

The experts, the 18-pounder battery commanders, were quite good at cutting wire, but it did need very careful laying because guns were rather inaccurate things in those days. They had what was called a 'hundred per cent zone'. That meant that, if you fired a hundred rounds from one gun, at, say, a range of three thousand yards and you then measured up very carefully the area in which all the shells had fallen, you would then call that the hundred per cent zone. But, although most of the hundred rounds – all laid in the same way, remember – would be more or less gathered in the middle, quite a few odd ones would have exploded out towards the extremities of the zone. So, it wasn't easy to go on plugging one gun into the same hole every time, however accurately you laid it. With the inaccuracies of ammunition and fuzes and even the guns themselves, you would get unavoidable errors.

It was quite literally a case of a hit or a miss. In the cloudy moonless nights before the assault, raiding parties, crawling in black-faced cohorts across to the German lines, brought back mixed reports. They had found the German trenches empty and the wire 'well cut'. They had found the wire impassable and the trenches heavily manned. They had found the trenches empty (except for an unfortunate sentry dragged back as a prisoner) but had heard the muffled singing of Germans in their dugouts. But the small bag of prisoners

---

[1] Further note by General Sir James Marshall-Cornwall: The disappointing effect of shrapnel shells in wire-cutting brought about the introduction in the following year (1917) of a new type of fuze (the 106 fuze). This was a highly sensitive percussion fuze which acted instantaneously as the shell hit the ground and scattered the fragments horizontally, thus effectively destroying the wire entanglements.

sent back for interrogation were cowed and visibly shaken by the unremitting nervous strain of the bombardment and, like Eversmann, sheltering in a deep dugout from the explosions rocking Thiepval Ridge, willing it to end.

It is night. Shall I live till morning? Haven't we had enough of this frightful horror? Five days and five nights now this hell concert has lasted. One's head is like a madman's; the tongue sticks to the roof of the mouth. Almost nothing to eat and nothing to drink. No sleep. All contact with the outer world cut off. No sign of life from home nor can we send any news to our loved ones. What anxiety they must feel about us. How long is this going to last?

Freiwilliger Eversmann, 143rd German Regiment of Infantry.

The answer was, 'not long'. Already the British troops were moving up to the assembly trenches. A few unfortunates, the first to move into position for the attack that should have been launched forty-eight hours before, had already been in them for two chilly and rainy days. There was no question of taking all of them back, for, in the country immediately behind the lines, every tent, every hut, every barn and every house in every village was crammed full of men who had marched up from the rear behind them. Now the weather had cleared. It was a fine night with the promise of a fine day ahead.

Greatcoats had been handed in, tied in bundles of four and, with two hundred thousand packs and three thousand or so officers' valises, were stacked in farm outbuildings all up and down the line. At last-minute parades, brigadiers had bawled through megaphones in cheering tones of encouragement. Commanding officers and adjutants, armed with the printed Summaries of Intelligence sent forward from Headquarters for the purpose, read extracts aloud to their battalions. Based, perhaps selectively, on captured documents, on the interrogation of prisoners, the reports of raiding parties and observations of the result of the bombardment, they pointed without exception to the demoralisation of the enemy, to the destruction of his defences, to his lack of fighting spirit, to the casualties he had suffered in the punishing shellfire. Listening to these words, as the shells roared and crashed in the distance, neither the officers nor the men found them difficult to believe.

In the early dusk of the previous evening Major-General Rycroft had gone forward to have a look for himself at the Thiepval Ridge where his 32nd Division was going to attack. Standing at the edge of Aveluy Wood he had no need of binoculars. The ground under his feet quivered with the vibration of the guns and for five days they had been trained on the Thiepval Ridge. Like the tall church and every other building in the village, the château had all but disappeared

under a heap of tumbled brick and rubble, half-glimpsed through
clouds of yellow smoke that enveloped the ruins with every salvo.
Away to the right, the face of the hill was pockmarked with craters.
On the skyline above, the clutter of wire and trenches, the forward
lines of the great redoubts, seemed to totter behind a curtain of flying
chalk. 'My God!' the General had to shout to make himself heard,
although the Commanders of his three Brigades were only inches
away. 'All we'll find in Thiepval, when we go across, is the caretaker
and his dog!'

The Brigadiers, pleased with the aptness of the General's sum-
ming-up, had passed it on to the infantry in their reassuring goodbye
messages. They all sincerely believed that it was true.

Now the troops were on their way, each man wearing on his
shoulder a flash in the identifying colour of his division. In a
spectrum of bright colours they fluttered from two hundred
thousand shoulders and on their backs, catching the last rays of the
dying sun, were two hundred thousand triangles of tin. Shining in
the sun tomorrow morning, they were intended to reveal to distant
observers the progress of the infantry's advance. It was the last tiny
detail of a million details of the painstaking planning that would
direct their destiny.

Even the assembling of such a mass of men had been planned with
such care that there was hardly a hold-up or a hitch. Coloured
lamps, glowing discreetly at ground level, guided the battalions
along their designated tracks to arrive at Divisional Assembly Areas
within minutes of the appointed time and with time in hand for a
little rest. Although the order had been 'March Easy', it had been
hard going; 'Battle Order' meant that every man was weighed down
with more than sixty pounds of equipment and, now, at forward
divisional dumps, they were dishing out still more spades, pickaxes,
and even, to some benighted Tommies in the second wave, rolls of
barbed-wire. Cursing at the weight of it all, the infantry could hardly
be blamed for failing to appreciate that this burden of extraneous
equipment was intended for its protection. After much mulling and
weighing of advantage against disadvantage, the Staff had decided
that its novice warriors would stand a better chance if they were able
to consolidate captured trenches with all speed, rather than run the
risk of a counter-attack while they waited for Pioneer Battalions to
come up behind them.

Hunched under their assorted burdens, the infantry moved up to
the line. Their excitement was mingled with nervousness, but at
least the waiting was over. At long last they would have a chance of
having 'a proper go' at the Hun. Despite the bellicose array of
weapons dangling about their persons, many Tommies had

thoughtfully provided themselves with knuckle-dusters, lengths of chain and even vicious knives as their personal contribution to the armoury of battle. Most had never yet seen a German face to face, but, as if anticipating some street corner brawl, they intended to be ready when they did. The fact was that, in spite of the long months of careful rehearsal, of lectures and training, of preparation and of orders, in the untried ranks of Kitchener's Army there was hardly an officer or a man who appreciated the difference between a raid and a general attack.

Part 2

The Big Push

'Old soldiers never die; they simply fide a-why!'
That's what they used to sing along the roads last spring;
That's what they used to say before the push began;
That's where they are today, knocked over to a man.

Siegfried Sassoon

Chapter 6

Morning crept over the Somme spreading a gentle haze that promised a fine day ahead.

The last hour of waiting was the worst.

At 6.35 the guns, which had been firing incessantly all night, roared out in the crescendo of the final bombardment. The shells were too high to be seen but they came screaming so thick and so fast over the front-line trenches that the men packed into them, with only the sky for a view, looked up in spite of themselves, as if expecting to see some thrilling visible sight, like the hail of arrows singing through the air at Agincourt.

In the trenches on either side of Gommecourt, the British troops hardly noticed the stepping up of their own bombardment because the Germans, convinced that the main brunt of the attack would take place here, were returning shot for shot. They were pounding the advanced trench, dug with such bravado well out in No Man's Land, where the first wave of the 56th Division infantry were waiting to go. They were hammering the old front line where the second wave were ready to follow them. Shells were crashing among the support trenches and raining down on Hébuterne where the reserve troops awaited the order to move forward. Captain Agius was there with B Company, ready to go across with bombs and ammunition and to establish contact with the leading companies of the 3rd Londons as soon as they were ensconced in the enemy's front line. In the open street outside the cottage that served as Battalion Headquarters there was no shelter from the bombardment. Brigade Headquarters was even further ahead, for Brigadier-General Loch was a man who liked to see for himself what was going on. The Brigade Orderly Sergeant, Harry Coates, in ordinary circumstances, rather admired his fire-eating Brigadier, but now with shells exploding all around the fine observation trench which was Brigade Headquarters for the battle he was not quite so sure. Brigade-Major Philip Neame, originally a Royal Engineer, was a fire-eater of equal calibre to General Loch, and had proved it a year earlier at Neuve Chapelle by winning the Victoria Cross. He had designed the trench, had supervised its construction and, last night, they had moved into it. Luckily, Neame's design had included a good dugout a dozen feet underground and they were sheltering there now. The Brigadier, Neame himself, Coates, and a clutch of runners, orderlies, telephonists and signallers, who were already hunched over their instruments testing the lines as the orderlies dished out the first of the dozen strong cups of tea that each man would drink in the course of the day ahead. The walls were vibrating with every explosion and the Brigadier was looking worried.

Across the two-mile stretch of land that separated the 56th Division from the left flank of the main attack, the two battalions of the 48th Division who were manning the trenches were having an equally bad time. They, at least, were not going 'over the top' although, to make it look as if they were, they had opened conspicuous lanes through the wire in front of their trenches and made the same visible feint 'preparations' as the Third Army on their left. But all they were required to do was to launch a smokescreen to hang like a curtain across the two miles between Gommecourt and Serre and thus to blind and confuse the Germans and their guns. They knew already that they would fail. The wind, which should have carried the smoke forward, had turned and now a gentle breeze blew towards the British from the direction of the German lines.

At Serre the Pals were in position. Waiting in the support trenches with the men of his Vickers machine-gun team, Sergeant Jimmy Myers checked the gun and its components for the umpteenth time and thought for the umpteenth time that, even broken into its component parts and with five men to carry the gun and its thousands of rounds of ammunition, it would be quite a job to hump the gun when they went over with the Bradford Pals. Still, that was more than an hour away. They had practised it all a thousand times – dismantling the gun, slinging the pieces on top of the trench while they clambered out, keeping up with the infantry and, when they reached their advanced position, re-assembling the gun with lightning speed and coming into action. They had got it down to a fine art and after the final rehearsals, the only observation made by Lieutenant Burrows had been a nod of quiet satisfaction. There was no need to worry about the trek across the width of No Man's Land. As the rehearsals had shown, by nine o'clock when they went over troops of the first wave would already be far ahead and the German outpost line, now staring down at them from the low crest of the hill, would long ago have been rendered harmless.

In the first wave, Willie Parker in the Sheffield Pals was probably the only man who had not rehearsed the battle. He had only been with the Battalion for two weeks. Since he had joined up with his young brother Reg on the very day the Battalion had started recruiting, his belated arrival was due, in his own view, to unreasoning wilfulness on the part of Authority. First they had trained him as a soldier and then, at the end of six months, had plucked him out of the ranks and sent him back to his proper trade as a skilled engineer. No one from Lord Kitchener downwards could have convinced Willie that the year he had spent making munitions at Armstrong-Whitworth's was more valuable to the war effort than his presence in the khaki ranks of the Sheffield Pals, armed with a rifle that he barely knew how to use. He had badgered the Army, he had petitioned the Lord Mayor, he had made such a nuisance of himself by pestering the factory manager that Armstrong-Whitworth's had given in and released him. The Army had taken Willie back into the fold and he had considered it the greatest piece of luck that a draft of men was on the point of leaving to join the Battalion in France in time for the Big Push. Waiting now in the front-line trench, clad in new khaki, taking pleasure in the unfamiliar weight of rifle and tin hat, Willie would not have changed places with the King himself.

Already they were placing the scaling ladders against the wall of the trench. At twenty-past seven the Sheffields would climb them and crawl out to lie in readiness in front of their own wire. At seven-thirty, when the whistles blew, they would be the first men across.

Over the Redan Ridge, ever since dawn, machine-gun teams to the left of Beaumont Hamel had been looking across at the German line through a tangle of grass and weeds. It was the closest view they had ever had, because they were now well out in No Man's Land on the very edge of the low plateau they called the White City. The British front line ran across it within forty feet of its furthest edge and, in the weeks before the battle, they had driven forward a series of shallow tunnels to within a foot or two of the sunken road in No Man's Land beyond. Just before dawn, they had broken down the last thin barriers of soil in its bank and camouflaged the openings with a thin curtain of tangled vegetation to hide the gun-crews from the prying eyes of any over-zealous observer who might raise his head in the thick of the bombardment. They lay so close – no more than a hundred yards away – that they could almost see the individual barbs of the wire entanglements that stretched across the field, guarding the rising ground where the German trenches furrowed through shattered orchards. The wire looked uncomfortably intact, but there were gaps here and there. Marking them with their eye, the men mentally plotted the rush that would carry them across the ground as they dashed out ahead of the infantry to put paid to any opposition and pave the way ahead. Meanwhile, they were waiting for the word of command to move back along the tunnel, dragging the guns to a safe distance, so that they would not be damaged nor the men concussed when the great mine exploded under the redoubt on the Hawthorn Ridge. That would be the signal to crawl forward again ready for the jump-off ten minutes later.

At twenty minutes past seven, the mine went up in a sheet of flame and a thunderous fountain of debris that leapt a hundred feet into the air. As it fell back to the earth and the last rumblings of the explosion died away, looking across from his observation position behind the White City, Dudley Lissenburg could see quite clearly on the ridge across the valley a small force of two hundred men rush forward and disappear into the cloud of black smoke on their way to capture the crater.

In the stunning aftermath of the explosion, despite the sound of the bombardment on the heights of Thiepval to the right, and a distant mutter of gunfire far, far away to the left, a strange silence seemed to fall. In the moments before the German machine-guns started up, it seemed to Lissenburg uncanny. Across the Redan Ridge the Pals of the 31st Division, crawling out to wait in front of the wire for the signal to go for Serre, remarked on it too. The bombardment which, more than two miles away had had to cease to allow two companies of troops to attack four hundred yards of the enemy's defences on the Hawthorn Ridge, had, by some error of judgement or misinterpretation of orders, stopped along the four-mile length of the 8th Corps Front. For the next ten minutes, not a single shot would be fired.

In their jumping-off trench at the edge of Thiepval Wood, waiting to move uphill across the slope to tackle the formidable line that lay in front of the Schwaben Redoubt, the Ulstermen of the 36th Division heard the explosion quite clearly through the roar of their own bombardment, and saw the tip of the cone of debris it threw into the sky. They were at a pitch of excitement. It was the 1st July and, according to the old calendar, it was the anniversary of the Battle of the Boyne. To the Ulstermen it was the best of all possible omens and they were raring to go.

A little way behind them, where the 109th Brigade were in readiness to follow up the first line troops as they left their trenches, Colonel Ricardo stood on the parapet of the assembly trench cheering his men on as they went through the two centre exits on either side. He wanted to wish them luck, but he needed a megaphone to make himself heard. 'They got going without delay; no fuss, no shouting, no running, everything solid and thorough –

just like the men themselves. Here and there a boy would wave his hand to me as I shouted "Good Luck" to them through my megaphone. And all had a cheery face. Most were carrying loads. Fancy advancing against heavy fire with a big roll of barbed wire on your shoulder!'

Away to the right, at the top of the hill, the ruins of Thiepval village were shuddering under the final tornado of the bombardment. The piles of dusty rubble seemed to hold as little threat as the bleached bones of a long-dead tiger. Not a man among the hundred-strong company waiting to clamber from the trenches across the tumbled terracing of the old château gardens and on to the shattered village beyond, had the slightest doubt that their job would be a piece of cake.

Away to their right, under the crest of the ridge, the vanguard of the 17th Highland Light Infantry was inching forward to lie close up to the belts of wire in front of the Wunderwerk. Somewhere beyond it, in these last moments of the bombardment, Freiwilliger Eversmann, waiting in battle order, was doubtless still wondering, 'When will it end?'

Round the promontory of the Leipzig Redoubt, where the 70th Brigade was also waiting nearly in the shadow of the wire for the bombardment to lift, the line took an almost right-angled turn down into the Nab Valley. Ernest Deighton, of the 8th Battalion King's Own Yorkshire Light Infantry, was the first man out and he had been out since before dawn concealed in a shell-crater halfway across No Man's Land. He had never felt so exposed nor so alone in his life. Deighton was a sniper and a marksman and, ever since it had been light enough to see, he had been training the telescopic sights of his rifle on a gap in the German wire, keeping his eyes peeled for any movement. The Jerries had been keeping their heads well down, and who could blame them, but he was pretty sure that he had bagged at least a couple and that there would be no trouble from that quarter when his comrades dashed across at Zero. The minutes dragged. He had no means of knowing the time – the chance glinting of a watch face might have given away his position – but, like Eversmann, he longed for the bombardment to stop, for the whistles to blow in the trenches behind him, to be on the move, to get going. As soon as the first line of troops reached him, he was to leap up and join them in the charge towards the German trenches.

A mile to the south, Brigadier-General Ternan was furious. Like General Loch at Gommecourt, he had gone to some trouble to make sure of having a good view of the attack and the Royal Engineers had constructed a fine observation post two hundred yards down on the forward slope of the Tara-Usna Ridge overlooking the Ovillers valley and with a fine view to the right over la Boisselle and the 34th Divisional Front. Here, with Brigadier-General Cameron, in command of the Tyneside Irish Brigade, he positioned himself just minutes before Zero, and he had just made the unpleasant discovery that, in spite of the elaborate preparations of the Engineers, it was impossible to see a thing.

The Brigadiers wished in particular to see the effect of the huge mines that were to explode on either side of the village of la Boisselle at Zero Hour. The infantry had already been pulled back to the reserve trenches to protect them from any untoward effects of the explosions and, as Ternan was unhappily aware, this meant that they would have a long way to go, and that they would be exposed to fire even before they started across No Man's Land. Pushing along an assembly trench to their right, the two Brigadiers discovered that, by climbing on the fire step and looking over the parapet, they had a good, if unprotected, view of the valley. Fifty yards down the slope ahead, Ternan could see the first line of the Tyneside Scottish preparing to leave their trenches. At seven twenty-eight the mines went up – one to the left of la Boisselle, a huge one to the right of it and a mile beyond, on the Fricourt Salient, a clutch of smaller explosions. As the noise died away, in a brief spell of comparative silence while the guns lengthened their range, he could hear a strange whining noise from the trenches down the hill. It was the pipers tuning up as they made ready to play the Tyneside Scottish over the top.

The attack of the 18th Division in front of Montauban started with a bang. At the advanced Battalion Headquarters of the 10th Battalion, The Essex Regiment, the waiting officers cheered as the mines went up at Kasino Point. There were casualties from the fall-out and, although it was in the second trench, a few far-flung chunks of debris even flew into their shack, but this was some compensation to Lieutenant Robert Chell who, newly promoted to Adjutant, had been rather disappointed that his place was at Battalion Headquarters rather than in the line with the men. But the men were surging ahead and the first prisoner arrived, incredibly, before the attack was five minutes under way. He was a pitiful specimen, unwashed, unshaven and, as Chell noticed delightedly as he telephoned the details of the prisoner's regiment back to Brigade Headquarters, he was unfed as well by the looks of him and still shaking from his ordeal of seven days in the front line under the bombardment.

This was the first of many reports of good progress that Chell was to send back during the course of the day.

Eight minutes before Zero, where the 30th Division met the French at the end of the British line, Stokes mortar batteries had thundered a hurricane bombardment. Here where the Germans least expected an attack, it was so powerful and so effective that, when it stopped, there was absolute silence from the German lines. As the whistles blew and the troops left the trenches, they presented a sight that would have gladdened the hearts of the Staff who had pored so long and so hard over the battle plans. Extended in lines of companies, a hundred paces apart, they crossed the width of No Man's Land in quick time with rifles slung – British Tommies on the left, French *poilus* on the right. At the point where the two lines met, Colonel Fairfax of the 17th Battalion, The King's Liverpool Regiment, and Commandant Le Petit, in command of the 3rd Battalion of the 153rd Régiment d'Infanterie, found themselves together. Grinning, the French officer crooked his elbow invitingly. Colonel Fairfax took it and, pushing forward, they led the advance arm in arm.

By half-past seven all along the straggling miles of the front the ground mist was beginning to thin. As the first hundred thousand men went over the top, the sun was already shining strongly enough to feel warm on the napes of their necks and it blazed on through the long summer's day.

Ordinarily, on the uplands of the Somme, just a week after midsummer, a balmy evening would have followed such a glorious day and turned imperceptibly into a warm cloudless night. But the night had fallen early, and it fell so thick with the dust and fumes of battle that you could almost touch it. It shook and quivered, blazed lurid yellow in the flash of the guns, swirling into black cloud shot with the flame of exploding shells, swelled into monstrous incandescence, as signal rockets soared through its turbulent mists. A hundred and fifty thousand men, living, or dead, lay out in the inferno.

Peering across at the furnace of Thiepval from the Artillery Observation Post, built four-square in solid concrete high on the Mesnil Ridge, anxious observers were still trying to make sense of the day's events. Their eyes had been glued to the Thiepval Ridge since early morning, but, for all they had seen, for all they had been able to interpret the course of the long day's battle, for all they had been able to make of the conflicting reports that had reached them, for all they were able to understand the significance of the signals and flares that lit the sky above the battle-line, they might have been blind and deaf. In spite of their best endeavours, they did not have the faintest idea of what was happening. But the sight of it awed the mind. The sound of it numbed the senses. And their only sickening certainty was that the position of the line had altered hardly at all since the troops had attacked from it in the morning.

But rumours of a break-through on the Somme had travelled fast and had been improved in the telling. Barely twenty miles to the north, in a sector of the trenchline between Wailly and Arras where the 6th Battalion the King's Own Yorkshire Light Infantry was in the line, Lance-Corporal Len Lovell and Private Bill Clegg were suffering from the effects of the exaggerated good tidings. The joke had been conceived on the spur of the moment back at Brigade Headquarters in the euphoria of the first optimistic reports of success in the south and the Brigadier, who was never averse to 'showing Jerry what was what', had sent for a sign-writer from the Pioneer Battalion and set him to work right away. He was to find a trenchboard and embellish it with a suitable inscription. Almost before the paint was dry, it had been sent gleefully to the Headquarters of the 6th Battalion, Kings Own Yorkshire Light Infantry with explicit instructions.

Len Lovell was no stranger to No Man's Land. It had become almost routine to him, and to Clegg as well, to strip off their insignia, to empty their pockets, to blacken their faces, to crawl through the wire and melt into the night.

There was no possibility of dragging the heavy notice-board. First Lovell, then Clegg had to carry it on his shoulders as they crawled, belly down, across No Man's Land, feeling for obstacles in front, freezing in the intermittent glare of flares, inching on when they died down. It took them more than an hour to reach the German wire. Now they had to be doubly cautious, ears cocked for the slightest sound that might warn of an enemy patrol, wary of coming too close to the wire, lest a vibrating 'ping' should give them away, or the inadvertent movement of an arm catch one of them fast in its barbs.

Ten interminable minutes passed before the board was embedded into the earth. It took five more to prime the booby trap, designed to give any Germans who tried to remove it an exceedingly nasty surprise. Then came the slow crawl back to the lines, the ticklish business of finding safe passage through the wire, the hoarsely whispered password. Tonight if was 'WITH' – an every-day word, chosen for its ease of pronunciation by any native-born Britisher, yet containing, in one simple syllable, two complex sounds guaranteed to stump the foreign tongue of all but the most practised linguist.

Experience had shown that a surprisingly large number of Germans had some knowledge of English, so there was little doubt that

Jerry would get the message – if not the joke – bright and early in the morning. The sign-writer had gone to some pains to make sure that it would be legible at a distance of thirty yards and, on its black-painted background, the white lettering stood out bold and clear:

10,000 MEN

AND

100'S OF GUNS

CAPTURED ON SOMME!

MORE TO FOLLOW

GOD SAVE THE KING!

A little way to the south, in the confusion of the thundering night, Intelligence Officers, trying to make sense of the day's events on the Somme, would have given a great deal to have been put in possession of such precise information.

At Bouzincourt, where the hundred reinforcements of the 6th Battalion, The West Yorkshire Regiment had been anxiously waiting all day without news, dusk was falling before a message from Brigade Headquarters ordered them forward to join the Battalion. It was not hard to guess that there had been casualties and that the Colonel was among them, for Major Scott, his Second-in-Command, was instructed to go up with the reinforcements and to take charge. Even more disturbing was the fact that they were to rendezvous not, as they might have hoped, at Grandcourt, three miles beyond the start line, but at the start line itself in Thiepval Wood. Now they were trying to get there and, although two hours had gone by since they had set off, they had only managed to get as far as Aveluy Wood and here, it seemed, they were stuck. It was almost impossible, even in single file, to make headway through a struggling tide of stretcher-bearers streaming up the narrow tracks against the flow of ration parties and reinforcements pressing down them towards the line. The road to Lancashire Dump was nose-to-tail with limbers, and Lancashire Dump itself was a bottleneck, teeming with supply parties and ration parties and endless small bands of reinforcements pouring out from all over the wood on their way up to the line.

Leaving the track they had followed with difficulty through the trees, the West Yorkshires had to wait while a straggle of walking wounded passed, and some from their own regiment, recognising them as they went through, called out to them, 'It's bloody murder over there, boys.' A signpost at the edge of the wood was confidently

marked THIEPVAL-BAPAUME-BERLIN. This time last night it had
cheered the troops on their way to the line; now, waiting beside it for
the last stragglers to catch up, Lieutenant Hornshaw found it less
than reassuring.

A peremptory arrow pointed to the track. It led across the marshy
valley to the bottom of the ridge, and to the single route to the
trenches below Thiepval which was invisible from the enemy positions above. It took the West Yorks more than half an hour to shuffle
across the mere half-mile to the opposite bank of the Ancre.

Sheltered by a steep bluff the track turned left, hugging the lower
slopes of the ridge, passing through the ruins of Authuille and,
beyond it, rising gently as it ran towards Thiepval Wood, a mile
ahead. Pushing against an ever-swelling huddle of wounded, of
messengers and runners clamouring urgently to pass, deafened by
the din, wearing gas-masks for the last half-mile, held up in front,
pushed forward from behind, the hundred men of the West Yorkshires struggled on as best they could through the rank, sour mist,
towards the edge of the wood and the rendezvous at Paisley Dump.

The British Military had taken over Thiepval Wood as surely as
they had taken over Aldershot. For the first year of the war, a
tottering signpost, drunkenly askew, had kept up a pretence that it
was '*Proprieté privé. Entrée Interdite.*' But it had long ago given up the
ghost. Now battered trenchboards nailed to the trees bore directions
in uncompromising English: 'To Johnson's Post.' 'To Iniskilling
Avenue.' 'To Hamilton Avenue, Campbell Avenue, Elgin Avenue.'
'To Belfast City.' 'To Paisley Dump.'

Here, at the foot of the ridge on the western edge of the wood,
communication trenches splayed out towards the firing line six
hundred yards above. Here, supplies were unloaded and ammunition dumped. Here was the meeting-place of every track from
Authuille, every causeway across the marshes. Paisley Dump had
regularly been chaotic. Tonight it was pandemonium.

The reliefs and reinforcements of two divisions were circling in a
sheep-like throng, at a loss to know just where, in the holocaust
above, their presence was so urgently required, and prevented even
from getting up the communication trenches by the rabble of
battle-worn soldiers, relieved from the front line, trying to throng
down. Some, at the limit of their strength, had given up the effort,
and the assembly trenches, where they had waited for the attack,
were overflowing with exhausted troops, lying literally in heaps, so
drained by strain and fatigue that they could sleep in the midst of the
inferno. The deafening sound of the battle above was blotted out by
shells screaming closer still, exploding among the men packed into
the clearing and exploding too among the still forms of the badly

wounded as they lay along the edge of the wood waiting to be evacuated.

As they neared the wood, between the roar of explosions, behind the sickening gas-soaked mist, in the forefront of the noise that raged at them from every horizon, the small party of the West Yorkshires became aware of another sound. It was like nothing they had ever heard before. Later – and for the rest of his life – Lieutenant Hornshaw was to remember it as a sound that chilled the blood; a nerve-scraping noise like 'enormous wet fingers screeching across an enormous pane of glass'. It was coming from the wounded, lying out in No Man's Land. Some screaming, some muttering, some weeping with fear, some calling for help, shouting in delirium, groaning with pain, the sounds of their distress had synthesised into one unearthly wail.

As midnight passed and the night of the first day of July turned towards the dawn of the second, as the gunfire died down, it seemed to fill the air. All along the front, from the orchards of Gommecourt to the heights of Beaumont Hamel, from the shoulders of Thiepval to the valley beyond la Boisselle, it rose from the battlefield into the night like the keening of a thousand banshees.

Holding grimly to the remnants of their battered trenches, the battered remnants of the Army shivered as they listened.

Chapter 7

At Gommecourt, Arthur Agius was back where he had started at the beginning of the battle, at Battalion Headquarters at Hébuterne, but this time he was inside it, huddled in a corner with his face to the wall. Technically, Agius was a casualty, but his legs had not been able to support him through a long wait outside the aid post in a crowd of walking wounded, who seemed to him to be in more urgent need of attention than himself.

Captain Arthur Agius, 3rd Btn., Royal Fusiliers, City of London Regiment, 56th Division.

I was shell-shocked, I suppose. At any rate, I wasn't much use – inclined to cry, if anything. In fact, I couldn't stop and, being rather young, I was somewhat ashamed of it. But it had been a total shambles. The first two companies had got across and, about an hour after they started, I was told to take B Company across to support them. We had no idea that the whole attack was a diversion. We thought that we were going forward. We had maps and plans of Gommecourt – we knew from information we'd got from the local people exactly where every house was. But the trouble was that Gommecourt stuck out in the middle of the line and we didn't attack it directly. We attacked on one side of the château park and the 46th Division were attacking on the other. We were supposed to encircle it and link up behind. But what we didn't know was that the Germans had so manoeuvred and organised their line that this part which we weren't to attack was really their strongpoint, and they simply had a clear field of fire on either side and nothing to bother about in front. And the shellfire was absolutely appalling. They were simply pouring shells down. We just couldn't get across. We didn't even get as far as the trench we'd dug – well, there was no trench left. It was all hammered to blazes. We got just about as far as our old front line and then it became quite impossible. The company in front of me said, 'It's no use. We can't get over.'

We got orders to turn and try to make our way back to the village. One of my subalterns was newly out. Such a nice chap. He must have had money and we used to tease him a bit because his batman was the family butler! This young officer jumped out of the trench to try to organise the men, pass the word and get them moving to the communication trench, and he was promptly killed. Just disappeared in an explosion. The whole of the valley was being swept with machine-gun fire and hammered with shells. We got the men organised as best we could – those of us who were left. So many gone, and we'd never even got past our own front-line trench! And then we found we couldn't get back. The trenches were indescribable! We were simply treading on the dead. Eventually my Sergeant and I got out on top – we were at the back of the Company. I heard a shell coming. I remember thinking, 'Imagine! Just imagine hearing a single shell in the middle of all this din!' It burst just above my head. The Sergeant was blown one way and I was blown the other. He was killed. I don't know how I got back. I simply don't know how I got back. It was murder.[1]

Trudging along the road away from the battle-line towards Sailly, 'Murder' was a word which Sergeant Henry Coates was finding it difficult to dismiss from his mind and he surmised that the thoughts of the man who was plodding along in silence by his side were probably running along the same lines. He was taking the Brigadier home. From Philip Neame's fine trench they had both had a grandstand view of the battle. The troops had gone over in fine style, behind a smokescreen so thick that they were through the battered German wire and into the front-line trenches almost before the Germans knew what was happening.

And that was the last they had seen of the advance, for the advance had melted away under the relentless German bombardment that had fallen all day on No Man's Land. After the first euphoric hour when markers hoisted above the German trenches triumphantly confirmed that the first wave of troops had reached its first three objectives, they had seen nothing but the perpetual flicker of signal lamps. They had flashed all day long, signalling over and over again the same urgent message: SOS BOMBS. SOS BOMBS. SOS BOMBS.

Looking back on the long day at Brigade Headquarters, Coates could not bring himself to contemplate the number of parties they had ordered out into the maelstrom to try somehow to get bombs and ammunition to the troops, cut off in the German lines, battling to hold on to their hard-won gains. Eventually the Brigade Staff had stopped trying. It was very clear, as the day wore on, that no more troops had reached the other side. Even through the tossing sea of

[1] The casualties of the 3rd London's on 1 July were four hundred and sixty-eight killed and wounded.

explosions, it was plain to see that the fighting was dying down. As dusk gathered in, the lessening flash of rifle fire, the intermittent sparking of a lone Lewis-gun, spoke all too eloquently of one last microscopic stand by a small band of survivors. Without ammunition, without help, without reinforcements, it was a miracle that they had lasted half so long.

As Coates stood in the trench peering at the last few futile streaks of fire, Philip Neame had appeared at his shoulder. 'I think you'd better accompany the Brigadier back.'

Coates had followed Neame down the steps to the dugout. General Loch sat slumped, staring at the low roof and the hanging lamp that swung and shivered with every crash of the bombardment.

Sergeant Henry
Coates, No. 510729,
14th (London
Scottish) Btn.,
London Regiment.

He was like a man in a dream. It was terrible to see him like that, because he was quite a chatty old boy, always talking about his little daughter, and friendly, though he could be severe sometimes. The Old Man was a daredevil. A real fighter. He wanted to be in strict control of all that was going on and that's why we had this magnificent dugout with the short trench above it, away in advance of the Battalion HQs. It saved all our lives. If it hadn't been for this deep dugout we'd all have been killed or buried alive. They were simply knocking hell out of us, nearly all day.

I'm sure the Old Man was shell-shocked. I know I was! He was broken. He made no objection to coming with me. He didn't say a word. He just got up, very, very slowly and, in a break in the shelling, we went out. They'd shelled our own trenches so much that the line was absolutely broken, and the trenches were all knocked in and chaps buried underneath. We were treading over dead bodies and all sorts of things going along. We just struggled back as best we could, past men going forward to try to get the wounded out of the trenches and out of No Man's Land, and past people going up to reinforce the front line – what was left of it! There was hardly anyone there. The Brigadier just followed me and eventually we managed to get through on to the road to Sailly au Bois.

It took them several hours to cover the four miles to Sailly and the old Brigade Headquarters and all the way, neither of them spoke a word.

A sentry snapped to attention as they entered Brigade HQ. The Brigadier hardly returned his salute. The bombardment was still thundering behind them. In silence they went down the steep stair to the cellar and, huddling in opposite corners, still without speaking, they settled down to pass what was left of the night.

Two miles south of Gommecourt, travelling at snail's pace along the congested road that would take them to the reserve trenches in the line in front of Serre, Reg Parker thanked God that he was with the Transport. Things had quietened down early on the Serre Front. By ten in the morning it had all been over. Two out of three of the men who had gone over the top had become casualties and lay dead or wounded on the gentle slope of ground between their trenches and the German lines. The Pals who had joined up in all the euphoria of the early weeks of the war, the lads from Leeds, from Bradford, from York, from Lancaster, from Sheffield, from Hull, had been slaughtered in the first short hour of the great battle. The last echoes of the cheers and the shouting, the last faint remembered notes of the brass bands that had sent them off from the towns and villages of the north, had died out in a whisper that morning in front of Serre.

It must have been two or three in the morning before we managed to get the transport and the rations up, though we'd been trying since early in the evening. We could see the fires as we went up. This little country village, this Serre, were a mass of fire that night. We had to take the stuff up to a place called Basin Wood and it was an exposed position, just about 600 yards behind our front line. And it was full of wounded. There were three doctors there, working flat out, and you could hear this groaning in the dark and see them lying round in the flash of the guns. They'd sent a party down to unload the rations but I'd got a water cart and you couldn't just chuck the stuff and get away. You'd got to wait while they emptied it and poured it in to petrol tins. You could see it had been a shambles.

I kept trying to find out about my brother. He'd only come to the Regiment a matter of days before the attack and he couldn't have come at a worse time. I didn't have time to wangle him on to the Transport. He was joined up with C Company, in the City Battalion, and he didn't have time to pal up with any of them. So nobody knew him. I kept asking, but nobody knew what had happened to him. While they were unloading the water I saw our Sergeant-Major and I tried to speak to him but he'd have shot me! He was brandishing this revolver. Berserk! Didn't know what he was doing. He was absolutely shell-shocked. They all were!

You weren't supposed to stop there. You'd got to get out of it before dawn and I just managed to. I never did find out what happened to my brother. He must have been blown to smithereens.

Private Reg Parker, No. 744, 12th Btn., York & Lancaster Regiment (The Sheffield Pals).

Willie Parker was just one of some two thousand men who had
fallen in front of Serre in the first hour of the attack.

Over the Redan Ridge in the Beaumont Hamel valley, blinking
monstrously under the flashing sky, the white chalk crater of the
mine on the Hawthorn Ridge glowered across at the British lines. It
was many hours since the small force who had captured it and, for a
time, held it, had been killed or pushed back. The Germans still held
Beaumont Hamel; they were still in firm possession of their line.
Save for the carpet of dead that lay in front of it, nothing had
changed since morning. The long toil of the mining operations, the
careful preparations, the high optimism, had all gone for nothing
and been cancelled out by the single monstrous error that had
silenced the guns across the whole Corps Front. Even now, at 8th
Corps Headquarters, Sir Aylmer Hunter-Weston was fuming over
it, and he was fuming because, in the course of a brief telephone
conversation, the Commander-in-Chief had made it plain that he
was displeased with the performance of the 8th Corps. Hours
earlier, in a few snatched moments between conferences, between
consultations and the hasty recasting of plans, Sir Douglas had
confided his displeasure to his journal:

> North of the Ancre, the 8th Corps[1] (Hunter-Weston) said they
> began well, but, as the day progressed, their troops were forced
> back into the German front line, except two battalions which
> occupied Serre village, and were, it is said, cut off. I am inclined to
> believe from further reports, that very few of the 8th Corps left
> their trenches.[2] . . .

They had 'left their trenches' all right, though not many had got as
far as the trenches of the enemy beyond. When the mine had gone
up and the bombardment had ceased across the whole length of the
8th Corps Front, it was the last signal of confirmation the Germans
had needed to warn them that the assault was under way. That had
happened, not at Zero, but ten minutes before the troops were to go
'over the top'. The Germans had ample time to rush up from
shelters and dugout, ample time to garrison their line, ample time to
set up machine-guns, to man their hidden posts, to train the guns on
the gaps in their own wire and also on the British wire, accurately
sighted on the narrow lanes, through which the Tommies would
have to pass into No Man's Land. As for the troops already lying

---

[1] The 8th Corps comprised the 29th Division, the 4th Division and the 31st Division.
[2] No troops had 'occupied Serre village', much less two battalions, although later there was
evidence that a handful had, incredibly, slipped through the German line and reached it.

beyond the trenches, awaiting the signal to go forward to the assault, it took far less than ten minutes to alert the German artillery and to bring a hurricane of shells crashing down on to the land they would have to cross.

It was incredible that any had succeeded in crossing it at all, and those who did had long ago been cut off, with no hope of reinforcement, of relief, or even of rescue.

Between the remnants of the Pals and the remnants of the divisions flung back at Beaumont Hamel, but far ahead of both at Pendant Copse, Sergeant Harry Butler and a dozen men were still holding on to a tiny stretch of captured trench. They spent the hours of darkness salvaging the rifles of the dead and propping them around the trench in the hope that, when morning came, the glinting bayonets would lead the Germans to believe that fresh troops had come up in the night to reinforce them. For the moment they were safe. There was no shelling to worry about. After the first two hours, after the attack had first dwindled and then withered away, the German guns opposite the 8th Corps Front had been able to swing about and add the full strength of their support to the sectors on either side.

They were still firing now, some northwards to Gommecourt where the last of the survivors were trying to crawl back from the German line under cover of darkness. The rest of the guns, ranged behind Beaumont Hamel, had swung their muzzles towards the Thiepval Ridge and were firing over open sights at the Schwaben Redoubt where a handful of the Ulsters who had captured it were still holding on.

Later, when the shelling stopped in order to allow the encircling Germans to close in, they managed to struggle back to the shelter of Thiepval Wood through the tiny opening that remained.

Machine-gun fire from Thiepval village was still stuttering into the night.

On the shoulder of the ridge beyond it, the body of Eversmann was lying spreadeagled in front of the Leipzig Redoubt, where the Germans had counter-attacked and been pushed back in the afternoon. Major McFarlane of the 15th Highland Light Infantry had taken A Company out to search for the wounded of the 17th Battalion. That morning, they had punched the Germans hard in the nose of the Leipzig Redoubt and were still, miraculously, holding on to the first two lines of the trenches they had captured. The rescue party stumbled across Eversmann's body. There was no time to spare for the dead; in particular – and in the view of the Jocks, scouring among the carnage of the morning's battle – there was no time to spare for a dead German. But there was always the chance that his pockets contained 'souvenirs'. Later, crouched in a shell-hole in Authuille Wood, two Jocks of the 15th Highland Light Infantry were going over their haul in the first light of morning. The small notebook with its incomprehensible German script might have been tossed aside as useless, but Captain Hunter happened to come along. They handed it over with a jerk of the head. 'We found it up yonder, sir.' It was Eversmann's diary. Hunter tactfully ignored the rest of their booty. The men had had a hard night. Between them they had brought in forty-two of the wounded.

Beyond the wood, across the dip of the Nab Valley, Ernest Deighton had not been quite so lucky for no rescue party had found him nor the four others who lay wounded beside him in the big shell-hole between the first German trench and the second.

Private Ernest Deighton, No. 25884, 8th Btn., King's Own Yorkshire Light Infantry, 8th Division.

I thought I was a goner. I didn't think I'd get back. I didn't think I'd *ever* get back.

Lying out there that morning I were within twenty-five or thirty yards of the German front line, looking through this telescopic sight at the gap in their trench. I could have touched it. I had my finger on the trigger all the time, not moving, and I saw a few of them laid to rest. But it didn't do our lads much good. As soon as they started across the machine-guns opened up. It seemed like hours before they got up near to me, but they kept on coming. I still dursn't move. These bullets are flying all over the place. It were Maxims they were firing and they were shooting across each other, with this hissing noise as they went past. I dursn't turn round, but I heard the noise behind me and I knew our fellows were coming. Some of them were getting hit and they were yelling and shouting, but they came on, and when the first wave got up to me I jumped up.

I were in the first row and the first one I saw were my chum, Clem Cunnington. I don't think we'd gone twenty yards when he got hit straight through the breast. Machine-gun bullets. He went down. I went down. We got it in the same burst. I got it through the shoulder. I hardly noticed it, at the time, I were so wild when I saw that Clem were finished. We'd got orders: 'Every man for himself and no prisoners!' It suited me that, after I saw Clem lying there.

I got up and picked up my rifle and got through the wire into their trench and straight in front there was this dugout – full of Jerries, and one big fellow was on the steps facing me. I had this Mills bomb. Couldn't use my arm. I pulled the pin with my teeth and flung it down and I were shouting at them, I were that wild.

'There you are! Bugger yourselves! Share that between you!'
Then I were off! It was hand to hand! I went round one traverse
and there was one – face to face. I couldn't fire one-handed, but I
could use the bayonet. It was him or me – and I went first! Jab! Just
like that. It were my job. And from there I went on. Oh, I were
wild! Seeing Clem like that![1]

We were climbing out of the trench, making for the second line,
and that's where they got me again just as I were climbing out,
through the fingers this time, on the same arm. I still managed to
get on. I kept up with the lads nearly to the second line. Then I got
another one. It went through my tin hat and down and straight
through my foot. Well, that finished it!

After a bit, lying there, I saw two fellows drop into some
shell-hole. I crawled after them and, of course, you couldn't see
much for the smoke but, next thing we *did* know, the Germans had
taken back all their front line again. There were no more of our
fellows about. So there we had to stop. When night came I were in
a deuce of a state. I must have been fainting off and on, what with
the loss of blood. You'd no idea of the passage of time. I didn't
know where I were. I only knew there were Germans in front and
Germans behind and I had no idea which way were the British
lines.

What with having nothing to eat and nothing to drink all day, my
tongue was getting as big as two. I could hardly close my mouth.
My water-bottle was gone. I couldn't realise where I was. Lights
going up all the time. All this noise. Them shelling from their side
and us shelling from ours, and machine-gun in between. What
worried me was getting caught in our own shellfire. I bothered
more about that. Well, they dropped in front of me and they
dropped behind me but they never put one into the shell-hole.

The long night flickered and thundered on. By mid-afternoon on
the previous day, sickened by the terrible sights half-glimpsed
through the smoke that rolled across the valley in the front of
Ovillers and la Boisselle, Brigadier-General Ternan had dodged
back through the shelling to his Brigade Headquarters in the lee of
the Tara-Usna Ridge. If any news was to come back from the line, it
would be brought – or telephoned, if there was a line intact – to
Brigade HQ. The fate of the 8th Division, attacking at Ovillers was
obvious to them all. Few of them had even managed to cross the wide
expanse of No Man's Land to get within shooting distance of the
village. As for his own Brigade, every single colonel of the Tyneside
Scottish had died at the head of his battalion, and almost every other

---

[1] Clem Cunnington is buried in Ovillers Military Cemetery.

officer had perished as they went forward to tackle the line at la Boisselle.[1]

Runner after runner had been sent across and had come back – if they came back at all – with no news. It was only now, in the deep dark, as some wounded fragments of the Tyneside Scottish were crawling painfully back from No Man's Land that they realised, with terrible finality, that the 1st and the 4th Tyneside Scottish had been virtually annihilated. Later, when a telephone line was established, Major Acklom reported that he had gathered the remnants of the other two battalions and was holding out in a small length of the German line. Both his flanks were in the air. His men were exhausted. He urgently needed bombs and water. He recommended 'an early relief by fresh troops'.

It was Tom Easton who had got the line going.

Private Tom Easton, No. 1000, 21st Btn., Northumberland Fusiliers, (2nd Tyneside Scottish).

I was in this tunnel with Major Acklom – it was one of the tunnels the Engineers had dug when they laid the big mine. The mine went up all right. We saw it go from the third line. We'd been pulled back because of the explosion and, as a signaller, I was there with all the Battalion Headquarters people.

I could take you to the spot where we set out from. You had a dip coming from Bécourt Château to where the crater is. We were in the deep dip. You couldn't see much when the mine went up, but the noise was terrible. The fall-out was tremendous as well, but it fell short of us. Then we got orders to advance. My Colonel had gone sick and Major Heniker was in charge. He got killed by a shell even before we started. Major Neven was Second-in-Command – a big, noble-looking fellow. He got killed too. They all got killed. All the officers. I couldn't do nothing but pray for my mother to protect us. As we went across I kept saying, 'Mother, help me. Mother, help me' – just as if I was praying to her. When we got to the wire, there was my Signal-Officer, Lieutenant McNeil Smith, lying dead. Then Major Acklom came along, and he took command. We didn't have an officer left – and there were few enough of *us*!

We climbed into the German front line. There were any amount of dead and wounded there, ours *and* theirs. We built a barrier in this line for our own defence on the la Boisselle side – the Germans were still in the trench on the other side of it. They'd had a great shock when the mine went up, but they'd found their feet.

---

[1] Lieutenant-Colonels Lyle and Sillery are buried in Bapaume Post Military Cemetery. The bodies of Colonel Elphinstone and Major Heniker were never recovered.

We were in this sap and we'd got the telephone lines in and, late in the night, I managed to get through to my Battalion Headquarters at Bécourt Château. The dugout was full of wounded. My Sergeant, Bob Wear, was there, badly wounded. The blood was draining out of him. When it got quieter, after dark, I said to Major Acklom, 'Sir, could I and one or two of the other men try to get this man across to our own front line?' It was only fifty yards away, because we were at the bit where the lines had been closest. Major Acklom studied a bit and then he said, 'Yes, you can go, providing you promise to return.' I said, 'You can have that promise now!' I got these two or three lads and we got a groundsheet. We couldn't carry him. We trailed him on the sheet. One or two shells were coming over. We laid him down to take a bit of a rest and he said, 'I don't know what the hell you're bothering about me for. I'm half bloody dead anyway. You're just risking your own bloody lives.' 'Well,' we said, 'we're going to bother.' We trailed him across to our own front line. We had to watch what we were walking on. We were absolutely trampling on the wounded. You couldn't help it. It's bad enough when you're getting bloody wounded, but it's bloody murder when they're trampling on you as well. Oh, they were crying out! I can hear them now. But there wasn't a thing we could do about it. Just get back to the sap, and hang on. Bob Wear died later.

Still more wounded coming past the guns, day and night. Two of our signallers and an officer who had gone through with the infantry charge return to us. The officer was slightly wounded and the two signallers suffering from severe shock, as they had been buried. Also one of the telephonists was missing and another badly wounded. The duty of this little party had been to run out a telephone wire to keep us in touch with the advancing infantry – but they met with disaster and failed. They say that many of our poor wounded were shot by the enemy while trying to crawl back to the cover of our own trenches. But, on the other hand, a German doctor and his staff was nicely captured whilst tending our own wounded. As nightfall approaches, our infantry are still fighting for la Boisselle, so we are still firing heavily through the night. La Boisselle is now alternately reported in our hands and then in the enemy's. The dogged courage and high fighting qualities of the enemy machine-gunners who had weathered our rain of shells and then breasted and checked the waves of our determined infantry is worthy of admiration. The suggestions one hears that the Germans have not fought well, is no compliment to our own gallant troops.

Gunner Frank Spencer, C Bty., 152 Brigade, Royal Field Artillery. (His diary.)

Beyond the loop of the Fricourt Salient still, as it had been that
morning, in German hands, and some four miles to the south-east,
the officers of the 10th Battalion, The Essex Regiment, were settling
down to enjoy a late dinner in the deep German dugout which some
of their Battalion had had the pleasure of helping to capture earlier
in the day. It was an extremely convivial occasion and, strictly
speaking, there were rather more officers present than there had any
right to be. But so many officers had drifted up from the transport
lines where the cadre of the Battalion had been left behind when the
rest went into action, and they were so anxious to savour the delights
of victory, so keen to sightsee in the captured German line, that
Colonel Scott did not have the heart to send them packing.

The dugout in 'Mine Alley' near Montauban, was the best part of
a mile from their jumping-off point of that morning. Their progress
had been swift, their casualties had been comparatively few and now
their satisfaction was enormous. The 18th Division had well and
truly broken the German line on the Somme and, even now, on the
other side of Montauban, the troops were probing even further
forward. There was no doubt that Jerry was considerably shaken, for
only one gun was firing in a desultory fashion from, they guessed, the
direction of Delville Wood. It didn't worry them much. They had
captured innumerable prisoners, run over a score of gun positions
and, once in possession of their new domain, the 10th Essex had even
had time to toss out a load of rubbish in the form of the spare
uniforms, stores and personal belongings of the previous occupants.
They had burned them in a celebratory bonfire. But they had taken
care not to dispose of interesting souvenirs or useful commodities.
Almost every man in the Battalion, from the Colonel to the cooks,
would be able to march out of the line festooned with the coveted
German helmets as well as lesser trophies.

Tonight they were having a wonderful time. There was only bully
beef to eat, supplemented by cheese and some watery soup, but
there was a copious supply of very acceptable German chocolate
and, for the officers, excellent German sparkling water to dilute
their whisky. General Higginson had enjoyed a generous tot when
he had come in person to congratulate them. Now, several hours
after his departure, the officers of the 10th Essex, together with those
signallers and servants who were lucky enough to be attached to
Battalion HQ in its luxurious new abode, were still delightedly
smoking good German cigars, celebrating their victory, and looking
forward to pressing on tomorrow. It was a whoopee of an evening.

Only the Adjutant, Captain Robert Chell, with his ear clamped to
the telephone, doing his best, in the rowdy atmosphere, heavy with
cigar-smoke, to comply with the demands of Brigade for precise

information, had half an inkling that, elsewhere, things had not gone quite as well as had been expected.

All along the front, of the hundred and fifty thousand men who had gone over the top that morning, more than fifty-seven thousand had been killed or wounded. By a prophetic irony of fate, when the Central War Charities Committee had allocated particular dates in 1916 to particular fund-raising bodies, the first week of July had been designated 'Women's Tribute Week'.

Chapter 8

For the people at home, the parents, the wives, the sweethearts, even the children, of the boys who had mostly gone into battle for the first time, the Big Push would be the story of the year. The Correspondents had watched it from a rise on the Amiens road a mile or so behind Albert.

Spangled with waving poppies and wayward clumps of mustard flowers on its verges, the road ran from Albert through the summer fields of Picardy to the town of Amiens, fifteen miles to the south-west – near enough to the battlefield to hear the constant rumble of gunfire in its streets and to see, from a top floor window, the glowing sky lit by the battle below. But Amiens was another world. With the influx of refugees and of French and British military, the number of residents had almost doubled since the war and they were further augmented by an ever-changing floating population, predominantly masculine and predominantly khaki-clad, drifting in holiday mood through its streets in search of civilian delights. Even after two years of war Amiens still had plenty to offer.

After a spell in the squalor of the trenchline, when a man had perhaps not removed his clothes for a fortnight, when his daily ration of water for washing and shaving had been easily contained in a half-pint mug, and whose head, for most of the time, had been clamped into a steel helmet, the pleasure of a visit to a barber was indescribable. The barber's shop in Rue des Trois Cailloux offered a whole range of sybaritic pleasures – a shampoo, a hair-cut, a shave, hot towels and, greatest luxury of all, a *friction d'eau de quinine* rubbed in until the scalp tingled and glowed. Next door at the parfumier you could buy Eau de Cologne to mask the unpleasant odour that clung to every uniform and person, buy French scent as a lavish present for your girl, or, against the happy day when it would be your turn for a bath, soap that bore no relation at all to the abrasive yellow slabs provided by the Army.

There was the bookshop where Madame Carpentier and her daughter, smiling on purchasers and browsers alike, did a brisk trade in indelible pencils and writing pads and an even brisker trade in copies of the saucy *Vie Parisienne*, whose cut-out pictures enlivened the décor of almost every dugout on the Western Front.

They also sold postcards galore and occasionally a book. There were smart cafés, mostly frequented by young officers, and bars in the side streets where drinks were half the price. There was an interesting museum and, although the glorious stonework of the Gothic cathedral had long since disappeared behind a pyramid of sandbags, it was still worth a visit.

Best of all, to palates numbed and wearied by army rations, there were restaurants – la Cathédrale, which specialised in good home cooking, the more expensive Godebert, presided over by the delicious Marguerite and, in a sleazy side street with the curious name of Rue du Corps Nu sans Tête, Josephine's oyster restaurant, cheap, cheerful and none too clean, was run by a virago of a *patronne* who clattered and banged about with the speed of a whirlwind and whom the Tommies had consequently nicknamed 'Hurricane Jane'. A few doors away an establishment which proclaimed itself in white-washed letters across the window to be an 'Officers Dining Room' was much patronised by junior subalterns.

By tacit consent the excellent restaurant of the Hotel du Rhin in the Rue Amiral Courbet was avoided by all but officers of the rank of major and above. There were far too many staff officers about, and staff officers, moreover, whose red-hatted grandeur was further enhanced by the green armbands of the Intelligence Service. They lived and worked across the road in a mansion owned by Madame de la Rochefoucauld but, despite the comfort of their aristocratic billet, despite the pleasant proximity of the Hotel du Rhin and its excellent cellar, despite the civilised surroundings of Amiens, they were not enjoying themselves. They were nurse-maids, or so they would have described themselves, to a group of British War Correspondents – or so *they* would have described themselves. To the Army they were 'writer chappies' and the Army, and in particular its Commander-in-Chief, thought them an infernal nuisance.

Always a professional soldier who regarded soldiering as a professional affair, impatient of what he saw as 'interference' by the uninformed (a category in which he included most civilians and all politicians), Haig had accepted the presence of journalists at the front with distaste and reluctance. Since the beginning of the war the military authorities had put every obstacle in the way of those who wished to report it but, by the time Haig had taken over command of the Army six months earlier, the presence of the journalists was already a *fait accompli*. But his attitude towards them was far from helpful.

Official Communiqués were telegraphed from GHQ each evening and, in the opinion of GHQ, they contained all the facts which newspaper readers required to know. Any embellishment by nonmilitary observers might, when published, give useful information to the enemy. More colourful stories were, after all, only 'written for Mary Ann in the kitchen'. Haig had been injudicious enough to say as much to the faces of some of the most distinguished representatives of Fleet Street when they had called on him at GHQ, and had caused deep offence. Faced with the patronising smile and formidable presence of this 'tall, handsome man who could not see why we wanted more facilities to record the progress of the war', only Philip Gibbs of the *Daily Telegraph* had the courage to speak up. He told the Commander-in-Chief, and in no uncertain terms, that he 'could not conduct his war in secret, as though the people at home, whose sons and husbands were fighting and dying, had no concern in the matter. The spirit of the fighting men, and the driving power behind the armies, depended upon the support of the whole people and their continuing loyalties'.

The Commander-in-Chief was not a man whose opinions were easily swayed, but Gibbs had given him food for thought and, at least on the face of it, his attitude had changed. The correspondents were given uniforms, the use of the upper storey of the splendid billet in Amiens, and the 'services' of a group of trusted Intelligence Officers as censors-on-the-spot, who were installed on the floor below. Their brief was to escort the Correspondents on their forays to the front, censor their despatches as they wrote them and, so that they might be despatched with all speed, no less a personage than a King's Messenger would carry them daily to London. The Correspondents were also led to believe that there was no part of the front they might not visit, that the Army had been instructed to this effect and that they might write whatever they liked, on the understanding that they might not mention place names other than in the most general of geographical terms, nor the names of individuals or units ever at all. As a final accolade, they too would have the right to wear the green armbands of the Intelligence Service.

It was a brilliant move. From now on, the War Correspondents, attired in the King's uniform, were, to all intents and purposes, Officers of the Army, conscious of their debt to it and conscious too of their duty to keep up morale and to reinforce that 'continuing loyalty' of people at home. It was natural that they should wish to prove themselves worthy of the Army's trust. Their facilities included the right to 'talk to anyone', and they travelled far and wide, doing just that, each accompanied by his Army Watchdog, viewing the battles from convenient vantage points and often taking considerable risks to get closer.

It was human nature that, in the light of their previous difficulties with the Staff, the ease of their new situation should float like a rosy gauze between the Correspondents and their observations. It was also human nature that, senior officers who condescended to speak to them, confined themselves to sanguine observations on what was apparent to anyone who took the trouble to read Official Communiqués, that field officers confined themselves to platitudes and that other ranks, invited by an officer of senior (if unrecognisable) rank to confide his impressions of the war, inevitably responded with such anodyne observations as would appeal equally to the sentimental heart of 'Mary Ann in the kitchen' and the patriotic fervour of her master at the breakfast table. It was human nature, but it was not journalism. If any breath of criticism ever escaped the lips of the War Correspondents none was detectable in the dutiful columns of print that breathed victory and hope to the 'people at home'.

In Madame de la Rochefoucauld's house in Amiens, the lights had burned into the small hours of the morning of 2 July as half a dozen typewriters clattered out a story which each Correspondent fervently hoped would convey the drama and flavour of his excitement better than any other. Robinson of *The Times*, having exhausted his repertoire of adjectives in eye-witness descriptions of some scores of previous bombardments during his two years in France, was now faced with the difficulty of describing one that outstripped them all. In an attempt to convey the number of shells which burst every minute he resorted, in desperation, to a technique which had all the elements of a parlour game.

> . . . counting was hopeless. Fixing my eyes on one spot I tried to wink them as fast as the lightnings flickered, and the shells beat me badly. I then tried chattering my teeth, and I think that in that way I approximately held my own. Testing it afterwards in the light, where I could see a watch face, I found that I could click my teeth some five or six times in a second. You can try it for yourself and, clicking your own teeth, will get some idea of the rate at which shells were bursting on a single spot. . . .

But there was no hint of 'chattering teeth' in the well-oiled lyricism inspired by the sight of the Tommies marching to battle.

> Long before they came close one heard the steady roar of their feet – tramp-*tramp*! Tramp-*tramp*! And always as they passed they whistled softly in unison. Some whistled *Tipperary*, some *Come back my Bonnie, to me*, and some, best of all in the place and surroundings, *La Marseillaise*. As we came back along that road, far behind the front, we saw more companies, more battalions. On the tree-shaded road it was too dark to see them, save only as

vague dark masses against the light background of the highway. One felt their presence and heard more than one saw them; always the steady tramp-*tramp*, tramp-*tramp* as they shouldered by; and they were always whistling. Now and again a laugh broke out at some unheard joke, a completely careless laugh, as of a holidaymaker . . .

The Correspondents had only been able to snatch an hour or two of sleep when the morning Communiqué arrived from GHQ. Now, as the censors breakfasted at this unseemly early hour on a Sunday morning, restoring themselves for their duty of scrutinising the despatches as they were ripped hot from the typewriters, the Correspondents were at it again, stiffening their skeleton impressions with a backbone of positive fact.

. . . North of the Ancre our principal success was the capture of the hamlet of Serre, which is regarded as an important tactical point; but by the close of the day the Germans had counter-attacked so violently that progress appears to have been partial. . . . Everything has gone well. Our troops have successfully carried out their missions. All counter-attacks have been repulsed and large numbers of prisoners have been taken. . . . The enemy apparently still hold Gommecourt, though our troops are on both sides of that village. . . . On either side of the valley of the Ancre the situation is unchanged. . . . Our troops were making effective progress near la Boisselle. . . . The general situation may be regarded as favourable. . . . Thanks to the very complete and effective artillery preparation, thanks also to the dash of our infantry, our losses have been very slight. . . . The first impression of the opening of our offensive is that our leaders in the field have amply profited by the experience of the last two years and that they are directing a methodical and well planned advance. . . . There are already indications that close touch must have been kept throughout, and that the attacking forces were well under control . . .

What else could they have written? Could they have told of the painstaking plans that had gone so badly awry? Could they have told of the awful consequences of the blunder which had stopped the guns firing after the explosion at Beaumont Hamel? Could they have criticised the Staff for underestimating the enemy's defences? Could they have dwelt on the supporting barrage of shells, so unalterable in its rigid timing that it went far ahead of the troops, lifting again and again, according to programme, until its shells were tumbling harmlessly miles behind the inviolable German line, leaving its own troops to the mercy of the enemy's machine-guns and shellfire? Could they have been expected to explain that no one had been able to interrupt the programme, to bring the bombardment back, because no one had known what was happening? And were the Correspondents in a position to judge that no reliable news had come back from the fighting line because the painstakingly elaborate system of communications had completely broken down? How could they have arrived at the bitter truth that, despite the plethora of failsafes – of pigeons and wireless and runners and flags, of markers and flashes and lamps and telephones and aeroplanes – in places where no messages had been received it was because no single officer or even sergeant had survived the slaughter to send one?

It was not that GHQ had suppressed this information. The simple fact was that the Army itself did not know. It would be many hours yet before the situation was fully understood. It would take weeks and months of agonised analysis and reappraisal before the truth of what had gone wrong was fully understood and appreciated. And the truth was that the Staff had not trusted Kitchener's Army. Leading it by the hand, it had left it so little room to manoeuvre that, in the end, it had been unable to manoeuvre at all.

Although the reports which were beginning to trickle back gradually from the front were becoming more and more disquieting there were at least some successes to report. It was natural that the GHQ Communiqués should dwell on them. It was in the front line that the troops were dwelling on the failure.

The biggest mistake that was made on manoeuvres and training was that we were never told what to do in case of failure. All that time we'd gone backwards and forwards, training, doing it over and over again like clockwork and then when we had to advance, when it came to the bit, we didn't know what to do! Nothing seemed to be arranged in case of failure.

Sergeant Jim Myers, No. 22745, 25th Co., Machine Gun Corps, 31st Division.

Whatever was gained, it wasn't worth the price that the men had paid to gain that advantage. It was no advantage to anybody. It was just sheer bloody murder. That's the only words you can use for it.

Corporal Harry Shaw, No. 12774, 9th Btn., Royal Welsh Fusiliers, 19th Western Division.

They said to us, 'You lot are moppers up, that's what you've got to do, follow in after the first wave and mop up.' But, they never told us what mopping up was, and we only had a vague idea. No training, as such, except that we were supposed to chuck bombs at these flags that were supposed to be dugouts. Well, when we got to

Rifleman T. Cantlon, No. 33419, 21st Btn., King's Royal Rifle Corps.

the real thing and we were supposed to throw them down real dugouts full of Germans when we got into the trench, the first thing was that the bombs weren't nearly powerful enough to do much damage. And the second thing was that they didn't go right down anyway because the Germans built the steps down with a bend to them, so half the time when you chucked your bomb down, it didn't go all the way down and explode at the bottom, it just went off, bang, against this bend in the wall. It maybe brought down a bit of dust, it maybe even blocked the entrance, if you were lucky, except that Jerry always had a back door to go out of, but, when you're rushing along like that, you don't go down to look and see, do you? You just chuck your bomb down, like you've been told. Well, half the time, when you moved on a bit, the Jerries would come rushing up at your back and get you from behind. That's what was happening on the first day and it was happening all over the place in our sector. It must have been, because, when you got into the second trench, and you were bombing away there, you'd get shots coming at you from the way we'd come and you'd turn round and there would be old Jerry at your back potting away, and some of them going for the next lot of troops coming up to this trench that we were supposed to have cleared. We simply didn't know what to do, and that's the truth of it. But we soon learned!

Still in his shell-hole between the Leipzig Redoubt and Ovillers and between the first and second German lines, Ernest Deighton was in no state to analyse what had gone wrong. He only knew, between bouts of unconsciousness, that the sun riding high in the sky marked his second day lying out on the battlefield, that he was in pain and that rescue was a long time coming. He also noticed, without much interest, that one by one his companions had died during the night. For a long time it was mercifully quiet, then, alerted by some movement, a machine-gun started up and the bullets were zipping dangerously close to him. The shell-hole was too shallow for safety but there was no possibility of moving even if he had been able to summon up the strength. A dead comrade was lying just below the edge of the shell-hole. Inch by inch and painfully slowly, using his good shoulder and his uninjured hand, Ernie managed to push the body up above the rim. He was only able to heave up the legs and a part of the trunk; the arms and the head still hung down into the shell-hole. As the gun swung through its traverse, Deighton noticed, almost absently, that the bullets smacking into the body sounded exactly the same as if they were thudding into sandbags. It was all one to the poor chap now and a few more bullets would make no difference but all the same he wished, as he crouched beneath the body and drifted back into unconsciousness, that the dead boy's upside-down contorted face was not suspended quite so near his own.

There were few church parades on the Somme that Sunday morning. Most padres had their hands full succouring the wounded as they were carried out of the line, lending a hand at aid posts or travelling along the still chaotic roads as their battalions were pushed forward, with all haste, to relieve the shattered troops in the line. Such public orisons as were addressed to the Almighty were spoken over the mass graves where, in communal funeral services, they were burying the bodies of severely wounded soldiers who had died at dressing stations. It was a dreary duty that would go on for days, for weeks and even months as the Army inched forward and the dead were gradually recovered from the captured ground. Already some padres, sickened and dispirited, were disinclined to comply with the clearly expressed wishes of the Commander-in-Chief, passed on to them, at his request, by the Deputy Chaplain General, Bishop Gwynne, . . . *that the Chaplains should preach to the troops about the objects of Great Britain in carrying on this war. We have no selfish motive, but are fighting for the good of humanity.* It was Haig's sincerely held belief that this was true and that the duty of the padres was to underline it constantly, to sustain the troops and bolster their morale just as, in the midst of his own difficulties and responsibilities, he himself was sustained and uplifted by the approval of Higher Authority, obligingly reaffirmed each Sunday in the sermons of Mr Duncan. This good man had no doubts about his mission and his duty and, that Sunday morning, he fulfilled both admirably and to the full satisfaction of the Commander-in-Chief. Early that morning he attended the simple Presbyterian service held in make-shift premises near his headquarters at Beauquesne. With the heavy responsibilities of the Commander-in-Chief at the forefront of his mind, Mr Duncan had chosen as his text: 'Ye are fellow workers with God'.[1]

The service was necessarily brief because there was much to be done. As early as yesterday afternoon, when Sir Douglas Haig had driven after luncheon to Fourth Army Headquarters at Querrieu to confer with Sir Henry Rawlinson, plans had been hastily recast in the light of the first reports. Even by then, it had been obvious that the attack all along the 8th Corps Front and also at Gommecourt had failed completely, while firmer and more detailed reports had

[1] It was a popular sentiment, but it is interesting to note that, on 28 June, in the House of Commons it had been stated, in reply to a question, that: 'The aims of the military machine and those of the New Testament are not compatible.'

indicated, beyond doubt, that in front of Mametz and Montauban, it had succeeded. It was clear that General Gough's Cavalry, jingling in reserve and ready to dash through to Bapaume, would not be needed in the immediate future – nor would the two held-back divisions (the 12th and the 25th) be required to accompany it forward. Until the situation became clearer, as Sir Douglas Haig tentatively suggested to Sir Henry Rawlinson, courteously leaving him to make the decision, it seemed sensible to concentrate all efforts towards exploiting the gains in the south and, meanwhile, to hold the attack north of the Ancre. By seven o'clock that evening, it had been decided.

Extract from the daily diary of General Sir Douglas Haig.

At 7 p.m., as the result of my talk, Sir H. Rawlinson telephones that he is putting the 8th and 10th Corps under Gough at 7 a.m. tomorrow. The 8th Corps seem to want looking after! Gough's command will be the 5th Army.

General Gough's command would therefore stretch from the Thiepval Ridge northwards to Serre. His most important task was to take Thiepval – and to take it at all costs. The Fourth Army, under Sir Henry Rawlinson, would be left free to concentrate on the rest of the line, to exploit the breakthrough on the right and push towards the Thiepval Ridge by its back door at Pozières. But they could not even begin this task, nor even move much further forward on the successful right flank, until they had driven the Germans out of Fricourt and la Boisselle.

Late in the afternoon GHQ received the gratifying tidings that the Germans had retired from the Fricourt Salient. Now, with all the force that they could muster, the troops must consolidate their 'gains' at la Boisselle, capture the village and renew the attack on its twin village of Ovillers across the valley.

At la Boisselle, practically all the force that the troops could muster was represented by some one hundred and fifty men in the small length of the trench they had captured between the big mine crater and the village, and by Major Acklom, Tom Easton, and a handful of others in the tunnel behind – so narrow that two men could only squeeze past each other with difficulty, so low that they could not stand upright and where their only link with the outside world was the single telephone line that Easton had managed to connect. It was the only means by which Brigadier-General Ternan could keep in touch with the sole officer of his entire Brigade who was still, to his knowledge, in the line. The Brigadier's cheerful bellow at the other end of the wire, his encouragement to 'hold on', his reassurances that help was on the way and that fresh troops would soon relieve them, was some slight comfort in their dilemma.

Ternan was far from feeling as cheerful as he sounded, for the ranks of the dead and most of the wounded were still lying out where they had fallen yesterday morning. Behind them the front line was tenuously held by a company of Pioneers. They were practically all that was left of the Brigadier's command.

The first priority if la Boisselle was to be taken was to get the survivors out, to get fresh troops in and to get them in fast. In all but name the 34th Division had ceased to exist.

Chapter 9

The theatre at Bavincourt some miles to the north of the battle was only a barn, but it was a pretty good one. While no one could pretend that it came up to the standard of the London Pavilion, the 37th Division had been in the area for almost nine months and in that time, even with a strenuous programme of normal duties of trench-digging and road-making, the Divisional Pioneer Battalion had had plenty of time to transform the building into a respectable facsimile of a real theatre for the benefit of the 37th Divisional Concert Party. There were curtains, there were footlights, there was a ticket-office and seating for up to three hundred on an assortment of pews and forms rescued from churches rather nearer the line which, having been 'ventilated' by German shells to an unhealthy degree, had been temporarily abandoned by their congregations. If the village of Bavincourt was not precisely the Shaftesbury Avenue of the Western Front, it was conveniently situated within a few kilometres' walk of half a dozen villages occupied as rest-billets by troops out of the line. But, such was the popularity of 'The Barn Owls' that the troops would have walked twice as far to see them.

It was a tidy step from Humbercourt – a good eight kilometres – and among the men of the 13th Battalion, The Rifle Brigade who had marched there the day before, on feet softened by a ten-day tour in the trenches, there were many who were more than content to stroll down to the *estaminet*, make a tour of convenient farmhouses in search of eggs, or simply to 'hang about' – an inexpensive pastime made all the more attractive by the fact that they had not been paid. It had been a miserable day of parades, cleaning up and kit inspections. And it had rained. It was still raining in the evening when a dozen stalwarts set out to tramp the eight kilometres to Bavincourt to enjoy an evening at the theatre and to get together after the show with two members of the battalion who were in the cast of the concert party. They spotted Bill Tylee and Telly Dillsen as soon as the curtain went up and the full company launched into the opening chorus:

> We are the Barn Owl Boys,
> We make a lot of noise,
> We come here nightly,

We just can't get to Blighty,
We are just divisional toys.

Don't think that we're just shirkers,
We fight like Leicesters or Gurkhas,
We've got our iron rations,
And all the latest fashions,
We dig like real good workers.

It was the prelude to a happy evening. For the Riflemen the highlight was a turn by Telly Dillsen who combined a splendid bass voice with a talent for lugubrious comic parody. Tonight he chose to render his own version of *Sentry! What of the Night?*

Sentry! What of the night?
The sentry's answer I will not repeat,
Though short in words 'twas with feeling replete.
It covered all he thought and more,
It covered all he'd thought before,
It covered all he might think yet
In years to come,
For he was wet and had no rum.

There was hardly a member of the audience, other than the Brass Hats in the front row, in whom these sentiments did not strike a sympathetic chord, and they raised the roof. Even Jack Cameron, flirtatiously representing a beautiful blonde, received no greater ovation although 'she' took half a dozen bows, eyelashes a-flutter, before the company joined hands for the closing chorus:

We hope you will excuse us,
If you didn't like our show don't abuse us,
For we tell you straight and true,
That like you we're soldiers too,
We don't get any suppers, not any more than you.

And why we're not in the trenches just now,
Is because our Gallant Staff,
Have sent us here to try and make you laugh,
But one and all,
We are ready for the call,
To join our regiments.

There was time for a beer afterwards when Tylee and Dillsen had changed back into uniform, and many handshakes, back-slappings

and backward shouts of 'See you soon', as the lads started back on
the long tramp through the rain to Humbercourt. They were to see
Tylee and Dillsen sooner than any of them expected and it was just
as well that they were 'one and all ready for the call to join our
regiments', because their orders were already on the way. The
following morning they would be saying goodbye to the greasepaint,
packing up their kit and making for Humbercourt themselves to
rejoin the battalion on the final stage of its journey to the Somme.

In all their sojourn in France, since they had arrived on the *Mona's
Queen* on 30 July almost a year before, and apart from a few jolting
rail journeys in unsavoury cattle trucks, it was the first time that the
Riflemen had not had to march. The buses arrived at ten o'clock in
the evening of 5 July. There were twenty of them to transport the
Battalion, and they had seen better days since they had trundled
around the peacetime streets of London, shiny red and cheerfully
noisy. They were still noisy, and here and there, where the drab
khaki of their wartime paint was chipped, a glint of red still hinted of
the days when they had plied along Oxford Street, travelling north to
Kilburn, or honked through Piccadilly and south to Kensington.
The windows were boarded up but, miraculously, on some the
conductor's bell was still functioning. And, as the boys clambered
aboard, one wag inevitably positioned himself on the platform and
rang the bell.

'Do you stop at the Savoy Hotel?' It was the old, old joke that Joe
Hoyles couldn't resist asking.

'No, sir!' The 'conductor' was equally familiar with the old
chestnut. 'Can't afford it! Did you say a twopenny one, sir? Comes
cheaper if you take a return.'

But for one in three of the boys it would be a one-way ticket.

It was not much more than thirty miles to their destination but it
took the entire night to get there. Two whole brigades of the 37th
Division alone were on the move and there were hold-ups and delays
which came as a welcome rest to the war-worn buses if not to their
passengers. For the first part of the journey, before the lateness of
the hour made it possible to drowse off even in the discomfort of
buses whose suspension had never been designed for long distance
travel, there was chat and banter and sing-songs – anything to pass
the time and to keep at bay disturbing thoughts of the ordeal ahead.
Although no one had informed them of the purpose of the journey,
the men had a shrewd suspicion that they were 'in for it'. Most of
them were excited at the prospect.

Joe Hoyles had a flowery turn of phrase which perhaps sprang
from the attachment he had formed for the death-and-glory

reputation of the Rifle Brigade as a lad before the war. It was not necessarily to the taste of some of his less flamboyant comrades and it was couched in terms which owed not a little to the prose of the Empire-building adventure stories he had read as a schoolboy, but he had fairly summed up the feelings of many others in the speech he had made to the Company Officers of the Battalion when they had attended the A Company Corporals' Christmas Dinner:

Gentlemen,

On behalf of my fellow corporals and myself, I welcome you here tonight. We are pleased that you have come to see us and regret that convention prevents your partaking of this meal which you have so thoughtfully provided.

We have invited you here tonight, to drink your health. We are fortunate in our officers, and when the time comes we shall show you how we appreciate our good fortune. Yes, gentlemen, when the time comes, when once again we go into the line, you will find us ever ready cheerfully to obey and completely to fulfil our duties. You will find us ready to uphold and, if possible, excel the high traditions of the Rifle Brigade and to emulate the noble example of Britain's sons.

Fellow corporals, I ask you to rise and drink the health of our officers, hoping they will be with us to the end of the war and may that end be speedy and gloriously victorious.

Joe's speech was a *tour de force*. Its eloquence was not unconnected with the generous libations of alcoholic refreshment with which most of the battalion had been toasting the occasion for most of the day. The 13th Rifle Brigade had had a whale of a Christmas at Hannescamps and, lurching in their unwieldy convoy past the end of the very road that led to that village, which otherwise had little about it to inspire nostalgic memories, they nudged each other and laughed as they remembered it.

B Company had done best of all. Between them they had collected twenty-five pounds towards the Christmas festivities which their officers had generously doubled. Having made their arrangements well in advance, they had actually sent to London to Fortnum and Mason's for special delicacies and, while most of the other companies contented themselves with pork, B Company had enjoyed turkey, pheasant and ham. The dinner started at lunchtime and, when it ended, late in the evening, transport, in the form of wheelbarrows, had to be pressed into service to convey some of the more enthusiastic revellers back to their billets.

Number 13 Platoon had excelled themselves in a way that might have caused some astonishment to those who had known them such a brief time before as earnest members of the Boys' Brigade.

Rifleman Walter Monckton, MM, No. 2765, 13th (S) Btn., The Rifle Brigade.

We all gave up our blankets to cover the walls of the barn and we covered the beams with evergreens and paper flowers. We got long tables with forms on either side and at one end of the barn we built a stage and draped it with white blankets and footlights made from biscuit tins and candles for a concert we were going to have later on. In the centre of the barn someone actually managed to construct a 'chandelier' with reflectors made of bits of cut-out biscuit tin and with several dozen candles in it. On the wall opposite the door in the middle of the barn Richardson had built a tablet on a draped blue blanket. At the top was a big Rifle Brigade badge with a Union Jack on one side and a tricolour on the other and immediately below this in huge letters: '13 R.B.' And underneath we had written: 'Its honour we will keep. To its glory we will add.' And we surrounded the whole thing with a shield shaped in cotton wool.

I can't remember where we got the cotton wool from, but we must have had plenty, because, on the wall opposite the stage, we had enough of it to stick up a whole poem of two verses. It took absolutely ages forming the letters of the poem with strips of cotton wool and sticking them on to the wall. It was Sid Daynes who made it up, and it said:

> *There is a good time coming some day!*
> *May that day be very soon.*
> *May we all enjoy that some day,*
> *That's the wish of 13 Platoon.*
>
> *This season is noted for wishes*
> *So here's one from 13 Platoon*
> *May you safely meet your dear ones,*
> *Safely and well and soon.*

It was not great verse and Sid Daynes, the proud composer, did not represent a threat to the status of the official Poet Laureate, but 13 Platoon were delighted with it and guests who visited their festivities were equally impressed, particularly the battalion Pioneer Corporal who insisted on pointing out this and the other insignia, slogans and decorations which beautified the barn, to each individual officer as he did the traditional rounds of 'men's dinners' on Christmas Day. The Corporal had evidently 'done the rounds' himself, but the officers overlooked his occasional stumbles in speech and in gait, took it in good part and dutifully admired it all. They toasted the health of the Platoon in whisky or champagne and presented them with several boxes of good cigars. It was a fitting end to the day. Not only had 13 Platoon dined on roast beef and Christmas Pudding, enjoyed chocolate biscuits and tinned peaches for tea but they had even had supper of cheese sandwiches, nuts, oranges, washed down by yet more champagne and white wine.

The concert was a fiasco but that was only because, by the time it was due to begin, most of the audience and some of the performers had disappeared under the tables.

Like the spring holiday month at Auxi, Christmas at Hannescamps shone like a bright beacon in the Battalion's collective memory as they lurched towards the Somme.

On a night journey most of the boys who could packed into the lower deck, although it got very fuggy in there, what with the crowd, and the smoking, and the windows being boarded up. In one way it was better to be on the top deck, but there wasn't much chance of sleeping. Even in July it was pretty cold and the top was completely open in these old buses. You went up a spiral staircase on the outside to get to it and packed into the wooden seats, completely in the open air. These old buses swayed like anything, especially with the number of troops that were packed on to them, and all our gear and, at times, when we went round a corner we really thought she was going over! Then, another hazard was the wires. There were so many telephone wires slung across the roads, and fairly low too, so we really had to crouch down low in our seats and keep our rifles down too, so as not to get caught up in them. There was a rumour going around, though I don't know how true it was, that one chap had been decapitated travelling on the top of a bus, so we were all scared stiff, but of course we made a joke of it. In spite of the cold, I dozed off a bit, but I remember waking up because I was sharing a seat with another chap and he suddenly stood up and shouted, 'Look, boys, the dawn!' And there was just that little bit of light in the sky in the east. But it was well after sun-up when we got to Bresle.

Corporal Joe Hoyles, MM, No 3237, 13th (S) Btn. The Rifle Brigad

The dawn was rising over the Somme and in the first half-light, still trapped in his shell-hole, half-starved, half-frozen and half-dead, Ernest Deighton was roused to consciousness by a sound he had been awaiting for four long days. It was the noise of thundering feet and in another moment a line of British troops rushed past towards the Germans' second line. They had already swept over the first, but Deighton had heard not a hint of the fight. Now he was fully conscious and now he knew from the direction of the attacking troops where his own trenches lay. He also knew that it was probably his last chance to get back to them.

Private E. Deighton, No. 25884, 8th Btn., King's Own Yorkshire Light Infantry.

I thought, 'Here goes, I'm off.' I knew I were a dead man if I didn't. I scrambled out and hobbled and crawled back as best I could and even then I don't know whether I'm going the right way or the wrong way. When I got to not far off the first trench, this voice cried out, 'Halt!' and I just tumbled into it. They couldn't help me back further, they'd just taken that trench and they had to stop there, so somehow I got out of it and I had to crawl all the way back across our old No Man's Land to our own front trench. I managed to get to the barbed wire and I found one bit of a gap and I went through it. It took me about two hours. It would have been twelve hundred yards altogether. And when I tumbled into that trench they said, 'Who are you?' and all I could say was: 'Orange.' That were our password on the first day. 'Orange.' And I was gone, straight away. Passed out. When I came round I were lying on the fire step and they said, 'The remnants of your lot are in Long Valley.' So the stretcher-bearers took me down to Long Valley.[1] There were none of our lot there. Just the MO. It was Captain Marshall and he says, 'Good God! This is 87 in now. There'll be no more!' After that they transported me down to the Canadian Hospital and I was down there six weeks.

Tom Easton was out as well. The 19th Division which had been in reserve on 1 July had moved up on the left of those who remained and Tom himself had signalled them in.

Private Tom Easton, No. 1000, 21st Btn., Northumberland Fusiliers (Tyneside Scottish).

It was about the middle of the forenoon after the attack. We were still down the dugout. We'd had no rations and nothing to eat except some tea. Major Acklom was a regular officer with the Highland Light Infantry and he knew all the tricks of the old soldiers' trade. He suggested that we should tease out some sand-bag rags, put them in a tin with some candlegrease, and set light to them with another tin on the top with some water in it. It took hours to warm up and it was nowhere near boiling, but we put the tea leaves and sugar in and let it all warm up together and eventually we got a fairly hot drink that was better than nothing.

Halfway through the next morning in came this Colonel from the 19th Division. They called them the Butterflies, but he was a hard nut. He said he wanted a signaller and I was instructed to go outside and take a signal flag with me, so out we went in front of what had been the first German line and still not very far away from the enemy. The officer gave me instructions. He said, 'I will

[1] Also known as Blighty Valley.

give you one letter and you must signal that to our own front line four times.' So he gave me the letter and I made the signal. Suddenly, very slowly and methodically, a whole armed company I'd no idea was there, jumped up and came forward in extended order with fixed bayonets and passed us and went forward to the line the Germans were still holding in front of la Boisselle. After a minute or two another letter was given to me and, with exactly the same precision, another company moved forward and passed on their way. By this time, of course, the Germans had seen what was going on and their guns had begun to roar out. But I went on signalling, steady, as he gave me the instructions. The third lot came over and then, after a while, the fourth. When they'd passed by, the Colonel turned to me and said, 'Well done, Signaller!' and then he turned and moved after his troops into the battle. I went back down into the tunnel.

Tom was only too happy to get out of the open for the German guns were now registered on the advancing troops and shells were falling too close for comfort. Roy Bealing was in the thick of it.

We'd been waiting in our old front-line trench. We'd had a rough time even before we got there. There's a ridge getting on towards la Boisselle and then there's a dip and the Germans were all on higher ground and they could see us all coming down in single file, perhaps a thousand of us going to this trench, and they started shelling. One shell pitched right in front of me and knocked out Sergeant Viney and two or three more. We had to keep going and we had to step over one and step over another to carry on. But we had to keep going. We were thankful to get into what was going to be our assault trench, but, what with the shells exploding and what with it being our first time over the top, we felt pretty damned bad as we waited there. It seemed like an age, and then Captain Reid came along the top of the trench – right out in the open! – I suppose it was the only way he could pass the word along the company and he must have had a couple of machine-gun bullets through his water bottle because the water was spouting out of it. He yelled down, 'Fix your bayonets and get ready to go over when you hear the whistle.'

I was beside a young chap called Lucas and he was a bundle of nerves. He was shaking, yes. He was simply shivering and shaking like a leaf. He could hardly hold his rifle, never mind fix his bayonet. So I fixed mine and then I said, 'Here you are, Lucas,' and I fixed his for him. It would have taken him a week to fix his bayonet, the state he was in! He wasn't one of a new draft. He was one of the older ones, and I was right sorry for him.

Private Roy
Bealing, MM,
No. 3/437, 6th Btn.,
The Wiltshire
Regiment, 19th
(Western) Division.

The worst of waiting in the trench was that the Germans had a
machine-gun trained on it going backwards and forwards, backwards and forwards, traversing and coming round every couple of
minutes, and the bullets were cutting the sandbags on the parapet
just as if they were cutting them with a knife. And, if a bullet didn't
get you, this shower of sand and dirt was going straight into your
eyes although the sandbags were a couple of feet above our heads.
Terrible feeling, knowing you've got to go over the top with your
eyes full of sand and watering and not able to see anything. We
were to the right of la Boisselle village and the stretch of trench
where we had to go across was just in front of this huge mine
crater. We didn't know it was there, nobody told us about that, just
that we had to go over and on past that line they'd captured, on to
the second line of German trenches and take them.

When the whistle went, I threw my rifle on top of the tench and
clambered out of it, grabbed the rifle and started going forward.
There were shell-holes everywhere. I hadn't gone far before I fell
in one. There were so many shell-holes you couldn't get round
them. But you had to go on so, every time I stumbled and fell in a
shell-hole, I just waited a quarter of a minute, had another breath,
then out of it and on again. I must have fallen half a dozen times
before I got to the first line, and there were lads falling all over the
place. You didn't know whether they were just tripping up, like
me, or whether they were going down with bullets in them,
because it wasn't just the shells exploding round about, it was the
machineguns hammering out like hell from the third German line
because it was on slightly higher ground. Lucas went down. He
was killed before he even got to the first trench – the one that was
partly in our hands.

I got to the parapet – it looked just like a parapet, chalk banked
up, and I flung myself over it. Well then, I didn't know where I
was! I went straight down sixty feet or more, sliding and slithering.
I thought I'd never come to the bottom! Of course it was this big
crater where they'd blown the mine. There were half a dozen of us
all rattling down, shouting. We picked ourselves up and Captain
Lefroy was there and Sergeant Stone and just about fourteen or
fifteen of us, at a glance, out of the whole company. Captain
Lefroy got us together and we clambered up the opposite side of
the crater and lay there, well under cover, halfway up it and
looking round to see if any more was coming in. We had two
brothers named Moxham and one of them was with us and,
looking across, we see his brother coming to the opposite lip of the
crater. He stopped and didn't throw himself over it like we had,
unexpected like, he just stood there looking down into it. We all

shouted, 'Come on, come on! Don't stand there! That bloomin' machine-gun'll come round. He'll catch you!' But he just stood there a moment too long – and it did get him! He was killed there. Of course his brother didn't know what to do with himself. But there was nothing we *could* do – just lay there. We couldn't get forward. There weren't enough of us anyway!

A while after that another chap called Bill Parratt came over and he was getting down the side of the crater, careful like, when a shell dropped almost right beside him. There was a big cloud of smoke and when it cleared we saw that it had dropped him right in the bottom of the crater. He was lying on his back and one of his legs had been blown off and it was two or three yards away from him. He was hurt bad. He must have been in pain and agony, but there was nothing we could do for him. As the day went on, and it got towards evening, he started to cry out. 'Captain Lefroy, come and shoot me.' He kept calling over and over again, 'Captain Lefroy, come and shoot me.' We got fed up with hearing him calling out. Makes you jangly, all this calling, 'Come and shoot me, come and shoot me.' So the Captain crawled down and went over to him and pulled a packet out of his pocket and it was morphia tablets. He knew he couldn't do nothing for him, just give him these morphia tablets, and he got them down Bill and after a bit he went quiet and gradually faded out.

There was nothing to do but to stay there. Huddled into the side of the crater it seemed to the small party of the Wiltshires that they were in the very cone of the volcano the crater so strongly resembled as the night flashed and roared around them. After a brief lull in the early evening, it had all started up again as another brigade of their division had moved up to renew the attack on the village of la Boisselle a few hundred yards away to the left. Although it was dark, with the merest hint of a new moon in the sky, the lines in front of la Boisselle were so close that the German sentries were alerted by a shifting shadowy mass of movement, by the unavoidable clink of equipment, by a hoarse suspiration compounded of a thousand whispers, as a thousand men crept out to lie in front of the British lines, ready to launch an attack. Nervous machine-gunners started firing indiscriminately ahead and, a moment later, the field guns opened up, sending a hailstorm of shrapnel over the waiting troops. The groans and cries of the wounded confirmed the Germans' suspicions, if any confirmation had been needed and, in the glare of the bursting shells, the eerie light of the flares that rocketed from their lines, the British were as visible as if they had been standing up in full view and on parade. In fact, they had their heads well down.

Crouched close to the evil-smelling earth, Fred Darby of the 10th
Battalion, The Worcestershire Regiment, found that he was sharing
his shell-hole with Tom Turrall, a bomber of C Company. Darby's
acquaintance with him was slight, for Turrall was a surly man not
given to conviviality and with the reputation of being a rebel. He had
spent the previous week in the guardroom – or what passed for a
guardroom in the village where the Worcesters had rested behind
the line – and although at Lieutenant Jennings' insistence he had
been released to go into the battle, he was still, officially, under close
arrest. It was far from being the first time that he had been
reprimanded and disciplined during his service with the Battalion,
and his crime this time had been '*insubordination to an NCO*'. Turrall
was a troublesome soldier out of the line. In the line, however, the
ugly streak of aggressiveness in his character which made him a
thorn in the flesh of the Battalion, also made him a formidable
fighter, and Lieutenant Jennings was well aware of it. Now, sheltering from the rain of red-hot shrapnel, noticing that Turrall was
carrying a bag of bombs that could easily be set alight, Fred Darby
did not regard him as the ideal companion in adversity.

Darby himself had had his own brush with Authority and,
although it had been no more than a minor misdemeanour, typical of
many a fed up Tommy, it had earned him eight days' field punishment, which had seemed to him a trifle unfair, because it had only
been meant as a joke. But the joke had a point. The particular chip
on Fred's shoulder was the sparsity of the rations and a shrewd
suspicion that a large proportion of the food intended for troops in
the line was being filched on the way up. The army biscuits which
were all-too-often substituted for bread were nutritious enough
once you got your teeth into them, but getting your teeth into them
was the problem. They were as hard as cement. Varnished, buffed
and polished, with a suitable cavity gouged from the centre, an army
biscuit made a handsome and durable frame for a snapshot of wife or
sweetheart. Soaked in water, and mixed with jam, or raisins if any
were to be had, they made a reasonably palatable slop. Wrapped in a
cloth and pounded with a mallet, they could be reduced to a state
resembling 'breadcrumbs' which, mixed with mashed-up bully beef,
resulted in a hash which was eatable if warmed up or – if there was fat
available to fry them in, and a Tommy who had the patience to
mould them – made into tasty rissoles. But the purpose for which
they were palpably useless was the very purpose for which they were
intended – to allay the pangs of hunger when nothing else was
available. Fred Darby had sent one home to his wife, Freda. He
wrote the message on one side: 'Your King and Country need You,
and this is how they feed you.' On the other he wrote his wife's name

and address, affixed a stamp and posted it from a civilian Post Office behind the lines.

It was the latter that caused the Army offence. There was no regulation which actually forbade defeatism in correspondence although, for obvious reasons, it was discouraged and could evoke a pointed rebuke from the censoring officer. But posting uncensored 'correspondence' – even an army biscuit – was a serious misdemeanour. Astonishingly, Freda had received the biscuit through the normal channels of the Post Office. Fred had received the backlash and, having taken his punishment, was not encouraged to repeat the experiment. He bore no grudge against the Army and the Army later demonstrated that it bore no grudge against Fred by awarding him the Distinguished Conduct Medal and wiping his 'crime' from its records. But, crouching together in their shell-hole under the bombardment, neither Fred nor Turrall could have guessed that Turrall, the *enfant terrible*, was about to earn even greater distinction.

They went over at three o'clock in the morning. It was less than forty-eight hours since the first general attack had been launched on the Somme Front and it had been much against the will of the British Command that the troops had gone over then in broad daylight. After Saturday's débâcle they were now doubly convinced that they had been right in disagreeing with the French who had pressed for a morning attack. It had been all very well for them to insist that their artillery observers needed daylight but it was glaringly obvious that the daylight had been on the side of the enemy. Now, with no interfering ally to thwart better judgement, the leading battalions rose from their shell-holes and surged forward through the concealing night to the trenches in front of la Boisselle. The 10th Worcesters were in the first wave.

Eight hundred and ten men went in. Four hundred and forty-eight came out.

But they had captured three lines of trenches and, although they had not succeeded in taking the whole village, by mid-day they had succeeded in winning enough ground to establish a line halfway through it and Tom Turrall had earned the Victoria Cross.[1]

---

[1] Turrall's citation read: 'For most conspicuous bravery and devotion to duty. During a bombing attack by a small party against the enemy, the officer in charge was badly wounded and the party having penetrated the position to a great depth, was compelled to retire. Eventually, Private Turrall remained with the officer for three hours under continuous and very heavy fire from machine-guns and bombs and notwithstanding that both himself and the officer were at one time completely cut off from our troops. He held his ground with determination and finally carried the officer into our lines after our counter-attack had made this possible.'
Date of Act of Bravery 3 July 1916   *London Gazette* 9 September 1916

It had not been so much a fight as a mêlée. The ruined buildings concealed fortifications, dugouts and hidden strongpoints as apparently invincible as any on the front, but the Worcesters had fought with bayonet and bomb. They had gone on fighting when the Commanding Officer, the Second-in-Command and almost every other officer had been killed or wounded and there was no longer anyone to lead the fight. In the first light of dawn Lieutenant Jennings had gathered some remnants of the men about him and was doubtless thankful to recognise Turrall among the scattered troops who, willy-nilly, had been separated from their platoons. They had pressed on through and beyond the village and into a storm of machine-gun fire. When it ceased, none of the party was left but Turrall and, lying a few feet away from him, his leg shattered and useless, Lieutenant Jennings. Turrall had dragged him into a shell-hole. He had bandaged the broken leg, using his entrenching tool as a splint and one of his puttees as a bandage. He had single-handed repulsed a bombing attack by a party of Germans creeping up at close range. He had survived a counter-attack, by lying as still and apparently lifeless as Lieutenant Jennings himself as the enemy swept past to try to retake the line. One German soldier had even stopped and prodded him with his bayonet, and still, with a monumental effort, Turrall contrived to appear oblivious. Throughout the day he lay with Jennings in the shell-hole at the further end of the village with the enemy in front and behind.

At first light as the fight for la Boisselle was at its height and as Lieutenant Jennings had been gathering up his party and preparing for the dash forward, the small force of the 6th Wiltshires, their number swelled by men who had crept or tumbled into the crater during the night, were facing the German lines on the further rim of the crater, 'standing to' in case the enemy should rush it in a dawn attack. Nothing happened and the fearsome noise of the fighting in the village a quarter of a mile to their left reassured them that, for the moment, the Germans had their hands full. But their first sight of what lay beyond the crater, glimpsed cautiously in the grey half-light, haunted them through the sweltering day. Sweating in the heat, parched with thirst, pressed against the gas-soaked slopes of the crater, dizzied by the fumes of explosions, in the forefront of the clamour of the fight to the left of them they could hear quite distinctly a sound that came closer to home. It was the buzzing of a million flies hovering and settling on the still bodies of the dead, lying in countless numbers beyond the crater. The smell, in the summer heat, was almost overpowering but all Roy Bealing could think of through the endless day of burning heat, was that every dead soldier lying out in front must have a full water-bottle strapped to his body. Their own were long since empty. They could only hope that, when nightfall came, rations would come too. Meanwhile, they could only hold on.

When the darkness deepened, Bealing scrambled over the rim of the crater and crawled in search of water among the ranks of the dead. The shelling had abated. In la Boisselle the fighting had died down. Both sides were glad to draw breath and draw strength for tomorrow. Flares lit the ground from time to time, but there was no fear that Bealing would be spotted. Creeping close to the ground among the huddled dead, he would simply be taken for one of them.

Some few hundred yards away, beyond the captured line that ran through the centre of the village, Tom Turrall was creeping back with infinite caution and also with infinite difficulty. He was carrying his officer on his back and Lieutenant Jennings was in a bad way. He had been wounded twice before Turrall had dragged him into the shell-hole and he had been wounded twice more while he lay there. Now, with his left leg shattered, with wounds in his right thigh and knee and a bullet wound through his left arm, he could do little to help himself. Tom Turrall was not, in general, an admirer of officers, but he admired Lieutenant Jennings. He liked the way he had tackled the first dugout, bombing it himself and capturing it almost single-handed which, in Turrall's opinion, was no mean feat. He had liked the way that he had led the men to the second line and kept on leading even after he was wounded and, when Jennings was beyond carrying on, he had astounded Turrall by his courage as he lay shattered in the shell-hole. Time after time he had fainted with pain and time after time he had roused and chatted in an almost social way and had even smoked a cigarette or two, allowing Turrall to light them but, with his one uninjured arm, waving away his efforts to place the cigarette between his lips. Turrall had liked that too, and he was determined to get Jennings back.

Jennings was a dead weight. He was weak with loss of blood. He was a taller man than Turrall and his one sound arm which Turrall had thrown around his own neck had little grip left in it. All that Turrall could do was to grasp it with one hand of his own, throw his other arm behind him around Jennings' body, and half-carry, half-drag him through the gaps between the German outposts, across the battered ground, to the new British line. There had been little chance to consolidate, and the sentries were edgy, alert to any shadow that staggered from the darkness of the night beyond.

'Halt! Hands Up!' And then, as Turrall raised his hands as far as he could without letting Jennings go, came the heart-stopping snap of the rifle bolt, 'That man behind you too! Quick!' 'For God's sake! He's wounded and I'm bringing him in!' Turrall was just in time to stop the sentry firing and raising the alarm.

Lieutenant Jennings survived long enough to be carried to the field dressing station. He survived the journey by ambulance to the casualty clearing station at Dernancourt. And he lived long enough to tell the story of what had happened and to recommend Tom Turrall for the Victoria Cross. He died of his wounds on the evening of 5 July. Some hours earlier, before Lieutenant Jennings had finally slipped into unconsciousness, they were able to tell him that the Germans had been pushed out of la Boisselle.[1]

The 19th Division was still in the line but now it was possible to bring out the Tynesiders of the 34th. The fragments of the battalions came out in pathetically small groups and were collected together in trenches on the Albert side of the Tara-Usna ridge. There was little shelter and, after a fine day, a chilly wind hinted at rain in the morning. They were very near the gun line but neither the roar of the night barrage, nor the absence of greatcoats and blankets disturbed them. Slumped where they had thrown themselves down, the Geordies slept the sleep of the dead.

Next morning, for the first time in five days, they had a hot breakfast to sustain them on the six-mile march through the town of Albert to Millencourt four miles beyond. It was a long slog along the congested roads but there were many welcome rests while they waited at the roadside for a convoy of buses or lorries to pass. All were carrying troops whose clean and cheerful demeanour, in spite of an almost sleepless night of travelling, contrasted vividly with the appearance of the soldiers newly out of the line. Filthy, bedraggled, sunken-eyed with fatigue, they stood by the roadside and grinned and waved back as the cheering convoys passed. Tom Easton, for one, felt that, for the first time, he truly understood the meaning of the word 'relief'.

---

[1] Tom Turrall survived the war and died in 1964.

Chapter 10

With the concentration of troops coming out of the line and whole brigades preparing to go in, the population of Millencourt which had amounted to a few hundreds before the war had expanded to that of a fair-sized town. There was no question that such billets as there were should be reserved for the exhausted ranks of the decimated battalions who, beyond anything else, needed rest. In the barns, stacked high with tiers of short wire-netting bunks, the weary men of the 34th Division lay asleep and replete too, for they had enjoyed a lavish meal. Some of the lads had managed to tuck away as many as four plates of stew and, for once, there had been enough bread to mop it up. With so few to be fed, there was plenty to go round.

Arriving late in the afternoon from his meeting with the Divisional Commander, Brigadier Trevor Ternan was reluctant to rouse the sleeping officers, but it had to be done. A day or so before he had addressed the officers of his Brigade *en masse* in the village school-room. Now there was more than room enough for them all in his office at Brigade Headquarters. Eighty officers had gone into action with the four Battalions of the Tyneside Scottish Brigade. Ten now remained.

In the Tyneside Irish, it was the same sorry tale. Mere drafts of reinforcements arriving in officerless battalions would be of little use. It had been decided, Ternan announced, that both Brigades should be transferred wholesale to the 37th Division to rest and recuperate, to regroup and retrain with new men in a quiet sector of the line. Meanwhile, two Brigades of the 37th Division would take their places in the 34th to continue the battle. Later, when they were up to strength again, he hoped that they would all return to the Home Division. But his listeners knew, as Ternan knew himself, that, whatever the future held, neither the Tyneside Scots nor the Tyneside Irish would ever be the same again.

The change-over had taken place while the men were sleeping and the 112th Brigade was already resting on the slopes behind the village preparing to move off.

A brisk half-hour's stroll away in the environs of the insalubrious village of Bresle, the boys of the 13th Rifle Brigade had enjoyed a day of comparative rest and, in the course of it, had learned that they were now part of the 34th Division. After their night journey from Humbercourt they had been bivouacking all day in the open and they were not sorry to be stretching their legs and leaving to march nearer the line. Earlier in the afternoon, the Battalion had formed an open square on the hillside, Colonel Pretor-Pinney had addressed them, cautioned them – if caution were needed – to uphold the tradition of the 'Golden Horseshoe' symbol of the 37th Division, even though they had been abruptly transmogrified to the 34th, and wished them luck. A number of the boys felt, superstitiously, that it was an inauspicious moment in which to be deprived of the lucky horseshoe.[1]

Now they were marching along the road, and they were singing. It was not exactly a marching song, nor one of the rousing airs which the popular mind had been led to believe by the War Correspondents made up the usual repertoire of cheery Tommies singing on the march. It was certainly not the *Marseillaise* – which one fulsome report had attributed to some anonymous battalion the week before. Although they were approaching the first anniversary of their arrival in France, the linguistic abilities of the Battalion did not extend quite so far as mastering the words of the *Marseillaise*, but there was nevertheless a distinctly international flavour about one tuneless dirge which was a favourite of theirs, if only because they had composed it themselves. In its genesis the melody had borne a faint resemblance to *Here We Go Round the Mulberry Bush* but with the passage of time infinite variations had rendered it almost unrecognisable.

> *We don't want a girl from Givenchy-le-Noble,*
> *From Givenchy-le-Noble,*
> *From Givenchy-le-Noble,*
> *If you go for a walk she will get into trouble.*
> *So we don't want a girl from Givenchy-le-Noble.*
>
> *We don't want a girl from Izel-lez-Hameau,*
> *From Izel-lez-Hameau,*
> *From Izel-lez-Hameau,*
> *She may be all right, but we don't care a damno,*
> *So we don't want a girl from Izel-lez-Hameau.*

[1] The 111th and 112th Brigade which were exchanged with the 102nd (Tyneside Scottish) and 103rd (Tyneside Irish) Brigades in the 34th Division comprised:

111th Brigade:	112th Brigade:
6th Bedfordshire	10th Royal Fusiliers
6th Leicestershire	13th Royal Fusiliers
7th Leicestershire	13th King's Royal Rifle Corps
11th Royal Warwickshire	13th Rifle Brigade

We don't want a girl who comes from les Comptes,
Who comes from les Comptes,
Who comes from les Comptes,
For they all eat onions, and their breath rather haunts,
So we don't want a girl who comes from les Comptes.

As they marched easy a familiar discussion arose in B Company among the bards of No. 13 Platoon. They felt that they should bring the melodic itinerary up to date by adding a verse in honour of the delightful female inhabitants of Auxi. But inspiration eluded them. No one could come up with a better rhyme than 'poxy' and it seemed singularly inappropriate to the place where they had spent such a pleasant time.

I can see us now – a long column of marching riflemen. We must have recaptured our high spirits of the night before because we're singing again. It was a fair step and the gaps between the platoons got noticeably wider and wider. We marched past a field gun battery, halted for tea. We could have done with a cup ourselves, and we let them know it as we went by! Then we marched past them up a steep bit of road and, as we got to the top of the rise, there were long stretches of canvas fastened to plane trees along the roadside to hide the traffic on the road from enemy observation and, beyond the hill, we could see the town of Albert down in the valley.

It was funny how the singing died away. Shells were bursting away to the north-east and there in front of us was Albert, looking fairly intact, but with the battered cathedral tower standing out above it and the figure of the Virgin holding the Child leaning over the town in this sorrowful attitude. I can still picture that stark outline in my mind's eye and it seemed to me then, as it always did afterwards when I looked back on it, that she seemed to be lamenting the folly of men.

Sergeant Howard Rowlands, B Coy., 13th (S) Btn., The Rifle Brigade.

Even before the war, the golden Virgin, triumphantly holding the infant Child in her uplifted arms on the soaring heights of Albert's Cathedral, had been a landmark. Now it was the very symbol of the war itself. Early in 1915, an unlucky shot from a German gun had struck the cathedral tower fair and square and the Virgin had fallen forward to lie precariously horizontal, face downwards above what had once been the market-place and was now the bustling centre-point of troop movements through Albert. It was an awesome sight.

As the shellfire intensified and the cathedral itself became more and more battered and knocked about, the tower with its leaning

Virgin remained intact. A superstition grew up among the French troops and it was adopted in their turn by the British when they came to the Somme. When the Virgin fell the war would end – and the Germans would have won! As the Virgin looked likely to fall at any time, an event which would be distinctly bad for morale, French Engineers were ordered to secure the statue with strong steel hawsers. So, there she hung, sorrowing or, according to the various imaginations of the troops, protecting or blessing them as they passed beneath.[1]

It was astonishing that there could still be civilians in Albert a scant two miles behind the British front line. It was the ridge that saved it, for Albert lay cupped in a valley. It was not so much a town as an outsize village and, although some houses were tumbled and ruined and shells had taken a bite out of many others, there was still a remarkable air of normality about Albert although, since the bombardment had started, there were fewer inhabitants to be seen and those who had stayed there were keeping judiciously under cover. There were some villas still intact on the western outskirts and, in the main street by the cathedral, a number of houses which, if a soldier was not too fussy, could provide a reasonably draught-free billet for the night. The individual platoons of the 13th Rifle Brigade were more or less left to fend for themselves, with the proviso that they must be on parade and in battle order in front of the cathedral at 7.30 next morning.

Sergeant Jack
Cross, No. 4842,
C Coy., 13th (S) Btn.,
The Rifle Brigade.

We had to break into the houses to get the lads under cover, but that was all right as long as the sergeants did it, so all the C Company NCOs got in one place and the company officers were next door. We thought that they were fattening us up for the kill, so to speak, because we actually got issued gammon rashers for supper. We had to cook them ourselves, of course, but nobody minded that. Well, I'd noticed that the garden next door had a fine crop of potatoes in it, just ready. So Fred Crease and myself, we slipped over the garden wall, took our bayonets and dug up these potatoes. They were lovely. We boiled them, fried the gammon rashers and had gammon and new potatoes that night for hot dinner. We hadn't had such a feed since Christmas.

The fact that the Sergeants of C Company dined so royally was probably because Jack himself had seen to it that the cooks always

[1] The hanging Virgin remained in this position until the late spring of 1918 when she was shot down by the British Artillery after the Germans had occupied Albert. They rightly concluded that the Germans would use the tower as an observation post, just as they had used it for this purpose themselves.

got a share of the warm garments so lovingly knitted by his fellow servants in Eaton Square. No one enquired too closely where the gammon rashers came from, but the C Company Sergeants did notice that the same appetising smell drifted from the C Company Officers' billet next door. The officers had not had the good fortune to enjoy the delicious accompaniment of new potatoes, although they had been brazenly filched by the Sergeants from the garden behind their own billet, and had to be content with beans.

The rest of the Battalion supped, that evening, on beans and bully beef. Bob Thompson was mixing it into a tasty mush in his mess tin and warming it over his personal, carefully guarded primus stove, when Major Sir Foster Cunliffe popped his head into the Corporals' billet.

'Lost your saucepan, Thompson?' They exchanged grins.

'Yes, sir. And no custard either!'

It was an old joke, dating back to the previous autumn when the Battalion had been occupying the line that ran through the orchards at Hannescamps. The trees above the communication trenches were heavy with apples, and it had given the signallers of D Company an idea, for they were partial to stewed apples and custard. There was no 'custard', of course; there was no milk to make it with; there was no sugar to sweeten it. There were apples in plenty, actually falling in showers into the trench when a shell happened to explode within fifty yards of them, but there was no saucepan to cook them in. It was Sid Whiting who supplied the deficiency.

We could get Quaker Oats – so I suppose the custard was porridge, really speaking – and bags of apples, but this question of a utensil really bothered us. One day, when we were out of the line, I was sitting in the barn at Bienvillers, when I saw 'Madame' bring out a saucepan of food for the dog. As soon as she turned her back, quick as a flash before the dog could get at it, I nipped over, emptied the food on the ground and 'won' the saucepan.

Next time up the line I was cooking our usual supper of stewed apples and porridge when our Company Commander, who was then *Captain* Sir Foster Cunliffe, came into the dugout and remarked how good it smelt. Well, I naturally asked if he would like some, and he said he would. He asked me how we came by the stuff. So I told him the whole story – including the story of the saucepan. We all thought it was a great joke, and the Captain really enjoyed his supper! But he never let us forget it after that! He said, 'Well, I've attended banquets and eaten off gold plate, but I don't think I've ever before eaten food cooked in a dog's saucepan.' Well, as we used to say, '*C'est la guerre.*'

Rifleman Sid Whiting, MM, No. S/4229, D Coy., 13th (S) Btn., The Rifle Brigade.

And '*C'est la guerre*' the boys were saying, as they put their shoulders to the door of a locked-up *estaminet* in the main street of Albert. Major Sir Foster Cunliffe, now Second-in-Command of the Battalion, was fortunately well out of the way, or had turned a judicious blind eye. And any officers in the vicinity later turned a deaf ear to the merrymaking when, pleasantly replete with free beer, Horace Smith and some other stalwarts of B Company, dragged the piano from the *estaminet* into the street for a sing-song. Breaking into private property had not over-worried them. If the place had not been locked up when the civilians had hastily evacuated, they would never have dreamed of helping themselves. They had been perfectly willing to buy the beer and, for once, they had money to pay for it. '*C'est la guerre.*'

Sergeant Jack
Cross, No. 4842, C
Coy., 13th (S) Btn.,
The Rifle Brigade.

Well, what the lads were a bit annoyed about was that we all got paid out that day. They could have done with the money a couple of days before when we were up at Humbercourt. You never knew for sure when you were going to get paid except if you were going into action. They always paid us out then because it was a chance to get rid of this money, so that the Quartermaster-Sergeant wouldn't lose it all in a fight. He'd see you got it first. There was a chap in my platoon called Wright and he used to run a Crown and Anchor board so he said, knowing that the lads had got money, 'I'll get the old board out, Sergeant.' Strictly illegal, of course, and as a Sergeant I shouldn't have had anything to do with it, but I said, 'All right, Arthur, you do what you like. Get the board out and I'll give you a start.' Well, all the lads gathered round and Arthur started on the job and I was putting my bits and pieces down and I was winning! I just kept putting my money down on the right spots. I've never won so much money in my life on a Crown and Anchor board. Four pounds ten shillings I picked up that afternoon – near enough a month's pay for a sergeant. I thought, 'Well, I'll stick it now and hold on to the money.' So, off I went. After a bit, when it got dark and they had to pack up, Arthur came along and found us in this billet and said, 'Sergeant, can you tell me where there's a Field Post Office?' I went out in the street and there was a Military Policeman coming along so I said, 'Say, chum, can you tell us where there's a Military Field Post Office?' He said, 'See that flag fluttering over there? That's it.' 'Right,' said Arthur. 'I'm going over there to get rid of this money. I'm not going up the line for somebody to pick my pockets when I get a bullet.' So he sent the money home in postal orders – and it was a tidy sum too!

It rained that night. It was the last straw for Joe Hoyles and the twenty others of his platoon who had not been fortunate enough to find a billet under cover. Wrapped in waterproof groundsheets they passed an uncomfortable night lying on the broken pavement round the church. They had not required to visit the Field Post Office to send their money home. In a sense, Arthur Wright had done it for them and the few francs that had passed briefly through their hands an hour or so earlier were already on their way to swell Arthur's savings at home. Between them they had lost every bean.

It was just as well that Colonel Pretor-Pinney had not been in the vicinity while the Crown and Anchor game was going on. He was a stickler for discipline.

But Colonel Pretor-Pinney was otherwise engaged, for Major-General Ingouville-Williams, the Commander of the 34th Division, and in spite of his exalted rank disrespectfully known to the troops as 'Inky Bill', had summoned the Brigadiers of his two newly acquired Brigades and the Commanding Officers of their eight Battalions to a meeting. It started at eleven o'clock. The General apologised for the lateness of the hour. As they were already on their way into the line, this was the only opportunity there would be to make mutual acquaintance and to discuss the plans that were to be put into effect tomorrow.

The particular plan for tomorrow was the renewal of the attack on the village of Ovillers, across the valley from la Boisselle, which, in spite of the terrible cost, had resisted all efforts to take it. Strictly speaking, it was not the affair of the 34th Division, because the assault was to be carried out by the right flank of General Gough's newly formed Fifth Army, but it was important that they should know of it because they were to be attached to the 19th Division still holding the adjacent sector and their own fortunes and progress would depend on the result. Unless Ovillers fell, it would be extremely difficult to exploit the gains at la Boisselle and to push on beyond it. Meanwhile, they would move up in support and, when the 19th Division was relieved, take over the front line and push ahead.

The night was heavy with cloud and heavy with noise, for the iron-rimmed wheels of the transport limbers clattered non-stop over the broken pavé, making the most of the hours of darkness to get the supplies up the line and behind the town the guns were roaring out a bombardment as fierce as any since the first day of the assault. Through the long damp hours between nightfall and dawn the men lay waiting for the morning. They knew that something was up and that, soon enough, they would find out what it was.

What was 'up' was that the Germans were answering back. Behind his line for the last few days the enemy had been engaged in very much the same reorganisation as the British behind theirs. After the first onslaught the German Army, which had put up such a rugged resistance to the British efforts to break their line, was exhausted and depleted by heavy casualties, and Royal Flying Corps observers were bringing back reports of long lines of ambulances, of troop movements and trains of supply wagons as units were reshuffled in and out of the line. Both sides had fought almost literally to the death and there was hardly a British or a German soldier coming thankfully out of the front line who did not feel a positive admiration for his opponent. It was impossible for the Germans not to admire 'Tommy' pitting his strength and his will against the steel and concrete of strongholds armoured and designed to be impregnable; it was impossible for the British not to admire 'Fritz', who had fought so valiantly in their defence.

The Germans had been chivalrous. The morning after the Big Push in many places where the attack had utterly failed and there was no fight left in the troops, unofficial truces had lasted for hours and the few troops who were left were allowed to move freely in front of their trenches to rescue as many of the wounded as they could in the time allowed. In front of Beaumont Hamel, a young soldier of the Worcesters who had crawled out concealed by the morning mist to search for a wounded friend and had, miraculously, found him, was seen by the Germans just a few feet from their wire when the mist suddenly cleared. There was a clatter of rifle bolts but, as both soldiers looked up, appalled, a sharp order was given and a German officer sprang on to the parapet of the enemy trench. He shouted across, in astonishingly perfect English, 'You must not stop there with that man. If you want to come in, come along. Otherwise you must go back to your own trenches.' And he added, as the boy hesitated, 'We will look after your comrade.'

'I'll go back to my own trenches, sir.' He didn't dare stand upright, and it seemed a long crawl through the shell-holes and the bodies, down a slope, across dead ground and up again to the British wire. But the Germans had not fired a shot at his retreating back. Nor did they fire at the line of British soldiers in their forward trench who, incautiously poking their heads above the parapet, anxiously watched his approach.

Now, days later, some thousands of dead still lay there and the weak waves and shouts of the wounded had long ago been stilled. Even in sectors where bitter fighting had pushed the line forward, the terrible detritus of the first day's battle lay blackened and decomposing in the open. Awaiting the 13th Battalion, The Rifle Brigade, on their arrival at la Boisselle was the task of burying them. Someone had to do it.

Above left: Boromée Vaquette, the first man to die on the Thiepval Ridge, lies in the family plot, under a modern headstone, in Authuille village cemetery.

Above right: '… the first one I saw were my chum, Clem Cunnington. I don't think we'd gone twenty yards when he got hit straight through the breast. Machine gun bullets.' (*Private Ernest Deighton*) Clem Cunnington's grave in Ovillers Military Cemetery.

Below left: Reg Parker (*on left*) with two comrades of the Sheffield Pals. He took the water cart up to the Battalion in the trenches at Serre on the night of the First of July but failed to find his brother Willie who had gone 'over the top' that morning.

Below right: Reg Parker's brother Willie who fought his way out of his 'reserved occupation' job as an engineer to rejoin the ranks of the Sheffield Pals in time to go over the top with them at Serre on the First of July. He was killed in the first wave of the attack.

A view of the still-visible trench-lines to the left of Contalmaison attacked alone by the 13th Rifle Brigade on the evening of 10th July. The chalk-pit in the centre of the photographs was in the 3rd German line. After word reached them that the abortive attack was cancelled more than half the battalion was wiped out by shell-fire as they struggled to get across the land in the foreground of the photograph.

The road from la Boisselle to Contalmaison, just to the right of where the 13th Rifle Brigade made their unsupported attack on 10th July.

Now that the Germans, like the British, had replaced their battle-weary front-line forces with fresh troops they had thrown them straight into the battle – not, like their exhausted predecessors, to defend their line but to wrest it back in the places where the British had bitten into it, and to stand fast. They had attacked at dead of night. They threw themselves against the tiny lodgement in their front line north of Thiepval and proceeded to throw the British out of it in short order. They had attacked beyond Thiepval, at the other end of the ridge, battering into the bloody nose of the Leipzig Redoubt and fought and bombed all through the night before their survivors were beaten back. And the Germans had been beaten back even beyond the trench from which they had started. Two companies of the 3rd Worcesters had pulled it off. They had succeeded at last in capturing the whole of the German front line in the Leipzig Salient, and they held it and continued to hold it though the Germans blasted a desperate bombardment back at them.

The Germans had also attacked at Ovillers, streaming out of the village and setting up machine-guns in No Man's Land an hour before the British troops were due to launch an attack themselves. But, by ten o'clock in the morning, by the time the 13th Battalion, The Rifle Brigade, had marched out of Albert up the long straight road to the Tara-Usna Ridge, which overlooked the valleys of Ovillers and la Boisselle, Ovillers had been taken. Or, rather it could have been taken, if there had been survivors enough to hold it. The cost of thwarting the German attack, of pursuing them back to the village, of subduing the nest of strongholds which had repulsed successive waves as a cliff-face repulses the sea, had been too high. Fourteen hundred men of the three Battalions had been killed or wounded. They took the first three lines of trenches but, by the time they had done so, there were not enough of them to hold the enemy. All that could be done, until reinforcements arrived, was to retire from the first line, consolidate the two behind it and hang on. But it was a start. And it was more than a start. It was a victory.

From their position in low-lying Ovillers, had they dared to raise their heads and look to their right, the victors could have seen, two kilometres ahead of them, at the top of the long shallow valley that ran through the gently rising ground, the thick belts of wire that protected the village of Pozières, lying beyond them astride the Albert–Bapaume road. Like Ovillers, Pozières was a fortress.

With the Army now pushing towards it from two separate directions, it seemed to Sir Douglas Haig that Pozières was the next logical objective. He had just discussed the matter with General Rawlinson when the news arrived that the capture of Ovillers was not complete and that the troops had merely gained a foothold in the village. No casualty figures were yet available, but it appeared, from all accounts, that the gain, though small, had been costly. More men must be brought in. Experienced men. Good fighters. The Commander-in-Chief accordingly issued his orders. He instructed General Gough to complete the capture of Ovillers with such troops as remained at his disposal, and he ordered the Anzac Corps in the Second Army to send two Australian Divisions south to the Somme. For the moment he would hold them in reserve. Later, when the way was open, he would push them in to attack Pozières.

In his conversation with General Rawlinson, the name of the Anzacs and the name 'Pozières' were linked for the first time. As long as battles were remembered, they would never again be separated.

In meadowland near Millencourt, flanked on either side by Major-General Ingouville-Williams and by the Corps Commander, Sir William Pulteney, Brigadier Trevor Ternan surveyed the ranks of his Tyneside Scottish Brigade. After a morning of roll calls the totals returned by each battalion had almost beggared belief, but they were amply confirmed by this afternoon's parade. The whole Brigade, drawn up in open square formation, barely occupied the space of a single battalion. The Generals warmly congratulated the men. Sir William Pulteney dwelt at length on the tactical importance of the part they had played. Their achievement might only be measured in yards, but they had broken the German line. General Ingouville-Williams dwelt on their splendid gallantry. He bade them Goodbye and Godspeed. He hoped that they would soon rejoin his command. Trevor Ternan, as sadly conscious of the absence of familiar faces as any man in the ranks, called for three cheers. A voice yelled out with statutory bravado, 'Are we downhearted?' The men obliged with a stentorian 'NO!' No one yelled it louder than Tom Easton. For the last six days he had been sick with worry about his brother Joe. This morning, in the decimated ranks of his battalion, he had found him. By some miracle he was whole – and alive!

At ten o'clock that evening, in pouring rain, the 13th Rifle Brigade left the reserve trenches on the Tara-Usna Ridge for the line at la Boisselle. It was less than a mile ahead, but the shelling was heavy and they lost thirteen men, killed or wounded on the way. Early the next morning, just after stand to, Walter Monckton and Joe Hoyles were brewing tea in the trench when the Colonel came along, accompanied by a Staff Officer. They both rose hastily to their feet as the two officers stopped beside them. The trench ran to the left of the big crater and now, since la Boisselle had fallen, it was a good distance behind the front line. It was exactly a week, almost to the minute, since the 34th Division had gone over the top, and most of them lay there still, with the bodies of the men who had followed them.

Climbing on to the firestep, the Staff Captain cautiously raised his head above the parapet and looked across. 'Good God!' he exclaimed. 'I didn't know we were using Colonial troops!' Pretor-Pinney made no reply. Hoyles and Monckton exchanged grim looks. 'Dear God,' muttered Monckton, when the Colonel and the visitor had moved away to a safe distance, 'has the bastard never seen a dead man before?' It was a rhetorical question. Lying out in the burning sun, soaked by the frequent showers of a week's changeable weather, the bodies of the dead soldiers had been turned black by the elements.

The Battalion spent the rest of the day burying them.

There was a terrific smell. It was so awful it nearly poisoned you. A smell of rotten flesh. The old German front line was covered with bodies – they were seven and eight deep and they had all gone black. The smell! These people had been laying since the First of July. Wicked it was! Colonel Pinney got hold of some stretchers and our job was to put the bodies on them and, with a man at each end, we *threw* them into that crater. There must have been over a thousand bodies there. I don't know how many we buried. I'll never forget that sight. Bodies all over the place. I'll never forget it. I was only eighteen, but I thought, 'There's something wrong here!'

> Corporal Joe Hoyles, MM, No. 3237, 13th (S) Btn., The Rifle Brigade.

My job was to take the identity discs off the dead men. Other people were detailed off to collect the rifles and other people collected the equipment and then there was a band of stretcher-bearers who picked up these dead gentlemen and took them to the edge of this crater and tipped them over, rolled them down and they buried themselves in the chalk before they got to the bottom.

> Sergeant Jack Cross, No. 4842, C Coy., 13th (S) Btn., The Rifle Brigade.

My lot, we had to collect the bodies off the old German wire. Over 200 we counted. And we dumped them in the crater. All the time we were getting shelled, and casualties were happening of course. Some of us was hoping they'd happen. I know I didn't mind it happening! Then I got it! I'd just jumped in a trench between two men, Gomer Evans and Dick Darling, and as I jumped in there was this terrific crash. I didn't know any more until I woke up a few minutes later, and there was old Gomer Evans, he'd got the top of his nut blown off, and Dick Darling, he'd got it in the back. His

> Corporal Horace Smith, MM, No. 3697, 13th (S) Btn., The Rifle Brigade.

kidneys blown out. We had to bury them both. But we didn't put them in the crater. We buried them just to the side of it.

Acting Corporal Ruper Weeber, No. 4477, 13th (S) Btn., The Rifle Brigade.

As far as you could see there were all these bodies lying out there – literally thousands of them, just where they'd been caught on the First of July. Some were without legs, some were legs without bodies, arms without bodies. A terrible sight. They'd been churned up by shells even after they were killed. We were just dumping them into the crater – just filling them over. It didn't seem possible. It didn't get inside me or scare me, but it just made me wonder that these could have been men. It made me wonder what it was all about. And far away in the distance we could see nothing but a line of bursting shells. It was continuous. You wouldn't have thought that anybody could have existed in it, it was so terrific. And yet we knew we were going up into it, with not an earthly chance.

The shells were bursting on the line where the troops were grappling with the enemy at Mametz Wood and, nearer still, struggling to capture the village of Contalmaison. It lay beyond them in the dark, three kilometres ahead of the big crater where the blackened bodies of the dead committed to its depths were sinking, by the weight of their numbers, into the crumbling chalk.

Chapter 11

The road that once flew arrow-straight from Albert to Bapaume bisected the battlefield. Before 1914 the traffic it carried had hardly changed since the Roman Legions had marched along it when France was Gaul. Half a dozen farm carts might trundle down to Albert or up to Bapaume on their respective market days. A bicycle might be seen from time time, free-wheeling down the hill from Pozières to la Boisselle, but the sight of an occasional motor car travelling at a dizzy twenty-five miles an hour en route to Albert or Amiens, was enough to interrupt work in the fields on either side for up to five minutes while the peasants goggled and gaped.

The peasants themselves travelled mostly on foot and mostly away from the main road. From the farms and smallholdings in the villages there were easier ways to get to market. The country was criss-crossed with tracks and lanes, linking the villages and running out to the surrounding woods and farmlands, tramped out by ten generations of feet going backwards and forwards to the fields, of woodcutters hauling timber, of women in shapeless country black, work-worn and weather-beaten, plodding to market weighed down by heavy baskets of farm produce. In the morning the oxen lumbered out to the fields; in the evening the cows were driven home for milking and at harvest time carts, heavy with hay or mangel wurzels, gouged ever-deeper the permanent ruts that had finally turned the tracks into roads and put them on the map. There were more roads in the Somme countryside than there were places to go. It was hardly surprising that its inhabitants preferred the by-ways to the hard pavé of the single highway. Living in close-knit communities in their separate villages, few of them ever had much occasion even to cross it.

But the main road was a landmark. A daughter who had married from Contalmaison or Bazentin and gone to live at Ovillers or Courcelette, twenty minutes' walk away, would be described as living 'à l'autre côté', as if she had gone to the other side of the Atlantic, while the residents of Thiepval and Fricourt, just six kilometres apart on either side of the main road, would refer to each other as 'ces gens là', as if they inhabited separate planets.

Things had changed only slightly since the coming of the railway

but, even in this respect, the country-folk south of the road felt a
certain superiority to those who lived to the north of it. Over there
the main line thundered through the Ancre valley on its way to Paris.
There were stations at Miraumont, at Beaucourt, at Hamel, where a
few local trains stopped once or twice a day. There was a single-line
track that climbed up behind Aveluy Wood to Mesnil and chuffed
behind the ridges past Serre to Puisieux, but it was nothing compared to the network of 'railways' that meandered through the fields
and villages of the country south of the main road, in much the same
manner as the wayward tracks and lanes. And, although the 'trains'
were little more than tram-cars, in this gentler terrain it had been
possible to lay a considerable network of track.

North of the Albert-Bapaume road the land swept up to the
dramatic bluffs and ridges, the steep slopes and deep valleys on both
sides of the River Ancre. South of the road, it dropped away and
unrolled a carpet of fields and meadows in a panorama of soft hills
and valleys, rising gradually to the horizon where the poplars,
marching along the high road to Peronne, stood sentinel on the
skyline. In this idyllic landscape, the last idyllic touch was its lush,
abundant woodland.

The woods appeared on the British Army maps in a strange
conglomeration of names. Mametz Wood, Bernafay and Trones,
presented no problem, although anyone who cared to look closely at
the pre-war maps might notice that the original 'c' of 'Troncs' had
been mis-read or misprinted as an 'e'. 'Thrones' or 'tree trunks' – it
made little difference to the troops who were fighting for it now.
Getting its name right was the least of their worries.

To the right of Montauban, Bernafay Wood and Trones Wood
had been the first big obstacles in the way of the advance when the
troops had broken the German line in the south. Even now, when
they had swept ahead of Montauban and the bloody stumps of
Bernafay Wood were in their hands, although the edge of Trones
Wood was only a couple of hundred yards away, they had captured a
mere toe-hold, at its southern end. Trones was shaped like a
pear-drop and beyond its elongated northern tip lay all the strength
of the Germans' second-line position. It was natural that the
Germans were going to fight for Trones Wood as savagely as they
were fighting to hold on to Mametz Wood away to the other side of
Montauban. There too the British troops had only managed to
capture the tip of one long spur of woodland projecting from the
thick mass of the wood itself, and they had not quite managed to
capture all of Contalmaison village lying off to the left.

Now that the Fricourt Salient had been pinched out, it was at
Contalmaison that the line swung round and, in a sense, linked up.

The four villages of Ovillers, Pozières, Contalmaison and la
Boisselle form a rough rectangle with a village at each corner
bisected diagonally by the Albert–Bapaume road, as its runs from la
Boisselle (in the bottom left, opposite Ovillers) to Pozières, astride it
in the top right 'corner', opposite Contalmaison.

If Pozières could be captured, then Ovillers would automatically
fall, and Thiepval, still standing impregnable on its bluff above the
Ancre, might be taken in the rear. With Contalmaison in British
hands, the way would be open to pour troops into Mametz Wood
from the left, to join up with the Welsh who were thrusting into its
southern flank and to push on together to crack the Germans'
second-line defences at a blow. By the evening of 9 July the line ran
through the southern edge of Contalmaison and, swinging northwards a mile to the left of the village, crossed the road that ran
between it and la Boisselle. That evening the 13th Battalion, The
Rifle Brigade, moved up from la Boisselle and into the new front
line. They were facing the open country that lay between the
strongpoint that was Contalmaison and the fortress that was
Pozières.

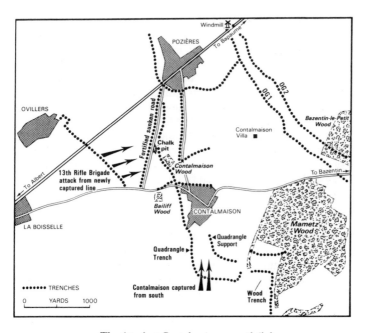

The Attack at Contalmaison on 10th July

It was a slithering, wet shambles of a night. The churning shellfire, the constant traffic, the frequent showers of the ten days' fighting had turned the trenches into ditches running with mud. Next morning, a slight steam rose above them under the hot rays of the sun. It was a beautiful day. It was also a day of hellish noise for the Welshmen of the 38th Division were hammering hard for Mametz Wood and, on the immediate right of the Battalion, the 23rd Division were attacking Contalmaison village. By half-past five in the afternoon the village had been captured.

At eight o'clock two battalions of the 111th Brigade were ordered to prepare to attack. The 13th Battalion in the front-line trench were to lead it. The Germans had last been seen streaming out of Contalmaison north to Pozières, protected by the trenchline on the left which was still in their hands, still strongly held and directly in front of the 13th Rifle Brigade. This was the trenchline the Battalion was ordered to capture. On their left, the 25th Division would attack astride the main road and, at the same time, part of the 23rd Division would attack on their right. There would be a heavy barrage to support them. They lined up, well back, on either side of the country tramway track. It was a beautiful evening.

Corporal Joe Hoyles, MM, No. 3237, A Coy., 13th (S) Btn., The Rifle Brigade.

It was a very bright hot day and we'd seen Contalmaison go up in the air. We'd seen the church go up in the air. Marvellous gunnery it was, our gunnery. *We* had to take to the left of Contalmaison. I was a section leader and Colonel Pinney came by the Platoon and he said, 'We're going over at 8.45. Set your watches.' Those of us in charge of sections had to take our sections over. Where I got my courage from I don't know. I suppose, being young, one had an 'Up Guards and at 'em', sort of feeling. Some men funked it of course. They went over all right, they had to or they'd have got my bayonet up their arse. But you could tell from their faces that a lot of people dreaded it. We went over with fixed bayonets and we all had a Mills bomb in our hands. It was a quarter or a third of a mile to the first German trench.

Rifleman Ed McGrath, D Coy., 13th (S) Btn., The Rifle Brigade.

I can see in my mind's eye, Captain Smith, watch in hand in the trench, just before we went over. He soon gave the order and over we went. I remember how I felt like Barnacle Bill, all dressed up like a Christmas tree. Rifle slung, spade in braces, and two bandoliers of ammo, one Mills bomb in my right hand, pin out, and two in a mess tin cover in my left.

Rifleman George Murrell, B Coy., 13th (S) Btn., The Rifle Brigade.

Some of us South African boys were told we were wanted at the other end of the trench. An officer called out, 'Lewis-gunners, over here.' My brother was with me, in the same team. We formed up and I found myself carrying a Lewis-gun pannier and many drums of spare ammunition – at a guess about 800 rounds. Sewrey then took my rifle to carry it and the next thing was – Over the Top! By the time we had got fifty yards or so Sewrey was hit and I was charging the enemy with plenty of bullets but no rifle.

I had a Lewis-gun team of about six men. We weren't in the front of the first line because, with a Lewis-gun and carrying ammunition, you're not able to do trench attacking really. You let your attacking infantry take the line, then you can go in, you see, because you can't defend yourself with a Lewis-gun. So we were in the second line, or what there was of us. I lost all my lot. I can still hear the bullets zipping up, like a lot of bees and tufts of dirt, thrown up in front of you where the Jerries were shooting. You could see them going zzzp . . . zzzp, like a lot of bees.

Corporal Bob Thompson, D Coy., No. 2756, 13th (S) Btn., The Rifle Brigade.

We impressed upon the chaps in the platoon, 'Don't stick together, don't bunch. Keep, apart. If you bunch up they'll pick you off like rabbits.' I was on the left of my platoon on one side of the tramway and Sergeant Laney was on *my* left on the other side, because he was the right man of No. 11 Platoon. It was only about a hundred yards, or maybe a hundred and fifty yards in front of us, the first German trench, and we'd got to go straight ahead and capture that position. The whistle went and away they went. As soon as they did you could hear the bullets whistling. I yelled at Laney, 'Look at that lot going through there!' There was a gap in the wire and the platoon in front of us converged on it and into the gap. They went down, just like that! I should think every man was mortally wounded.

Sergeant Jack Cross, No. 4842, C Coy., 13th (S) Btn., The Rifle Brigade.

I always remember saying to my section, 'Come on Rifle Brigade! The first time Over the Top. Here we go!' And off we went. We were in the first wave, and our platoon officer, Fitzgibbon, was away out in front of us. They just mowed us down! People were falling on your right and your left and of course you had to keep going forward.

Corporal Joe Hoyles, MM, No. 3237, 13th (S) Btn., The Rifle Brigade.

We hadn't gone very far and our section got less and less until there were only two of us left. I remember calling to the chap I was with, 'I think we're the only ones who are going to get through this lot!' Then I got a jolt in my thigh and my leg came up and hit me in the face. It literally hit me in the face! Down I went!

Rifleman Ed McGrath, D Coy., 13th (S) Btn., The Rifle Brigade.

Rifleman George
Murrell, B Cov., 13th
(S) Btn., The Rifle
Brigade.

There was no artillery barrage and so every sniper and machine-gunner had a marvellous target as we advanced in short rushes. I was so laden that I had difficulty in keeping up and I must have made a good single target at times. But all the time I tried to keep up with my brother. Then he went down beside me and I yelled, 'What's the matter? Are you hit?' And he looked up at me, in an absolute fury, and shouted, 'No! I'm picking daisies, you bloody fool!' We had to go on. You couldn't stop for a wounded man – even if it was your own brother! I carried on about thirty yards or so and then suddenly my legs went from under me. I hadn't felt anything. I thought I'd stumbled into a shell-hole. Then I found that my left leg was quite useless. I couldn't move! In the meantime the advance had continued.

Murrell was not alone in noticing that there was no artillery barrage. Pretor-Pinney noticed it too. It had not worried him that there had been no preliminary gunfire, for the attack had been mounted hastily. But the orders which had reached him at eight o'clock had stated clearly that the guns would support the troops as they went across, that the 13th Royal Fusiliers would come up, straight away behind them, that the 23rd and 25th Divisions would be attacking to the left and to the right of them. Now, dodging the bullets, seeing his Battalion falling all around him, even with the hammering of the machine-guns and the cries and the noise of the fight, Pretor-Pinney was not so deafened that he could fail to observe that they had no supporting barrage. Nor was there a barrage to the left or to the right of his Battalion where the other troops should have been attacking. Furthermore, as he glanced anxiously behind him from his position in the last wave, he could see none of the Royal Fusiliers who should have been following on their heels coming up to support them.

There were no troops advancing to support them. There were no troops advancing simultaneously on left and right. In the evening sunlight, the Battalion was advancing alone against the full strength of a triple line of German trenches. This was the long-awaited moment; the climax of the last two years; the first real trial of strength; the first time 'Over the Top'.

In all the rhetoric of the war, like the words dauntless, dogged and gallant, 'at all costs' was an oft-repeated phrase that rang through every report, every Communiqué, every citation, every tale of heroic adventure and misadventure, every celebration of success, every letter of condolence, every justification of failure.

Now, The Rifle Brigade were determined, 'at all costs', to capture the lethal stretch of line. The Germans were equally determined 'at all costs' to hold on to it.

Even without support they made it. Even though men were falling at every step, the survivors kept on. They took the first German line. They bombed and battled their way into the second. With super-human effort, through a maelstrom of bullets whistling down the hill from the line in front of Pozières, a small force had even got into the strongpoint in the third German line. It appeared on the map as a 'strongpoint' – but, in reality, it was a fort constructed around a small chalk quarry halfway down a sunken track that linked the road from la Boisselle to Contalmaison with the road from Albert to Bapaume. The sunken lane was now a trench, lined with concrete pillboxes. The 'chalk pit' was riddled with dugouts. From its lip machine-guns were firing at pointblank range. They were firing at Tom Jolly and a handful of 13 Platoon as they bombed their way towards it.

It was just about this time that the runner caught up with Colonel Pretor-Pinney as he stopped in a shell-hole to take stock of the situation and to watch as the flurry of fighting intensified around the chalk pit a couple of hundred yards ahead. The runner had only breath enough to gasp, 'Attack cancelled, sir.' And in bleak con-firmation he thrust the written message into the Colonel's hand. It had been sent out from Divisional Headquarters, and passed on in good time by Brigade. It had reached the artillery in time to prevent them firing the barrage. It had reached the 23rd Division, which had been preparing to attack on the right. It had reached the 25th Division on the left. It had reached the 13th Royal Fusiliers, in time enough to stop them moving forward in the second wave. Now, belatedly, it had reached the 13th Rifle Brigade.

There was no means of signalling to the men who were already fighting in the German trenches. No flags could be waved without signing the death warrant of the man who waved them. Nobody, in any event, would be looking back for such a signal. No whistle, no bugle, no shout or warning could possibly be heard. Nothing could be done but to send more runners forward, to get word to the boys and to tell those who were still fighting to get out and come back.

There weren't over-many of us there in the third German trench. I'd lost my Lewis-gunner somewhere or other, and I was on my own for ten minutes or a quarter of an hour and then I picked up another Lewis-gunner. We all knew that, once you occupy a trench, you have to set up a post to consolidate it and defend it in case the Jerry attacks again. Well, we were looking round for a place to plant our gun over the Jerries' side of the trench and, walking round it, I found a Jerry who was wounded sitting on the ground. As we walked up to him very carefully, with a bayonet at

Corporal Bob Thompson, Lewis-gunner, D Coy., No. 2756, 13th (S) Btn., The Rifle Brigade.

the ready to stab him if he started being naughty, he looked up and he said, 'Water, Tommy, water.'

He was badly wounded. What could you do but give him water? So, I slung my rifle and told the other chap to keep watch, and I took my bottle and gave him a drop of water. And then, when he'd drunk it, in a very strange manner – he hadn't got a steel helmet, they had little round hats – he took his little blue hat off and he handed it to me and, in good English, he said, 'Lucky souvenir, you, Tommy.' And he died. Just died, there and then. I was glad I'd given him the water. I stuck the hat in my pocket and forgot all about it. We'd found a place and started setting the Lewis-gun up when Sergeant Holford came running across along the trench beneath us and he shouted, 'The thing's cancelled! We've got to make our way back.'

Corporal Joe Hoyles, MM, No. 3237, 13th (S) Btn., The Rifle Brigade.

Every officer was wounded or killed. We only had one officer left, Captain Reviere, and he shouted across to me, 'Corporal, gather some men together and capture that machine-gun post that's doing the damage.' We went up this German communication trench and we found this machine-gun. There were only about six of us left in the section and I went ahead and, when I saw the Boche there round the corner, I said, 'Right, lads! Get rid of your bombs!' And over went the bombs! We killed those poor chaps. We captured one prisoner alive. I sent him back, and, just with that, we had the order to retire. It was about ten o'clock by then. Just getting dusk – and after all that massacre, after we'd taken the trenches, we had to retire.

Sergeant Jack Cross, No. 4842, 13th (S) Btn., The Rifle Brigade.

How these bullets were whistling! I can still hear them! Now and again a shrapnel shell would burst in the air and these bits of shrapnel showered down, hitting the mud and going flop, flap, flip over the mud. Laney went down. Then he got up and off he went again, and I was going on with him when, suddenly, I got hit and it lifted me up in the air and dropped me flat on my face, just like you see in cowboy films. It knocked me out. I fell down flat on the grass and I stuck my head forward and tipped my steel helmet to the front. I thought, 'I'll hold that on there, and then I won't get one through the napper.' Suddenly, the firing ceased and the machine-guns stopped spluttering just for a moment. I hopped up, doubled back and dived into this shell-hole. I knew I'd just passed one, and as I dived into it my leg came up in the air and I felt a sting in the calf of the leg and I'd got a bullet there as well.

I turned myself round, and faced the enemy and got my head down into the shell-hole and somehow I wiggled my entrenching tool out of the back of my belt and I scratched a hole so I could get deeper down and get the side high between me and the bullets and they still kept singing round the top of this earth around me. After a while, everything went quiet, so I thought, 'This is it, Jack. Now you make your way back to that dressing station – if you can!' And I started crawling back.

I lay there for a long time. For a while I could hear the Lewis-gun firing in front of me, but the Number One couldn't have had more than one drum of ammunition, because I knew all the rest of the section had been wounded and they'd been carrying the spare drums. When it stopped, I didn't know what had happened. I thought maybe it had only run out of ammunition because the Jerries' guns were still going. But then the remains of the Battalion began to come back past me. One of them stopped to see how I was and he told me it was all over. He couldn't help me. He was a little chap and he was wounded in both arms. After a while it got dark and, although I could hear voices, I didn't know whether they were friends or enemies. So, I just had to stop there.

Rifleman George Murrell, 13th (S) Btn., The Rifle Brigade.

As the wounded lay waiting for rescue or waiting for dusk to cover the long crawl back and, as the survivors were leaving the captured lines to get back as best they could to their own, the barrage started up. It was fired by the British guns and it was a devastating barrage.

It was not the fault of the artillery. They had been notified in good time about the cancellation of the attack and, as no news had reached them to the contrary, they had no reason to think that it had gone ahead. The guns were firing in response to an SOS signal from troops in Contalmaison. Seeing the affray in the trenches above them to their left, they had assumed that the Germans were about to counter-attack the village from that direction. The guns, trying to balk the counter-attack before it could get going, registered with uncanny accuracy on the trenches the Rifle Brigade had just attacked and also on the ground beyond, where the remnants of the Battalion were struggling to make their way back. Despite the awful losses on the way across, it was under their own bombardment that the 13th Rifle Brigade died, as a battalion, on the way back.

It was dark when the barrage lifted and in the terrible silence that followed those who remained alive and could still move, dragged themselves back to the line.

A little later, the shaken Germans sent a reserve company forward. They trickled down the hill from Pozières to rescue their wounded, to remove their dead and to file back into their empty line to the left of Contalmaison.

The 13th Battalion's own Medical Officer had been killed and, in the nightmare conditions at the Field Dressing Station – a dugout in a deep cutting on the side of the road to la Boisselle – it was impossible to give more than cursory first aid to the wounded. It was not even possible to crowd more than a tenth of them into shelter and so they lay, waiting to be carried back, in the open roadway, sprayed from time to time with bullets from a German machine-gun, firing along the road on fixed sights. It was not a pleasant experience. But they were the lucky ones. They were not so lucky as the men who had escaped uninjured, now gathered in small exhausted groups in the support trenches, but luckier by far than the wounded men who still lay painfully out in front, with little hope of rescue. 'Old Chelsea' was there, and there he would stay for five days and five nights until he was picked up – still alive – when the line advanced.

Ed McGrath lay out for a whole week. Ted Murrell was in, but his brother George was still out. For three days he would be crawling between the lines, dragging his useless left leg, unsure of his direction, until, on the thirteenth, by a happy chance, he struck the outlying trench of a neighbouring unit.

Company Sergeant-Major Croucher was back, but only because he had been brought in by his sworn enemy, Welch, the most disreputable man in his company whom the Sergeant-Major had personally put on many charges. Inadvertently firing off his rifle on parade while drunk was the most serious of a whole catalogue of Welch's misdemeanours and the very sight of him had been enough to send Croucher into a fury. Now, Welch was at the Field Dressing Station with Croucher on his back, demanding that he should have attention and refusing to take no for an answer. He personally saw to it that the Sergeant-Major was the first casualty to travel down the line. Thompson had followed and, sometime during the night, so had Jack Cross, Weeber and Monckton, among a hundred or so others. Colonel Pretor-Pinney, his left arm mangled by machine-gun bullets, was the last to go.

Most of the officers had been killed, among them all four Company Commanders. Horace Smith kept seeing them in his mind, conferring together in one shell-hole, after the order to retire had reached them. He had also seen the explosion that wiped them out. When the small force of survivors took stock in the morning, there was no sign of the Platoon Commanders. Lieutenant Reviere was the only officer in sight – apart from the Second-in-Command, Major Sir Foster Cunliffe. They would not have seen him had he not tied a handkerchief to his swagger-stick. Now he was waving it above the shell-hole where he lay far out in No Man's Land, close to the German front line. Looking through binoculars, they could easily identify him for the shell-hole, steep on the German side, was shallow where it faced the British.

Fred Lyon and Joe Hoyles stood side by side looking across and Lyon muttered, 'There'll be a VC for whoever brings him in.'

It was broad daylight now. It would be certain death to go back alone. Hoyles was almost too exhausted to shake his head. 'I've had enough, Fred. Enough.' Like Lyon, like Jolly, like Thompson, like Smith, he had got right up to the third line and he had even gone back to it, just before the Germans reoccupied the trench, to rescue his badly wounded officer, Lieutenant Fitzgibbon. Hoyles was not interested in winning the Victoria Cross. He was even a little surprised, when they came out of the trenches, to find that he had been recommended for the Military Medal.

Arthur Wright, burglar, reprobate and King of the Crown and Anchor Board, who had gone out three times to bring in wounded comrades, had earned one too. So had eight others.

Gradually, over the next few days, what was left of the Battalion moved back by stages to the trenches behind the Tara-Usna Ridge. It was just ten days since they had marched into them on their way up the line.

Sergeant Howard Rowlands had gone up with the boys, but almost immediately he had been ordered back again to Albert to join Headquarters Detail as orderly sergeant. He had spent an anxious ten days. No one at Headquarters knew quite what had happened 'up there' – only that there had been some kind of mess. After a scratch roll-call, all that could be done in the trenches was write the ominous letter 'M' after most of the names. 'M' stood for 'missing'.

Brown . . . *Missing.* Smith . . . *Missing.* Jones . . . *Missing.* Robin-son . . . *Missing.* The dreary litany carried on through three hundred names, or more – for no one knew, in the confusion of the aftermath, who was alive, who was dead, who had been wounded and evacuated and who was still lying or dying out in the horrid scrubland that lay between the Battalion and the German line. It would be many weeks before the battlefield could be cleared and bodies – or those that had not been blown out of existence – could be identified and buried. It would be weeks before the names of the wounded, so hastily evacuated, would appear on the returns of clearing stations close to the front, of hospitals at the coastal base and even across the Channel at home.

In the meantime, Howard Rowlands took it upon himself to find out what he could. From morning until night, on foot, near the line and, further afield, on a borrowed bicycle, he scoured every aid post, every dressing station, every casualty clearing station, not once but many times, asking the same questions. 'Any 13th Rifle Brigade here?' 'Any 13th Rifle Brigade been here?' 'Any 13th Rifle Brigade burials here?'

Even the unofficial list that Rowlands was able to compile, appalled him. And it appalled Colonel Pretor-Pinney. Rowlands had found the CO after four days, still in the big dressing station outside Albert, and too ill to be moved. It shook Rowlands, as nothing else had, to see his stiff and disciplined Commanding Officer in tears; to hear him say, over and over again, 'What a mess they've made of my Battalion! What a *mess* they've made of my Battalion.'

On 19 July, the Battalion marched back to Albert, and stopped there for the night. When they marched out again on the road to Bresle, they looked – at least in numbers – something like a battalion, for a large draft of new men had met them in Albert and had been hastily grafted on to the ranks. A new Commanding Officer rode in front of them. Colonel Prideaux-Brune showed his mettle during the march. It was the front ranks who heard him. As they were approaching a village, Keene, who, since his predecessor was 'missing', was now acting Regimental Sergeant-Major, passed the order: *March to Attention.* Prideaux-Brune put a stop to that with an impatient wave of his hand. 'Cut it out, Sergeant-Major! And the men can smoke if they like.' The Battalion appreciated that.

The road back to Bresle seemed considerably longer than it had seemed eleven days before on the way to the line. But then they had been singing and no one was singing now. Even the men of the new draft were silent and half-embarrassed. But the Battalion stuck it out. They only broke when they got to Bresle. The Colonel had to allow the Sergeant-Major to march the men to attention, for the Divisional Band had paid them the courtesy of turning out to meet them, and it was only good form to 'put on a show'. The band struck up what must have been felt, in all innocence, to be an appropriate tune, and played it in quick time to keep pace with the Riflemen's brisk ceremonial march. The tune was all the rage, and, from a hundred sing-songs, the boys all knew the words.

> *Here we are! Here we are! Here we are again!*
> *There's Pat and Mac and Tommy and Jack and Joe.*
> *When there's trouble brewing –*
> *When there's something doing –*
> *Are we downhearted? NO! Let 'em all come!*
> *Here we are! Here we are! Here we are again!*
> *We're fit and well, and feeling as right as rain.*
> *Never mind the weather.*
> *Now then, all together,*
> *HULLO! HULLO! HERE WE ARE AGAIN!*

There are still traces in the foreground of the line that formed the Fricourt Salient. Beyond it the line swung east and from the slopes above Fricourt in the top-right of the photograph the British attacked almost straight ahead to capture the villages of Mametz and Montauban.

Contalmaison Château in 1917, a year after its capture.

Right: Entrance to a (possibly British) dugout, one of a line in a sunken road near Contalmaison.

Below: Reserve trenches on the Somme.

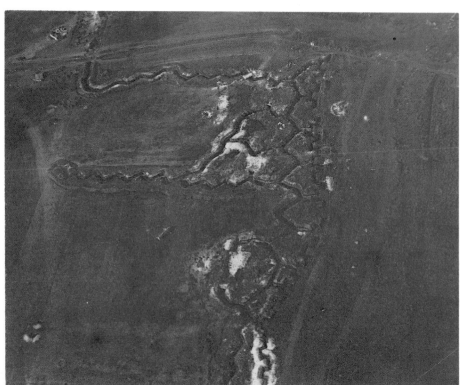

Percy Eaton, the only one of the 'South African Mob' who had returned unscathed, found that tears were gushing from his eyes. As they were still marching to attention, they had to gush unchecked. He was not the only one. Not many of the boys had yet reached their twenty-second birthday and it was all a little too much for them.

Part 3
'High Wood to Waterlot Farm, All on a summer's day'

High Wood to Waterlot Farm,
All on a summer's day,
Up you get to the top of the trench
Though you're sniped at all the way.
If you've got a smoke helmet there
You'd best put it on if you could,
For the wood down by Waterlot Farm
Is a bloody high wood.

E. A. Mackintosh, August 1916.
(written as a parody of
Chalk Farm to Camberwell Green)

Chapter 12

It was 14 July and neither the Battle of the Somme, neither the struggle still raging at Verdun, nor even the war itself was sufficient reason to deflect the French from celebration of their national day. Before the war, in towns and villages all over France, local bands had turned out, there had been picnics, merrymaking, much toasting of the Republic and, weather permitting, dancing in the streets. Now, in addition to the traditional celebrations, there were military parades, medals were presented, local heroes were fêted and a fever of patriotism added point and poignancy to the occasion. France, always quick to rouse herself to a pitch of nationalistic fervour, had more reason than ever to do so. The French were united in a common hatred of the German invader who had jack-booted across the frontier, just as he had done less than fifty years before, and they were united in their intention of kicking him back where he belonged. So, Bastille Day this year – the second since the war began – had taken on a greater and deeper significance than ever before. In Paris, parades marched down the Champs Elysées, cheered on by crowds who reserved their loudest cheers for the contingents of marching *poilus*, many of them veterans of Verdun, who obliged them, when the parade was over, by peeling off and allowing themselves to be marched into cafés by enthusiastic bystanders, who were only too anxious to buy them drinks and to join them in toasting France and Victory.

More sedate, but no less fervent toasts, were drunk at official ceremonies and receptions at the Hôtel de Ville and also at the Elysée Palace, where the President of the Republic received a large company in which military dignitaries almost outnumbered civilians. There was, after all, something to celebrate. If the Germans had not yet been defeated at Verdun, their defeat, it seemed to its stalwart defenders, was only a matter of time. There was the victory on the Somme, where the French Army had advanced gloriously through the German lines and, so some thought privately, would have advanced a good deal further, had it not been for the less magnificent performance of the British Army beyond their immediate left. But, before the end of the President's reception, Lord Esher was able to give him news which he had just received at first hand by telephone from GHQ. In a series of dawn attacks on a wide front, the British had broken through to the Germans' second line.

But, whatever satisfaction Lord Esher may have felt in conveying such gratifying tidings to President Poincaré in Paris, it was nothing to the satisfaction with which the British on the Somme battlefront itself were able to inform the neighbouring French Army that their attack had succeeded. The French, and in particular General Balfourier, had been bitterly opposed to the whole idea of a night manoeuvre, involving some thousands of troops – and inexperienced troops at that. In their view it was madness to contemplate such a thing and they had forcibly made the point. The sheer assembly of such a force behind the battle-line in darkness, the very idea of sending them stumbling through the night to attack the enemy line, was unutterably foolish. To expect them to make a considerable advance, to capture the bulwark of the Germans' second-line position at a single bound, was insanity. Failure would be inevitable and, in the confusion of the aftermath, the whole front would be left wide open and vulnerable to a German counter-attack. The French feared that the enemy might even be able to seize back most of the ground he had lost and wipe out the gains which the infantry had won, inch by slogging inch, in the first two weeks of July. Further-more, such a failure would leave the French flank on the right of the British dangerously exposed.

General Balfourier was an advocate of classic warfare. He was a soldier of the old school. He had seen no need to modernise his uniform from the style of the attire in which he had graduated from the military college at St Cyr some forty years earlier. In his high-necked blue coat and wide red trousers, looking much as he might have looked had he been a general in the army of Napoleon III halfway through the reign of Queen Victoria, he had shaken his grizzled head in doubt and consternation and, via his liaison officer, Captain Spears, he had sent repeated messages, begging the British to reconsider.

Captain Spears, weary of fruitless discussions on the same subject, weary of pressing General Balfourier's case with the passion felt by the General himself, weary of bearing back a succession of diplo-matic but repetitious replies, returned on the evening of 13 July, having received Fourth Army's last word on the matter from the lips of Major-General Montgomery. 'Tell General Balfourier, with my compliments, that, if we are not on the Longueval Ridge at eight tomorrow morning, I will eat my hat.' Like Captain Spears, Major-General Montgomery had had enough, but, although he had not intended Captain Spears to repeat the message verbatim, the general jubilation at Fourth Army Headquarters was enhanced by much amusement when General Balfourier telephoned through, with Bastille Day bonhomie, to congratulate Major-General Montgomery on having avoided the unfortunate necessity of making such an indigestible breakfast.

General Haig had also telephoned his congratulations early in the morning and they were particularly appreciated by Sir Henry Rawlinson for, as he well knew, Haig had shared the misgivings of General Balfourier and he had made his feelings on the matter very clear. They had come as close to altercation as urbanity and military etiquette would allow and, in the end, Rawlinson had had to insist on going ahead with his plan. Now he had been vindicated, and vindicated triumphantly.

This time there had been no long preliminary bombardment to warn the enemy that the troops were coming. This time there had been no long lines of soldiers advancing in brilliant daylight. The troops had assembled in darkness. Five minutes of brisk and violent bombardment had been sufficient to get the Germans' heads down and send them to their dugouts and, almost before they had time to realise that it had ceased, before the dawn was more than a grey hint in the sky behind their trenchline, the attack was upon them and on a front of more than three miles the German second line was overwhelmed by Kitchener's Army.

Taking off from the northern edge of Mametz Wood, wrested at terrible cost from the enemy's hands, the troops had wheeled east and captured the woods that protected the villages of Bazentin le Grand and Bazentin le Petit in as many hours as it had taken days to capture Mametz Wood. Launching forward into the mangled remains of Trones Wood, they had driven the Germans out of it and carried on to capture most of the village of Longueval in the shadow of Delville Wood and had even penetrated a little way into the wood itself. Now was the moment to press on, and that, as the 7th Division put it to Fourth Army Headquarters, was precisely what they wished to do.

The village of Bazentin le Petit was easily cleared. By nine o'clock, all was quiet. Ominously quiet. In the shelter of the sloping ground – hardly worthy of being called a ridge – which rose beyond a valley on the eastern edge of the village, headquarters had been set up in the village cemetery and in the little quarry which lay conveniently beside it. Quickly, and for once unimpeded by shellfire, cables were run down and communications established. Soldiers filtered down from the village to assemble in the valley while, behind them, Royal Engineers set to work immediately to consolidate the captured line. Officers conferred. Patrols were cautiously sent forward to reconnoitre whatever might lie on the other side of the hill. They brought back astonishing reports. There was not a German to be seen. The commanders decided to look for themselves. General Potter of the 9th Brigade of the 3rd Division, with Lieutenant-Colonel Elliott and Major-General Watts, Commander of the 7th Division, were not so foolhardy as to expose themselves by walking along the track at the top of the slope but, hugging the shelter immediately below, clambered along to the ruined windmill, a hundred yards or so to the right. Beneath the jagged outcrop of its rubble, the Germans had constructed a strongpoint with a dugout running deep down, but it had been hastily vacated and was as still and empty as the scene that met their eyes as they squinted across from the shelter of the ruin. They were looking across the gentlest of valleys, where the ridge on which they stood sloped down to a hollow and rose almost imperceptibly to the dark mass of High Wood itself, less than a thousand yards from where they stood, gazing incredulously across fields of waving corn. Here, behind the Germans' second line, where the seed corn had dropped from ears heavy with grain in the quiet autumn of 1915, the unhusbanded crop of 1916 was growing thick and lush and ripening fast. Some had already been prematurely harvested by the guns and, only hours before, broad tracks had been trampled through it when the Germans had beaten their hasty retreat from Bazentin to the shelter of High Wood. But there were great patches, still untouched, still standing yellow and rich, and, where the earth had been tumbled by shellfire, red poppies shone through the standing corn. Off to the right, shells were screaming on to Longueval village and Delville Wood, the smoke of battle hung thick in the air, but ahead all was quiet. Nothing stirred in the cornfields. High Wood was silent.

The officers grew bolder. Tentatively at first, and then, with rising confidence, they walked down to the little valley, stopped prudently halfway across in the concealment of a low chalk bank and, peering through binoculars, surveyed the land ahead. Then they crossed the cornfield almost to the edge of High Wood. Not a shot was fired. High Wood was empty.

Jubilant, excited, and anxious to push ahead, they almost ran back to the line. The troops were fresh and ready to go, General Watts had a brigade of fresh troops in reserve and he could get all four battalions across within the hour, with more ready to follow.

Fifteenth Corps Headquarters – although congratulatory – was not impressed with his plan. They had a plan of their own, or rather, GHQ had a plan, and Thirteen Corps had no choice but to fall in with it. If they were correct in the belief that the enemy had retired, it would be pointless to send the infantry forward to take possession of the wood. An infantryman can move only as fast as his feet will carry him; a cavalryman can move as fast as his horse, and therefore they must wait for the cavalry – the fast-moving mobile arm which could exploit the breakthrough and, who knows, with the infantry behind them, could speed through High Wood, fan out to Martinpuich, and gallop through le Sars to the very gates of Bapaume. It was a chance too good to be missed and it was the chance that both Rawlinson and Haig had been waiting for.

It was unfortunate that the cavalry did not arrive until five o'clock in the evening. For two weeks now they had been ready, waiting and eager to go – but the Indian Cavalry, which had been earmarked for the job of pushing through in this locality, if the opportunity arose, was waiting at Morlancourt, and Morlancourt, four miles south of Albert, was separated from High Wood by many miles of shell-battered ground. It took the cavalrymen a long time to negotiate it. They had started to move forward not long after eight o'clock in the morning, and by mid-day they should have been at Carnoy, just behind the old front line of 1 July, a good seven kilometres from High Wood but with a clear run towards it from the left of Montauban. By a quarter-past twelve, although the fight still raged a mile away at Longueval, High Wood and the valley beyond still lay tranquil under the hot noon sun.

At Fourth Army Headquarters there were anxious conferences. In the absence of the cavalry, should the 7th Division be sent forward to occupy the wood? Yes. The order was issued and almost immediately cancelled in the light of new information that Longueval village had not been completely captured. Now the cavalry was reported to be arriving in the Carnoy valley, but would it not be dangerous to send them forward on a great gallop across open country towards High Wood when they would have to pass between Longueval and Bazentin le Grand? It was unfortunate that early reports had been misleading and that it now appeared that part of the wood north of the village was still holding out. Could they commit the cavalry, fast moving though it was, to pass between the Scylla and Charybdis of two embattled points where the enemy was acting in a manner that was very far from tranquil and where the situation was not, as yet, fully understood? It was decided to hold the cavalry back and to wait.

Like the calm epicentre of a whirlpool, the corn in front of High Wood waved on throughout the long afternoon.

Slowly, cautiously, unable to believe their good fortune, the Germans filtered back into High Wood and took up defensive positions, and snipers and machine-gunners crawled out in front to lie low among the thick corn, on the *qui vive*, for the first hint of attack.

It had been such a day of confusion, of orders and counter-orders, of brilliant successes and partial reverses, that in the hasty issuing of last minute orders it was not entirely surprising that some failed to reach the units concerned. The 33rd Division arrived in the area at two o'clock in the afternoon when the situation was at its most muddled and were happily ensconced in the devastated valley at Fricourt, a good seven kilometres away, and they were resting before moving up to the front line early in the evening. The only orders their Divisional General had yet received were that they were to attack through the 21st Division the following day and to consolidate the line beyond High Wood after the cavalry had swept across it and put its German garrison to rout.

For the infantry, there was time enough to rest for a bit, but their guns were already moving forward up the newly constructed plank road to positions less than a thousand yards behind the new front line. Ahead of them went Second Lieutenant Fred Beadle. As Forward Observation Officer in the Divisional Artillery, his job was to survey the ground and to assess the target so that the guns might be ranged and registered for the barrage that would usher the infantry across. Accompanied by a signaller to send back information to the battery, he went up through the battlefield. It was a long trek over unfamiliar ground. Even a map was not much of a help and in a maze of captured trenches it was not surprising that they lost direction. Where two half-obliterated tracks met at Crucifix Corner they took the wrong road, and, instead of leading to the forward observation post in the British line, the old German communication trench led directly to the corner of High Wood. It also led, late in the afternoon, to Fred Beadle's first encounter, face to face, with the enemy, for the Germans were reconnoitring, and one man well out in front of the patrol was creeping down from High Wood as stealthily as Fred Beadle and his signaller were creeping towards it in the opposite direction.

2nd Lieutenant
F. W. Beadle, Royal
Artillery, 159
Brigade, 33rd
Division.

I had no idea that we were so near the Germans, but the mass of trenches there were so involved that we had the utmost difficulty and really were simply taking a chance. There was a terrific noise going on with shellfire and it seemed to me extraordinary that this trench was more or less abandoned. We were being very cautious as we went and I had my revolver at the ready – ready for trouble! Then, as we turned the corner of one of the traverses of the trench, there, approaching me, was a German soldier armed with a rifle. The extraordinary thing was that he had his rifle slung on his shoulder and the other odd thing was that he was wearing an overcoat and this was July, although it had been showery.

He saw me at exactly the same time as I saw him and he raised his rifle, but he must have been impeded by this overcoat because he couldn't get it up to his shoulder quick enough. I knew jolly well that if he had I should have caught it. It was either him or me. It was the first time I'd ever fired my revolver in anger, so to speak. The first time I'd ever seen a German soldier, apart from prisoners. I killed him with one shot.

I felt nothing. All I felt was relief. I knew I had no option, but I didn't stop to think of the morality. It was either him or me. Afterwards, I often wondered who he was and where he'd come from and whether he was married and whether he had any family. I've thought about that very often but, at the time, I didn't think of anything except where on earth were we, and where on earth was the infantry we were supposed to contact?

It seemed incredible that the German had been on his own. But his companions, if he had had any, alerted by the shots in front, had beaten a hasty retreat. Five long minutes passed. Resisting the temptation to scuttle back down the trench, Beadle carefully raised himself above the parapet and looked across. He saw with horror that he had brought his signaller more than two-thirds of the way across the valley to within three hundred yards of High Wood, and as he looked he saw the cavalry galloping into action. They were the Deccan Horse, and the 7th Dragoon Guards, and, far across the valley, the infantry were moving towards the northern corner of High Wood to support them.

It was seven in the evening, and the British were attacking more than twelve hours after the Germans had been driven back across the meadows and cornfields to the shelter of High Wood.

It was an incredible sight, an unbelievable sight, they galloped up with their lances and with pennants flying, up the slope to High Wood and straight into it. Of course they were falling all the way because the infantry were attacking on the other side of the valley furthest away from us, and the cavalry were attacking very near to where we were. So the German machine-guns were going for the infantry and the shells were falling all over the place. I've never seen anything like it! They simply galloped on through all that and horses and men dropping on the ground, with no hope against the machine-guns, because the Germans up on the ridge were firing

2nd Lieutenant F. W. Beadle, Royal Artillery, 159 Brigade, 33rd Division.

down into the valley where the soldiers were. It was an absolute
rout. A magnificent sight. Tragic.

The cavalry had advanced in classic historic style with lances
glistening in the sun. They entered High Wood. They killed a
number of infantry and machine-gunners in the crops in front of it,
and killed them with the lance. They captured thirty-two prisoners.
When darkness fell they lined the road between Longueval and the
corner of High Wood, and held this position through the night.
Some must have wondered what had become of their comrades.
The fact was that the two remaining cavalry brigades had never left
the rendezvous and were now ordered to go 'back to bivouac'. The
First and Third Cavalry Divisions waiting all day well south of Albert
had received no order at all. The casualties that the cavalry inflicted
on the Germans were precisely two less than the casualties they
themselves had suffered. The troops were in High Wood – but only
just, and now the Germans were answering back with all the fire
power they could muster.

By seven o'clock the 33rd Division was in position at Bazentin with
the 100th Brigade in front ready, according to the orders they had
received, to 'attack through the 21st Division' on the following
morning, and they were feeling distinctly uneasy now with the noise
hammering from the other side of the slope and shells falling a great
deal too close for comfort. At a quarter to eight, while Beadle and his
shaken companion were scuttling back, this time in the right
direction, Brigadier-General Baird, having seen his troops disposed
and having made contact with the 21st Division, now received a nasty
surprise. He visited the headquarters of the 91st Brigade in the 7th
Divisional sector on his right and he was not greeted with open arms
It came as news to the Brigadier that the 7th Division had been told
that his troops would be supporting them, that they had been
expected to take part in the attack which was even now in progress
and, not to put too fine a point upon it, where the hell had they been
and where the hell were they now?

They were bivouacked along the western edge of the wood behind
Bazentin le Petit, but they did not stay there for long. Baird had had
enough of Army, enough of Corps and even enough of Division. He
did not even trouble to refer to HQ for revised orders. There was no
time to shilly-shally. On his own responsibility, he ordered two
battalions of the 100th Brigade forward to hold the dangerous gap
that now existed in the line between High Wood and Bazentin le
Petit. So, on the right of the valley, the Glasgow Highlanders moved
up into the communication trench so recently and hurriedly vacated
by Fred Beadle and, on the left of the valley, the 1st Queen's took up

a line along a sunken road. By midnight he had succeeded in moving both battalions into those positions. Only then, as an after-thought, he transmitted a brusque uncompromising message to Divisional Headquarters, informing them that he had done so. Darkness had fallen, the Germans were back in High Wood and all night the shelling and the fighting never abated.

The 16th Battalion of the King's Royal Rifle Corps, although part of the 100th Brigade, had remained behind and were glad of the respite of a night's comparative rest, even in the open air, even on the *qui vive*, even with the din of shelling in front of them at High Wood and away to the right at Longueval and Delville Wood. They were the 'Black Buttoned bastards' of the 100th Brigade and were as proud as the Rifle Brigade of the traditions of their adopted regiment and of their quick step and rifleman's bearing. Like the 13th Rifle Brigade, the 16th King's Royal Rifle Corps were merely riflemen 'for the duration' but this did not deter them from patronising the Rifle Brigade in the well-founded knowledge that they were the senior regiment, nor from perpetuating the traditional rivalry between the regiments which, since 1858, had expressed itself in emotions ranging from friendly sparring to downright animosity. Even the Kitchener's Battalions of the Rifle Brigade had been quick to learn the taunting words that went with their regimental march, composed by some wag years before any of them had been born and they were quick to launch into it whenever they came within jibing distance of a battalion of The King's Royal Rifle Corps.

> *The Rifle Brigade is going away*
> *To leave the girls in the family way.*
> *The KRRs are left behind,*
> *They've two and six a week to find.*

This sentiment, with all its bawdy implications, and even the strong language of the term 'Black Buttoned Bastards' might reasonably have been expected to bring a blush to the cheeks of the 16th King's Royal Rifle Corps for they had been recruited from the ranks of the Church Lads Brigade. But, such piety as they had harboured in the far-off days of peacetime, had been well and truly knocked out of them during the two years they had spent in Kitchener's Army and, in particular, by the eight months almost to the day that they had been serving in France and in the trenches. This was a matter to which the Battalion's Padre had become resigned. It was many months now since he had gone looking for a party engaged in digging trenches behind the lines. He had come upon Jack Brown's platoon and announced, as he jumped down among these black sheep of his flock, 'I knew where you all were. I couldn't see you but I knew where you were from the language that was coming up. I knew it was the Church Lads Brigade and I've never heard anything like it in all my life.'

It was fortunate that the Padre had not been within earshot that afternoon at Fricourt. The Church Lads had marched eighteen kilometres to get there and their feet were killing them.

Corporal Jack Beament, MM. A Coy., 16th Btn., King's Royal Rifle Corps (Church Lads Brigade), 33rd Division.

It was a terribly hot day and we'd only had ten minutes halt in each hour all the way up. Everywhere was devastated but we spotted a stream and we made for it. There was Jack Brown and old Billy Thompson and his pal Charlie Thompson from West Hartlepool and myself. Billy wasn't a very big chap but how he could swear! I always remember him, after that march taking off his equipment and taking off his boots and socks and swearing like hell. 'Those fucking, bloody bastards! Those bloody fucking bastards!' Between us we said more than a word or two, because it was so hot and we had full equipment and 120 rounds of ammunition to carry. I'll never forget the relief of it, coming to the edge of this stream and bathing my poor bloody feet. We weren't there long, and there was a bit *more* swearing when we were told to pick up our stuff again and march up the line. We regretted having taken our boots off, because it wasn't so easy to get them on again!

I shall never forget that scene as we went up the line. As we marched along there was a corpse of a soldier with no head plonked up against the side of this sunken road, and a bit further on, sticking up above the ground, a hand and obviously a body underneath it, but all you could see was a hand, and, on the lefthand side, just lumps of flesh with the innards and remains of a poor horse all rolled up there together. A shell must have got them. There were bodies all around. You can't describe it! That massacre had happened fourteen days before we got there. It was horrifying. We were all only about twenty years of age and you're a bit callous then. It's a cruel age really. You have no sort of feeling. But it must have made some sort of impression because I can still see it all in my mind's eye, this terrible scene as we went up the line. But we had to take it all in our stride because we couldn't do anything about it. We'd got to go forward. That was our job.

Rifleman Jack Brown, MM, No. 3 Platoon, A Coy., 16th Btn., King's Royal Rifle Corps

We was going to High Wood. That's what we was told. It was a hot day and the stench was something awful. The guns were there firing and all the artillery blokes had got their shirts off. There was two banks, one on either side of the road, about chest high – if you could call it a road! And when we actually looked, they weren't banks at all! They were heaps of overturned waggons, dead horses, broken equipment and, not to tell a lie, dead bodies as well. The smell was terrible. We went up to a place and, believe it or not, they called it Happy Valley! On the way up there was a trench at right angles to where we was, and it was full of dead Germans, just standing there where they'd been shot. You could see their heads and shoulders, just stood up there where they'd been firing from. They hadn't fallen down and they'd gone as black as pitch.

(Church Lads Brigade), 33rd Division.

You didn't worry when you got in the Army. You didn't – straight! Well I didn't anyhow. I was carrying the rations and I got a bit fed up with them, they was so heavy. So we was told to sit down for a rest and I said, 'What about some of you carrying these rations for a while?' Nobody seemed to want to, so I just said, 'Well, I don't suppose any of us'll want much rations tomorrow.' I dumped them, and that's the last I saw of them. Didn't care really, not among all that. I don't mind saying it, on the way up there, what I did was, I just said a little prayer for myself. I always did it before we went into action, but on the way up there to High Wood, looking around at those terrible things, I just kept saying this little prayer. I suppose it must have been answered, or I wouldn't be here now!

A few little prayers went up from the Church Lads Brigade that night as they waited in the shelter of Bazentin le Petit Wood to go over the top in the morning. From Jack Brown's platoon, at least, they were intermixed with imprecations of a more down-to-earth nature and even Jack himself now rather regretted having dumped the rations. Appetites which had been temporarily sickened on the march to the line had nevertheless been sharpened by the long day's exertions and, with the prospect of going into action in the morning, a little food – even bully beef and army biscuits – would have been a comfort. Jack himself managed to scrounge a bite from his mate Jack Beament in Number One Platoon, but it was as much as his life was worth to let the rest of his own platoon see that he had done so.

It wasn't the first time the two boys had shared a meal. Even before the war, when both had been working for John Dickinson's Paper Company at Croxley Mill, they had shared their lunchtime sandwiches. But munching the dry army biscuit, or sucking it as best he could, that was not what Jack Brown had in mind. He nudged Beament. 'Remember those feeds at Miss Harper's?' 'Yes,' replied Jack Beament, 'And remember the fleas?'

They both well remembered the fleas in the first billet they had shared at Denham. Even the beds had been full of them. It was not that the spinster, Miss Harper, and the two bachelor Harper brothers were anything less than scrupulously clean and they themselves seemed to be impervious to the fleas, doubtless through years of custom, for they were dog breeders to Colonel Wyld and it was on his estate that the Church Lads had been concentrated when the battalion was first formed, with the Colonel (then Major) as Second-in-Command of the Battalion. The boys had arrived in detachments from all over the country, some from as far away as Scotland and the north. They were a good bunch, but Jack Beament who, despite having been a senior sergeant in the Church Lads Brigade, was a youth whose physique it would have been charitable to describe as lanky. When he had first tried to join the Army in August 1914 the Army had described his chest measurements in rather less kindly terms and turned him down flat. Now he was rather glad of it. It had been September before it had been suggested that the Church Lads Brigade should form its own battalion and there were thirty-two past or present 'Church Lads' working together at the paper mill at Croxley Green. To lose them *en masse* would certainly make a hole in the work-force but the manager, Mr Charles Barton-Smith, was all for it. He was over Army age himself but he had served as a captain in the Church Lads Brigade, so he connived, encouraged them and even supplied a lorry to take them up to London.

Corporal Jack Beament, MM, A Coy., 16th Btn., King's Royal Rifle Corps (Church Lads Brigade), 33rd Division.

Every one of us passed the test – including my vital statistics! There was even one lad, Charlie Rogers, who was practically blind in one eye and, when he had his eyes tested by the Colour Sergeant, we were seated on a form at the back. When they covered his good eye and it came to his bad one and he had to read out some numbers off the chart, we were all whispering, 'Twenty-four, forty-eight, nineteen, twenty-eight,' and Charlie repeated them. It's a wonder the Sergeant didn't hear, because he was standing right by Charlie. But if he did, *he* turned a blind eye, so Charlie's blind eye got through. All thirty-two of us got through.

Rifleman Jack Brown, MM, No. 3 Platoon, A Coy., 16th Btn., King's Royal Rifle Corps (Church Lads Brigade), 33rd Division.

We got our calling up papers a few days lays later and we had to go to Sardinia House, Kingsway in London. The mill gave us a lorry and it was waiting outside the Red House, which is the pub at Croxley, and we all bundled in there and it took us to Watford Junction to get the train, not knowing where we was going or anything. We found Kingsway all right but we didn't know where Sardinia House was or anything else but we found it and we got introduced right away to the army regulations. There was a

Regimental Sergeant-Major and he took our names and particulars and we got lined up and we marched through the streets. I'd got an old flute and I was playing it. I was playing *The Girl I Left Behind Me* and I played it all the way through London to Paddington Station. We stepped out on that march! Because the Church Lads wasn't just a religious organisation. It was a bit like the Boys Brigade, you did drill and all that, and we made a pretty good job of that march to Paddington – or so *we* thought.

Of course we didn't know where we was going and everyone was guessing, would it be Durham, or would it be Bristol or anywhere at all? Anyhow we got in the train and away it went. By this time we'd been all day on the journey because we left Croxley Green quite early in the morning and, blow me, about half an hour later we ended up at Denham – just about seven miles away from Croxley Green where we'd all started out from!

By some miracle, although the Battalion had had its share of trench warfare and casualties, the original thirty-two were still together. They were older, harder, fitter. Even Jack Beament's chest measurements had expanded by a good two inches, but their link with Denham was as strong as ever. 'Lizzie Wyld', as the Battalion had disrespectfully nicknamed their Commanding Officer, was the local squire and, although they had moved on to Clipstone Camp near Nottingham within three months, the residents of Denham still regarded the 16th King's Royal Rifles with proprietary affection as 'their Battalion'. Other troops who had followed them after they had moved north to Nottingham had a kindly reception but the proceeds of every concert, every village fête, every bazaar and jumble sale and the product of hundreds of knitting needles, clicking through miles of khaki wool, was intended for the benefit of the Church Lads and the Church Lads alone. The coffers of the Battalion's Comforts Fund swelled, the Battalion Stores bulged with a plentitude of socks and scarves, gloves and knitted helmets, and there was hardly a man of the original contingent who did not also receive a regular supply of letters and parcels from his old billet at Denham.

Altogether the Battalion was spoilt and Jack Beament was more spoilt than any. He had a share in the collective parcels sent by the Harper household at Denham and parcels from Heanor as well, where he and Harry Chapman had been billeted in Mundy Street with Mr and Mrs Buxton. A parcel had arrived only yesterday. In it was a small tin of patriotic design, adorned by a picture of the King, and Mrs Buxton had filled it with chocolate. Jack had put it in his haversack and now his haversack was on the parapet of the old German trench where they were preparing to pass the night. He considered sharing the chocolate with Jack Brown and Charlie Rogers right away, and then thought better of it. He would keep it for tomorrow.

Machine-gun fire was coming from High Wood across the valley, slowly traversing in the dark in the hope of catching troops assembling for the big attack that would surely come in the morning. It was a random bullet, almost spent, that hit the haversack. It went straight through the tin of chocolate which thus, facetiously, became the first of the Battalion's casualties in the battle for High Wood. Beament was nervously conscious of the fact that, had he not placed the haversack on the parapet, that casualty might have been himself.

Chapter 13

Only two days ago, give or take the occasional spot where a stray shell had created havoc, the trees in High Wood had been in full leaf. But twenty-four hours of fighting and shelling had taken ghastly toll. The leaves were limp and yellowed by cordite. Branches hung splintered from lurching tree trunks. Whole trees had been uprooted and sent crashing into the trampled undergrowth, and the tangle of branches, now seeming to spring out of the ground, gave fine cover for snipers firing from behind them and, looming up fearful and grotesque in the light of the green star shells that rose and fell in the heart of the wood, barred the way to the infantry blundering forward.

It should have been a sylvan scene, the half-full moon riding high on a summer's night over the woods and valleys of the Somme. To observers in the British line, looking across the valley to the wood that swelled and sank in an inferno of flash and fire, the moon, the stars, the warmth seemed strangely incongruous.

Repeated reports had claimed that High Wood had been captured by the 7th Division, and General Baird, in command of a Brigade of the 33rd Division, had sent his men into it with orders to consolidate the line. 'Consolidate' meant 'dig', and on a line running diagonally through the wood, they dug for half the night, cursing the undergrowth, cursing the tentacles of roots that entangled spades and entrenching tools, and cursing the fact that, for all their orders and all the reports and assurances that the wood had been captured, machine-gun bullets were spraying them as they worked. In lulls between the bursts, they could hear voices very close in front of them shouting orders in a language that was unmistakably German. And, occasionally, the alien commands seemed to come from behind their backs.

It was a gruelling and frightful night of fear and crucifying labour. In the first light of the dawn, the weary men were ordered to filter back out of the wood, to abandon the new line, and to prepare the line up outside High Wood for a fresh attack. The long night's digging had gone for nothing.

In spite of the insistence of Headquarters that High Wood had been captured – or nearly so – by the 7th Division, it was obvious to

Brigadier-General Baird, from the experience of his own troops during the dreadful hours they had spent in it, that this was not the case. Furthermore, the new orders were that the whole division should pivot to face north and, with High Wood on its right, attack the trenchlines that lay between it and Martinpuich. The Glasgow Highlanders were to start out on this affray from the western corner of High Wood and, as no one knew better than the Glasgow Highlanders themselves, the western corner was still clenched in the hands of the Germans. Their orders were therefore inviting them, if not to turn their backs on the enemy, at least to launch into an attack which would bring them, in a matter of yards, within a hail of enfilade fire.

It was suicide to think of attempting it. In remarkably restrained, but pungent terms, General Baird pointed out this fact to Divisional Headquarters and pointed out furthermore that, no matter how his troops were positioned, the attack could not hope to be successful unless the enemy had been cleared from High Wood. Judging by the experience of his troops in the night, this was palpably not the case. Divisional Headquarters was unperturbed. The troops had perhaps been edgy. It had been categorically claimed as long ago as ten o'clock the previous evening that High Wood had been captured, and the casualties which Baird's Brigade had unfortunately sustained, the difficulties they had encountered during the night, must have been due to isolated pockets of resistance – nothing that a little 'mopping up' would not put right. His opinion, they informed him in placatory tones, would be recorded. But the attack would go ahead.

In a lather of impotent fury, all that General Baird could do was to send a company of the King's Royal Rifle Corps up to the wood itself. When the main attack began they, with the remnants of three platoons of the Glasgow Highlanders, would attack through High Wood. At best they would clear the remaining 'pockets of resistance'. At worst they would divert the Germans' attention from the right flank of the 33rd Division as they pushed towards the north.

The attack was due to start at nine o'clock. The bombardment started at 8.30. It sounded loud and impressive. It had no particular effect.

Rifleman J. Brown, MM, No. 3 Platoon, A Coy., 16th King's Royal Rifle Corps (Church Lads Brigade).

We'd laid there all night in these little shelters what we'd dug and they were just bringing up the breakfast and the order came to march, so we never got no breakfast that morning. Cor' Blimey, I was frightened. Just thinking, 'Hope I'll get out of it.' But my legs worked, so I got up and walked out with the rest. We went across the valley and got up to High Wood and when we got along the side of the wood we lay down there and had a look down this valley what we'd come up. There was a Jock regiment marching up the road in fours and Jerry opened up on them and I remember two or three shells dropping right in among the column and they just closed ranks and came on – never faltered! Then our own bombardment started and, as usual, they was dropping short. They was falling in the fields behind us. Our own guns! I don't believe one of them went into High Wood and that's what they were supposed to be bombarding before *we* went in. They was too far away to hit us, because we was right up against the wood, and they certainly didn't hit the wood! I don't know what they was aiming at or whether they'd just had a good rum ration the night before! I reckon they were trying to ricochet off on to the target!

Just picture a lovely July sunny day. As we were waiting so many paces apart, I noticed there were hazel trees growing on the edge of the wood – hazel trees, with nuts on them. I was a stretcher-bearer in this attack and I was with George Illife who was my partner, the other stretcher-bearer. Then the Very light went up, which was the signal, and we had to go into the wood. Illife had got wounded while we were waiting and he cleared off, so I was there on my own.

Corporal Jack Beament, MM, No. 1 Platoon, A Coy., 16th King's Royal Rifle Corps (Church Lads Brigade).

The order come. Away we go! I remember Major Cooban – he was our Company Commander – going into High Wood bent forward, like, on the trot, with his revolver in his hand, and that's the last I see of him! We follow on. There was some troops dug in about twenty yards inside High Wood, in little shell-holes, leaning forward on their arms, because the machine-gun bullets was whizzing about something awful. We went through past those chaps, but we didn't get much further. Me and another fellow got into a shell-hole, because there was no point just going on against these machine-guns and bullets spitting everywhere, so we had to sit there for a time and wait to see what was going to happen and if anyone in front was going to knock these machine-guns out so that we could get forward.

Rifleman J. Brown, MM, No. 3 Platoon, A Coy., 16th King's Royal Rifle Corps (Church Lads Brigade).

Major Cooban was a very, very brave man. He ought not to have been in that attack at all. He had lumbago so, technically, he was unfit, but he would insist on leading our Company. I never saw him after we got into the wood. It was an absolutely raging inferno. Shells and rifle fire, machine-gun fire, but, strangely enough, looking back on it, I don't think I felt all that frightened. You couldn't let fear get into your brain. You'd go berserk! All you could do was hope for the best and get on with the job. You hoped

Corporal Jack Beament, MM, No. 1 Platoon, A Coy., 16th King's Royal Rifle Corps (Church Lads Brigade).

you wouldn't get killed though! I came across a chap who came from Cork, he was an Irishman and he was wounded in the head – badly, but I got him into a shell-hole and bandaged him out and he managed to get out of the wood and cleared off. Then I went on a bit further, looking for more wounded but I had to take shelter, which is what all the boys were doing. I don't think that we really got twenty or thirty yards into the wood.

Rifleman J. Brown, MM, No. 3 Platoon, A Coy., 16th King's Royal Rifle Corps (Church Lads Brigade)

All of a sudden something hit me in the back. I thought it was the Jerries up behind me with a mallet! So I puts my hand round on my back and it was covered with blood. I thought to myself, 'I'm going to get out of this!' But when I tried to move my legs, they wouldn't go. I was all on my own in this shell-hole and – this is God's truth! – I lay down, put my arms under my head, laid my head on my arms and laid myself down to die. All I could think of was, 'Fancy training more than fifteen months for this!'

Corporal Jack Beament, MM, No. 1 Platoon, A Coy., 16th King's Royal Rifle Corps (Church Lads Brigade).

I got a bullet in the left shoulder, so I packed up. I started to crawl back where we'd come from and, while I was doing so, I came across a fellow from Redhill called Johnny Redman. He was wounded. He was a very tall, heavy man, but I got hold of him and I half-dragged him and half-carried him out of the wood. I got him somehow on to my shoulder and I remember wondering if the Germans had machine-guns up in the trees because, as we were getting back, I remember the bullets hitting the ground, just like heavy raindrops. They couldn't have been spent bullets from a distance, because they were so near and of course the Germans were shelling as well. There were explosions all over the place. It wasn't very pleasant. But I just had to struggle on as best I could and hope to God we would get back. What a shambles it was. I didn't get more than thirty yards, or forty yards at most. We just couldn't make any advance at all.

Rifleman J. Brown, MM, No. 3 Platoon, A Coy., 16th King's Royal Rifle Corps (Church Lads Brigade).

I was really resigned to dying and I just lay there quiet. After a while I said to myself, 'I'm a long time getting unconscious! I'll have another go.' So I had another go and my legs worked. They told me afterwards that the nerves in my spine must have been numbed with the bang of the bullet in my back, and they'd recovered a bit by then. It wasn't easy, but I chucked my equipment off and my rifle and left it in the shell-hole and when I looked at my haversack as I took it off (I'd got a primus stove in there, one of them little ones) and whatever it was that hit me had smashed that and it was full of petrol. It's a good job it never went up! So I started to crawl back out of the wood and, when I got clear of it, I was able to stand up a bit – but still creeping along like a half-shut knife because of this thing in my back.

It was a good struggle back over the open with this chap Redman over my shoulder – the one I *hadn't* got the bullet in! When I got out of the wood I was carrying him over open land. There were no trenches there, and I was going through the remains of this Cavalry. I remember a poor horse with no guts – guts all hanging out – and I had to pass that and get down somehow to the aid post. I passed Colonel Wyld on the way. I couldn't help feeling sorry for him. 'Lizzie Wyld' we called him. He became our CO when we got out to France and he used to ride round and, if he saw something he didn't like, he would bellow, 'I can see you all from my horse and I have the power to send you all home.' It was a joke in the Battalion; we made up a song, or a kind of a song and we used to sing it.

I can see you all from my horse
And I have the power
To send you a-a-all home!

Well! To see him then, I really felt sorry for him. There was a bank halfway across, just a low bank. He wasn't in the wood with us, because he was in charge of the four Companies and the other three were going in the other direction and only 'A' Company had gone into this part of the wood, to fix the Jerries on the right flank, you see. And so he had to stay outside to co-ordinate and give them the orders. He'd had to get messages somehow to each Company as to what action they could take. But things were going so badly against us that I suppose the poor devil didn't know what commands to give! And that look of anguish on his face! Poor old Lizzie! I suppose he must have been a bit shell-shocked. He was sent home after that.

There was a little doctor's shelter thing dug into the side of the hill, so I went in there and got bandaged up and that's where I did see Jack Beament. He'd just brought this chap Redman in and he'd got wounded and all. But the doctor said, 'Can you make it further back on your feet?' We both said we could, so we set off back together. What with the loss of blood, we was both feeling pretty queer by the time we got down to Happy Valley and there was a battery of guns firing there, just over the top of a steep bank. You wasn't supposed to go that near the guns but we was just plodding on. Anyhow they stopped firing and let us go by and then

Corporal Jack Beament, MM, No. 1 Platoon, A Coy., 16th King's Royal Rifle Corps (Church Lads Brigade).

Rifleman J. Brown, MM, No. 3 Platoon, A Coy., 16th King's Royal Rifle Corps (Church Lads Brigade).

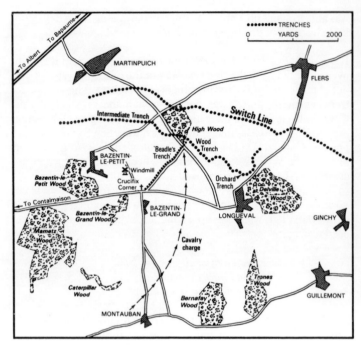

The Ground Attacked on 14th/15th July

they started again when we'd got past. We get down to the dressing station eventually and then we was shipped off to the casualty clearing station in an old general service waggon. The Padre was at the dressing station asking us all when we came in if we'd seen anybody get killed and who they were. See anybody get killed! I should say we did!

Corporal Jack Beament, MM, No. 1 Platoon, A Coy., 16th King's Royal Rifle Corps (Church Lads Brigade).

It was a horrible, terrible massacre. We'd lost all the officers out of our company. We lost all the sergeants, all the full corporals and all the NCOs right down to Herbert King who was the senior Lance-Corporal. He was my pal and he brought 'A' Company out of the wood. He rallied them and brought them out. There were more than two hundred of us went in. And Herbert brought them out. Sixty-seven men. That was all.

It was 15 July. It would be exactly two months to the day, 15 September, before High Wood would be taken.

The trouble was the Switch Line, so long, so deep, so formidable, so heavily manned, so closely interlinked to the trenches that lay in

The ground attacked on 14th and 15th July, with the two stumbling blocks of High Wood and Delville Wood.

As Forward Observation Officer Fred Beadle lost his way and turned up this German communication trench to the right of the Crucifix Corner. To his horror he found that it was leading him straight to the enemy line at High Wood.

On the left are the remains of the windmill which concealed a deep dugout. It was from here that astonished British officers were able to look across the waving corn to High Wood and, exploring further, found it empty.

From the windmill above Crucifix Corner, Bazentin, looking across to Longueval and Delville Wood. Although there was still fierce fighting and shelling at Longueval the cavalry galloped across this open country to make their abortive attack on High Wood witnessed by Fred Beadle. The long clump of trees above the remains of the windmill in the foreground is the approximate site of the German communication trench in which Fred Beadle accidentally found himself.

when I tell you he was only out 16 days in all, and he was attached to the Middlesex Regt on the Friday 6th & sent into the trenches the same afternoon and attacked on the Sat at 2-30 in the afternoon, when he was killed, it all seems to quick to give them a chance. Forgive this long letter but it helps one to bear there sorrow to be able to write of it.

from
Yours sincerely
Ethel Bath

2nd Lieutenant Reginald Bath, killed in action in Leuze Wood.

Above left: Bill Turner of the 15th Highland Light Infantry with his girl-friend Maggie Gaffney. They were photographed together two days before he was to leave for France – but he was hauled off the train at the last minute when his mother revealed that he was under age.
Above right: Jack Beament of the Church Lads Brigade.

Below: Some of the Church Lads of the 16th Battalion, Kings Royal Rifle Corps. Jack Beament (*second from left, middle row*) and Jack Brown (*fourth from right, back row*) later crawled together out of the debacle at High Wood.

front of it by a network of fortifications, that it was virtually impregnable. It ran from the village of Martinpuich along the valley, through the north-eastern corner of High Wood and out beyond it, slicing across the open ground to pass behind Delville Wood and to form a bastion in front of the village of Flers. Switching direction as it went, with High Wood and Delville Wood beyond it, the Switch Line was an iron gateway, defending Flers and Martinpuich as a portcullis might once have defended the gateway of a castle against a besieging horde. So long as they held the Switch Line, the Germans would hold High Wood. From whatever direction they attacked – frontally or from the boundaries of the wood to the south or to the north – blundering through the thickets and briars or down the long rides that divided it, no matter how they scraped, dug, entrenched and consolidated, no matter how often successive lines of attack swept over the front line that stretched from the north-west to the south-east corner of the wood, no matter how they hacked and battled their way beyond it, again and again the troops came up against the deadly strong triangle that still held out at the corner of the wood. The cavalry who had galloped into the wood with pennants flying, the soldiers who had fought their way through it on 14 and 15 July were the vanguard of a whole host who were to fight in High Wood and to die in it.

At Delville Wood, just along the road, the story was even more appalling. Here they had pushed in the South African Brigade and, together with Scottish troops, they had taken the wood and had held it. But it had been held at a terrible cost. The South Africans had gone in three thousand strong. At roll call, when they eventually came out, seven hundred and sixty-eight men answered their names. The South Africans had suffered more than two thousand casualties – and, in this case, casualties meant dead. It was possibly the greatest sacrifice of the war.

In 'normal' battle conditions the proportion of casualties was reckoned to be, on average, four men wounded or taken prisoner for every man who was killed outright, or died within hours of his wounds. Even on the first black day of July, when the final casualty list had numbered more than fifty-seven thousand, appalling though the total was, roughly one man in every three casualties had been killed. Proportionately, the South Africans' losses had been far greater. Of the three thousand soldiers of the South African Brigade who went into Delville Wood, the handful of wounded were out-numbered, four to one, by the dead. None was taken prisoner.

Sunday, 15 July, dawned a fine morning in Winchester. The cathedral was packed and in the streets outside, the pavements were crowded with bystanders. Accustomed though they were, even in peacetime, to seeing soldiers about the city, the townspeople of Winchester still dearly loved a parade. So they lingered in the warm sun, feathered hats nodding, shoes polished to Sabbath brilliance, to enjoy the sight of the Reserve Battalions of The King's Royal Rifle Corps and The Rifle Brigade as they marched the short distance from the barracks to the cathedral. The soldiers had been roused at dawn and it had taken hours of preparation and spit and polish before their turn-out had achieved the standard of smartness necessary to satisfy the critical eyes of sergeant-majors and inspecting officers. It was no ordinary Church Parade. Even the King, although not actually present in person, would be represented at the head of the city's dignitaries, by the venerable Field-Marshal, Lord Grenfell, and as many of its congregation as the cathedral would hold were admitted after the troops and official guests had filed into their places.

In spite of the glorious music and singing, it was a sombre service, dedicated to the memory of the soldiers who had a special bond with Winchester, the home of their Regimental Barracks. They were the officers and the men of The King's Royal Rifle Corps and of The Rifle Brigade who had fallen on the field of battle since the war had begun almost two years before. There were too many of them to enumerate. Besides, precise statistics might have been lowering to morale and might also, perhaps, have taken the edge off the note of ringing patriotism that crowned the solemnity of the service with a full-blooded rendering of the National Anthem.

As the second verse began and the verger swung open the big oak doors, the notes of the anthem spilled out of the cathedral into the streets. Passers-by froze where they stood; men removed their hats and most of them joined in:

> *O Lord our God, arise,*
> *Scatter his enemies,*
> *And make them fall;*
> *Confound their politics;*
> *Frustrate their knavish tricks;*
> *On Thee our hopes we fix,*
> *God save us all!*

There were rather more of the fallen of The King's Royal Rifle Corps to honour than if the service had been held two days earlier. And a hundred and fifty miles away, on the scarred uplands of the Somme where the same morning sunlight shafted through the crippled trees of High Wood, more King's Royal Rifle Corps were dying, even as the patriotic notes swelled through the sunlit streets of Winchester.

The lucky ones, the boys who had been wounded and had dragged themselves or been carried away from the wood, were pressing towards the dressing station. By five in the evening, some one hundred and fifty of them had managed to reach it and had passed through it down the line.

Jack Brown ended up in the mortuary. Such was the chaos and disorganisation, such was the flow of casualties pressing towards the second-stage dressing stations in the rear, where ambulances would take them to casualty clearing stations on the other side of Albert, that the walking wounded were literally queueing up for treatment. It was a long wait and, having just received an anti-tetanus injection, Jack was feeling distinctly queer. An orderly ducked out from a tent as the long line of men shuffled slowly past, and, through the flap, Jack glimpsed the still forms of wounded soldiers lying on stretchers inside. It did not occur to him that the soldiers lay very still indeed, only that there was one stretcher unoccupied. 'This'll do me!' he thought, as he slid discreetly from the throng of wounded into the dim half-light of the tent and painfully, gratefully lay down.

It was many hours before he awoke, and, even then, he only had the energy to open one eye, half-blinded by the swinging lantern in the hand of the orderly who bent over him. It was not until he heard the orderly yell as he ran out of the tent that Jack woke up fully and realised that something was wrong. The mistake was soon put right and, early in the morning, Jack was sent off in the first of the day's convoys to the casualty clearing station at Warloy on the first stage of his journey to a long convalescence at home. The unfortunate orderly, whom Jack had scared out of his wits, helped to load him into the ambulance. The parting glance he cast upon him was not a friendly one.

Jack Beament was already on his way to a base hospital at Rouen. His wound was not so serious as Brown's, and, in normal circumstances, his chances of getting home at all would have been slim, but the circumstances were far from normal. For, even two weeks after the disastrous first day of the battle, casualties who had been lying out from the first and later attacks were still being rescued and brought in and the seriously wounded men who had been rescued early from the battlefield, or who had been wounded in the line, were not yet fit to be moved by train, ship, and train again on the long haul back to Blighty. The situation had improved since the first calamitous forty-eight hours of the offensive, when the overflow of wounded arriving at casualty clearing stations was so great that even the vast reserves of spare stretchers were soon used up and, all around the big marquees, men were laid in patient rows on the bare earth, without even the benefit of a blanket to cover them.

It had been a miracle of organisation that all had received emergency treatment and had been swiftly sent on to the superior comforts of base hospitals at Rouen or on the coast. But the base hospitals themselves were now packed far beyond their capacity. Beds were moved together, so close that there was barely room for the nurses to pass between them. When the beds ran out, stretchers were pressed into service, laid crossways at the foot and, in the largest marquees, in rows down the middle. And still more wounded were arriving all the time. It was the lightly wounded who came off best – the men who, otherwise, would have been treated for a week or so at the base hospitals, sent to convalescent camps for a few days and then returned to their units in the line. But there was no longer room for them. They, at least, could stand the journey and must be shipped off as quickly as possible to make room for the serious cases. Such fortunate soldiers found little to object to in this arrangement and simply thanked their lucky stars that they were out of it.

In the desperate aftermath of the big attack with every dressing station, casualty clearing station and hospital in France strained ten times beyond its limit, with every orderly, nurse and doctor working hollow-eyed around the clock, some men had not even passed through the base hospitals at all. The transport authorities, at their wits' end, had sent three train-loads of walking wounded straight from the front to the harbour at Boulogne, and, to the delight of their passengers, loaded them directly on to hospital ships bound for home. A few were 'accident cases', suffering from nothing more serious than a sprained ankle, but, now that they had been packaged into the system, they could be sure of at least a few days' rest in a Home hospital, of a period of sick leave and then the blessed respite of a few weeks at their Regimental Base Camp before being drafted back to France and up the line.

Jack Beament, sent to hospital at Rouen, was not quite so fortunate in the short term, but he was nevertheless in for the greatest surprise of his life. It was also the greatest coincidence.

Corporal Jack Beament, MM, No. 1 Platoon, A Coy., 16th King's Royal Rifle Corps (Church Lads Brigade).

It was a hutment hospital on Rouen Racecourse and I was directed to Ward C.3. I could move under my own steam, because my legs were all right. When I got there, the nurse met me at the door and said to me, 'That's your bed over there on the right-hand side.' I thanked her and, as I was making for the bed, I heard a whistle and I looked round. On the other side of the ward, almost immediately opposite my bed, there was my brother Stanley! Just imagine! In all the scores and hundreds of hospitals in France, with all their scores and scores of wards in every hospital, I ended up in the same ward as my brother Stanley. And the even more amazing coincidence was that he had an almost identical wound to mine, only it was in the opposite shoulder. What a reunion that was! And how delighted the nurses were too! They simply couldn't get over it and they made a terrific fuss of us both.

Stanley Beament, in the 20th Battalion of Jack's own regiment had joined up, on reaching military age, a year after Jack himself, and, as the 20th Battalion of The King's Royal Rifle Corps was a Pioneer Battalion, might have been expected to be immune from wounding by rifle fire. But, twenty-four hours before Jack had been wounded at High Wood, Stanley's company had been attached to the 8th Brigade of the Third Division where they stood in the line ready to launch the dawn attack in the early hours of 14 July. It was while they were consolidating the line between High Wood and Delville Wood, while the Pioneers were digging a new communication trench, that Stanley had been wounded. On his way back to the dressing station, he must have passed within yards of his brother Jack as the Church Lads, in their turn, marched up towards the line. Now, in the hospital at Rouen, the two brothers compared wounds, swapped experiences, gloated over their luck, and, in between painful dressings, thoroughly enjoyed being petted and fussed over and treated as minor celebrities. On 22 July they were bundled aboard a hospital ship and travelled home together.

On the same day, the most illustrious casualty of Bloody July met his death on the Somme. It was Major-General Ingouville-Williams, in command of the 34th Division. He died at Mametz Wood, killed by the explosion of an unlucky shell, as he moved up to reconnoitre the ground for the next stage of the hoped-for advance. It was a severe blow to the Army, for the Somme fighting had taken a heavy toll of colonels and brigadiers who had gone into the line with their troops and had been killed or wounded, and even a colonel or a brigadier was more easily replaced than an experienced major-general in command of a Division. The General's body was brought back and he was buried at Warloy with full military honours. Transport columns and gun batteries were scoured for black horses to draw the gun carriage bearing his coffin and two matching pairs were eventually found in 'C' Battery of the 152nd Brigade.

23 July: Good progress reported as a result of the strafe and batches of prisoners are continuously marched back to the rear but no definite news is obtainable. We now suffer a great loss by the death of our Officer Commanding our 34th Division – General Williams killed by a shell bursting last night. Our No. 2 black team is used for removal of the body (Fritz leaves us alone,

Sergeant Frank Spencer, No. 1113, 'C' Bty., 152nd Brigade, Royal Field Artillery.

being evidently too preoccupied in dealing with infantry as great progress is made during the day.)

There had been another night attack on High Wood, and this time by the 51st Division.

Lance-Corporal David Watson, No. 3721, 9th Btn., Royal Scots, 51st Division.

We were marched up through Fricourt, which was badly battered. That was the first real sign of war we had come through and, when we reached Mametz Wood, we cut through the wood across the valley and went into a trench behind the Bazentin le Petit wood. That was the assembly point for the 'do'. And the battle order was that, if the attack failed, we had to come back to this trench. When we reached the road at Bazentin village we turned left and moved up the road. We were in extended order right up that road and, oh, the German guns were knocking us down wholesale and the same with these machine-guns. We took up position along the wall and, at two minutes past twelve, we jumped the wall and ran down the hill to take, according to orders, a few minutes rest in a valley. To me it was like a dried-up water course. A dip. Water would be there in the winter. And then we were to form up about fifty yards from High Wood to rush it. The Corporal and three of us, three privates, we reached the fifty yards spot but no order came to charge the wood. The corporal decided to go and see what had happened but we saw him knocked down about fifty yards away from us. And he had given us an order, 'Don't move from where ye are until I get back.' But we couldn't move because we were pinned down with machine-gun fire. Bullets were flying all roads and men were dropping on each side. In fact, I saw Sergeant Thomson who was badly wounded being helped by a Lance-Corporal who had got down on one knee and had the sergeant sitting up against him, and a big shell splinter came across and sliced the Sergeant's head off. That poor Corporal, he was nearly demented. He was inches away from him.

We took up position ready to get into the wood. Nothing happened and our guns didn't seem to hit the wood at all because they should have been able to knock out these machine-gunners. They kept firing for a long time and there were only three of us left. One lad lost patience with the strain of waiting, just got up on to his feet and ran away and he went down. He was hit. You saw the flashes coming out of the machine-guns, pointing directly at us. They knew where we were but they hit everything bar the two of us. We could hear the bullets going into the ground in front, behind and at the side. Just never seemed to get us. We decided the best way was just to lie still because it was level ground and the bullets were whizzing over and hitting the earth all round about us. And it took us two hours before we got back to the assembly trench. After it seemed to quieten down a bit, and it was obvious the thing had failed completely, and we gradually – just one at a time – moved back a little – we took just turn-about moving because, if one movement had been spotted, we would both get it. And we got down into this dip that was at the foot of this steep hill. There was a crucifix at the crossroads – and we got back down to the crucifix, down the road from Mametz Wood and then we climbed the hill behind the Bazentin Wood to get back into the trench. There were only eleven of us left. We were no good to anybody.

That was a stupid action, because we had to make a frontal attack on bristling German guns and there was no shelter at all. We were at the back, but C Company really got wiped out. We had a lot of casualties but they lost all their officers, all the NCOs, the lot – cleaned out! We knew it was pointless, even before we went over – crossing open ground like that. But, you had to go. You were between the devil and the deep blue sea. If you go forward, you'll likely be shot. If you go back, you'll be court-martialled and shot. So what the hell do you do? What can you do? You just go forward, because the only bloke you can get your knife into is the bloke you're facing.

Sergeant Bill Hay,
No. 1459, 9th Btn.,
Royal Scots,
51st Division.

There were dead bodies all over the place where previous battalions and regiments had taken part in previous attacks. What a bashing we got. There were heaps of men, everywhere – not one or two men, but heaps of men, all dead. Even before we went over, we knew this was death. We just couldn't take High Wood against machine-guns. It was ridiculous. There was no need for it. It was just absolute slaughter.

When it marched out of the line, the Battalion was a shadow of its former self. They passed through Fricourt in a straggling column, pathetically few in number and a piper marched at their head. He belonged to the Battalion. He knew the terrible toll that High Wood had taken and, doubtless, his mind was on the bodies of the comrades they had left behind. Since the days of Culloden *The Flowers of the Forest* had been the traditional Highland lament. He chose to play it now. It seemed appropriate to the occasion.

As the Royal Scots marched away from the battle, the Australians were preparing to go into the attack. Their orders were, at all costs, to take Pozières.

Chapter 14

Although the first contingent had arrived only at the end of March, the Australians were already a familiar sight in Northern France – tall men, most of them, broad of physique, hard of muscle, with lean, brown faces tanned to leather by the blistering suns and winds of two seasons on the Gallipoli Peninsula and by their scorching sojourn in Egypt after the evacuation.

True to the British tradition of turning defeat of a kind into victory of a kind, the evacuation of British and Colonial troops from the peninsula had already passed into legend. So carefully had it been planned, so thoroughly had the Turkish enemy been duped, that it had been accomplished without the loss of a single man.

Silence was the essence of the plan. The armada of ships was already moored in the straits and around them bobbed a fleet of lighters ready to creep towards the coast after dark to pick up the men from the narrow beaches at the foot of the cliffs. In places, the tracks that led down to them from the gulleys above were steep and so narrow that some thousands of men would have to scramble down them in single file, boots wrapped in sandbags to muffle the sound of their feet, moving slowly, carefully, so that the inadvertent clink or jingle of rifles and accoutrements, multiplied a thousand times, might not give them away.

But it was equally obvious that, if silence fell too suddenly in the trenches above, the Turks would be alerted, might guess what was happening and might open up their guns and bombard the beaches and the rescue fleet beyond. With infinite cunning the Allies planned a great deception. For some hours after the last of the men had filed out of the trenches, it must appear to the Turks that it was still 'business as usual'. Over the last few weeks, they had changed the pattern of activity to accustom the enemy to long periods of silence, alternated with busy periods of fire. At Sari Bair, where the Royal Engineers had been tunnelling for months towards the Turkish lines, preparing a mine beneath the enemy trenches to be blown in conjunction with a big attack which would now not take place, the possibilities of an explosive farewell were not lost on the minds of those who planned the evacuation. The mine could still be fired at the very last minute, as the last man left the trenches. From the deck of a cruiser in the bay, General Birdwood had the satisfaction of seeing 'an eruption that seemed to rival Vesuvius' and to hear, for hours afterwards, a fusillade of fire as the Turks wasted considerable amounts of ammunition firing at the now-empty Allied trenches.

It was a long time before the enemy woke up to the fact that the opposition had melted away, for the troops had exercised considerable ingenuity in order to deceive him. All along the trenches, up and down the length of the peninsula, ready loaded rifles had been left in position with strings of varying lengths attached to the triggers and lighted candles, so positioned that the rifles would fire automatically when the flames burnt through the strings. Similar devices would shoot flares into the sky, carefully timed to reproduce 'normal night-time activity', so carefully established over the past weeks.

As the last troopship bearing the rearguard of the Gallipoli force slid silently down the straits, and the sheer cliffs to starboard began to loom grey in the first light of dawn, the 'Jokes Department' could still plainly be heard drawing enemy fire. With an enormous effort, the troops restrained themselves from spoiling the effect by raising a triumphant cheer. It was a glorious end to an inglorious episode and the story of the *sangfroid* and cool-headedness of the departing warriors had improved in the telling.

Tall stories about the Australians were circulating in France long before they arrived there themselves in the late spring. Most of them could be traced to the Pals Battalions of the 31st Division who had been soldiering alongside them in Egypt. They had every reason to feel slightly resentful of their Anzac comrades. On their arrival in Egypt, the local traders had been quick to notice that the Anzacs, with their six shillings a day, were more affluent than the British troops whose cost of living had immediately rocketed. Oranges, previously obtainable at fifteen for one piastre, soon cost one piastre per orange. The Anzacs, flush with back pay accumulated during service in Gallipolli, rode in taxis while Tommies slogged back to camp on foot or clung precariously to the last tram-car. Prices at the Café Egyptien increased twenty-fold overnight and, within days of the arrival of the Australians, it was rumoured that the sawdust on the floor was swept up by the grasping Egyptians in the small hours of every morning and squeezed between sheets to recover the beer that had soaked into it during the evening's carousal. Souvenir sellers made clear their disdain of customers unadorned by slouch hats and upped their prices accordingly. Touts roamed the streets and cafés to inveigle the well-breeched Australians into dives and dens in sleazy back streets where the charms of women of a dozen different hues and nationalities were available, if not for the asking, at least for the price of one day's Colonial pay.

The Australians were mostly country boys, many of them from the far outback, and it was the first time that they had had the opportunity of indulging in such dubious pleasures. Many had cause to regret it. Within weeks, a huge barbed wire compound was built outside the Mena Camp containing some hundreds of disconsolate Anzacs, mooching about – between doses of unpleasant remedial treatment – as they waited to be shipped home 'in disgrace'. Later the Army took a more realistic view of human frailty and turned its mind towards prophylaxis as well as supplying remedial treatment for venereal disease. But in 1916, 'sin' was supposed not to exist among the upright, adulated troops of Great Britain and her Empire.

The 'sin' which did exist, in the view of the Army, and which must be stamped on hard, was the unforgivable assumption on the part of the Australian soldier that he was the equal of any man whether he wore the desert-stained uniform of a private or the immaculate turn-out of a superior being endowed with the King's Commission. Horrified officers indulging in a civilised aperitif in the palatial bar of Shepheard's Hotel, who had been chummily invited to 'Have one with me, mate' by a slouch-hatted, none-too-clean Australian ranker, had speedily had the hotel put out of bounds to other ranks and, when a whole series of British officers found themselves unable to dine almost anywhere because all the tables had been reserved for convivial parties of noisy Australian troops, other hotels followed suit and were henceforth reserved for 'Officers Only'. There was not much else but 'dives' of dubious reputation where Anzacs and Tommies alike were unmercifully fleeced.

The Australians were nobody's fools and it did not escape their attention that the Egyptians were only too willing to take advantage of their open-handed *bonhomie* and to defraud them at every opportunity. But they seldom got away with it. There were well-authenticated stories of Australians – justifiably enraged by blatant profiteering – overturning market stalls, forcing some unfortunate over-optimistic orange vendor to distribute his entire stock free and administering such corporal punishment to impertinent taxi drivers as their inflated demands deserved.

Real retribution had been reserved for sellers of liquor who had evolved the ingenious ploy of boring a hole in the bottom of a full whisky bottle, draining the contents, filling it with amber-coloured liquid – often urine – and replugging the hole with a ball of molten glass. Few Egyptians tried this ploy more than once if an Aussie caught up with him. He was a lucky man if he escaped with no more punishment than having the bottle broken over his head. The

Aussies looked on it as 'safeguarding the interests of future tourists'.

Soon every Egyptian, venturing on a commercial transaction with an Anzac, was demanding, 'Gibbit money first!'. Among the Anzacs this expression became a catch phrase and a huge joke. Months later in France, the veterans of Gallipoli and Egypt were still bandying it in *estaminets* whenever money changed hands, to the accompaniment of roars of laughter and total incomprehension on the part of the various 'Mamzelles' who served them with the cheap white wine or thin beer which, while it still fell a very long way short of Australian standards, was at least better than the unmentionable liquid which had passed under the name of beer in Egypt.

The Anzacs liked 'Mamzelles'. They prided themselves on their success with the fair sex and fostered the rumour that their turned-up hats were so designed to allow a feminine head to rest comfortably on a broad Australian shoulder and to facilitate kissing, without discommoding the object of admiration by disarranging an elaborate *coiffure* with the broad brim of an Australian hat. The Aussies also prided themselves on their toughness as fighters and now that they had arrived in France they intended to prove it.

It was unfortunate that their first blooding should have been at Fromelles in an attack that turned out to be a catastrophe. Fromelles was not on the Somme at all; it was across the Aubers Ridge in front of Neuve Chapelle and Laventie. The Anzacs were occupying the trenches facing Aubers in what, since the autumn of the previous year, had been a quiet sector and they had been sent here on their arrival from the East to harden them to the harsher climate, and to accustom them to the trenches and trench warfare on the Western Front. Even before the Allies had attacked on the Somme, it had been decided that a subsidiary attack would be useful and that it should be delivered by the 5th Australian Division and by the 61st Division, standing on either side of the Sugar Loaf Salient, both newly arrived in France.

The real tragedy was that it need never have happened at all, for General Monro had been authorised by the Commander-in-Chief to cancel the attack if he saw fit.

From the beginning, Fromelles had been an on-off affair, planned initially to take place on 8 July to pierce the German line towards Lille in one demoralising blow that would exploit the advances on the Somme. That idea had long gone by the board, but it was the very failure to make a significant advance on the Somme Front which now made a diversionary attack even more desirable. This time it would have quite a different objective. If it were a success, if the preliminary bombardment were strong and powerful enough to induce the Germans to believe that it was the prelude to a major

attack, it would have the beneficial effect of preventing the enemy
from moving reserves from his line at Aubers Ridge to reinforce
his troops facing the hard-pressed British on the Somme Front.
But the scale of the attack itself was reduced. There was no
possibility of a break through to Lille. Even if the small number of
available troops had succeeded in the impossible task of breaking the
German line, there were no reserves available to follow up and
exploit their success, for every man, every gun, and every available
resource to back up the infantry was needed on the Somme where
the urgent necessity was to relieve tired divisions and replace them
with fresh troops and reinforcements from other parts of the line.
The objective must now be limited to the capture of the first three
German lines that faced the troops at the foot of the Aubers Ridge.

It was a sad and desolate piece of territory, battered and bruised by
the fighting more than a year before, when the troops had tried in
vain to capture the low ridge, crowned by the villages of Aubers and
Fromelles, and to gain the high ground that guarded the city of Lille.
They had failed, but the scars of the fighting, only slightly
camouflaged by the sparse green growth of irrepressible summer,
still lay like pockmarks on the flat land that separated the British line
from the Germans. It was not only flat but muddy. This country had
little in common with the dry, chalky landscape of the Somme some
thirty miles to the south. It was Flanders, and Flanders meant mud –
a deep solid stratum of heavy earth that was the devil to dig in, quick
to absorb water, slow to drain. And the weather had broken.

Even on the Somme the deep, dry trenches now had two or three
uncomfortable inches of liquid mud at the bottom and the ground
above them, churned up by the passage of troops and supply wagons,
was now slippery and treacherous. At Fromelles the effect of the rain
of the last few days was even more devastating. There were no
trenches, dug deep with high head-cover, such as the Aussies had
known in Gallipoli. Crouching behind breastworks of mud-filled
sandbags, in weather that, even in Flanders, was unseasonable for
mid-July, concealed by the mist, the troops took cautious glances
across the four hundred yards that lay between their own breastworks and the Germans'. The steady drizzle was seeping into the
earth, trickling into every old shell-hole, swelling the brook that
meandered across part of the front, and turning every crumbling,
ancient trench and ditch into a water course. Remembering the
deep, dry entrenchments on the Gallipoli Front this time last year,
the damp and dreary Australians felt that they would willingly put up
with the clouds of mosquitoes, the legions of bugs that made their
lives accursed misery, if they could exchange them for the miserable
ditches they now inhabited as they waited to 'have a go at the Fritzes'.

The attack had already been postponed twice while the Command dithered as to whether it should take place at all. Now, with the break in the weather, it was postponed again. The drifting rain and mist hanging over the line had blinded the artillery. Even experienced gunners would have found it impossible in such conditions to register the guns so that the bombardment would fall accurately on the German lines and cut the wire in front of it so that the infantry could get through – and these gunners were far from experienced. Few of them had ever fired a gun in France.

The bombardment was the keystone of the plan. Cunningly applying the bitter lesson that had been learned on the First of July, assuming that the Germans had not failed to notice the rigidly timed 'lifts' when the guns lengthened range with each stage of the attack, the architects of the action hoped to dupe the Germans into thinking that they were using the same technique. But there would be an all-important difference. Giving the Germans five minutes to man the parapets of their front-line trenches against the coming attack, the guns would be brought back to tumble shells among them and, it was hoped, 'to reduce the defenders to a state of collapse before the assault'. As an added refinement, at the moment when the Germans might have expected them to leave their trenches, the troops in the front line were to hoist dummies above the parapet to simulate the vanguard of the attack.

If the Germans had been occupying the line that the gunners were so confidently bombarding, it might have worked. But they were not. They had long abandoned the rain-swept flatlands and, apart from keeping a few fortifications and outposts, had wisely climbed back to the drier ground on the slope of the Aubers Ridge behind. Even if the Australian and the 61st Division succeeded in capturing the line which, according to the trench maps, was still the German Front, they would hardly have improved their position. Their advance would simply bring the line nearer to the foot of the ridge where the Germans, with the advantage of observation, would be able to pick them off as easily as a boy with a catapult. The fact was that the objective of the attack was so limited that the advantage in gaining it would be nil.

General Haig had taken the trouble to make sure that General Monro clearly understood that the operation was no longer urgently needed, and also that he had absolute discretion to cancel or postpone it because of the adverse weather or for any other reason. As the rain continued to fall, as reports brought the disturbing news that not all the Australian gun batteries were yet in position, General Monro began to have serious doubts. Unaccountably, he failed to avail himself of his permission to cancel the attack on his own authority and, on the morning of 17 July, reported to GHQ that he proposed to postpone the attack because of the bad weather and that, unless it cleared up soon, he would have to postpone it again. All things considered, he thought it best to cancel the operation. Was he authorised to do so? He was passing the buck. In an ambiguous message, the Commander-in-Chief promptly passed it back again.

The Commander-in-Chief wishes the special operation . . . to be carried out as soon as possible, weather permitting, provided always that Sir Charles Monro is satisfied that the conditions are favourable and that the resources at his disposal, including ammunition, are adequate both for the preparation and the execution of the enterprise.

It squarely placed on General Monro's shoulders the responsibility of deciding whether or not the attack should go ahead and also hinted that, if he cancelled it, his reasons for doing so would not pass unquestioned. Either way, it must have seemed to General Monro that he could not win. He decided to proceed with the operation.

It was a fatal decision and one that left a legacy of bitterness that the passage of time would never expunge. Bitterness in the mind of General Monro, removed from command of Eleven Corps, as he brooded far away in India over the disaster at Fromelles. Bitterness in the minds of the Australians directed, perhaps fairly, against the Staff and unfairly against the 'Pommy bastards' of the 61st Division, in the unshakable conviction that they had been let down.

Unlike the Australians who threw themselves over the parapets in a wild enthusiastic rush for the supposed German line, the 61st had been forced to emerge from their wire by sallyports, so few, so narrow, presenting such a target to German machine-gunners, that, in some places, half the men were killed or wounded within yards of their trenches. Unlike the Australians, bronzed, fit and up to strength, the men of the 61st Division could hardly be described as the pick of the bunch. The Division was less than five months old. It had been formed in January 1916 from Reserve Battalions of the second-line whose manpower, ever since their formation, had been bled for reinforcements needed by their first-line battalions in France, and their numbers had been made up at frequent intervals by drafts of raw recruits. Their training had been long-delayed by lack of equipment, and was, at best, sketchy. With sixty-plus divisions to supply, against Australia's five, it could hardly have been otherwise.

Half the Australian force had seen service in Gallipoli and were toughened to trench warfare, while hardly a man in the 61st had even seen a trench a month earlier. For the last few days of that month half its strength in men and energy had been expended, in nights of slogging labour, in carrying out from the trenches to a safe distance behind the line fifteen hundred heavy gas cylinders which, days before, they had laboured to carry in. Only two companies of each battalion were fit to go into the attack.

On the extreme flanks of the attack both British and Australians had forged across in fine style. It was in the middle, where they were supposed to meet in the Sugar Loaf Salient, that the real disaster happened. All but a handful of the British failed to get there.

Away on the left flank the Australians were unable to recognise, in any of the tumbled ditches, the German line which had been so clearly marked on the trench maps but, determined to capture something, they had pressed on, in spite of awful casualties, to 'capture' and to hold anything that resembled a trench, a sap, or an outpost. Away on the right, the British had swept across the shattered wire of the line which, according to the maps, had been bombarded by the artillery, but they had ground to a halt against the uncut wire of the actual German line. Before nine o'clock, on that dull evening, dusk had fallen. Long before it did, it had been shatteringly apparent that, apart from ragged fighting by scattered groups of Australians, who were literally choosing to die rather than go back, the attack had fizzled into failure.

There was one ray of hope. The Australians were still fighting in the Sugar Loaf Salient and, if this strongpoint could be captured, some advantage at least might be gained from what was otherwise a débacle. Late in the evening it was decided to renew the attack on Sugar Loaf, and, in conjunction with one battalion of Australians advancing on their left, to send the depleted Reserves of the 61st Division across to the Sugar Loaf to 'help the Australians'. In a final demonstration of the dithering that had characterised the action since its inception, the attack was cancelled – and cancelled so late that word did not reach the Australians until after their 59th Battalion had advanced, alone and unsupported, to share the fate of their few remaining comrades, still battling at this strongest point of the German Line.

It was a terrible repetition of what had happened to the 13th Battalion of the Rifle Brigade at Contalmaison nine days earlier and it created a breach between the Australian fighting troops and their British comrades, which would never be completely closed. It was a sad outcome of the first engagement in which British and Australian troops had fought side by side in France.

For months, for years, for successive decades, the feeling of the Aussies that they had been 'let down' was constantly reinforced by citing the casualty figures as indisputable proof of their own sacrifice and of the British failure.

On the face of it, they looked stark enough. Australian, five thousand three hundred and fifty-five. British, one thousand five hundred and forty-seven. But it was not a comparison of like with like. The 61st Division had gone into the assault at half-strength, and, with fewer than half the number of men engaged, their casualties were proportionately almost as many.

But, for the Australians fighting in France, it was a terrible beginning and no one was more aware of this than the Commander-in-Chief. He kept to himself his thoughts on Fromelles, but, three days later, on 22 July, Haig took the trouble to visit General Gough at his Headquarters 'to make sure that the Australians had only been given a simple task'. He left presumably less than reassured. The following day, the First Australian Division would be attacking on the Somme. Their 'simple task' was to capture Pozières.

Chapter 15

The thronging of troops and supplies into the battlefields reached astounding proportions and the Pioneer troops were slaving night and day to keep the battered roads from disintegrating altogether under the strain of the constant trundling of wheels, the incessant tramping of feet, the pounding of shells that the enemy sent over in unremitting nervewracking salvoes. Wherever they fell along the roads, they were sure of finding some target.

The road through Fricourt was the single route towards High Wood, Delville Wood, and Guillemont, which, for most of the way, was not overlooked by the enemy. By branching off through Bécourt and going by way of Sausage Valley to the right of la Boisselle, the troops could reach the line in front of Pozières in comparative safety. During the twenty-four hours when the Anzacs were moving into the line, between nine fifteen on the morning of 21 July to nine o'clock in the morning of the 22nd, the traffic control post at Fricourt Cemetery took a census of the troops and vehicles that passed. The night was dark. The enemy soaked the road with tear-gas and, for a six-hour stretch, the census-takers were forced to wear goggles. This, they explained, accounted for the incompleteness of their returns. But, in spite of this handicap, they had managed to count two thousand four hundred and twenty-three motor vehicles in a steady stream of lorries, motor cars, buses, motor bikes and ambulances, throwing up clouds of white dust that blinded the horses and irritated the eyes and throats of almost four thousand drivers of horse-drawn waggons that rumbled slowly along the road. Five thousand four hundred and four mounted officers and one thousand and forty-three men riding bicycles, stumbled or dodged as best they could through the long column of transport. The Control Post unfortunately did not manage to make a complete count of the infantry moving to and from the line. The nearest approximate figure which could be arrived at was twenty-six thousand five hundred and thirty-six.

These troops who passed through Fricourt in a single span of twenty-four hours, outnumbered by some hundreds the total force of British troops engaged in the Crimean War. One of them was George Middle.

George Middle was a temporary Anzac. He was also very much a 'temporary gentleman'. Despite his First Class Degree in Mathematics and Physics, obtained in 1914 at the tender age of twenty, he had been a humble lance-corporal until a few months ago, and he had only attained that rank because Army protocol frowned on a humble Sapper lecturing to officers, no matter how much of an expert he might be. George was decidedly an expert, not so much in Maths and Physics, but in the infant science of wireless which he had taken as a subsidiary subject. But his youthful looks had worked against him. Early in the war, the pundits who had interviewed him in the august surroundings of Room 417 at the War Office itself, had not been inclined to offer him a commission, but they had been sufficiently impressed by his qualifications to send him as an Instructor to the Wireless Section of the Royal Engineers Training School at Worcester.

Less than a year later, attitudes had changed. In three short months, Middle had risen from lance-corporal (unpaid) first to the dizzy heights of second lieutenant, Royal Engineers and then, with startling rapidity, to the sole command of his own unit of sixty-four men. No one was more surprised than George himself. He had been in France for less than a month and, within days of his arrival, he was ordered to report to Bailleul as Wireless Officer of the First Anzac Wireless Section. It was a daunting task, because the First Anzac Wireless Section did not exist. What did exist was a nucleus of sixty-four burly Australian volunteers without an NCO among them and with precious little in the way of qualifications and experience. Furthermore, the orders of the 'Wireless Section' were that it was to move to the Somme Front on 10 July, which gave Second Lieutenant Middle just forty-eight hours before its departure. He spent most of it interviewing the men, informing himself as to their all-too-scanty experience and, in desperation, winkling out which of them, if any, had done any kind of job in civilian life that would make him useful now. The results were discouraging but among the assorted bunch of sun-toughened warriors, among the one-time jackaroos and salesmen, clerks and sheep shearers, was Harper, who had at least been an electrician at a Melbourne theatre, and whom Middle promptly promoted to temporary acting-sergeant, and there was a handful of army signallers who could act as lance-corporals. It was little enough, but it was a start.

Equipment was another matter. Having disposed his 'command' into sections, having moved them down to the hinterland of the Somme and seen them installed in billets, having instigated some kind of rudimentary training to occupy the waiting time, Middle's real work began. There was plenty to be done, because the 'First

Anzac Wireless Section' possessed hardly a single piece of apparatus and Middle himself had to travel mile after weary mile on a far from reliable motor bike, collecting apparatus, conferring with his superiors, checking the equipment and, finally, going into the zone of the battle itself to set up wireless stations in preparation for the coming attack. He had some hair-raising journeys. It was hardly surprising that all was not complete before the Australians went into their first fight on 23 July.

There was an avalanche of paper work to be dealt with, lists of stores to be checked, men to be apportioned to sections, orders to be read, noted, and initialled. In the middle of July, he received a memorandum with disquieting implications.

DIRECTOR OF ARMY SIGNALS
CIRCULAR MEMORANDUM NO. 114

Issued From:
General Head Quarters,
11th July 1916

A memorandum has been issued by the General Staff calling attention to the very serious consequences which have undoubtedly resulted from the enemy overhearing buzzer or telephone messages, and directing severe punishment to be inflicted on anyone communicating in clear by these means information which will be of use to the enemy.

These instructions apply equally to the Signal Service. Signal Service Officers will ensure that all operators including wireless operators are aware of the strict orders against conversation over the wire.

The telephone, or buzzer, or wireless, is not to be used for sending any Service Messages which give in clear the names of Units, their formation, or where they are located. A great deal may depend on the strict observance of these orders and every effort must be taken to detect and punish any disobedience.

(Signed) J. S. Fowler
Brigadier-General
Director of Army Signals
(Noted 17/7/16 by Officer I/C Wireless, 1st Anzacs)

It was not surprising that the Army was edgy about signals. In the last few days it had had several unpleasant revelations and the most unpleasant of all had been at Ovillers where troops who had gained the first foothold in the village had established themselves in a deep dugout, once the German Command Post. In it they had found a complete, verbatim copy of the operation order for the First of July attack at Ovillers, with a German translation appended. A similar unpleasant discovery had been found in similar circumstances at la Boisselle, where the British Corps Commander's 'Good Luck' message to the troops had been read 'in clear' over the telephone to the front line on the eve of the battle. Taken together they explained why the Germans had been ready and waiting, why enemy shells had bombarded the assembly trenches before the attack and why so many of the men, whose bodies were still lying unburied on the battlefield, had met their deaths. It was terrible confirmation of a suspicion which had been growing in the minds of Intelligence Officers for many months. The Germans, with superior equipment, had been listening in on British communications.

It explained too why, for so long, battalions taking over the trenches had been astonished when the Germans had greeted them by name. The latest example was still fresh in everyone's minds. It had happened only days earlier while the Australians waited to attack at Fromelles and, in impotent fury, had shot away the notice-board cheekily hoisted above the German trenches. It read:

'ADVANCE AUSTRALIA – IF YOU CAN!'

And, although they were to exist in Army mythology for many years, although every man who served on the Western Front would continue to believe them for the rest of his life, they demolished the Spy Stories at a blow. The soldiers had been convinced that certain French civilians were in the pay of the Germans and stories of their perfidy abounded. The hands of a Town Hall clock, not far behind the line, which went mysteriously fast or slow when a relief was under way. The sails of a windmill which appeared to take up a significant position when an attack was imminent. A farmer who unaccountably changed direction in ploughing a field, who switched one of his pair of brown horses for a grey one or put one white animal in a grazing herd of black cows. Even the French housewife, in some hilltop village, innocently spreading bed-linen to bleach in the sun as a contingent of troops went past, was not above being suspected of signalling to the Germans, and many a volubly protesting Madame had been reported and interrogated by Intelligence officers.

Now, it seemed that there might be a simpler solution. In literally thousands of miles of telephone wires stretching right up to the front line, and even beyond it into forward saps, there was ample opportunity for enemy patrols to creep across No Man's Land after dark and to attach a wire of their own to a junction in the jumble of British cable. In the Somme it was even easier. The chalky sub-soil was ideal for induction and, by using quite simple listening devices, the

Germans could pick up signals and conversations with very little difficulty. One unguarded remark, one exchange of friendly badinage between officers of two different units in the line, could give useful, even vital information on plans or dispositions. It was now outrageously evident that the enemy had made good use of his superior technical skill.

Henceforth all this must change. Frivolous use must no longer be made of the telephones and, where possible, wireless must be used and messages transmitted, not simply in Morse Code, but in coded Morse Code. It was not easy to get this message across to the troops and the Army very soon realised that, for every signal circuit set up to serve the troops in the line to send back information during the course of an attack, another must be set up as 'listening circuit', not to listen to the Germans, but to monitor the traffic in their own lines and to trap the unwary and the indiscreet alike.

But George Middle's job was to provide communications for the Australian attack on Pozières. The First Anzac Wireless Company was to serve the 1st and 2nd Australian Divisions as well as the 4th New Zealand Division, but by 23 July when the Australians went over the top, Middle had barely had time to set up the receiving post on Tara Hill and to select the sites for two forward posts. One, code-named U.M., was at the head of Sausage Valley; the other, U.L., was roughly on the line from which the 13th Rifle Brigade had launched their disastrous attack towards Pozières on the 10 July. The position of the line had hardly changed since.

Lying astride the Albert-Bapaume Road, the ruined village of Pozières was an island surrounded by deep wire-entangled entrenchments. Strongpoints bristled on the high ground, dominating the land to the south-east, where Sausage Valley ran towards Pozières from the direction of la Boisselle, and to the south-west where Mash Valley crept towards it up the hill from Ovillers. The most formidable was the fortified house – so fortified that it was virtually a concrete tower – which the Germans had christened the 'Panzerturm' and the British troops nicknamed 'Gibralter'.

The Australian attack on Pozières was part of an ambitious exercise. With the 48th Division attacking up Mash Valley on its left, the Australians were to capture Pozières, while, it was hoped, other attacks on their right would have secured the whole of the Bazentin Ridge beyond. The prizes of Delville Wood, High Wood, the Switch Line and even Martinpuich would then be in the hands of the Allies and, if the Australians could capture Pozières and press on a few hundred yards to capture the fortified windmill on the ridge itself, the troops all along the line would be virtually in sight of Bapaume.

Again, it was a night attack, but, on the right, the attack failed. The troops were newly in the line. There had been no chance to reconnoitre. Conflicting orders had changed the timing of Zero Hour and, at the eleventh hour, changed it back again, so that some of the troops were in position barely minutes before the attack was due to begin. Haze and cloud had hindered artillery observation, so the guns had not prepared the way. The fighting troops, many back in the line for the first time since the start of the battle, had been hastily reinforced, but they sorely felt the absence of the experienced officers and NCOs who had led them into the attack on the First of July and who had never come out.

The Australians, on the other hand, were fresh. They were at full strength, they were raring to go and they roared into Pozières. Almost in the first wave they captured the outer trenches of the bastion of Pozières. In an hour they were fighting through the shattered gardens and outbuildings of the houses on the right of the Bapaume road. Here, or just beyond, they should have linked up with the 48th Division attacking from the other side of the Bapaume road. It was just as well that they did not wait for them.

On their own initiative, the Aussies dashed across the road and battered their way through the fortifications on the other side. They conquered 'Gibralter' even while the 48th Division – or what was left of its men after the Germans had bombarded them in the assembly trenches – was still creeping forward in the face of terrible opposition from the posts beyond. To all intents and purposes, the Australians had captured the village of Pozières. What they had not managed to do, on their right flank, was to subdue the formidable trenches to the north of the village and to strike towards the windmill two hundred yards away.

But the Commander-in-Chief was delighted.

The diary of Sir Douglas Haig. *Sunday, 23 July:* A general attack was made at 1.30 a.m. The 5th or Reserve Army on our left advanced well to the west of Pozières village with 48th Division, while the First Australian Division captured the village of Pozières itself as far as the Albert-Bapaume Road and reached within two hundred yards of the windmill on the hill north-east of the village. . . . The Fourth Army was not so fortunate.

General Haig had received the news early and in time to impart it at breakfast to his illustrious visitor, Lord Northcliffe, who was making one of his frequent visits to the front. Lord Northcliffe was particularly favoured by the Commander-in-Chief, at least by comparision with other journalists. Although he had started in a very small way as a reporter on a provincial newspaper, in the view of General Haig

Lord Northcliffe hardly counted as a journalist at all. It was true that he had founded his fortune by means of a magazine of dubious reputation entitled *Answers*, whose content was directly aimed at 'Mary Ann in the kitchen', but, via the *Daily Mail*, he had long ago attained respectability. Now he was proprietor of *The Times* and was a Viscount to boot. Haig was delighted to entertain Lord Northcliffe, and very happy when, after breakfast on the dull, cloudy morning of 23 July, Lord Northcliffe accepted his invitation to accompany him to Mr Duncan's service at the makeshift Church of Scotland. Before leaving, Northcliffe gave the Commander-in-Chief even greater reason to have confidence in him.

Lord N. was, he said, much pleased with his visit, and asked me to . . . send him a line should anything appear in *The Times* which was not altogether to my liking. He also said that Repington had now no influence with *The Times*. They employed him to write certain articles but he (Lord N.) knew that he was not reliable.

The diary of Sir Douglas Haig.

Tim Repington had incurred the displeasure of the Commander-in-Chief by publishing certain views which emanated more from his own observations and deductions than from the Communiqués and official views of the Army regarding the conduct of the war. He had now been replaced as regular correspondent by Robinson (he of the 'chattering teeth'). Altogether General Haig, if journalists there had to be, found Robinson more to his taste. He was certainly more to his taste than 'John Bull', in the person of the redoubtable Horatio Bottomley, a campaigning journalist who made it his business to find out a good deal more than the Army wished him to know and broadcast it in the vociferous columns of his magazine which the soldiers themselves were beginning to refer to by its unofficial title of 'The Soldiers' Friend'. Already rumours of the débacle at Fromelles had reached Bottomley's ears and already he was drafting the article which would dub the 61st Division 'The Sacrifice Division'.

Meanwhile the Australians were bracing themselves for a fresh attack on Pozières, to consolidate their gains in the village and to attack beyond it.

Our Brigade came in and we had to take over from where the 1st Division were to carry on the fighting and go as far as we could. The place by this time was one shambles of destruction – a wreck. Our headquarters, where I was with the CO of the Battalion, was in a fort called Gibralter. It was a German concrete dugout with a

Private Fred Russell, No. 524. 22nd Btn., AIF, 6th Victoria Brigade.

six-foot tower above the ground, right in the centre of the village of Pozières and all the rest of the houses round it were absolutely smashed to pieces.

Orders came along, 'We're to move off at a certain time and we'll advance on the village of Pozières.' Our artillery guns were mounted in a place called Sausage Valley and they were continually firing and, of course, we had to go through them. The main impact of an 18-pounder gun firing is the compression of the shell leaving the muzzle as it goes forward. When you were in front of the guns, you got into that compression. Of course the shell was going up in the air but you got the full blast, where you were, and it was a very hard experience to put up with.

Then we came into the counter-fire of the Germans. The shells were lobbing all over the place. We didn't know where on earth we were. We got into a chalk pit and guides met us there, fellows who were trained for the purpose. They led each party up. There was no front line as such, just a series of shell-holes and timber – no front, no back, no lines of demarcation. It was just an open devastated area. The companies didn't know where they were. You had to put yourself into position and say, 'Well, where are we?' And our CO said, 'Well, you take up fifty yards from here to here – say down to that broken-off tree – and the next company will have to take on from there and co-ordinate it that way.'

That went on all night, with the shelling still going on and they were throwing over big stuff. We got into this Gibraltar HQ – I had to be with HQ, because I was a signaller. We weren't in there ten minutes when a nine-inch shell landed on top of it. There were about twenty or thirty of our fellows down below in there – and down fifteen or twenty feet in a very solid concrete-lined job. But the compression was terrific. All night long they were calling for stretcher-bearers. Every time a salvo came over, after the explosion, you could hear these calls going up outside, 'Stretcher-bearer! Stretcher-bearer!' We took an awful lot of casualties that night, even before the boys went over.

Five days had passed since the first attack. George Middle had got his wireless stations going and they were in position ready for the attack to begin. With the advance of the line, U.L. had moved up and was installed in the chalk pit where the vanguard of the 13th Rifle Brigade had fought so valiantly eighteen days before. The trouble was, that they could not make contact with U.M. a few hundred yards behind, at the head of Sausage Valley.

The signal reached Middle at his station on Tara Hill at 11.25 a.m.: *Am not in contact with U.M. Corporal Love and two men are there but owing to very heavy shelling in that quarter, presume it impossible to erect aerial.*

There was no doubt that the shelling was heavy. It was falling so thick around the island of Pozières that it seemed to the troops advancing that the approaches were encircled by fire. On the right of the road, the Australians were pushing towards the village as best they could and, on the left, the 48th South Midland Division were struggling as best *they* could in a pincer movement up Mash Valley.

My lot went up with the troops and we had to go over with rifles. Our own bombardment was terrific. This place, Pozières, was up on top of the ridge and in front of us there was nothing but one sheet of explosives. We went straight up. You grip your rifle and you say, 'Come on, you silly fool, you've got to go.' But all you could do was go a few yards and then drop down as the shells came around, then up again and on, and down again. The only thing you thought of was getting out of it. We engineers had to be there, because the idea was that as soon as we captured a trench we would consolidate it, reverse the parapet so that we'd be able to fire at the Germans from that side. What was even worse than going forward, was trying to keep on working. You drove yourself to it. You made yourself go on but there they were firing at you all the time.

I admit that I was windy. I remember being in a shell-hole and I was clawing at the ground to get my head into it. That's all I was interested in, to get my head right down into the ground. We captured one trench, and then a bit of another. But we didn't get much further. We didn't get to Pozières – and we could see it there, just in front of us. Or, at least, we could have done if you'd dared to look up but all you wanted to do was get on with your job and get out of it.

Sapper A. E. Comer, No. 474, 48th South Midland Division, Royal Engineers.

On the other side of the road, by half-past one, U.L. had succeeded in getting its aerial up and the message went back to Middle, anxiously waiting on Tara Hill: *Everything okay.*

The message should have gone no further. It was unfortunate that a signaller, unnerved by the noise, the barrage, the confusion of his first day in battle, inadvertently sent it on to Divisional Headquarters. It was unfortunate, too, that the message was taken at its face value to mean that the attack was going well, because under the punishing bombardment neither the Australians nor the South Midland Division were able to make much headway.

2nd Lieutenant
George Middle,
Royal Engineers,
Wireless Officer, 1st
Anzac Wireless
Section.

It was really a practice message and it was simply a fluke that it went through to Divisional Headquarters who'd planned the attack. I was still in the dugout at Tara Hill, an hour or so afterwards, and my immediate superior, Major Gordon, came down. I couldn't repeat the language he used. He said to me, 'What the so-and-so and so-and-so is the so-and-so meaning of this so-and-so thing?' And he was flapping this signal. I was a bit taken aback to begin with, but I immediately realised what had happened and said, 'This should never have got to you.' But it didn't do much good. He did belabour me because, as it so happened, everything was far from 'okay' and it had given Headquarters an entirely false impression of what was going on. It was a very bad start because, in a sense, we were demonstrating the use of wireless at that 'do' and supposedly showing how superior it was to telephones and land-lines that were so easily smashed by shell-fire. As a matter of fact, at Pozières, the shelling was so intense that all the lines were shattered and, apart from runners, wireless was really the only communication there was.

By evening, the Australians had borne such casualties and were so exhausted by the ordeal of shelling and fighting that the 2nd Australian Division was ordered into the line to relieve the 1st and, in the early hours, as the relief was taking place, the 17th Royal Warwicks, of the 48th South Midland Division, struggled through and linked up with the Australians to the north-west of Pozières. The village was secured, but the terrible obstacles to the north, trenches O.G.1. and O.G.2., still held out. Until they were captured it would be impossible even for the hard-fighting Aussies to fight their way towards the windmill a few hundred yards beyond. By 29 July, after four days in the line, after repeated efforts, the 2nd Australian Division had lost three thousand five hundred men – and still the windmill held out.

The Commander-in-Chief was sincerely impressed by the performance of Australia's fighting spirit and by the calibre and dash of the Australian soldiers. He was less impressed with their staff.

The diary of Sir
Douglas Haig.

Saturday, 29 July: The attack by the 2nd Australian Division upon the enemy's position between Pozières and the windmill, was not successful last night. From several reports I think the cause was due to want of thorough preparation.

After lunch I visited HQ Reserve Army and impressed on Gough and Neill Malcolm that they must supervise more closely the plans of the Anzac Corps. Some of their Divisional Generals are so ignorant and (like many Colonials) so conceited, that they cannot be trusted to work out unaided the plans of attack.

I then went on to HQ Anzac Corps at Contay and saw General Birdwood and his BGS General White. The latter seems a very sound capable fellow, and assured me that they had learnt a lesson, and would be more thorough in future.

General Birdwood, although an Englishman, like George Middle, was an honourary Australian, and popular with his troops. He had gone with them to Egypt and he had brought them to France. In the aftermath of the disaster at Fromelles, he had been following with anguished pride every stage of his Aussies' ordeal at Pozières. Now, in the face of the reproof of the Commander-in-Chief, he kept his own counsel. It was unlikely that he agreed with Haig's opinion that: 'Luckily their losses had been fairly small, considering the operation and the numbers engaged − about a thousand for the whole twenty-four hours.'

Considering the total strength of the Australian force, considering that the AIF had sustained five and a half thousand casualties at Fromelles, considering their losses in the six days since they first launched their strength into Pozières, one thousand men seemed a very large number to have been swallowed up by the maw of the war machine as it ground inexorably towards the end of Bloody July.

On that very day, 29 July, while Haig was in conference with Generals Birdwood and White a letter to the Commander-in-Chief was being written in London. It came from Field-Marshal Sir William Robertson, Chief of the Imperial General Staff, and after the initial euphoria of the 'Big Push' and the heroic stories which had stirred the imagination of the British public, it reflected the unease which was beginning to be felt at home. It was all very well to bandy about the names of villages and ridges as if they were places of metropolitan importance; it was all very well to talk in glowing terms of 'advances', 'leaps forward' and 'captures'; it was right and proper that the troops should be praised for their endeavours, for no praise was high enough, but maps were being published alongside communiqués from the front and the maps were drawn to scale. Assiduous newspaper readers did not have to be geographers or military experts in order to realise that, in terms of distance, if not in terms of strategic importance, the advances were small and that, in some cases, gains of as little as thirty yards were being hailed, in print, with as much enthusiasm as if Berlin itself had fallen to the Allies.

It was equally obvious that the price was high. The whole country had been virtually mobilized to cope with the streams of wounded arriving from the Somme. There had not even been enough

ambulances to transport them and even now huge numbers of
casualties were being nursed in an extraordinary assortment of
temporary premises ranging from village schools and church halls to
private houses. They had been pressed into service as temporary
hospitals when the civilian and military hospitals had been swamped
by the ceaseless convoys of wounded, and every day the Rolls of
Honour, those long lists of soldiers reported missing or killed, were
growing ever longer.

The letter from Sir William Robertson hinted at the doubts of the
powers-that-be and invited the Commander-in-Chief to reply to
some pointed questions:

> Will a loss of three hundred thousand men really lead to great
> results? If not should we revise and limit our plans?
> Why did it seem that the British were now bearing the brunt of
> the fighting and the French seemed to be doing little?
> Has the primary object of relieving the pressure on Verdun not,
> at least to some extent, been achieved?

The Commander-in-Chief carefully phrased his reply and sent it
immediately to London. Yes, the pressure on Verdun had been
relieved. In addition the enemy had been prevented from transfer-
ring troops from the Western Front to the Eastern, thereby aiding
Russia. He stressed the 'public-relations angle'. The Somme
Offensive had proved to the world that the Allies were capable of a
vigorous offensive and of 'driving the enemy's best troops from the
strongest positions'. This must certainly have shaken the faith of the
Germans and those who sided with Germany. It must also have
'impressed on the world, England's strength and determination, and
the fighting power of the British race'. The offensive must be
maintained and would eventually result in Germany being over-
thrown.

The Commander-in-Chief was not perturbed by the casualties.
In his view they were not inordinate. Making careful calculations on
the expected 'natural wastage' of trench warfare from shelling and
skirmishing, he was satisfied that the casualties in the July fighting
were only 'about one hundred and twenty thousand more than they
would have been had we not attacked'. This, in Haig's opinion,
could not be regarded 'as sufficient to justify any anxiety as to our
ability to continue the offensive'.

He made it perfectly clear that he intended to continue it and that
he expected to be able to maintain the offensive 'well into the
autumn'.

General Haig had omitted to take into consideration the fact that the casualties, which the Army was pleased to refer to as 'normal wastage', contained a very much higher proportion of wounded to killed than had been experienced on the Somme since the First of July. By the end of the month the casualties amounted to one hundred and sixty-five thousand. The casualties alone were almost double the entire strength of the British Expeditionary Force which had set off in August 1914 to meet the Germans at Mons. And forty thousand of them were dead.

Chapter 16

At Abbeville, many miles from the front, the lock gates on the River Somme refused to open and divers sent down to investigate found that they were jammed by the bloated bodies of French soldiers carried along by the current of the river as it flowed through to the sea. They had been dead for many weeks.

Although precise casualty figures for each stage of the fighting had not been disclosed, it was common knowledge that they had been heavy. In Britain, parents who had been rather proud of schoolboy sons who had lied their way into the Army, began to bombard the authorities, literally brandishing birth certificates in their anxiety to have under-age soldiers sent back from the front. The Army, while unwilling to remove any of its sadly depleted forces from the line, had no choice, but they had no intention of sending the enthusiastic juveniles home again, still less of discharging them from the Army. Some were, after all, within months of their nineteenth birthday when they would officially come of military age, and, in the meantime, they could be usefully employed at various base camps where every day a thousand or more reinforcements were arriving from Britain in transit to the front. They were flooding into France to replace the early casualties of the Somme and, in the great tract of land that stretched between the Somme battlefield and the coast, the weary battalions which had been struck hard in the first few days fighting were being rested, revitalised and brought up to strength with new drafts of men. The trouble was that, in the opinion of the Kitchener's Battalions, they were the wrong men.

In the flag waving days of August 1914, when local battalions surged into being on the tide of National enthusiasm, when local boys from Cornwall to John O'Groats had marched arm in arm to join their ranks, almost every battalion had its unique local identity. Now, with a hotch-potch of new arrivals sent to fill the gaps in the ranks of the Kitchener's Battalions with what the troops looked on as arbitrary disregard for their spirit and origins, resentment began to grow. After their ordeal at Gommecourt, the Queen Victoria's Rifles were particularly incensed when the very train that brought a draft of 'stangers' to reinforce them also carried a contingent of men of their own regiment bound for an entirely different unit. The

Queen's Westminster Rifles were amused when they were joined by a large batch of the under-sized Bantam soldiers and good-humouredly scrounged for empty ammunition boxes to raise the fire-steps of their trenches to a more convenient height, but they were infuriated when their own comrades, coming back to the front on recovering from their wounds, were posted to 'foreign' regiments. Trevor Ternan was equally enraged when precisely the same thing happened to the remnants of the Tyneside Scottish.

The Army allowed it to become known that it was anxious, in the future, to cultivate an 'Army Spirit' rather than the old-fashioned regimental or battalion loyalty. But there were more cogent reasons behind the decision. After the holocaust of the July attacks, local newspapers all over the country were carrying page after page of photographs of local boys who had been killed, casualty lists that were a terrible litany of familiar names, and story after pathetic story of brothers or cousins of one family who had been lost in a single attack. There were rumblings in Parliament where MPs, whose constituencies had been particularly hard hit, were beginning to ask awkward questions, and, despite the country's brave acceptance of what amounted to a mass bereavement, the policy of diluting what was left of Kitchener's Battalions, of spreading the risk by splitting up the ranks of boys who all hailed from one town or area, smacked strongly of deliberate political policy.

It was the Scots who took it as a personal insult. It was bad enough when their own Scottish drafts were sent to English regiments, but it was even worse when Scottish battalions were forced to receive 'foreigners' into their ranks and it was particularly resented in the kilted battalions. A large draft of the Fifty-First Division had been relegated to khaki-trousered ignominy in the ranks of the York and Lancaster Regiment, while their Scottish Division was augmented by a contingent of reluctantly kilted warriors who were actually Barnsley men in disguise. Once they had got used to the unaccustomed ventilation of their lower regions, they were not entirely displeased with their metamorphosis. It was a well-known fact, as the Argylls were quick to inform them, that the Germans referred to the 'Kilties' as the Ladies from Hell and that the very sight of the tartan put the fear of God into them.

But, as a Cockney born and bred, Bill Turner found the kilt a distinct embarrassment and, 'Ladies from Hell' or not, was inclined to feel at times that he would just as soon be fighting the Germans in the trenches, than his comrades of the 4th Highland Light Infantry in the only slightly less belligerent territory contained within the walls of Maryhill Barracks in Glasgow. The Scots were of the opinion that the masquerading Englishmen were fair game, an opinion which was not shared by Bill Turner nor by his friend George, who suffered the additional impediment of the surname 'England'. They became philosophical about being the butt of rough jokes. In the barrack room they quickly learned to judge just how far they could go in an argument and to dodge the flying boots and less savoury missiles that were hurled at their heads if they miscalculated. They became resigned to the fact that they were the first to be picked on by the Sergeants, could rely on being on Defaulters' Report as often as three times a week and that the only way to get off fatigues was to empty their pockets and bribe the Sergeant with all the money they had. But the Cockney contingent did not, on the whole, look forward to Friday evenings when the Highlanders invariably got drunk and, in their cups, considered it great sport to chase the lads with their 'dirks'. Being younger, lither and sober, they usually managed to escape with no more than a volley of imprecations and, once at a safe distance, hurled back taunts of, 'Who won at Bannockburn?' and, 'What about Flodden?' But this they would only risk when at a very safe distance indeed.

It hardly seemed fair. Bill Turner had not asked to be in the Highland Light Infantry. He had joined the Royal Artillery, and, strictly speaking, at the age of seventeen, he had no right to be in the Army at all, and here he was – not only a serving soldier but, what was more, a Regular.

After a dozen attempts to join up, after a dozen recruiting sergeants had turned him away with a smile as patronising as a pat on the head, it had seemed to Bill like the answer to a prayer when, passing Wandsworth Town Hall, he saw an announcement of a special enlistment scheme for boys under nineteen to join the Royal Field Artillery.

Corporal Bugler
· William Turner,
No. B. 21097, 15th
Highland Light
Infantry (City of
Glasgow
Corporation
Tramways
Battalion) 32nd
Division.

First thing off, I was sent to Maryhill Barracks in Glasgow. We was up there three months in the riding school and then we got called out on the parade ground. It was just after the Battle of Loos and the Highland Regiments had got badly cut up there, so they wanted seventeen hundred volunteers to join to refill them. Hardly anybody volunteered. In the afternoon we was called out on the square again and the CO says, 'Right. As I call your names and numbers out, fall in over there.' Blow me, he called out practically everybody's name and number! I was in a bunch of three hundred and fifty that was transferred to the Highland Light Infantry. And that was that! It was real hell for us Cockneys! You was picked out for the least thing. Up the Orderly Room, three days CB. We were never out the Orderly Room!

I managed to work myself into the band. It was a pipe-band, of course, but they trained me as a bugler and drummer. It had advantages in the band, and it had disadvantages too! The worst thing was that we weren't a kilted battalion, but the band was all dressed in the kilt. We didn't like it at all. Of course, being young things, we were after the girls, but we were frightened to go out to meet the girls wearing these things. We weren't allowed to wear anything underneath and it *was* cold. We felt half-naked – embarrassed as much as anything – and we knew the girls would see our white knees and that would give away that we were rookies. Even when we could get a pass to go up into the town, we didn't go for weeks. We used to stay in and get hold of some cold stewed tea, or get some permanganate of potash from the chemist and sit there trying to stain our knees to look as if we'd just come down from the Highlands. Then, when we thought we looked respectable, out we went.

I got to like the kilt very much. It was McKenzie tartan and there was eight and a quarter yards of material in it with pleats. They were lovely after a time and really kept you warm when you got used to them. By the time we moved down to Haddington, I felt a real swell and my knees were *really* brown by then. What with playing in the band and swinging around in the kilt, I was a real Cock of the North. I got off with a lovely girl called Maggie Gaffney. She was just about my age and I got very fond of her.

Then came the Battle of the Somme and I was put on a draft to go overseas to replace the casualties of the 15th Highland Light Infantry, which was the Glasgow Tramways Battalion, and they'd got very badly cut up on the First of July. So off I went home to London on four days draft leave. I was all spruced up in my kilt – a real Highland Soldier! There was a well-known tattooist on Waterloo Bridge, name of Birkett, and a lot of the other chaps, the older soldiers especially, they'd got the regimental badge tattooed on their arm. So when I got to Waterloo Station, I went across the bridge and popped in there and took off my tunic, rolled up my shirt sleeve and got this chap to tattoo the Highland Light Infantry badge on my arm. I got home, proud as Punch in my highland uniform, kilt and everything. I took my tunic off and rolled my sleeves up and was flashing my arm about. My mother caught sight of it and she says, 'What's that you've got on your arm?' I says, quite nonchalant, 'That? That's the Highland Light Infantry badge, same as I wear on my hat.'

I didn't half come down to earth then. My mother laid into me. 'How dare you?' she said. 'How dare you get a thing like that put on your arm! Making yourself common!' I said, 'I'm proud of that badge!' 'I'll give you proud!' she said. And she did too! She gave me a good hiding! She really did. Army or not, soldier or not, Highlander or not, she gave me a damn good hiding! And she kept nagging me about my leave. It was well-known that you got four days before you went abroad. She kept saying, 'Is it draft leave?' Of course I kept saying it wasn't – but she went on and on about it.

All in all, Bill's leave had not come completely up to his expectations. He was not sorry to say goodbye and to set off back to Haddington and the charms of Maggie Gaffney. Maggie was on the station platform two days later when the draft left for France. Almost the whole population had turned out to see the lads go. There were many girls like Maggie who claimed a last clinging embrace before the troops piled into the train, slung their kit and rifles on to the racks and struggled in a ten-deep mass behind the open carriage windows in a concerted, futile attempt to shout individual farewells. The shouts were inaudible. A pipe-band, drawn up in front of the train between the soldiers and the tearful tiptoeing civilians, was playing at the pitch of its breath the plaintive strains of *Will Ye No' Come Back Again?* Such of the civilians as were not entirely overcome, were mouthing the words and were disconcerted when the band droned to a halt in the middle of a bar as the train began to move out of the station. It had hardly moved a yard before it came to a jerking halt.

Now the Sergeant-Major was walking up and down the train and calling at the top of his voice, 'LANCE-CORPORAL TURNER!' At the fourth or fifth call, Bill Turner managed to squeeze his way to the window to answer the summons.

Corporal Bugler William Turner, No. B.21097, 15th Highland Light Infantry (City of Glasgow Corporation Tramways Battalion), 32nd Division.

He said, 'Fetch your kit and your rifle and come on out here.' I still didn't know what was happening, but I got my stuff and got out and he said, 'Come with me!' He took me up to an officer who had some papers in his hand and the officer said, 'Turner? How old are you?' I said, 'Nineteen.' He said, 'Don't tell lies! I've got a letter here from your mother. You're under age. Get your equipment on, and get back to your billet.'

Maggie Gaffney, interrupted in the full flood of an emotional farewell, was unsure whether to laugh or cry. Plodding back, humiliated and ashamed, with the sound of the cheering and the band and the hoot of the train growing fainter behind him, Bill himself could have wept with disappointment. Six months later, when he had wangled his way on to another draft for France, he made very sure that his mother would not have the least suspicion. This time he had missed his chance, and what galled him most was that he had missed it by just two minutes.

Some under-age boys had joined up with the approval of their mothers. In the case of Jim Dwelly the approval had been strictly conditional on his joining a 'safe' unit, and he had dutifully enlisted in the Army Service Corps. In ribald mockery of its initials the ASC was popularly known in the Army as Ally Sloper's Cavalry. Ally Sloper was a fictional character, of dubious behaviour, the blundering hero of a popular comic strip.

In the opinion of the front-line infantry, the ASC led the life of Riley behind the lines. They firmly believed that they had first pick of the rations, unlimited perks, total protection from the attentions of the enemy and, altogether, led a cushy life. But, without the often gruelling labour of Ally Sloper's Cavalry, the infantry could not have been maintained in the trenches for as much as twenty-four hours. It was the ASC who unloaded the supply ships and loaded the provisions on to divisional trains. Behind the lines it was the ASC who came in for most of the dirty jobs and a great deal of very hard work. At the front, delivering supplies to the line, they were exposed to quite as much dangerous shelling and had rather less protection than the infantry in the trenches. Their tasks were manifold, if humble. They were the underdogs of the Army and their theme song was not only plaintive but pathetic:

> *We are the little ASC*
> *We work all night, we work all day.*
> *The more we work, the more we may,*
> *It makes no difference to our pay.*

The tune, like a thousand other Army parodies, was a hymn tune, but unlike many of the others it did not have much of a lilt to it. *We are but little children weak*, possibly had a certain charm when warbled by infant Sunday School voices, but rendered in the deeper tones of Ally Sloper's Cavalry, it was distinctly dirge-like. It hardly mattered that it was not a tune that encouraged men to stride out on the march. The ASC did very little marching and many of them hardly knew how. Like Jim Dwelly, the vast majority had been shipped out to France after a mere three weeks in the Army and, with a hundred thousand infantry to be trained, they had been left largely to their own devices. They had mastered the rudiments of saluting, and very little more.

The most exciting thing that happened to me during the Battle of the Somme was when a sentry-box blew over on the quayside at Boulogne and broke a man's leg. We were down there loading. That was my job at the time, loading up meat – or, rather,

Private J. C. Dwelly, No. 274, Army Service Corps.

supervising the bokes who were loading it, because I couldn't even have lifted one of these huge sides of meat. It was all frozen and it came over by the boat-load, was brought off the ship and dumped on a siding. I had the job of working out the quantities for each division to send it up the line. It would be two thousand pounds of meat for one division and maybe one thousand four hundred and twenty for another, and the quantities were changed every day or two when the divisions were in the line because, of course, they were suffering casualties.

Being there on the Maritime Station we saw a tremendous number of casualties. All that coastline was full of hospitals and there were ambulances driving non-stop past the siding where we were working, taking the wounded to the hospital ships. I felt a bit badly about having a good time in Boulogne. We used to start work at four o'clock in the morning and we were finished by lunchtime and didn't do anything at all for the rest of the day.

I got fed up. I'd only joined the ASC to please my mother and I didn't want to be in it, so I decided to apply for a transfer. So many blokes had been killed that they were asking round all the camps for people who wanted to transfer to a line regiment, so I took my chance.

Jim Dwelly set his sights high. He requested an interview with the Regimental Sergeant-Major at the base camp and announced that he wished to transfer to the Guards. The RSM could hardly conceal his astonishment. He stared at Dwelly in disbelief and said, 'You must be bloody mad!' It was an understandable reaction for the only outward attribute possessed by Dwelly which might remotely qualify him to join the élite of the Army was that he was six feet tall. But quiet persistence had its way. Still marvelling at the very nerve of it, the RSM forwarded Jim's application and it was a moot point which of them was the more astonished when he was accepted by the Grenadier Guards. By the time she found out, his transfer was an accomplished fact, and his mother was slightly mollified by the knowledge that he would spend three months in safety while he trained in England. But, while Jim was waiting for orders to report to the Guards Depot at Caterham, they sent him to the Somme, and to his immense delight they sent him to join up with the Guards.

Private J. C. Dwelly, No. 274, Army Service Corps.

I had to report to the Guards Divisional Headquarters at Maricourt. Of course, I wasn't yet in the Guards officially, but they knew I was going to be transferred, so they thought I might as well be with the Division while I waited for my training. The first night I got there, I was put into a room with no roof to it or anything. It was open to the world, all smashed up with bombs and shells. There were a few other blokes in there and I told one of them I was waiting for a transfer into the Grenadier Guards. He said, 'You must be mad! Why didn't you stop where you were?' I said, 'Well, I got a bit fed up with being in the same place and I just thought it would be a change.' He said, 'You're crackers, mate, you really are!' Looking around me, hearing those shells booming away not so far off, I began to think I must be.

They made me clerk to the Veterinary Officer. They had all their horse lines there and the Veterinary Officer was in charge of any that were sick and I had to keep a record of all the things that went wrong with them, stiff legs, wounds, all sorts of things. And I had to keep a record of the horses that were sent away sick and the new horses that were examined when they came in. I was there all the rest of the time the battle was on and even long after. I didn't get to Caterham until April 1917.[1]

The health of horses was of prime importance and every division had its veterinary officer. The Army depended on horses and by 1916 there were more than half a million on military service in France. They came from America, from South America, and the vast numbers that had been requisitioned in 1914 from farmers and stables in Britain, were constantly being augmented by fresh 'drafts' from home. They came in a variety of sizes, shapes and breeds from the magnificent charger ridden by the Commander-in-Chief, to the humble mule teams pulling field kitchens along the cobbled roads in front of the marching battalions. There were huge draught horses, Clydesdales and Shires, to drag the heavy guns and ammunition waggons. There were fast-moving steeds for the Cavalry and Hussars, good mounts for colonels and senior officers and less refined beasts for other officers who needed transport to get around the countryside in a scattered command. There were humbler but powerful teams of hacks and mules to draw the horse-drawn limbers that were part of the transport column of every battalion. They ran into thousands, for the mountain of supplies which was required to keep the Army in the line was gargantuan.

Ammunition, rations and equipment could be taken as far as the nearest railhead; from there they were transported by motor columns to divisional dumps, but it was then up to the humble horse transport of brigades and battalions to make long cross-country

---

[1] Dwelly successfully passed the rigorous training at the Guards Depot in Caterham, was sent back to France in September 1917 and fought in the Guards until the end of the war.

journeys to fetch and carry back their own supplies of ammunition and rations for men and for horses. Forage was bulky and it caused the officer in charge of horse transport a good deal more trouble to ensure that his horses were well fed than any battalion quartermaster encountered in supplying rations to the men. A soldier could get by on a tin of bully beef, half a loaf and sufficient tea and sugar for a few brew-ups. Depending on its size and the work expected of it, a horse required between sixteen and thirty pounds of forage a day. The daily requirement of each division was thirty tons.

All over northern France blind horses were being put to the plough, for horses were too badly needed to be shot when they became casualties if there was the slightest chance that they would recover and, even if they were no longer of use for Army purposes, a useful deal could be made with French farmers in return for food or forage. Now that it was harvest time on the Somme, the troops as well as the horses were working in the fields, but on a strictly unofficial basis. There were certain commanding officers who, having marched the remnant of a battalion out of the battle to rest and absorb fresh drafts before going in to the fight again, considered that a day spent in a sunny cornfield engaged in healthy and useful activity in the congenial company of civilians, would do his men as much good as the long periods of drill or route marching laid down by the Army.

The troops and the French civilians got on amazingly well and although neither the French peasantry nor the Tommies, on the whole, were skilled linguists most of the soldiers had picked up enough fractured French to make themselves understood after a fashion, although '*No compree*' was probably the most frequently used expression in the pidgin French that served as the *lingua franca*.

The French themselves astutely appreciated the convenience of adopting the Tommies bowdlerised version of their native tongue and had quickly come to understand that a soldier who might be confused by the polite refusal, '*Il n'y a plus, Monsieur*', would certainly get the message of a blunt '*Napoo!*' and reply with a resigned '*San fairy ann*', whose meaning he plainly understood as '*it doesn't matter*' and which came close enough to '*ça ne fait rien*', to be equally understood by the French. It was more practical, too, when a farm had been cleaned out of produce by some ravenous battalion, to scrawl regretfully on the archway of its courtyard '*Napoo doolay. Napoo oofs*,' which was understood by all to mean 'No more eggs. No more milk,' rather than '*Il n'y a plus d'oeufs. Il n'y a plus de lait*,' which would be understood by few. There were occasional misunderstandings. One soldier, anxious to convey his urgent desire to purchase eggs, squatted and strained in elaborate pantomime of a laying hen, and was astonished and embarrassed to find himself conducted to the outside privy.

On the whole, given their limited vocabulary, the troops managed to communicate exceedingly well with their allies. One farmer's wife, hearing the shout, '*Doolay promenade, Madame!*' had no difficulty in understanding that her errant cow had wandered off. More sophisticated attempts at French construction often resulted in blank incomprehension and the soldier who had taken the trouble to study a booklet entitled *What you want to say and How to say it in French* (kindly supplied free of charge by the manufacturers of Wincarnis who also recommended their tonic wine '. . . *for the relief of nerves in the trenches*'!) occasionally found it more difficult to make himself understood than if he had left well alone and stuck to 'Tommies' French'. One was a soldier of the 51st Division whose uncompromisingly Scottish mind had vaguely registered that the complexities of the French language contained both masculine and feminine nouns. It was the Medical Officer, Major Rory, who overheard him exchanging pleasantries with the lady of the house in the yard of a farm not far behind the lines. She was admiring his kilt and fingering the pleats with a Frenchwoman's appreciation of quality. The Jock, a little unsure of her intentions, was anxious to change the subject and, gazing upwards for inspiration, caught sight of an observation balloon climbing slowly into the sky.

'Voilà, Madame! Voilà le sausage!'

Madame did not follow his meaning. The Jock racked his brains.

'Well, voilà *la* sausage then!'

The Labour Battalions, recruited from all over the world, added an exotic touch to the cosmopolitan population which inhabited the French hinterland behind the lines. At the peak of their strength, in late 1916, they numbered three hundred and eighty-seven thousand and, although it was chauvinistically reckoned that it took three foreign labourers to do the work of one European, by undertaking the navvying, road-building and mending, tree-felling and work on the railways – all essential to keep the evergrowing Army in the field – they released several thousand fighting soldiers for service at the front. There were battalions of huge Fijiians and Maoris; there were black labourers from South Africa and, strictly segregated from them, a Cape Coloured battalion. There was a battalion of Egyptian labourers and there was the Indian Labour Corps which had been kept in Europe when the main body of the Indian contingent had been sent to the Middle East, and were dying like flies in the harsh northern climate. There were certain Canadian labour battalions, chiefly working in the forests, where the lumberjacks could hardly keep up with the demand for wood for the trenches, huts and dugouts, for plank roads that could be quickly laid across the mutilated battlefields and for sleepers for the ever-lengthening miles of railway track that carried ever-larger quantities of supplies to the front. There was the Middlesex Labour Company, British in name only, composed of naturalised British subjects, many of German origin, who were not eligible to serve in the fighting ranks of the Army. Most numerous, and most exotic of all, were the Chinese Labour Battalions. They were also the most troublesome, for the large majority of the labourers had been recruited from Chinese prisons, induced by the promise that their sentences would be remitted and that they would be rewarded by untold riches in return for labour on the other side of the world. 'Untold riches' amounted to payment of a franc a day but, by the exercise of oriental wiliness, some of the coolies amassed considerable sums. Thieving and gambling were the most lucrative pursuits and the ones that caused the Provost-Marshal's biggest headache.

Like the other Labour Battalions the Chinese were clustered in camps around Montreuil, and among the camps, the hospitals, the training grounds and Army camps that filled the narrow strip of coastline that ran from Calais to le Havre. The Chinese knew nothing of the war and cared even less. What they did know was that, by the terms of their contract, they were not to be exposed to shell-fire, a clause they were apt to cite when occasionally there was an air raid, demanding extra pay as 'danger money'.

By 1916 there had been so few air raids in the region of Montreuil that it was generally believed an agreement existed. The Germans, it was said, would refrain from bombing the British General Staff if the British refrained from bombing the German Staff – a deal, cynics remarked, in which the Germans came off best both ways. The cynics, however, were mostly to be found in the ranks of the Headquarters troops and Pioneer Battalions attached to them and among the Tommies who, having been fortunate enough to be transferred to the Chinese Labour Corps, found themselves suddenly elevated from under-dogs in the eyes of the Army, to divine personages in the eyes of the Chinese.

Sergeant John Ward, No. 49747, 12th Btn., King's Royal Rifle Corps, and 53rd Company Chinese Labour Corps.

After I was wounded I was reclassified C.3., and sent to a base camp at Etaples, doing office work. One day we were paraded and the officer called out, 'Anybody speak Chinese?' I stepped out of the ranks and he said, 'Right, you can come to my office after you dismiss.' When I got there, he said, 'Is it true you can speak Chinese?' Well, of course, I couldn't speak a word of it, but I was fed up with my job and I thought it would be a change so I said, 'No, sir, to be honest, I can't. But I like languages and Chinese is really one I'd like to master.' He said, 'Bloody sauce!' But after a bit of to-ing and fro-ing he said, 'Well, just for your cheek, I'll transfer you.'

They sent me to a big Chinese camp at Crècy, where there were about seven hundred of them. I was in clover! For every twenty labourers there was a Chinese ganger who really did all the work so far as organising the coolies was concerned, and of course there were interpreters and one or two head-men. And there was quite a number of English NCOs, like myself. We all had batmen! Mine was called Yat-shay-bat-chipa. That wasn't his name. It was his number (14870). None of the Chinese had names, only a brass bracelet with a number on it. The first thing I did was to learn the Chinese for one to ten and it went something like this:–

Yat, Ye, Sam, Shay, Ng, Lok, Chat, Bat, Gow, Sap and *Pa*, which was a hundred. After only about a couple of days I was able to call out a dozen men just by using their number. It falls off your tongue when you know it.

This camp was a convalescent camp for Chinese who had been sick or wounded accidentally and they nearly all suffered from Trachoma – weeping red eyes. But that didn't prevent them from working and we used to send them out in gangs on different jobs every morning – light jobs, mostly, until they had fully recovered.

I had a good time with the Chinese Labour Corps. The only Chinese I ever learned was '*Koydy fidee!*' – and that means 'come on, quick!' They were damned good, hard-working and faithful, if they took to you. But, if they *didn't*, they could slit your throat or do anything. Across from our camp was the 186th Company which was a Prison Company, and all the men in it were under punishment for some crime. They had their own Military Police and they all carried a truncheon.

I was in charge of the Chinese Pay Roll. It was my job to pay them out – a franc a day, but we paid it once a month, so they got thirty francs. That's when there was trouble, when they got all that money. It was a fortune to them! One time we had the office safe broken into and all the money went. No one knew who had done it but of course the Chinese in my own camp had to take the rap for it and I had the unpleasant job of getting all the money back off them. They didn't like it a single bit! Everyone had to pay so much in, because several thousand francs were taken and they all had to contribute to pay it back.

The Chinese were terrible thieves. If I wanted anything at all I just had to mention it to my servant, who spoke a bit of pidgin English, and he'd get it. I never enquired where it came from. But

Private Norman Mellor, No. 41728, 4th Bedfordshire Regiment.

he would never pinch a thing from me. I'd go down in the village
the odd time and get tight. Go back to my hut – I'd got a hut of my
own – and sling my things off and my money would be lying all
over the place and I'd get into bed. Next morning, there he'd be
with a cup of tea and the hut all tidied and not a thing touched.
And then he'd shave me in bed! He'd do anything for me. It was a
life of luxury, and no mistake!

One thing I never ever saw was a drunk Chinaman. Everything
else they'd do, but not drink. They liked money, but they didn't
like spending it. They'd save it all up, and then someone else
would pinch it from them and there'd be trouble over that. Even
murder! The only murder we had in our lot was over a girl. One of
these coolies had taken a fancy to a French girl who served in
some *estaminet*, and he thought one of our Sergeants was just a bit
too friendly with her. So one night he went round when everybody
was alseep and slit open the NCOs' tents until he found this
Sergeant and he bashed his head in. Then he took off! I never
heard whether they caught him for it.

The most notorious murder was at Montreuil and it was a murder
over gambling debts. After that, an edict from GHQ strictly forbade
the Chinese to gamble. GHQ might as well have forbidden them to
breathe. Crouched in circles round every corner, the Chinese played
Fantan by the hour – and working hours, at that! And they bribed
their interpreters to inform the authorities that this was a Chinese
religious observance which must be respected. It didn't work for
long! The only people who seemed to be able to keep the Chinese in
any sort of order were some members of Pioneer Battalions who
convinced the Chinese Labourers that their crossed-axe sleeve
badges, a symbol of their status as skilled tradesmen, proclaimed
them to be official executioners, with the right to summarily chop off
the head of any recalcitrant 'coolie'.

The notorious Chinese Secret Societies had come to Europe with
the Labour Corps. Every coolie had his own 'Tong' and every coolie
was convinced by his Tong leader that a Chinese who died of illness
in a European hospital had been foully done to death. So, it followed
that, when a coolie fell ill, two men went out of action, for the patient
refused to go to hospital unless he was accompanied by a member of
his Tong to see that he got a fair deal and that he came out again.
This was also the aim of the medical authorities, for a dead
Chinaman could be as much of a nuisance as a live one. It was up to
the Chinese themselves to conduct the elaborate funeral rites but it
was up to the authorities to find a suitable place of burial and

'suitability' was spelt out precisely in an official memorandum on the subject of Chinese graves.

> *The ideal site to secure repose and drive away evil spirits is on sloping ground with a stream below, or gully down which water always or occasionally passes. The grave should not be parallel to the north, south, east or west. This is particularly important to Chinese Mahommedans. It should be about four-feet deep, with the head towards the hill and the feet towards the water. A mound of earth about two feet high is piled over the grave.*

It was not always easy to carry out these instructions to the letter for, at the height of the Somme Battle, the Labour Corps as a whole was suffering almost a thousand casualties a month, and many of them were Chinese. Although they were protected from 'war risk' and were therefore not supposed to be employed within shelling distance of the front line, nothing had been said about salvage operations and during August 1916 salvage was a matter of prime importance to the Army. As the troops fought forward, the Pioneer and Labour Battalions followed behind clearing the ground of unexploded ammunition, recovering lost equipment and rifles lying useless on the ground where there had been heavy casualties during an advance. In packing them and sending them back to the base there were many accidents.

There were fifty-thousand rifles lying out on the battlefield. The Pioneers used to go and fetch them in when the conditions permitted it. They came to us in open trucks and we had to clear them quick. I had a fatigue party of half a dozen men. They were all stood up on the truck passing the rifles down a line and, of course, coming straight off the battlefield, there were live rounds left in them. You grabbed them and threw open the bolt – didn't trouble to look at it – there simply wasn't time – and out flew the rounds, all over the place. The fellows in the truck were just throwing them out one after the other. We had two rifles every three seconds, day after day, and we were working flat out. One day I had thirty-two thousand rifles pass through my hands! I worked it out. Four tons, one load. The only vehicles that could take that load of rifles was the Foden steam engine with a very sturdy truck behind it and even with that we had to have a special steel bar made so that the sides wouldn't bulge.

If the rifles were all right, we just tossed them on to this waiting Foden and they went straight off down the line to the workshops, where they were checked for bent barrels and any faults and then

Staff Sergeant James Kain, No. 2282, Army Ordnance Corps.

they would be issued to the troops and straight back up the line. But of course we got badly damaged rifles, bits of rifles, all sorts of things and we packed them all together and put them in crates and took them out to sea and sunk them. Some of the others had tight bolts and you would give it a smash with a hammer to make it fly open, or sometimes the catch wouldn't be strong enough to eject the bullets still in it and one would be stuck live in the breech. Once every three weeks or so, one would go off and of course you'd always had to be sure to turn the breech away from you so that the explosion would blow the other way. There was one fellow killed, and one horse was killed and one fellow had his arm shattered, all through the same thing. But that was all the casualties we had, which was remarkable when you think how many rifles we were handling.

Once or twice a day a fellow would have to come round with a broom and sweep all the live rounds up and tip them into a wooden barrel and, further down the road in a field, were four French ladies and they sat there all day long with a special gadget which they stuck into the cartridge and eventually the bullet came out and fell into a box. They emptied the gun powder into a big barrel and their job was to put all the brass and nickel bullets in separate piles to go back home to be remade. Then, every night, they poured the gun-powder out into a heap in the field, ran a fuse to it and it just went up in a puff of smoke.

Kain was one small cog in the vast machine controlled by the Controller of Salvage at GHQ, known unkindly to his fellow officers as 'Old Rags and Bones' or more succinctly as 'Swill'. It was the responsibility of the Royal Engineers to recover their own miles of telephone cable and to return it to the base where it had to be tediously rewound on to cable drums by the signallers themselves. Almost everything else came under the aegis of 'Swill'.

Clothing was cleaned and repaired, or, if beyond redemption, sent back to the United Kingdom as rags. Entrenching tool heads were cleaned and sharpened. Steel helmets were cleaned and relined if they were whole, or, if too battered and holed, were sold as scrap iron after the chin straps had been removed for sale as old leather. Water-bottles were re-covered with a new felt and supplied with new corks. Webbing equipment was dry-cleaned on motor-driven brushes, darned and repaired by local labour or, if beyond repair, had their metal fittings removed and were sent back to the United Kingdom as cotton rags. Leather equipment and saddlery was washed and treated with fish oil, which was also used to restore suppleness to old boots. Even boots whose useful life was at an obvious end, had their studs removed for scrap metal before they were abandoned.

There was no item in the detritus of battle which was too insignificant to escape the attention of General 'Swill' Gibbs. He ran the Salvage Corps with an almost missionary zeal, in the firm conviction that every recovered horseshoe nail was another nail in the coffin of the Kaiser and he did his best to transmit his enthusiasm to the troops at the front. Soon, battalions coming out of the line were confronted with notices which demanded in peremptory terms: 'WHAT HAVE YOU SALVED TODAY?' The replies of the troops were invariably colourful, if not particularly helpful.

There were cogent reasons for not throwing empty bully beef tins over the parapets of trenches, as careless Tommies were apt to do. It was hardly sanitary. It encouraged flies and rats and, in places where the trenchline had remained static for many months, the clatter of piled up tins in No Man's Land could seriously imperil patrols creeping out under cover of darkness. But a soldier in the fighting line was disinclined to carry his debris with him when he left it, and, even in billets in villages behind the line, it was easier to bury empty tins and bottles than to drag them laboriously to the salvage dump.

The survivors of the July attacks on the Somme, sensing the rapid approach of the day when they would be marching back again, were less inclined than most to concern themselves with the trivia which seemed to them to weigh unduly on the minds of their superiors. In the case of some fortunate battalions, their immediate superiors took the same view and interpreted the periods of drill and fatigues which the Army was pleased to call 'rest' as 'rest' in the civilian sense of the word. Even where a certain amount of route marching and physical training was required to be carried out according to regulations, they organised swimming parades in lieu of PT, and country strolls, thinly disguised as route marches, to pleasant picnic spots or places of interest.

The Colonel of the 1st Queen's Westminster Rifles, whose ordeal by shell-fire at Gommecourt had been followed by a gruelling month of almost uninterrupted fatigues and carrying parties in and out of the trenches, went a little further. The Battalion had had a long slog to get to the back areas. The weather had been intensely hot. Three-quarters of the strength were men newly-arrived to replace the casualties of the First of July and the remainder had done no marching to speak of for a long time. Many of the men had fallen out and Colonel Shoolbred was of the firm and sympathetic opinion that they badly needed a rest. He gave them a whole day off to do nothing but sleep and, if they felt like waking up, to eat. The following day under the guise of the obligatory 'route march' he kindly organised a diversion for his battleworn men. It was a mere stroll, not more than two or three miles along cool forest pathways to the battlefield of Crècy. On its arrival, by prior arrangement with their Colonel, the Battalion was met by a certain Professor Delve, who spent a long time courteously explaining the various points of interest on the field and expounding on the finer points of the battle fought by their predecessors in 1346, nearly six hundred years before. The old hands of the Battalion, who had recently had a little too much of battles, listened bemused. They were, nevertheless, grateful to their Colonel. It was a kindly thought.

Colonel Shoolbred's own superiors had to consider the welfare of the 56th Division as a whole and reports had reached Divisional HQ that the performance of the troops on the march out of the line had not come up to the standard to be expected of a Territorial Division – even one which was diluted by a large proportion of raw troops. It was all very well to be sympathetic to men who had had a rough time in the trenches, but their ultimate objective was to go back to them and, for their own good, the time spent at 'rest' must be used constructively – to reimpose discipline, to embark on a programme of vigorous training that would weld new and old troops into a disciplined whole with due regard to the requirements of the war. There must be no slackness, no matter what the excuse. It was not enough to make the men fit, they must be fighting fit. Divisional Headquarters issued its orders accordingly, and commanding officers were obliged to carry them out and pass them on.

After his mild shell-shock on the First of July, Arthur Agius had been kindly treated by his own Commanding Officer, who had arranged for him to spend the last few weeks pleasantly engaged on a not-too-arduous training course at an Army School at Auxi-le-Château. Now, fit and bronzed and fully recovered, he was back with the 3rd Londons. He had rejoined them in time to get to know the new men of his Company, and to take sad stock of the gaps in its old ranks, before the move back to the Somme. It would be a long hike back to the battle and, on 18 August, Agius received the first indication that their 'holiday' was over.

To OC 'B' Company

MARCH DISCIPLINE

The CO wishes all officers to pay particular attention to march discipline. The men should know that it is a disgraceful thing to fall out on the line of march unless absolutely necessary. Straggling is to be considered an offence.

Company Commanders will see that an officer marches in rear

of their companies who will check all straggling and take the names of any men who fall out.

On arrival at Destination, companies will render to the Orderly Room a list of names of men who have fallen out.

The battalion has always been known as a good marching battalion and the Commanding Officer feels confident that this good reputation will be maintained.

(Signed). R. D. Sutcliffe,
Captain and Adjutant.
3rd London Regiment.

Two days later, as they were literally packing up for the move, another edict arrived from GHQ:

DISCIPLINE

A practice appears to have arisen of one soldier only saluting where more than one are passing an Officer. This practice must cease. When several soldiers pass an Officer, unless they are being marched as a party, they will ALL salute, whether there are NCOs among them or not.

When two or more men are sitting or standing about, and an Officer passes them, the senior NCO or oldest soldier will face the Officer, call the rest to attention and alone salute.

Soldiers will salute in the manner laid down in the training manuals.

Officers must return the salutes of their subordinates with a definite motion of the hand and not perfunctorily. Officers will check lack of discipline in saluting and will report to the unit concerned the names of men who fail to salute them. Such men will be severely dealt with.

(GRO1736, Republished above for compliance
by all ranks, 20 August 1916)

Agius conscientiously clipped both orders to the squared pages of the notebook he reserved for Battalion Orders, but he was not over-worried. He was rather more concerned about what they were marching back to than about discipline on the march itself, but at least he could set an example. The Colonel and the senior officers would be mounted but Agius chose to travel the long road back on Shank's Pony – like the men, on his own two feet.

It was good marching weather. Although there had been rain and storms in the middle of the month, it had turned fine. There was a stiff breeze but on the march that was all to the good and better by far than the heat in the early part of the month which had caused so many men to fall out on the way from the line to the rear. Now, marching back again, they were in better fettle and the spirits of the survivors were high enough to inspire them to sing as they went. The new arrivals were shortly introduced to the Battalion's marching song. Being a familiar music-hall ditty it did not take them long to get into the swing of it and, as the Battalion, now back at full-throated strength, passed through the villages of the Somme to the familiar strains of *I'm 'Enery the Eighth I am*, it seemed almost – but not quite – like old times.

Chapter 17

The colonel of any battalion on the march back to the Somme encouraged the men to sing. It whiled away the time between the hourly ten-minute stops – when one hour could feel like two in the dog days of August to men who marched weighed down by pack and rifle, tin helmets slung under rolled-up greatcoats, through clouds of dust that smarted the eyes and settled in a gritty layer at the back of a thousand parched throats. A song was no balm to a battalion of feet, swelling and sweating in woollen socks and heavy boots; it did nothing to lighten the cumbersome weight of equipment on weary backs, but a good song could lighten the spirits and discourage pensive contemplation when boys were going into battle for a second time, still haunted by all-too-vivid memories of the first.

The Tommies had their own ideas of what constituted a good song, and they seldom coincided with those that people at Home fondly imagined them to be singing as they swung along the roads of France on their way to the fields of battle and to victory. Least of all did they coincide with the ideas of a certain Mr Ainger whose patriotic fervour had inspired him to produce a booklet entitled *Marching Songs for Soldiers set to well-known tunes*. The words were appropriately updated and in every syllable they breathed bellicosity and patriotic intent. For the modest price of one shilling – 'all proceeds devoted to the Belgian Relief Fund' – the *Marching Songs* could be purchased in a full-size edition 'with pianoforte accompaniment' and, in the first months of 1915, it sold in such quantities as to suggest that family musical evenings all over the country were being enlivened by the strains of such ditties as:

> *D'ye ken John French, with his khaki suit,*
> *His belt and his gaiters, and stout brown boot,*
> *Along with his guns, and his horse, and his foot,*
> *On the road to Berlin in the morning.*

The pocket-size edition (price twopence) had outsold the original several times over and, lovingly tucked into parcels by mothers, sisters and sweethearts, each anxious to lift the spirits of her own particular warrior, the songbooks had arrived in France by the

thousand. On the whole, the songs had not caught on. Few battalions of Tommies were to be heard marching to the ringing words:

> *To arms! To arms! We bring the Jubilee.*
> *To arms! To arms! The Flag that calls the Free.*
> *For the right the foe to smite alike by land and sea,*
> *While we go marching to Germany!*

Marching, if not directly to Germany, at least back to face Germany's soldiers on the battlefield of the Somme, even if the words
had not seemed a trifle inappropriate, the strains of *Marching through
Georgia* did not exactly fit the Tommies' stolid progress across the
miles of 'marching easy' that carried them eastwards. Slower, more
lugubrious melodies fitted the pace and were more attuned to their
mood. *John Brown's Body* was a favourite, although Mr Ainger, who
had matched the melody to his favourite theme (*'Belgium has been
harried with fire and with sword . . .'*) might have been pained to hear
the less elegant version preferred by the troops:

> *John Brown's baby's got a pimple on its bum,*
> *John Brown's baby's got a pimple on its bum,*
> *John Brown's baby's got a pimple on its bum,*
> *And the little bugger can't sit down.*

He would not have been alone in his disapproval. The Commander-
in-Chief himself took a priggish interest in the songs warbled by his
now largely youthful army. It was rumoured that General Haig
found even the official version of *Mademoiselle from Armentières*
offensive to his well-bred ears, even though it had already become
popular in the most respectable circles at Home. The Tommies,
however, preferred the infinite variations of less respectable ver-
sions, and the younger soldiers, in particular, newly drafted to
France and into the ranks of the fighting battalions were first aghast,
then amazed, then – in most cases – delighted at the bawdy free-
masonry of which they had so suddenly and felicitously become a
part. Some schoolboy faces, unable to cast off the shibboleths of
their rigid and sheltered upbringing, blushed, stayed silent and, as
hymn tunes had been so frequently adopted to accompany words
that were less than religious in feeling, worried on occasion that the
whole blasphemous battalion might be struck down by an avenging
thunderclap from Above.

General Haig was more concerned with moral tone than with
avenging thunderclaps. No battalion would have ventured to march
to a ribald song within miles of his headquarters. No colonel within a

considerable radius of any spot where there was a likelihood of meeting a staff officer would have allowed his battalion to march, even in the heat of an August day, with tunics undone and shirt buttons loosened and still less would he have relieved his own sweltering discomfort by replacing his stiff army hat with a khaki handkerchief knotted at each corner in the style of a day-tripper to the beach at Southend. It was unfortunate for one particular Battalion marching towards the Somme that it happened to present precisely this appearance as it passed through a village where a senior Ordnance Officer had his headquarters. It was unfortunate that the Commander-in-Chief, concerned about supplies of ammunition for the coming Push, should have been visiting the Ordnance HQ in person – unfortunate too that the Battalion should have been in full vocal flood and rendering a particular chorus compared to which the bawdiest version of *Mademoiselle from Armentières* might have been considered a suitable serenade for a maiden aunt:

> *Do your balls hang low?*
> *Do they dangle to and fro?*
> *Can you tie them in a knot?*
> *Can you tie them in a bow?*

They had reached the fourth line before the full sense of the words got through to the Commander-in Chief. It got worse, as he listened:

> *Do they itch when it's hot?*
> *Do you rest them in a pot?*

He crossed to the window and stared in disbelief as the unwitting Battalion shambled past. 'Just as I thought,' he said. 'It's the rear companies! Fetch my horse!'

The Battalion straggled, easy marching, over almost a mile of road. By the time Sir Douglas Haig had mounted and started to trot up the long column, they had started all over again, this time in harmony, for the beauty of their favourite tune was that it could be sung in parts.

> *Do you get them in a tangle?*
> *Do you catch them in the mangle?*
> *Do they swing in stormy weather?*
> *Do they tickle with a feather?*

One by one, as the marching platoons spotted the unmistakable upright figure of their Commander-in-Chief trotting purposefully past to reach the head of the Battalion, their voices trailed away into embarrassed silence. But the men at the head of the column were still lustily singing.

> *Do they rattle when you walk?*
> *Do they jingle when you talk?*

The Colonel had a fine voice. Riding in front of his Battalion, he was singing louder than any of his men – so loudly that he either failed to notice the falling-off of the merry chorus behind him or, putting it down to fatigue, sang louder than ever to encourage his men across the last lap of the hour's march. Just as General Haig caught up with him, he had flung back his handkerchiefed head and was bawling in a rousing, oblivious crescendo:

> *Can you sling them on your shoulder*
> *Like a lousy fucking soldier?*
> *DO YOUR BALLS HANG LOW?*

Haig had to shout to make himself heard. 'I must congratulate you on your voice, Colonel!'

The unfortunate Colonel could only stare back open-mouthed, fumble at his unbuttoned tunic, call the Battalion to march to attention and, as an afterthought, snatch the handkerchief from his head.

'No, no!' Haig raised his hand. 'The men may march easy.' With the last of his voice the Colonel croaked the command. Haig, on his great black charger, a full hand higher than the Colonel's horse, trotted beside him and bent down for a private word in the Colonel's ear, but his orderly, riding just behind, heard – and later reported – every word.

'I like the *tune*,' he said, 'but you must know that in any circumstances those words are inexcusable!'

The discomfited Colonel, having now replaced his hat, managed to salute but before he could stammer an apology Haig was gone, with a final nod of rebuke, trotting back past the chastened Battalion to resume his interrupted business. It was a full five minutes before anyone broke the silence. Then, a wag halfway down the column dared to introduce another song. It was a song beloved by their virtuous Victorian grandmothers and he sang in notes of pure innocence:

After the ball was over. . . .

The Battalion exploded. Those of them who were capable of singing took up the refrain. Even the Colonel had to laugh.

In the summer of 1916 soldiers going on leave discovered that London was wriggling, Latin-style, to the strains of *La Cucuracha* and dancing soulfully to *I ain't got Nobody* . . . but the song that struck the mood of the moment was *Roses of Picardy*:

> *Roses are shining in Picardy,*
> *In the hush of the silvery dew,*
> *Roses are flow'ring in Picardy,*
> *But there's never a rose like you. . . .*

In Picardy itself the song was not unpopular. In the dusky August evenings it echoed tinnily through a thousand barnyards from the gramophones of a thousand sentimental young officers who never tired of listening to it, hands clasped behind their heads as they lay on some makeshift bed, thinking, remembering, dreaming of some real or imagined 'Rose' waiting in a world far removed from the smelly discomforts of the real Picardy they now inhabited where the noise of battle grumbled and roared round the horizon. But the romantic appeal of the song was irresistible and it was a smash-hit at every concert.

At more makeshift entertainments, where a clutch of soldiers out of the line sat together in a barn or *estaminet*, whiling away an evening with talk and stories and with the occasional song to the quavering accompaniment of a mouth organ, a new mythology of song and doggerel was growing up. There was a verse-smith in most battalions and, although their rough and ready efforts were seldom destined to be included in post-war anthologies, the boys liked them and listened intently as long-ago warriors might well have listened to the 'Odes of Horace', or a Viking Saga, with the feeling that it was their own history, their own experiences that were being immortalised and, to an extent, honoured.

Recovering from their ordeal at High Wood, the remnants of the Church Lads Brigade were particularly struck by the effort of their particular bard. In a sense he was anonymous, because by the time the verses had been passed round the Battalion and almost every man had scribed out a copy in his own handwriting, no one could remember who had composed them in the first place:

There's a Battalion out in France
Its name was spread afar.
And if you want to know its name
It's the 16th KRR.
They trained for months at Denham
Which made every man quite fit
Then on 16th November
They embarked to do their bit.
The ride it was fairly long
And I'm sure it was no treat.
For the only food that we could get
Was biscuits and bully beef.

Now the first time in the trenches
It was not so very bad,
But on the second of January
A lively time we had.
The shells flew all around us,
Yes, there were many a score!
And the only shelter we could find
Was to lay flat on the floor.

Of course, you know, we lost a few,
Which I am sorry to say,
But we will have our own back
On the Allemands one day.
Since then we've seen the trenches,
Yes many and many a time,
And some of our dear comrades
Got buried by a mine.

And then we went into High Wood.
Of that I cannot speak.
We lost the flower of our flock.
It left us sad and weak.
But still we have to carry on,
Of work we do our share
And unless we have an R.E. fatigue
You seldom hear us swear.

Now when the War is finished
And we return once more,
If they take us back to Denham
There will be a treat in store.
But we shall not forget the lads
That we have left behind,

And we all hope they will rest in peace
Where the sun will always shine.

Now here's good luck to all of us
No matter where we are,
For we know the name will never fade
Of the 16th KRR

To the Church Lads Brigade, High Wood was just part of the saga of the Battalion's collective History. But the 6th Wiltshires, with the memory of their ordeal at la Boisselle still searing their minds, wrote a Battle Song, and Roy Bealing, who had the 'voice' of his platoon, usually led the singing:

T'was on the first day of July,
In the year Nineteen Sixteen
When the Germans held some trenches
And to take them we did mean.
We started with Artillery,
Two thousand guns or more,
And then the lads of the Infantry
Went over with a roar.
And side by side they fought their way
And side by side they fell,
Did those gallant lads of the Infantry
For the Battle of la Boisselle.

High Wood, la Boisselle, like Thiepval, Beaumont Hamel, Serre and Contalmaison, were in the past. Another name had moved into the forefront of the epic of the Somme where, since the beginning of the month, the troops had been pitting the weight of their effort against the citadel of the Germans' second line at Guillemont.

August. High summer on the Somme, but the sounds of summer were lost behind the warring of the guns. Only one insistent sound vied with the thud of the drumming bombardments – the incessant humming of bluebottles, sated and fat as pigs, preying on the bodies of the dead and hovering above them in black droning swarms, so that in places they seemed to blot out the sky itself.

The bluebottles buzzed everywhere. They infested the trenches. They clung in infuriating clouds around the heads of the men, entered the noses, eyes and ears of soldiers who lay asleep, settled in thousands over sandbags containing rations. Swarms of bluebottles hung permanently above makeshift latrine-saps in a sinister, give-away cloud that was as good as a signpost to any alert sniper who merely had to set his sights beneath them, keep his eyes peeled for the flicker of movement that caused the swarm to disperse momentarily, and squeeze the trigger. An efficient marksman could bag up to a dozen luckless soldiers in the course of one patient day and there was no means of avoiding the danger for, by August, all the troops had diarrhoea. The flies carried the pestilence, alighting on the carrion of the bloated dead, breeding on the decaying flesh and hatching fresh generations to prey in their turn on every crumb of food a soldier ate and to cling and crawl round the rims of tin mugs sticky with the vestiges of a dozen or more brews of strong sweet tea.

In the line a man had precious little chance of washing his face, let alone his mug. In the heat of August, fresh divisions moving up to the line, through the carnage and debris of July, had found the lack of water almost the worst thing to bear. Water-bottles were filled every morning with foul-tasting chlorine-treated water, but they were soon emptied. Later in the month, when sudden thunderstorms turned the shell-holes into stagnant pools, troops in the reserve trenches were tempted to crawl out to augment their meagre water ration. This activity was strictly forbidden and, rightly, because gas had permeated the shell-holes and, floating up through the rainwater, it lay in a green, lethal scum on the surface. The troops were well aware of the danger but some, tantalised beyond endurance, were willing to take the risk. The technique was to lower a mess-tin into the water with the upper half clamped tight-shut, to slip it off just far enough to fill the tin with unpolluted water, and replace the lid before lifting it out again. The boys became adept at this trick and there were only a few casualties from stomach upsets and, occasionally, inadvertent gassing.

Signaller W. H. Shaw, No. 12774, 9th Battalion, Royal Welsh Fusiliers, 58th Brigade, 19th Division.

I managed to put twelve signallers in hospital when we were out on reserve. Our cook was away for some reason, so I volunteered to do the cooking. I managed to 'find' a bag of flour lying hear a certain officers' mess, and some currants and sultanas had come up with the rations, so I decided to give the lads a treat by making a plum duff. We had a bit of sugar and a bit of bacon fat so I mixed it all with the flour and a tin of condensed milk. Then came the question of boiling it. We weren't short of water but the hand of the NCO, who put the chlorine in it, was so heavy that sometimes it just wasn't possible to use it. This was one of the times! So I went out scouting and came across a shell-hole filled with lovely clear water. But, it was a well known fact that all water had to be purified and so I filled my big dixie with water and gave the water a good boil up, then I got hold of a clean sandbag, dumped the pudding into it, tied the top well round with string and boiled it up for hours, hoping for the best but, alas, all my precautions were of no avail. The lads thoroughly enjoyed their unexpected treat but, two hours later, they were all groaning and holding their stomachs and the air was blue with them telling me what they thought of my cooking! I was in just as bad a state myself, because we'd all made pigs of ourselves. The Medical Officer was sent for and he took one look at us and packed us off to the nearest First Aid station. What a scene that was! They had to use stomach pumps on the lot of us – and none too soon either. It was gas! A gas shell had made contact with that particular shell-hole, and after our CO had made contact with *me*, I lost my job as cook!

We were only in hospital for a few days, but, if the lads had carried out what they said they wanted to do to me, I'd have been there for months! But, unpleasant though it was, it was a relief to get out of the line for a bit – even the reserve line. It was only days since I'd been in Mametz Wood when the rations came up and I was standing, holding a loaf of bread in my hands, just about to divide it out, when it was shot to pieces – just crumbled and disappeared! It was a miracle that I wasn't hit myself, and I suppose the loaf saved me, but it gave me a very nasty turn.

In the early days of August it was the 55th Division which was bearing the brunt of the battle. At the beginning of the month they had moved into trenches in front of Guillemont and it was on Guillemont that the attention of the Command was now focussed. The shattered village of Guillemont, its ruins strengthened and fortified as strongly as any front-line positions of a month before, lay a thousand yards beyond the splintered vestiges of Trones Wood on the road that had once led from Mametz to Combles, with Delville Wood away to the left of Guillemont and the tiny village of Ginchy at the apex of a triangle between them.

The line had changed little since the middle of July and from Serre to Thiepval it had changed not at all since Kitchener's Army had broken its back against its granite strength on the first day of the battle. A great bite had been gnawed out of the Leipzig Redoubt. The Australians were in tenuous possession of Pozières village. Contalmaison and the Bazentins had gone. But, beyond them, High Wood held out as obdurately as ever and, despite the valiant efforts of the troops who had gained the greater part of it, a lethal rim still held by the enemy around the edge of Delville Wood stood like a wall of iron between them and the Switch Line. On the road from Delville Wood to Guillemont two unremarkable landmarks of peacetime (a sugar beet factory and, a little further on, the sleepy tramway halt they called Guillemont Station, a lane's length away from the outskirts of the village) were still bristling defiantly behind thickets of barbed wire – links in the menacing chain of defences that lay in formidable strength beyond the British line.

The British line ended just beyond Guillemont and beyond stood the French, cramped into an uncomfortably narrow echelon. Unless Guillemont fell and Ginchy with it, the French could not move. It was no longer a case of breaking the line, but of breaking the impasse, giving the French room to breathe and preparing the way for a concerted push over a wider front. This was the dearest desire of the French General Joffre. General Fayolles, on the other hand, who commanded the force that was jammed into the bottleneck between Guillemont and the River Somme, was rather more concerned that the British should help to relieve the pressure on his immediate area and the British Commander-in-Chief was on his side.

The first priority, as Haig saw it, was 'to help the French forward' by attacking Guillemont and Ginchy in a combined operation, carefully prepared and planned. 'Preparation' meant bombardment and, since the 55th Division had moved into the line, its artillery had been ceaselessly pounding the German trenches and the Germans had been retaliating with indiscriminate bombardments of their own. They were directed against the British gun batteries and also against the unfortunate infantry as they waited eight long days for the attack.

Gunner George Worsley, No. 690452, C Bty., 276 Brigade, R.F.A. (2nd West Lancashire Brigade), 55th Divisional Artillery.

The night we took over we had a terrible time going up the line. There was a tremendous bombardment going on and we were getting nearer and nearer to it. We had to move into a gun position to the right of Trones Wood, alongside the road, with Guillemont just in front and the battery we were taking over from was firing right up to the last minute. Then they pulled out and we pulled in and started firing. We only had five guns to fire with, because even before we started one gun was knocked out. I was in the Signallers' dugout, so I didn't see it, but we heard the shell exploding and saw a stretcher being carried past. A little while later, we got a signal through from Dublin Trench. It said *Please send down a burial party at once to 1/3 West Lancashire Field Ambulance Regimental Aid Post* and it was signed by the Medical Officer of the 277 Brigade, a Major Reilly. It was naïve of him really. But it was his first night in there and he probably didn't realise the situation. We had no one to spare to send a burial party for one man! When the daylight came, there were bodies all over the place – bloated bodies, they hadn't been able to clear away. The guns were literally wheel to wheel and we were firing, firing, firing twenty-four hours a day. There were gun lines everywhere – a continuous row of them. There was no end to them – and all of them were firing almost non-stop, right round the clock.

It began to get on your nerves after a while. It wasn't so much that we were being shelled – although we were, because the Germans used to put over these big 5.9 shells and then they'd follow them up with shrapnel shells to catch anyone who was running away. But what really began to get me was the sound of our own guns. The sound waves were going over your head all the time, like a tuning fork being struck on your steel helmet. A terrible sound – ping, ping, ping, ping – this terrible vibration day and night and this noise in your head, just like a tuning fork being rung again and again. It went right through you. You couldn't get away from it. It went right down into your nerves.

On the 8th, the infantry went for Guillemont and the French attacked simultaneously on their right on a front that stretched across the valley to the high spur and beyond that to the River Somme. Just as they had done on the morning of the First of July the two armies went forward shoulder to shoulder. But this time they did not sweep all before them. The French edged forward on their right but, where their line met the British, they were stopped by a hail of enfilade fire. In spite of attacking with two divisions ranged against the short line on either side of Guillemont, in spite of a week's backbreaking work digging advanced trenches for the jump-off, in spite of a carefully planned protective barrage, the German bombardment had stopped the British soldiers in their tracks. A few gallant parties, pitifully small, broke through and were annihilated by storms of machine-gun bullets, streaming from Waterlot Farm, from Guillemont Station, and from the trenches that stretched in front of the village itself. The whole débacle was horribly reminiscent of the attack at Serre just five weeks earlier and the lessons which had been learned there seemed already to have been forgotten. Once again the 'supporting' barrage went ahead in a series of predetermined lifts in accordance with a rigid timetable. Once again no messages came back. Once again the infantry attacked with all the panoply of visual communications, bearing on their backs those shining markers, the cut-out diamonds of tin that would glint in the sun as they made their way forward, carrying the flares that would signal their position to patrolling aeroplanes.

But there was no sun. There were no aeroplanes. There was mist – heavy, thick mist that mingled with the smoke and fumes of the crashing bombardment and swirled and clung round the infantry in a blinding suffocating curtain as impenetrable as the German line itself.

Later, when darkness fell, when the reliefs came up and the remnants of the shattered battalions stumbled back to the rear to lick their wounds, to hold scratch roll calls, to make the first sickening estimates of how many of their number had been killed or wounded or were missing, the rumour began to spread that, in the mist and confusion, two British battalions had attacked each other.

The bombers of the 5th King's Liverpools had somehow managed to work their way forward, had somehow managed to capture a length of trench, but they were sharing it with the Germans. They blew in part of the trench to block the passage and somehow managed to hold on. They called it Cochrane Alley, and its capture was the only real gain of the day. Some troops had managed to penetrate the field of heaped-up rubble that once was Guillemont village, where – as at Thiepval, as at Ovillers, la Boisselle, Pozières and Beaumont Hamel – every tumbled ruin concealed a warren of deep dugouts and fortifications. Sure of their own terrain, German reserves attacked through the mist and the smoke and the British battalions were overwhelmed. They could ill be spared, for these were no amateurs, no lambs sent in the innocence of inexperience to the slaughter. The 8th King's were the Liverpool Irish, like the rest of their brigade, hard-fighting, experienced Territorials. The 1st King's were Regulars and they had been in France since the first days of the war.

The 8 August was a black day and an inauspicious day for the King's arrival in France. Sir Douglas Haig would have liked dearly to show him a victory.

The King had reached Boulogne by destroyer in the same morning mist that enveloped the troops attacking at Guillemont and motored to Montreuil where he lunched at GHQ before driving on to Haig's advanced headquarters at Beauquesne. The Commander-in-Chief was waiting to receive him with his mounted escort of the 17th Lancers and a guard of honour of fifty Artists' Rifles. The two men were old friends. Ten years earlier while on leave from India Douglas Haig had met and, after an uncharacteristically whirlwind courtship, had married Miss Dorothy Vivian who was Maid of Honour to Queen Alexandra and a close connection of the Royal Family. The wedding had been held in the private chapel at Buckingham Palace, graciously offered by the King and Queen, who were delighted to see their protegée marry a distinguished soldier whom King Edward held in high regard.

The intimacy had continued into the next reign and now, after inspecting the troops drawn up to await him, after exchanging courtesies when the General presented his Staff, King George V was anxious to broach a subject which he suspected might be troubling the mind of the Commander of his armies. It was 4.30 in the afternoon. The two men repaired to Haig's writing room and tea was brought.

The Commander-in-Chief gave the King a general outline of the situation along the front, touching on Guillemont, where Cochrane Sap was still being held, where some troops were reported to be in the village and more were holding out round Guillemont Station.

If the attack had not been an overwhelming success, the scant information which had reached GHQ gave no reason to suppose that it was a total failure either. It was, after all, only a local engagement designed to assist the French – and the matter was still not concluded. Fresh troops of the Reserve Battalions would be attacking again tomorrow. They might well succeed. Short of omniscience Haig could hardly have given more information.

The King had confidence in his Commander-in-Chief, but, like Haig, he was subject to the Government. Already there had been rumblings in the Cabinet, but it was an outsider, Winston Churchill, who was causing the most trouble, and the King was furious.

Churchill had written a carefully considered paper criticising the whole conception of the Somme offensive and, weighing the awful cost of losses against gains measured in yards rather than miles, against stalemate rather than advance, and against the grand strategy which had been swept away on a tide of bloodshed, he had concluded that little or nothing had been achieved and questioned the wisdom of continuing what he saw as a vain sacrifice of life and endeavour for what appeared to be no forseeably fruitful result. Churchill had circulated the paper to every member of the War Cabinet and the Cabinet had been just sufficiently perturbed to make polite enquiries of the Commander-in-Chief as to his intentions. That very day (although Haig had penned his answer on 1 August) his reply was being read to the War Committee by Sir William Robertson. The occasion was recorded in the Minutes:

> The C.I.G.S. read a letter from General Sir Douglas Haig dated August 1st, giving his appreciation of the general military situation, more particularly as affected by the offensive of the Allies on the Somme. It was agreed that the C.I.G.S. should circulate it to the Cabinet.
>
> It was further agreed that the C.I.G.S. should send a message to General Sir D. Haig assuring him that he might count on full support from home.
>
> (August 8th)   War Office

The following day Sir Douglas would have the gratification of receiving that message. In the meantime he had the natural gratification of hearing the King express the utmost personal confidence in him and the very human satisfaction of hearing him refer to Churchill and his 'cabal' at length and in terms of robust disapprobation which entirely coincided with the General's own opinion. Thus fortified and encouraged Haig bowed his monarch off the premises to be driven off to a château near St Pol forty kilometres to the north, well away from the battle zone and behind the 'quiet sector' at Arras.

This billeting arrangement had not in the least suited the King who, short of running the unconstitutional risk of going into the actual firing zone, was anxious to get as near the battle as possible. A message from Buckingham Palace, a day or so before his arrival, had made this fact plain and had asked for a change to be made. But Haig had quietly insisted that the present arrangement should stand. He confided his annoyance to his diary:

Extract from the diary of General Sir Douglas Haig.

Friday, 4 August: A château in the area of the battle further south is desired. These courtiers at home evidently do not realise the congestion of troops and the dust on the roads when fighting is in progress.

Even miles back from the line, with the constant movement of troops, of long slow cavalcades of transport, of speeding despatch riders and powerful staff cars carrying supplies and ammunition, the roads were a nightmare of flying chalk, grit, dust and eternal sweating hold-ups. And, all along the roadsides, the spectral dust-covered figures of Pioneer troops and sullen patient German prisoners leaned on shovels as they waited for a gap in the traffic which would let them resume the endless task of repairing surfaces which, as fast as they worked, were ground back in the same old shambles of ruts and potholes with every passing day.

Beyond the old front line where battered tracks ran across land that had been wrested from the enemy, the shambles reached horror proportions. There were miles of abandoned trenches, pounded almost out of recognition. There were old artillery positions surrounded by mountains of empty shell cases that advertised the weight of fire thrown back at the Germans. There were live shells too, the duds that had failed to explode and they lay in disturbing quantities wherever the plodding battalions looked. There were shattered limbers, dead mules, tumbled mounds that once were villages, splintered sticks that once were woods. And there were the dead.

I was a driver. I'd been a driver before the war, and a fitter as well. I had a licence but, in those days, it didn't matter if you didn't have any legs on, if you didn't have any arms or even any eyes, if you wrote up for a driving licence and sent five shillings you got one.

I joined up in 1915. There was an offer advertised in the papers – six shillings a day for drivers and fitters if they joined the Army. Well, the Tommy was only getting a shilling a day, and if I joined up I knew I'd get my choice of job. But if conscription came in, that would be that! It wasn't just the money. I wanted to go into something where I didn't need to use a gun.

It was all right until the Somme got really bad. We were running from a village just outside Doullens, and we had twenty-four lorries parked in the main street. We used to run the rations up to the line, or as near as we could get. We used to help the Tommies too, because there was a tremendous number of troops going up. And one of the worst jobs I used to have was when a division was going up (they were marching up of course) and we would relieve them of their blankets, so that they wouldn't have to carry them. Well, they was all rolled up and it wasn't a case of, 'This is my blanket, that's your blanket.' You got a blanket and it didn't matter whose it was when you got to the end of your journey. Of course these were all stuffed into my lorry until it was completely full. It wasn't so much a lorry full of blankets as a lorry full of lice! We were all covered. They were all over us! And that happened again and again.

I was attached to the motor transport department of the Army Service Corps and it was mainly supplies we were taking up to the dumps. We used to load up in the afternoon and deliver in the morning and there was every kind of thing we had to carry – including food and stuff for the horses and mules, because the horse transport was further up the field than we were. One day you would load up with coal for the cooks to cook the meals with. The next day, perhaps, you would be on tinned stuff. That was all in boxes. Next day you would be on hay. If you got that you were well away because we had to sleep on our lorries after we'd loaded up – sleep literally on top of the load. One night we had frozen sides of beef!

There were so many casualties that they kept trying to run the ambulances up nearer and nearer the line and these ambulances kept breaking down or they got damaged by shelling or knocked out. But the further the ambulance could get up to the line, the better it was for the wounded men, so they decided that they would have an advanced workshop and, being a fitter, I was sent up to it. It was at Mametz – an old barn that was more hole than

Corporal O. W. Flowers, No. 133480, Motor Transport Section, Army Service Corps.

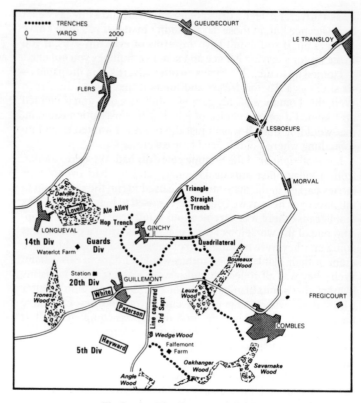

The Battle of Guillemont and Ginchy

wall – and it wasn't a case of the ambulances coming in there, we had to go up to fetch them. I was running to Guillemont, just to the right of Delville Wood.

There was no road at all – neither road nor anything else! It was a track for the ambulances and I don't remember ever seeing another lorry other than my own. They were all a lot further back. Well, there were horses, mules, men, bodies strewed all over the place. If ever hell was let loose, it was let loose then. A few of those nights I went out I used to dread going, not so much because of the danger to myself but because I didn't know what damage I was doing to other people. You couldn't see them. It was too dark. Sometimes a Very light would go up and it would just give you a glimmer of light, for a second or two, and then it was out. But by that time it was too late. You'd gone over somebody. I don't know how many people I may have killed with the lorry, but I'd known

Left: Death Valley and, running away from it on the right, Caterpillar Wood and valley. It was the only sheltered route to the line as the fighting progressed and the ground still shows the battering it received from the passage of troops and guns.

Below: Looking across to Longueval and Delville Wood from the corner of Trones Wood on the road to Guillemont. The tower-like building in the centre is Waterlot Farm (now a sugar-beet refinery) and the rebuilt Guillemont Station is on the right. Since the railway track has been abandoned it is once again falling into ruins.

After the War the deep dugouts and galleries the Germans had burrowed into the depths of the chalky uplands of the Somme were filled up with the debris and rubble of the ruined villages and the entrances levelled. But this one at Guillemont was overlooked. The kennel-like concrete entries, close to the earth, lead steeply down to a double-chambered German command post, once part of a more extensive underground system.

The remains of a machine-gun post in the Triangle, attacked by the 6th West Yorks. on 3rd September, still looks across the fields to their jumping-off line on the edge of Thiepval Wood.

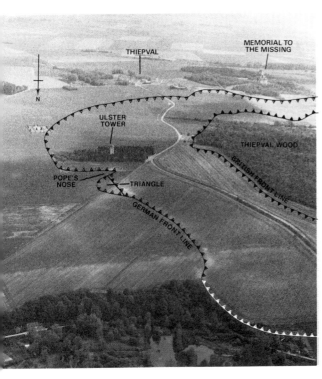

This panorama of the Ancre Valley and the Thiepval Ridge clearly shows the area where the West Yorks. attacked from the edge of Thiepval Wood on 3rd September, and both the Pope's Nose (although the trees surrounding the Ulster Tower mask part of its area) and the infamous Triangle can still be picked out by their outlines on the ground. (*Photograph Richard Dunning*)

The first message to be transmitted by the 1st Anzac Wireless section, under the command of George Middle, during the battle for Pozières.

The statue of Sir Douglas Haig at Montreuil-sur-le-Mer which was British General Headquarters from 1916 to 1919. The statue was destroyed by the occupying German army in 1940, re-erected after the War and narrowly escaped destruction for a second time when extracts from Sir Douglas Haig's private papers were published in 1952 and what were deemed to be uncomplimentary references to the French Army received wide publicity in the French newspapers, caused a national scandal and violent demonstrations by groups of *anciens combattants* demanding the removal of the statue. The row was smoothed over by the Mayor of Montreuil (the same Raymond Wable who, as a schoolboy, had seen Haig in Montreuil during the War) and the statue still stands today in the market square in front of the old Theatre which was the Army's telephone exchange and main communications centre. As an extra precaution there were duplicated lines in a deep dungeon in the Citadel.

A view of the land between and beyond Ginchy and Guillemont, the scene of the September fighting.

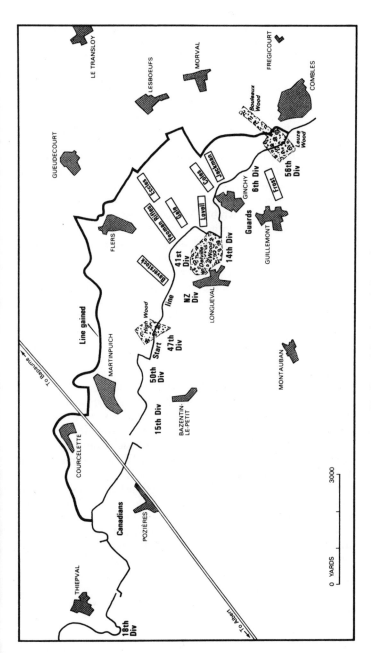

The General Attack on 15th September

I'd gone over them because I'd felt the bump. I didn't hear screams, and I tried to cool myself down with the fact that I'd have heard them if they'd yelled out. I tried to cool myself down with the idea that they must have been dead when I went over them.

Up there at Guillemont it didn't matter where men dropped, they just stayed there with nobody to pick them up. It was days and days before anybody dared to go out to pick them up and bury them. The bodies were piling up all the time, piling up by the roadside.

One particular night it was a real horror. I was going towards Delville Wood, and what a bombardment there was! There were ever so many ambulances knocked out. They were little ambulances, Tin Lizzies, and they only held two or three wounded, but they were very manoeuvrable. You could just swing your tow rope round the axle and loop it over your hook and away they'd go. Some had tyres blown off and some even had a wheel blown off and I've many a time towed one with three wheels on. (You could do it with a Ford as long as you changed the weight so that there's no one on the side where the wheel's come off.) But that night!

Quite a few ambulances had had a direct hit and we couldn't do much about those, but some of the others had been pretty well splintered with shrapnel and the wounded men they'd put inside had been wounded again after they'd been put in the ambulance. When you looked inside you got the shock of your life! All we could do was load them into the lorry, try and get them back as quick as you can, because this shelling's going on all the time. When we got back there were five dead in the lorry and the lorry floor was swimming with blood. We made six runs that night towing in ambulances and taking these poor wounded chaps out of the ones we couldn't shift. When I got back from the last run, my mates in the advanced workshop, said, 'What's the matter with you? You look like a ghost!'

I simply couldn't speak. It was a long time before I could speak, I was so terrified. Once we'd handed the wounded over I just crawled into the lorry and lay on the floor and went to sleep. The following morning my uniform was soaked in blood, sodden with it. They had to give me a new one. I looked at it and I can remember thinking, 'If the British people could see what I've seen and experience what I experienced last night, this war would stop. They wouldn't have it!'

I've never been able to stand the sight of blood since. If I prick my finger, I feel sick, even after sixty-five years and more.

The next night, when I had to go up, my heart was in my mouth every foot of the journey – driving in the dark all the time, not knowing where you were going, not knowing what you were hitting. But you just had to do it. You know it's your duty. It has to be done and there's men there that may be in the ambulance and we had to get those ambulances back. It was as simple as that. They were going down by the hundred. It was a blood bath, running up to Guillemont. It was a terror. And the shelling never ceased.

The Germans were shelling indiscriminately behind the immediate front line with far less accuracy of registration on distant targets (as they themselves admitted) than the British. During the Battle of the Somme the Royal Flying Corps exulted in the fact that it 'had the sky to itself' and it was only a slight exaggeration. Far above the duelling guns, the fliers of both sides were duelling in the air in a battle of quite another kind. Few German reconnaissance planes got far behind the British lines without being challenged by a buzz of British fighters swooping in pursuit like a swarm of angry bees and, far above the battle, soundless and graceful as kites, the fighting machines soared and dipped, circled and manoeuvred and were cheered to the echo by watchers below when a burst of flame, a spiralling stream of smoke, signified a kill.

No one greeted a kill with more enthusiasm and relief than the men who were the eyes of the guns, the Observers, swinging lonely in fragile baskets beneath the gas-filled balloons riding cloud-high behind the British lines. They were particularly vulnerable to attack from the air. One burst of machine-gun fire, even a well-aimed rifle shot, could destroy the balloon in a fiery explosion that sent its cable whiplashing to earth and its observer to Kingdom Come.

British reconnaissance planes flying with fighter escorts behind the German lines were not allowed to go about their business entirely unmolested but they managed, to a far greater degree than the enemy, to produce vast quantities of photographs of fine definition which, even taken from high altitude, pinpointed with extraordinary accuracy the enemy's supply and ammunition dumps, his transport depots and gun positions, the roads which carried his soldiers to and from the line. The Army cartographers were consequently able to produce maps so finely delineated that the guns were able to range and fire on such targets with a precision that was distinctly disturbing to the Germans. In a secret report, later captured by British Intelligence, the Germans observed:

It is worthy of remark that our enemy's guns apparently have a much smaller zone of dispersion than our own. He also appears to have better and more accurate data for shooting from the map than we have. This seems to be proved by the fact that, in weather that excludes all possibility of observation, and under conditions very different from those prevailing during previous shoots, he obtains hits on small targets with great accuracy.

The Germans' answer during the bloody days of August was to keep firing with every gun they had in continuous bombardments – haphazard, but so intense that, raking and ranging methodically back and forth behind the British line, the sheer intensity of the fire-power was bound to wreak destruction somewhere and lower the morale of the British troops as much as it raised the morale of their own men. On one such night of thundering retribution, they scored a hit that sent the morale of C. 276 Battery plummeting to the edge of despair.

In the Signallers' dugout a little way behind the guns, George Worsley and Fred Sharples were only twenty yards from the ammunition dump when the shell hit it and if the 2,000 eighteen-pounder shells had gone up in one almighty bang, they would not have lived to tell the tale. It was bad enough that it started a fire.

Gunner George
Worsley, No.
690452, C Bty., 276
Brigade, Royal
Field Artillery, 55th
Division.

It was like all hell let loose – an absolute inferno! It was like someone throwing fire crackers into a fire, but multiplied a million times. All the ammunition was exploding in the heat and flying over our heads. There were no officers there and no order was given.

There were three of us stood in a trench and, of course, the top of the trench was crumbling in all the time until our ankles were covered and I screamed at this NCO even though he was a bombardier. I took charge. 'We'll get killed whatever happens!' I screamed. 'We'll be killed whether we stop here or whether we run away. For God's sake let's be killed trying to get out of it.' And he said, 'Right-o, George.'

It was every man for himself. We ran like hell. The dump was blazing, lighting up the sky, and there was nothing else to do but run because, as soon as the Germans spotted it – and you could see it for miles around – all their guns would be trained on it.

There was a young officer staggering round blinded and screaming and, as we ran, I saw our cook – just his head sticking out of the earth where he'd been buried, and he was screaming too. Not that you could hear anything in the terrible roaring of all these explosives, but you could see by men's faces if they were screaming. And you could see that this man had gone stark staring mad by the frenzy in his face.

You couldn't do anything for him. The idea of digging amidst all that would have been sheer lunacy and everyone was running just to get out of it. I didn't expect to get out of it. I didn't expect to be alive a few seconds afterwards. We ran like hell until we were out of range. Then we dropped down and lay on the ground and watched this thing – a great lurid light, lighting up the whole sky. Blazing!

At dawn, when the fire had burnt itself out, the few survivors, sleepless, shocked and white-faced, began to stumble back towards the guns. But there were no guns to be seen and nothing but a few tangles of twisted metal among the smoking debris to hint that a battery had ever stood there. There was no sign of the cook. No sign of the blinded officer. No sign of a single survivor among the mangled bodies in the wreckage.

A little later a visitor arrived. His appearance was strangely incongruous in the blackened desolation of the burnt-out gun sites and contrasted oddly with the tousled looks of the shocked and filthy gunners. It was a warm morning and the Staff Officer was jacketless. His shirt sleeves were neatly rolled up, his breeches immaculately pressed, a cane tucked under his arm. He was clean, newly shaved and looked as if he had enjoyed an excellent breakfast before setting off on the difficult journey up to the gun-line.

He presumed to give us a lecture. Nobody formed up or stood in a line or anything, we just looked at him and I can remember every word he said. He said, 'Well, men, I can see you've had a terrible night. But you haven't seen the worst of war yet.' (We looked at each other as if to say, 'You should have bloody well been here last night!') He said, 'It's when you see women and children killed. That's the worst of war. Now, while you're here, I want you to forget about your wives and your sweethearts and your friends. Concentrate on the job in hand, so that, when the time comes for you to march out, those of you who are fortunate enough to be left can march out with your heads held high.'

What a lot of rot! We just exchanged looks. So far as we were concerned, he could have had England for twopence at that moment! By the time we went out of the line, of the original forty-two in our battery, there were only six of us left.

Gunner George Worsley, No. 690452, C Bty., 276 Brigade, Royal Field Artillery, 55th Division.

In the course of the day a few more survivors drifted back. They included the Sergeant who, to Worsley's later chagrin, was awarded the Distinguished Conduct Medal for 'putting the fire out'. New guns were hauled up and dug into fresh positions; new gunners arrived to replace the casualties and later in the day there was a well-meaning attempt to provide the men with a hot meal. Worsley's portion was a mess-tin of what appeared to be warm water with raw mutton fat floating on the top. His stomach, churning with the stench of the dead, revolted. Captain Smith happened to be passing and Worsley, shoving the mess tin under his nose, snarled, 'Look at that.' The Captain took a step back. Worsley followed, remorselessly holding the unsavoury dish under the officer's nostrils. 'Go on! Look at it! It's not fit for swine. If we have to be killed, for God's sake let us die with something in our bellies.'

It was an extraordinary breach of discipline and protocol, but Smith and Worsley had served together since the beginning of the war. The Captain knew his man, though it was difficult to recognise the young Territorial of two years before in the strained, dishevelled figure who confronted him now. For more than ten days Worsley, like his comrades, had slept – when sleep was possible – in his clothes. Like his comrades, for the past twelve days he had neither loosened his puttees nor undone the laces of his boots. Like his comrades he was at the point of exhaustion and, as Captain Smith doubtless realised, nearing the end of his tether. The Captain nodded sympathetically, looked at the 'soup' in the mess-tin and murmured, 'I'm sorry.' There was little he could do about it.

Some twenty-five kilometres away, where the King was a guest of honour at a luncheon party at Fourth Army Headquarters at Querrieu, the menu was more elaborate:

MENU

Déjeuner

Oeufs Glacés à la Russe

Poularde Rotie

Viande Froide

Salade

Mousse aux Fraises

Compôte de Framboises

Desserts

The meal had been planned to appeal to the most refined tastes for, besides the King, the party included some senior Commanders of the French Army. In deference to their Gallic appreciation of good food the dishes had been prepared with elaborate care; in deference to the King's wishes, no alcohol was served. At the beginning of the war the King had set an example of sacrifice and abstemiousness to the nation by announcing that neither wine nor spirits would be served at his table until the day of victory. Certain disgruntled courtiers, offered a Hobson's choice of flaccid soft drinks, entertained the ignoble suspicion that the 'ginger ale' served to the King bore a strong resemblance to whisky and soda and that the fizz in Queen Mary's 'fruit cup' owed more to Champagne than to lemonade. Their disgust was as nothing compared to that of General Joffre when Haig's butler, Shaddock, with as much aplomb as if he had been offering Hock or Chablis, invited him to state his preference for ginger beer or orange juice.

Sir Douglas Haig was fond of 'Papa' Joffre; the two men got on well and Haig's excellent French combined with an instinctive ability to handle Marshal Joffre, had amicably resolved numerous arguments and smoothed many feathers which had been ruffled by disagreements on Allied policy. But he could not resist teasing the old man. His orderly, Secrett (who combined his duties as personal servant to the Commander-in-Chief with those of mess servant when his master dined or entertained guests) was consumed by amusement behind a suitably impassive countenance.

Like Secrett, Sir Douglas had observed from the corner of his eye the meaning look Joffre cast at the waiter, with a half nod towards his empty wine glass.

Haig beckoned a waiter. 'I think Marshal Joffre wants the bread!' The waiter dutifully presented the silver bread basket to Joffre who politely accepted, taking the opportunity of lifting his eyebrows, rolling his eyes towards the empty glass and then staring the waiter directly in the face in an endeavour to communicate the telepathic message that man – or at least a Frenchman – cannot live by bread alone. With the oblivious exceptions of the King himself and the President of France on his right, the whole party was now aware of Joffre's predicament. The *entrée* was brought in and served. Still Marshal Joffre's wine glass remained empty. Sitting on the King's left, impressed by the proximity of Majesty, he achieved the difficult feat of appearing to give his full attention to the royal conversation conducted in the King's schoolboy French and, as soon as His Majesty turned to talk to the President on his right, pantomiming to waiter or butler in discreet dumb show, and venturing – as if absent-mindedly – to toy with the stem of his empty glass.

'I think,' remarked Haig jovially, 'that the Marshal would like some more bread.'

Again the waiter presented the bread. Again Marshal Joffre snatched a piece, glaring at Sir Douglas Haig across the table. It was plain to all that he would have dearly liked to throw it at him.

As soon as the meal was finished and the King was safely closeted in another room in private conversation with President Poincaré,

Haig's secretary, in response to a nod from the Commander-in-Chief, discreetly drew Marshal Joffre aside, explained the circumstances and offered him 'a little something'. Joffre refused with disdain. If he could not enjoy a glass of wine with his meal like any civilised man he would take nothing at all.

This slightly unfortunate episode did not advance the cause of Anglo–French understanding. However, it had, on the whole, been a satisfactory afternoon, particularly for Sir Douglas Haig. He had been able to assure President Poincaré, who was '. . . most anxious, before the approach of winter, that we should have made some decisive advance in order to keep the people of France and England from grumbling . . .', that he expected at least ten weeks of good weather before winter set in, that he was unequivocally optimistic that a great deal would be accomplished, and that he and General Foch were in entire agreement about future plans. He had also had the honour of playing host to the King at an excellent lunch which had been sauced by a good joke and, after the French visitors had left, Sir Douglas Haig had the ultimate gratification of being presented by the King with the Grand Cross of the Victorian Order. This honour was in the King's personal gift and, although the immaculate tunic of the Commander-in-Chief already carried several rows of well-earned campaign and service medals, none could approach the value of this mark of his Sovereign's personal esteem and appreciation.

The King, equally pleased with his visit, took his departure to spend a few days with his armies in the north before returning to London. Accompanied by the Prince of Wales, his personal ADC and Major Thompson (an ADC provided by the Commander-in-Chief) the King was driven back to St Pol in a staff car set aside for his personal use. It was a glorious evening. At the King's request they travelled with the hood down. Motor cyclists of the Military Police travelled well ahead to make sure that the road was clear of congestion and the troops, waiting on either side for the royal party to pass, were cheered and delighted with their brief glimpse of the King.

On 14 August, the weather broke.

Chapter 18

It poured with rain on the Somme. On the thinly held front of the Reserve Army from Serre to Beaumont Hamel, where the line was still stuck precisely where it had been before the First of July, the troops crouched in the trenches, sheltering – if they were lucky – under hastily rigged-up canopies of waterproof sheets that bulged under the weight of the rain and occasionally treated an unfortunate Tommy to an unexpected shower-bath. There was little to do. Apart from the occasional rattle of machine-gun fire from the drier and more comfortably accommodated Germans, and the occasional random salvo of shells designed to keep 'Tommy' from getting too complacent, watch-keeping in daylight hours was more or less confined to keeping a gloomy eye clamped to a trench periscope and watching, through the raindrops that splashed steadily on to its mirror, the same depressingly familiar view of No Man's Land where for six long weeks the bodies of the dead had lain still and silent and beyond recovery. Now, as the rain beat down, a sudden squall would lift some muddied rag of uiform and wave it in grim salutation.

The River Ancre, long liberated by shell-fire from its battered banks, swelled and sent tributaries groping across the valley so that the swamp turned into a lake and water lapped inches above the surface of the wobbling duckboard tracks leading to the line in Thiepval Wood. Below the dripping rubble of Thiepval village, where the Germans were busily pumping out their trenches, gravity carried the water downhill. It ran down the chalky slopes to Thiepval Wood, trickled down through the jagged tree stumps and turned the steep communication trenches into glissades of slime and mud, soon stirred into a squelching soup by the constant passage of soldiers slithering to and from the line.

Above the village, on the wide expanse of the Thiepval plateau, there was no shelter from the elements and the wind drove the rain across in curtains from the Leipzig Redoubt, where the British were still trying to increase their hold, to Mouquet Farm, soaking the exhausted Australians still doggedly striving to capture it. But they had won the old windmill to the north of Pozières and, in other parts of their sector, had gained the top of the rain-swept ridge that ran

away to Martinpuich, to High Wood and to Delville Wood beyond.
Protected by two great redoubts and by the Switch Line behind
them, Martinpuich held out. High Wood held out and the Germans
were still clinging on to the edges of Delville. They were clinging on
everywhere with exceptional tenacity, fighting back and charging
forward in powerful counter-attacks that rocked and sometimes
broke the newly captured line.

The Germans were not in an easy situation. Five experienced
divisions had been transferred from the Somme to the Eastern Front
and, to the fury of General Von Falkenhayn, their replacements had
been of such inferior calibre that he had been forced to send them
straight back again. At Verdun the French had gained the upper
hand. They were now taking the offensive and the Germans,
spreading their troops as thinly as they dared, were hard put to it to
maintain the illusion that the German Army was as strong as ever.
Supplies and transport were a constant headache, and every man
going into the line now had to carry on his own person sufficient
rations and water for the five days he would remain there. It all added
up to the first crack in the mighty armour of the German war
machine that had growled into action on the Somme almost two
years earlier.

In the British trenches, the Tommies were unaware of the
problems that beset the German High Command. They detected no
crack in the armour, no lessening of the enemy's fighting spirit.
Under the onslaught of his counter-attacks, numbed by the ferocity
of his shelling, they were not given to analysing the broader strategy
of the battle, still less of the war itself. They no longer lived from day
to day, but from hour to hour, minute to minute. Few had a thought
to spare for anything but the next man at his shoulder, the next hot
brew-up, the next relief. Letters, lovingly penned in ink that ran into
blue rivulets under the rain, had an air of unreality. News from
home, news of births and bazaars, of deaths and dances, of gossip, of
shopping, of all the trivia of everyday events, had little significance.
And the pleasure of any brief release from the dank and gloomy
trenches was mostly overwhelmed by the knowledge that there
would soon be another attack.

The next attack was on 18 August, four squally, stormy days later.
Ted Gale's Battalion was attacking to the left of Delville Wood and
their objective was Orchard Trench. It was part of a general attack
on the line from Guillemont to Thiepval Ridge and, this time, surely,
High Wood and Delville Wood would be finally secured and the way
ahead would, at last be opened. The 18 August would be the fiftieth
day of the Battle of the Somme and two years, all but five days, since
the first engagement of the war – the battle of Mons.

Ted Gale had been at Mons. He had been in the Army in the days when, in his opinion, it *was* an Army and he never tired of regaling grumbling comrades who had joined up 'for the duration' with tales of pre-war discipline as a Regular Rifleman: of having been confined to barracks for five days for being two seconds late on ration parade; of the regular duty of polishing the barrack-room floor with brick dust and lead; of having been given pack drill for failing to shine the *soles* of his boots. His companions were not particularly impressed by Ted's early hardships. They thought he had been amply compensated by the enjoyment of a cushy war, for he had twice spent long periods in England. Admittedly he had suffered the loss of all his teeth when a horse kicked him in the mouth early in 1915, but that unlucky episode was followed by several months of safety and comfort at home, while his mouth hardened sufficiently for the Army to fit him with dentures. This fortunate circumstance had resulted in his missing the Battle of Loos. Only a few months later he had gone down with rat poisoning, through eating infected rations, and after the initial discomfort had been blessed with another pleasant period of relaxation and recuperation in Blighty. It was five months now since he had been posted back to France to the 7th (Service) Battalion, The Rifle Brigade, and, after six years of soldiering, he was about to go over the top for the first time.

The 7th Battalion, The Rifle Brigade, were to attack to the left of Delville Wood on the right flank of the 33rd Division, which had been given the ambitious task of capturing the remainder of the ground between Delville Wood and High Wood and securing High Wood itself.

It was the waiting to go over that was the worst, because we didn't go over until almost three o'clock in the afternoon. There was a whole brigade waiting to go over on a battalion front, so we were crowded up like anything. During the morning, the Sergeant came round with the old rum jar and gave us a dessertspoonful of rum, just to put Dutch courage in us. It was strong, that Army rum, and I think he had two or three spoonfuls to our one – or more!

We really needed that rum, waiting to go over the top! Our own guns had put down this terrific barrage but, because we were a bit higher up than the Germans, in order to hit them they'd had to sight the guns so that they would just skim the top of our trenches and there we were, crouching in this terrible noise, and these terrible shells going over us just inches above. You can't describe the feeling! You can't describe the noise! A couple of our own chaps were killed. One fellow had the top of his head took off with

Acting
Lance-Corporal
E. Gale, No.
3774, 1st (later 7th)
Btn., The Rifle
Brigade, 41st
Brigade, 14th
Division.

one of our own shells. His brains were all over the place. But the artillery couldn't help it. They had a terrible job to get the elevation right and just had to try and skim the top of our trenches and this poor chap Dixon got it. He was only five or six yards away from me. It didn't do much for us to see that sort of thing before we went over!

Five minutes after we went over the top we were finished! The German machine-guns went through our lines just like a mow goes through a field of corn. I don't think we got two hundred yards before we were so mucked up that we just had to lay out in No Man's Land. I was in a shell-hole with the Sergeant – the one who'd been sampling the rum. We were absolutely pinned down but he kept jumping up and shouting, 'Why don't we advance? Why don't we advance?' He was absolutely hollering. How could you advance when there was three of you there and you couldn't see anybody else? I shouted back at him, 'Why don't you keep down? You'll be drawing the guns on us!'

D Company had gone across first and C Company were supposed to be following behind us. From this shell-hole we looked back and we could see C Company there lying on the ground spread out in extended order, just as they'd gone across. We couldn't understand why they weren't coming up to support us. There was just the three of us in the shell-hole – the Platoon Sergeant and Jack Hall, who was the Lance-Corporal, and myself. And the Sergeant said, 'Why the hell don't they come on and give us a hand? We can't go in there on our own!'

This old Sergeant wasn't half going on, nothing would keep him quiet. He was an enlisted man – he wasn't a Regular. There was only two of us Regulars in The 7th Battalion, but the Sergeant had been in the Marines before the war, so he should have known better. Of course he had all this rum in him. Then the third time he jumped up they got him! A bullet went straight in his ear and blew half his face away. Me and Jack had to lay there with him. We lay there for hours and hours and hours with all this clatter going on around us and when it got dusk we started to crawl back.

It was a terrible crawl back and, hunched close to the ground, his ears ringing with the sound of the explosions as the Germans continued to bombard the British line, Ted Gale had not gone far before he realised why C Company had not come up to support them. They were still lying in extended order as he crawled past them – and almost all were dead.

Lieutenant Hall was alive, but only just. He said, 'Can you help me! I've got a bad wound in my hip. I can't move.' I said to Jack, 'Can you hold my rifle and I'll pick him up?'

I picked him up and I carried him back to the trench – it was all of a hundred yards and it took a long, long time, because we had to be careful moving; the whole thing was still like an inferno although it was getting well dark. When we got into the trench, I laid him on the fire step. A few yards beyond him, laying out there, we'd come across a chap we called Corporal Gussie – a machine-gunner. He was badly shot in the stomach and I didn't suppose there was much hope for him, but he was in a bad way. I couldn't do anything, having the Lieutenant with me, but I said to the Corporal, 'I'll come back for you, Gussie.' So, when I'd laid the Lieutenant down and someone else came to see to him, I said, 'Right. I'm going out again.' But the officer wouldn't let me go. I felt very badly about it, because I'd promised Gussie I would go back, but the officer said, 'No you're not. You've had quite enough for one day.' It was nine o'clock at night by then, so I suppose, in a way, he was right. But I tried to insist and, I remember, he said to me, 'Anyone who's left out there isn't worth picking up now!'

He was right. There were twenty-three of us left alive out of my whole company. I don't know how they missed us. It was a miracle! It was a miracle that any of us got back. I don't believe I'd ever cried in my life, but, when I got back and found out what had happened, how many men we'd lost, I cried then. I was a Regular and they were all Volunteers, but we was all mucked in together. I cried then.

Acting
Lance-Corporal
E. Gale, No.
3774, 1st (later 7th)
Btn., The Rifle
Brigade, 41st
Brigade, 14th
Division.

Their Battalion was the only one of the Brigade to have failed and they had only failed because the right of the 33rd Division had not succeeded in pushing forward. The Germans still held High Wood. The Tommies had inched forward in Delville, but it would be weeks yet before the wood was finally and permanently in British hands.

Far away on the left flank, across the Albert–Bapaume road, the Australians had punched their way a little nearer to Mouquet Farm; some lines of trenches beyond the Leipzig Redoubt had been captured and, far away to the right, the troops had crept a little way up the valley to the right of Guillemont and the French had increased their hold on the village of Maurepas on the opposite slopes.

The small gains had been won at the cost of high casualties, but the Staff were satisfied. It was at least something.

Extract from the
diary of Sir Douglas
Haig.
Saturday, 19 August: The operation carried out yesterday was
most successful. It was on a front of over eleven miles. We now
hold the ridge south-east of and overlooking Thiepval. Nearly five
hundred prisoners were taken here while the battalion which
carried out the attack only lost forty men! During their advance
our men kept close to the artillery barrage.

The artillery and the Staff who ruled the destiny of infantry and
gunners alike, had been thinking on their feet and there had been
time, since the catastrophe of the First of July, for shrewd reappraisal
of the effectiveness of rigidly timed barrages with 'lifts' so inexorably
predetermined. A new technique was now being tried – the 'creeping barrage' which would literally travel like a curtain in front of the
infantry as it advanced, so that, when the barrage moved on from the
German front line, the infantry would be there, on its heels, ready to
engage the enemy, rather than advancing in full view two hundred
yards away or more. Perhaps the most satisfactory thing about the
limited successes of 18th August was that the technique of the
creeping barrage had worked.

But the hard nuts were still holding out. The hardest of all was
Guillemont and it was obvious that it would take a full-scale battle
and much preparation to capture it. It was equally obvious that,
before the Allies could push forward, Guillemont must be captured.
There was just the faintest indication that the citadel of the German
line was beginning to crumble – but it could be compared to the
merest trickle of brick dust on the outer curtain wall. There was a
long way to go.

Meantime the survivors of the troops who had been engaging the
enemy must be relieved, rested and revived for their next endeavour.
So the great chess game of moving troops and transport across the
grassless waste of the battlefield, now swept intermittently by rain and
winds and thunderstorms, must start all over again. The exhausted
troops stumbled thankfully out of the line and, with some trepidation,
fresh divisions slogged up through the desolation to take their place.

Alex Paterson was a born soldier, although, unlike Ted Gale, he
had not been a Regular before the war. Nevertheless, he had
reached the rank of Sergeant in the 11th (Service) Battalion, The
Rifle Brigade and furthermore had turned out to be a 'natural'.
Officers and men alike depended on Paterson. He had common-
sense. He had a steady nerve which inspired confidence. He was a
man's man.

Sergeant A. K.
Paterson, DCM,
I took to it like a duck to water, which was remarkable because
when I joined up I'd never even heard of The Rifle Brigade. I went

up to London, to Waterloo Station, and walked across to Scotland Yard and there was a great big Recruiting Sergeant there. I told him I wanted to join the Royal Engineers. He said, 'Well, you can't join the Royal Engineers. They're all full up. But I can give you a jolly good regiment to join.' I said, 'What regiment?' He said, 'The Rifle Brigade.' I told him quite straight that I'd never heard of it. I thought it was the Fire Brigade! It might as well have been the Fire Brigade for all I knew about it!

It was 8 September 1914, and I was still well under military age – I had to lie to get in – but a year later I was Platoon Sergeant and I took my platoon to France.

MM, No. 52574, A Coy., 11th (S) Btn., The Rifle Brigade.

In the course of his year's service in France, Sergeant Paterson had become adept at trench warfare. He had become a veteran leader of patrols and, for many months in the line in front of Laventie, he had practically lived in No Man's Land. In his view, it was a good deal to be preferred to sitting in a dugout waiting to be shelled. He made it his personal responsibility to cut the zig-zag gaps in the wire in front of the trenches through which the patrols could pass undetected at night. He made it his business to see that every man in his platoon was familiar with the alien land on the other side of the wire. After dark he would take them silently 'over the top' to lie beyond the wire and perhaps to creep a little way ahead, so that they became accustomed to being at large, vulnerable, unprotected by the high sandbagged parapets, with nothing between them and the enemy just two hundred yards away. He taught them to be ready to freeze when a flare went up; ready, when it died down, to scramble back noiselessly through the wire, knowing that such experiences would make his men less apprehensive about leaving the shelter of the trenches when a fatigue party was needed to strengthen the defences or to repair entanglements broken by shellfire.

Daylight patrols called for even greater nerve and skill, but only by daylight could the enemy's positions be properly reconnoitred, his strongpoints observed, his dispositions sketched. Day after day, in the hot September month of 1915, Paterson led his patrols out through the long grass towards the German line. The line was newly dug and information was badly needed.

The grass was just like hay, so anything that was dark or anything that was too light or was coloured would show up. We had to wear as little equipment as possible – no belts or buckles or anything that was likely to glitter in the sunshine. We had to really think about camouflage. We had to brown our hands and faces and, with my black hair, I had to wear a khaki handkerchief over my head

Sergeant A. K. Paterson, DCM, MM, No. 52574, A Coy., 11th (S) Btn., The Rifle Brigade.

with knots at the corners to keep it on and, because the weather
was so hot and we knew that our faces would be wet with
perspiration – and even *that* could glisten in the sunlight – we
covered our faces with grass seed. We crawled on our tummies
and we didn't keep to a straight line because, if we'd done that, we
might have furrowed the grass as we went through and that would
certainly be seen by troops using periscopes on the other side. So
we had to move to the left and then to the right on our bellies and,
as we got near the line, we had to keep very close so that we could
whisper to each other and discuss things that we saw. We even had
brown paper instead of white to write our notes on – just a
four-inch square which we put in our pockets and then, if there
was a bit of a shell-hole, we would get into it and very cautiously
make a sketch or two of any sniper posts in the parapet, or any
places where it seemed as if they'd got some activity in saps.
Sometimes people were captured. We lost an officer and another
Sergeant who were a bit too bold. They actually got into one
of these German saps. They thought it was empty, but there
were Jerries there, or at least they got there pretty soon! Only
six officers out of eight got back that day and we didn't know
what had happened. There was a certain amount of firing,
but firing was going on all the time, all over the place,
and you couldn't distinguish one particular lot of fire from the
other.

In the best part of a year's foraying in No Man's Land, Alex Paterson
had gained a great deal of valuable experience, a Military Medal, and
a certain aplomb which was about to be distinctly useful in the
trenches in front of Guillemont, for the troops were there to work,
to dig, to push the line well out into hostile territory, to push out
saps and communication trenches and to so improve the position
that when the big attack came they would jump off with every advantage.

Paterson was in his element. Night work suited him. No Man's
Land suited him. In spite of harassing fire from the Germans the
work went well. Paterson took considerable satisfaction in what had
been achieved and was more satisfied than ever when the Brigadier-
General came up in person to inspect the results.

Sergeant A. K.
Paterson, DCM,
MM, No. 52574, A
Coy., 11th (S) Btn.,
The Rifle Brigade.

General Shute was the finest offensive officer I've ever come
across and he was a man who wanted to be in the line and to know
exactly what was going on. The Colonel came with him, and the
Adjutant, and they handed him over to me and said, 'Sergeant,
will you take the General and do what the General says.' And the

GUILLEMONT

WATERLOT FARM

LONGUEVAL

QUARRY

The formidable defences of the German Second Line at Ginchy – still clearly visible as chalk-marks on the ground – captured by the Guards Division. The small quartery to the right of the village served as Brigade Headquarters.

Ginchy, Autumn 1982. Almost seventy years on the farmlands of the Somme still yield an annual harvest of steel.

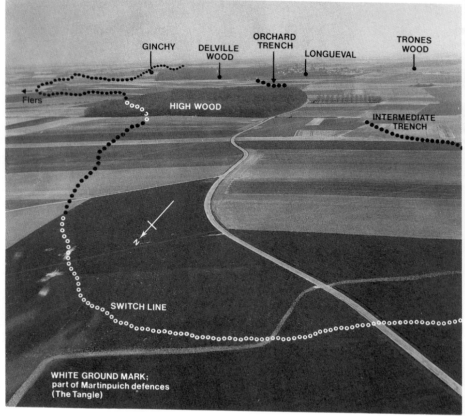

Where the Switch Line ran.

The site of the Triangle and the Quadrilateral from the Guards Memorial on Ginchy Ridge.

Christchurch Boys' High School cricket team in 1908, the year in which they won the Heathcote Williams Shield for the best team in the Dominion of New Zealand. Four of the eleven were killed in the War. Rupert Hickmott is seated left of the shield.

Above: The menacing Quadrilateral which blocked the advance from Guillemont (*in background*). Nearly seventy years later its massive concrete positions still stand – successive attempts to blow them up have merely tilted them.

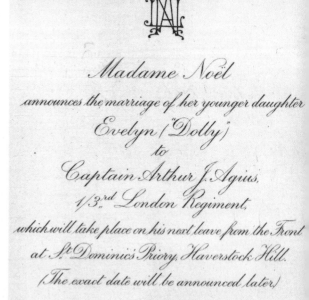

𝒩𝒜

Madame Noël

announces the marriage of her younger daughter

Evelyn ("Dolly")

to

Captain Arthur J. Agius,

1/3rd London Regiment,

which will take place on his next leave from the Front

at St. Dominic's Priory, Haverstock Hill.

(The exact date will be announced later)

45, Compayne Gardens,

Hampstead, London, N.W.   *September 1916.*

Right: The invitation to Arthur Agius's wedding.

General said he wanted to see on the other side of the wire and take a close look at the German line. Well, we had tunnels under our parapets running up through the wire and beyond. So I said, 'Right, you follow me.' He was on his own. I lifted up the sack on one side of the tunnel, I got in and said, 'Now, you come in.' So he came through. Two yards further on was another sack hanging down in the hole in front because, if you left it open all the way through, the Germans would spot the light shining through the other side. I lifted up the curtain at the front end of the tunnel and got through and held it up while he came through. He was a good six feet tall – a big man, taller than me. He went to his right and lay there and had a good look. I said, 'Keep down, sir. You'll have to go right down on your tummy and don't go any distance because there's no cover. I'm going to the right and I'd like you to follow me there, because you can see more.'

I talked to him like my uncle, and he knew perfectly well what I wanted him to do. I crawled along to a safe place and the Brigadier followed me, and I said, 'This is as far as I'm going. You can see all you want to see from here. Now, what do you want to know?' We stayed there for a good five minutes and I pointed things out and he asked me questions. When he'd seen all he wanted to, I said, 'We'll go backwards now. Don't turn round, because you'll be making a target three or four times the length. You go backwards on your toes and your knees, into the same curtain and I'll follow you backwards. Don't turn round and put your boots to them!' So we went back, just like that, and, when we'd crawled through the tunnel into the trench, he stood there and he chatted to me and he thanked me and he shook my hand in front of the Colonel and the Adjutant and everybody. They stood there just like stuffed dummies! But the General spoke to me man to man. He was a marvellous chap!

General Shute was no milksop, no remote, godlike figure so detached from his men that he saw them as pawns or statistics. They had done a good job. They had prepared the advanced positions with care. They were tired with long labour and had suffered much from shelling and sniping. Because of the bad weather which had caused the battle to be postponed twice they had been far too long in the line, and General Shute was absolutely determined that they should have a rest before it started. There was very little time, for the assault was now scheduled for 3 September and August was almost at an end. But Shute insisted. On 31 August his Brigade filed out of the trenches and moved back, for two days holiday, to camp in the Carnoy Valley.

They knew that it would be for a mere breathing space, that in forty-eight hours they would be back – but it was a relief to be out of the line, away from the discomfort of dripping clothing that was soaked again as soon as it began to dry out, away from the gruelling labour of digging trenches that the rainstorms turned into muddy streams even as they dug. Away from the dripping gloom, away from the stench, away from the eternal sound of the guns and the shells that whined through the leaden skies. Yesterday evening, just before dusk, the awful weather had crashed to a climax so furious that it had silenced even the guns. Two observation balloons were struck spectacularly by lightning and exploded. The torrential downpour soaked every man to the skin and turned trenches that had been rivers of water into seas of mud. Duckboards which had provided dry standing of a sort or, at the very least, a foothold, sank a foot or more into the glutinous depths. That night, between sunset and dawn, thirty-seven lorries of supplies and ammunition stuck on the Carnoy-Montauban road alone, and next night, as the boys trudged back towards their unexpected rest, rope-gangs of the ASC were still trying to haul the last of them out.

The night was clear, the rain had gone off, but the Germans chose to send over gas to cheer them on their way. Next morning the sun came out but few of the boys woke up until it was high in the sky. It had not been possible to find them accommodation in a proper camp, even if there had been time to take them so far behind the line. The Brigade found itself lying on the open ground in the vicinity of the Carnoy craters at Casino Point where, exactly two months ago today, in the wake of the exploding mines, the 18th Division had broken the line and forged exultantly ahead with the French at its shoulder.

It was hardly a camp, but, among the debris of abandoned ammunition boxes, the litter of empty shell cases that marked the old gun positions, wigwam-like bivouacs of canvas and canes had been improvised to shelter the men, some captured dugouts served as accommodation for the officers and two big marquees had been put up to serve as dining and recreation halls by day and dormitories by night. There was bacon for breakfast, and plenty to go round, for – discounting the sick – the Brigade had lost six hundred men in its nine-day stint in the trenches in front of Guillemont. There was dinner to look forward to – doubtless only 'His Majesty's stew' but a good deal more palatable than His Majesty's jaw-breaking biscuits, cold beans and bully beef, which was the unvarying diet in the line. Before dinner there was an issue of cigarettes and later the mail came up with letters and parcels from home. The guns still hammering the front two miles away were an unpleasant reminder of what awaited them but, as they lounged on groundsheets on the squelching earth, rapidly drying out under the warm sun, the boys inclined towards the opinion that it all added to an almost perfect day. The officers, as preoccupied as the men with drying out and catching up on sleep, had kept well out of the way; no sergeants had appeared with lists of obligatory fatigues and, towards evening, Brigadier-General Shute came up himself from Brigade Headquarters to look round with a benevolent eye and see that all was well. By his personal order the boys received a rum ration to which, being out of the line, they had, strictly speaking, no entitlement. When darkness fell, although the sky behind them quivered and pulsated with the glare of battle, almost extinguishing the efforts of the stars to shine through the warm night, although they were allowed no lights, the boys sat on in the open air, reluctant for the day to end.

Fred White and Freddie Stevens (more commonly known in the Army as 'Nobbler and Jerry') sat together replete with sweet biscuits. They did a good Cockney double act – perhaps not quite so good as the original 'Nobbler and Jerry' who had won fame in Fred Karno's Concert Troupe, but good enough to have earned their nicknames. They had been friends since their not-so-long-ago schooldays, near-neighbours at home in Camden Town and members of the same breezy bunch of mates who, on halcyon Sunday evenings before the war, used to walk across Hampstead Heath to Jack Straw's Castle to spend a convivial evening for the price of a glass or two of beer. This outing had been the highlight of the week and, rather more intoxicated on high spirits than on alcohol, they used to swing back across the heath, singing in exaggerated harmony:

> *We were sailing along on Moonlight Bay,*
> *We could hear the voices ringing,*
> *They seemed to say*
> *'You have stolen my heart,*
> *Now don't go 'way!'*
> *As we sang Love's old sweet song,*
> *On Moonlight Bay.*

The weekend the war began they had been singing this favourite as they tramped home in Bank Holiday mood. After that the two Freds had not felt much like singing, nor even like a tramp across the heath. Things had changed after their mates went into the Army. 'Nobbler and Jerry' were equally anxious to join. They had attained the military age of nineteen but what they had not attained was the necessary height. Stevens – with the advantage of one inch over

White – was barely five feet four and in the choosy days of August 1914 the Army still stuck to the minimum prewar requirement of five feet seven. It was a sore subject.

Rifleman F. C. White, No. R8529, B Coy., 10th Btn., The King's Royal Rifle Corps, 59th Brigade, 20th Division.

Most of our mates were in the London Territorials. Of course they went away immediately the war started and Freddie and I and my brother and one or two others who wasn't in the Territorials always used to march with them wherever they went, so we marched with them to Waterloo Station. That was 4 August, when war was declared. We was all as excited as anything. We all wanted to join up. My brother, who was taller than me, joined up and went in. I went up. They said, 'No, don't want you! You're too small!' Same thing happened to Freddie.

It came to the last day of 1914, and there was only Freddie and me left of the whole bunch. Freddie's brother had just got killed (he was a Regular in the King's Royal Rifle Corps) and me and Freddie was mooching about and we was fed up. We said, 'Come on, let's have another go!' So we goes to a recruiting office in Crowndale Road, St Pancras. Freddie goes in first, up to the Recruiting Sergeant, and I'm standing behind him.

'Yes?' says the Sergeant, 'what do *you* want?'

'Join the Army.'

'What do you want to go in?'

'King's Royal Rifles.'

'You can't go in there. They're full up.'

'Why not? My brother was killed in there!'

The Recruiting Sergeant softened a bit at that, and he says, 'All right. Sign here, take your shilling and away you go.'

Then it comes to me, but I got a flea in my ear! He said, 'You come back when you're a bit taller. We don't want you!' I thought, 'That's good! Freddie's in, I'm out, left on me own – the lone bloke.' When we got outside, Freddie and me talked a bit about what we should do and we decided to have another try. So we walked about three miles from St Pancras to Holloway Road to another recruiting office. I goes in there.

'What do *you* want?'

'Join the army.'

'What do you want to go in?'

'King's Royal Rifles.'

'You can't go in there. Full up!'

'Well, I ain't going in anything at all,' I said. 'My pal's going in there tomorrow.' So, he says, 'Oh, all right. Sign here.' Didn't measure me or anything! Off we went next day, down to the depot at Winchester, and we stuck together all the way along. Never was parted! Of course, later on we had different jobs with the battalion. Freddie went on the Lewis-guns and I stayed in B Company with the bombers. But every time we was out of the line we got together and stuck together.

That evening, sitting under the stars near the Carnoy Craters, was the last time the two Freds would meet until after the war. Tomorrow night they would be on their way back to the line and the battle that loomed ahead. Tonight they were thinking of old times. 'Nobbler' White's mouth organ was worn and battered by long service in the Army and a year or more in the trenches, but he could still squeeze a tune out of it. For most of the evening he had been playing the accompaniment to a selection of the bawdy choruses that had enhanced the Tommies' musical education since their arrival in France. Now he changed the mood.

We were sailing along on Moonlight Bay . . .

Freddie Stevens took up the words but they seemed inappropriate to the circumstances. After a little thought and a few false starts he came up with a better version. The lads liked it, and one by one, they joined in.

> *I was strolling along in Gillymong –*
> *With the Minniewerfers singing*
> *Their old sweet song*
> *And I said to old Fritz,*
> *'We're here to stay!*
> *And we'll kick your arse from here*
> *To Moonlight Bay.'*

The best that could be said for it was that it was a good tune.

On the following evening, as they prepared for the long trek back up the line, the boys felt less inclined to sing, and they did not much like the Padre's choice of hymn. Doubtless he meant well, but their thoughts were on the battle ahead and in the circumstances the sentiments expressed in *Nearer, my God, to Thee* struck a little too close to home. The singing was, to say the least, ragged. The boys stood bare-headed in the low rays of the evening sun waiting for dusk and the order to march off and it was noticeable that the Padre's voice boomed above them all.

Nearer, my God, to Thee,
Nearer to Thee,
E'en though it be a cross
That raiseth me;
Still all my song shall be,
Nearer, my God, to Thee,
Nearer to Thee!

In a few minutes' time they would be shouldering rifles and turning their faces towards the sound of the guns. In a few hours they would be going over the top. The 59th Brigade was well under strength, for there had been no time to reinforce them and they were under no illusions as to what lay ahead. Under the circumstances only the most resigned of Christian souls in their ranks could join in the hymn-singing with enthusiasm – and even the voices of that select band trailed off when it came to the third verse.

There let my way appear
Steps unto Heaven.
All that Thou sendest me
In mercy given,
Angels to beckon me,
Nearer, my God, to Thee,
Nearer to Thee!

Still, the boys had had a good feed and a good rest and, as the smallest man in the battalion, Fred White was suitably grateful. It was fortunate that he was wiry as well as diminutive for, as a company bomber, he was carrying excess weight in the form of a bomber's jacket with no less than eight Mills bombs tucked into its individual pockets and he was tired already. For most of the day the Bombers had been hard at it priming countless boxes of bombs in preparation for the battle, while their mates had been taking things easy. But one unexpected happening had cheered Fred up. In one of the boxes he had found a note tucked neatly into the top row of bombs. It gave the name and address of the girl munition-worker who had packed them and added the interesting information that she was blonde, blue-eyed and aged nineteen. The message ended encouragingly, *Good Luck, Tommy.* Fred had taken the note as a good omen and was carrying it into battle, tucked like a talisman into his breast pocket, beside a letter from his sweetheart, Ethel.

Chapter 19

Next day the sun shone and the troops splashed across the steaming mud of No Man's Land to capture Guillemont.

It was difficult to see the sun through the fumes, the smoke, the flying debris, the spouting columns of liquid mud that filled the sky and fell back to soak and blind the Tommies as they pressed forward on the heels of the creeping barrage. There was still a 'fixed barrage', a careful timetable of 'lifts', that would move steadily ahead to fall on the second and third German lines as the troops advanced – but this time they were advancing under the umbrella of a second barrage, moving smoothly ahead less than fifty yards beyond them, leading them to the objective and screening them from the enemy as they went.

It was not easy to keep going at a steady pace when every instinct nurtured by training and experience urged every man to throw himself flat. It took one sort of bravado to sing of 'strolling along in Gillymong' but, in the growing mistrust between gunners and infantry, most of whom had tragic experience of the worn-out guns firing short, it took bravado of quite another sort to go forward steadily behind a curtain of explosions in the unswerving belief that they would keep their distance as you progressed.

The mounds of brick dust and rubble which appeared to the naked eye to be all that was left of the village of Guillemont were no longer so innocent-looking to the eye of the Command. With the events at Thiepval, at Ovillers, at la Boisselle, disturbingly fresh in their minds they had no doubt that, beneath the field of ruins, the enemy was waiting in a Pandora's box of tunnels and shelters and dugouts, and that, when the lid was opened, they would be ready to catapult to the surface with the impetus of a tight-coiled spring, suddenly released. The nub of the British plan was to open the lid first – from the outside.

You went down steps to these places, but the steps didn't go straight down. They would go down, say, three steps to the left, then three steps straight followed by four to the right, until they reached the bottom – the idea being that nobody could throw a bomb directly down the hole of the entrance. Ordinary bombs,

Sergeant A. Paterson, DCM, MM, No. 52574, A Coy., 11th (S) Btn., The Rifle Brigade.

demolition bombs, would just burst halfway down and the worst they would do would be block up the passage, and they always had an escape route. So our job was to demolish the front of them, break down the doors and entrances, open them up a bit so that the Bombers could get at them. Well, the Jerries weren't just going to sit there and let us hammer away demolishing the front of these dugouts, so, first thing, we had to throw down phosphorus bombs – smoke bombs. You'd strike the smoke bomb on an ignition brassard you had strapped round your arm and fling it down the steps. The bombs gave off a thick suffocating smoke which, being heavy, flowed down the winding steps and spread out in the large spaces below so that it would either drive the Germans out or suffocate them.

We had to carry extra haversacks full of these phosphorus bombs and, as well as that and extra ammunition and all the rest of our normal equipment, every man had to carry either a pick or a shovel, one each. It was a wonder we were able to get out of the trench, because we had to get over a big bank that we'd made ourselves in front of our trenches for cover, and then beyond that was all the wire and water.

Zero Hour was supposed to be midday. The idea was that, about ten minutes before Zero Hour, our bombardment of their lines increased in volume and, when that noise stopped, which meant that your covering fire from the field guns was lifting ahead, that was your signal to go over the top. Well, maybe the firing stopped. If it did, nobody noticed it, because the Germans were still bombarding our front line and the shells were bursting all over the place and the shells of our heavy barrage were going over our heads. The noise was so deafening that, days later, it was still resounding in our ears – and we were supposed to listen! We went over by the time on our watches and my platoon was leading, in extended order, three to four paces between each man. You couldn't say, 'You go straight across that way.' You'd have to go round huge holes and, with more shells falling all around, it was very difficult to keep going in a straight line. Very difficult to keep the men together in any kind of formation. Very difficult to know what was happening.

What was happening was that part of the 59th Brigade, having started off fractionally early, was advancing into the line of its own barrage. It was the 10th Battalion of the King's Royal Rifle Corps, making straight for Guillemont village, who started earliest of all and who took the greatest punishment. But those who survived to reach the German wire and push through gaps to the first objective just as the barrage lifted, had the advantage of surprise.

There was me and this other bloke and our instructions was to make for the church gates at Guillemont. When we got to the church gate there was no church gate! All there was was a pile of bricks! Anyway, we'd been told there was a deep dugout under the church – because there always *was* one in a village church, with the vault and all. We was armed with about half a dozen Mills grenades in a waistcoat in the front of us, and we found the dugout entrance and I stood at one side of it and this other bloke, he stood opposite. There was no door on it – it was open and I got hold of a bomb, pulled the pin out, flung the bomb down. Nothing happened! He pulled the pin out and *he* slung a bomb down. Nothing happened! I got another bomb out, pulled the pin out, flung it down and, as soon as it went down this time, the bloody thing comes straight up again and exploded on the stairs! It didn't half give us a turn! So, I said to this bloke, 'Come on, we'll go somewhere else. It's too hot here!'

Rifleman F. C. White, No. R.8529, B Coy., Bomber, 10th Btn., King's Royal Rifle Corps, 59th Brigade, 20th Division.

We had to take six German lines and it was all plain to be seen. There was a sunken road, then there was another line of trenches and then there was a pillbox which was the entrance to a line of deep dugouts and a machine-gun was blazing away from it, but the bombers took care of that, and on we went. Every time we got to the next objective there were fewer and fewer men. At about one o'clock, we'd just taken what had been the Germans' support line when I found that our Company Commander had been killed and that the Second-in-Command was severely wounded in the head. Our reserves were just passing through us to take the next objective, which was a sunken road, and that gave us an hour's break, so I spent the time scrounging around in all the smoke and all the deafening noise trying to find out just who was there and who wasn't. There was nobody! No officers to be seen, no other platoon sergeant besides myself, so there was nothing for it but to take charge of the Company because time was going on and we had to line up with the 6th Battalion of the Ox and Bucks Regiment ready to go on to the next objective and over the top again at half-past two. The next objective was supposed to be Wedge Wood Valley. Wedge Wood was the landmark. But there was no Wedge Wood. It had completely disappeared. That was our final objective, on the other side of Guillemont – the line on top of the valley, facing the apex of Leuze Wood.

It was late in the afternoon by the time we got there and I started

Sergeant A. K. Paterson, DCM, MM, No. 52574, A Coy., 11th (S) Btn., The Rifle Brigade.

the riflemen digging a new line near the top of Wedge Wood Valley. By dusk the job was finished after a fashion. In my spare haversack I carried conical-shaped flares, yellow and red, and we had to lay them along the line of our position at three-feet intervals. We lit them when it got dark enough, just as a spotting aeroplane flew over, to show the position of the new front line.

After the flares had died down I took the roll call. Out of our whole company we mustered, besides myself, the Corporal, one Acting Corporal and thirty-seven men, including two stretcher-bearers. I sent one man back to Headquarters with a list of the names and inspected the rifles. Then I posted some sentries and lookouts a short way down No Man's side of Wedge Valley and, after a bit, I called the roll again – just in case anyone had come in or caught up. No one had.[1]

Rifleman F. C. White, No. R.8529, B Coy., Bomber, 10th Btn., King's Royal Rifle Corps, 59th Brigade, 20th Division.

It was getting dark and we come across some troops in a slit trench. They were the 16th Irish Division and one of them had found a full bottle of rum. They was all blotto! This was outside Guillemont. Beyond Guillemont. We was through Guillemont by now, digging in on the final objective. We felt rough – rough, I'll tell you! Actually that was our first real experience of warfare. Three or four times they had a go at Guillemont and they couldn't get it! But we got it!

In the general attack that had taken place along the length of the line, they had taken Guillemont – but they had been intended to take more.

For more than two months Thiepval village had scowled from behind the keep of its defences on the summit of the Thiepval Ridge and it seemed to the Tommies, creeping slowly towards it from the direction of the Leipzig Redoubt, and to the Aussies battering out from Pozières to take it in the rear by way of Mouquet Farm, as dauntingly impregnable as it had been on 1 July. So long as the Germans held Thiepval, they would be able to overlook almost the whole British advance and direct their guns to crush it.

From its heights, Thiepval could look over her shoulder to the high ridges that climbed up beyond Mametz – to Delville Wood, to High Wood and to Martinpuich. Just behind her back, the captured

[1] Sergeant Paterson, who three months before had earned the Military Medal, was awarded the Distinguished Conduct Medal after the Battle of Guillemont. The citation read: 'D.C.M. For conspicious gallantry in action. When both the officers of his Company had been wounded early in an attack, Sergeant Paterson collected and reformed his Company and pushed on to the final objective. He was twice wounded but displayed the utmost bravery and resource.'

village of Pozières was in full view with the windmill up the hill beyond it and, beyond even that, the land that swept in a bleak uninterrupted vista to Courcelette was clearly visible. Nearer still, Mouquet Farm held out and, as long as it did, Thiepval would hold out too. Looking out from Thiepval village across the treeless swampland of the Ancre Valley, the Mesnil Ridge, blasted and pockmarked by continuous bombardment, was bald of vegetation and, to the vigilant German observers, the chalk-white furrows of the spiralling communication trenches scarring the face of the hill pointed unerring fingers to the network of cable communications, and signposted with awful precision the journeyings of the passage-ways that led the British troops towards comparative safety and dubious shelter on the other side of the ridge.

The longest and most tortuous of the communication trenches, so steep that in places steps were built into it, was nicknamed Jacob's Ladder. But it was hardly a stairway to Paradise. By day it was bombarded with high explosives; by night unfortunate wayfarers were sprayed with shrapnel. Mingling with the burst of the explosions was the soft dull plopping of the gas shells that, night after night, soaked the Mesnil Ridge with deadly fumes. The last straw, in the back-breaking ascent, was having to sweat it out in the stifling confines of a gas helmet. The trench petered out into a muddy lane at the village of Mesnil.

The 'muddy lane' was a sunken road that ran from Mesnil past 'Brock's Benefit' to the trenches facing Beaumont Hamel. Radiating from it, other tracks and even a light railway ran towards the shoulder of the hill where the trenchline face Y Ravine. One day's fighting and more than two months incessant bombardment had reduced the battlefield to a wasteland and razed the British trenches almost out of existence. The task of a thousand unfortunate working parties had been to build them up again.

Working under the eyes of the enemy on the ridge beyond it was no easy job.

It was impossible to clear the land between the lines of its gruesome burden of dismembered dead. Even the old front line was so damaged and so choked by bodies, that it could only be held as an outpost and garrisoned by small parties of men. In the few places where the parapet had not been completely shattered, they stood guard, nauseated by the sight and smell of carnage as the working parties laboured to rebuild the line. The few hours of darkness between the long summer evening of one July day and the dawn of the next, were all too brief for the job because there was hardly a foot of trenchline in the sector between the Ancre and Serre which had not been damaged. During the last two weeks of August, in a final spurt of effort, the work on the trenches had been completed and now, on 3 September, the 39th Division filed into them to take part in the general attack from Thiepval to Guillemont which it was hoped would prepare the way for the Big Push that would finally break the line.

Their orders were to attack and capture three lines of trenches on the spur of high land south of Beaumont Hamel Valley; their real task was to cover the 49th Division across the Valley of the Ancre, as they went forward from Thiepval Wood to capture the Schwaben Redoubt and the line that linked it to the village of St Pierre Divion in the valley below. It was almost a blueprint of the attack of the First of July. But a new jumping-off line had been dug precociously near the German line, so close that it seemed inconceivable that, even against this now legendary rampart of steel and fire, the attack could fail. On the night of 2 September, the 6th West Yorks were back in Thiepval Wood – not, this time, in reserve but in the forefront of the attack. Now they were required to bloody the Pope's Nose.

The unflattering soubriquet had been coined, as might have been expected, by the 36th Ulster Division to describe the ugly little salient that thrust out, jagged with defences, to within yards of the British lines. It was armoured to the teeth and it adjoined another fortified strongpoint, dubbed the Triangle, which lay astride the old track that ran through the fields to St Pierre Divion. Concrete machine-gun posts dominated every possible approach but, from the new jumping-off trenches, audaciously far advanced beyond the old ones on the edge of Thiepval Wood, it seemed that one short sharp rush behind the creeping barrage would overwhelm the Pope's Nose and the Triangle at one swift decisive stroke. Meanwhile troops up the hill to the right would rush the German line and swarm across the Schwaben Redoubt. They had done it before. They could do it again. This time they would hold it.

But it was the few remaining old hands who had done it before. The new men, drafted in to fill the gaps in the decimated ranks of the 49th Division, were raw and inexperienced, newly out from home, so innocent that, when the principle of the creeping barrage was explained, there were anxious, mutinous mutterings, exclamations of disbelief. Misunderstanding the concept, the rumour spread that they had been earmarked as a suicide force and were intended to 'draw fire' by walking into the enemy's barrage. The misapprehension was resolved but, in the suspicious minds of the troops, a lingering doubt remained.

Even the officers and experienced NCOs anticipated the attack with misgiving. They knew that their men were exhausted. For the last six days they had spent every waking hour – including many, in the dead of night, which should properly have been devoted to sleep – humping ammunition and reserve rations from Aveluy Wood, across the Ancre and along the slogging miles of Black Horse road to forward dumps in Thiepval Wood. At the end of every exhausting trip, they were put to work again. The advanced trenches and saps had to be dug and there was no one else to do it.

They returned an hour or two before dawn so exhausted they could hardly walk and would have laid down in hundreds on Speyside or Paisley Dump, anywhere, but for officers and NCOs who were compelled to urge on the men to other fatigues and preparations during the daylight. Moreover, the Battalion was no longer the Territorial Unit of July First, but a mixture of reinforcements from twenty-seven different battalions from all parts of England, who had had no opportunity of shaking down into one efficient unit during the past few weeks of trench warfare. It was said that, if the men reached the assembly trenches on the morning of the battle, it would be a feat worthy of praise! And the most that was hoped for was that, with an extra rum ration, and the excitement of the moment, the attacking waves would reach the enemy support line and remain there from sheer physical inability to go back.

Captain E. V. Tempest, DSO, MC, 1/6th Btn., West Yorkshire Regiment, 146 Brigade, 49th Division.

The experience of my platoon was an average one. When we marched into support on 27 August this platoon was thirty-three strong and in fair condition. After a week of working parties, etc., there remained to go over the top eighteen decrepit old men. The rest were dead, wounded or in hospital. It was my unfortunate duty to wake my men and parade them for the fatigues. They lay like men drunk or dead. For instance, there was one decent average man who, I knew from experience, always pulled his last ounce. One night I could wake him by no ordinary means, and in the end he had to be pulled on to his feet, held there, and kicked into consciousness. He said, 'I can't do it, Sergeant! I'm done!'

I knew he was done, but there were sacks of trench mortar bombs to carry across the marsh up to the line and I had seen men do miracles before. He made an effort to pull himself together, and he moved off with the party. He collapsed after a few steps – but he was one of the eighteen in my platoon who went over the top two days later!

Sergeant J. E. Yates, 1/6th Btn., West Yorkshire Regiment, 146 Brigade, 49th Division.

Talking together, the Platoon Sergeants had come to the disquieting conclusion that any remote possibility of success would depend on one of three remote contingencies. First, that the enemy had been completely exterminated by the British barrage. Second that he was shocked into a state of instant paralysis at the very sight of them. Third, a miracle. Even without a miracle, if the Duke of Wellington's, on their right, had succeeded in capturing the Pope's Nose there might have been some flimsy chance of the West Yorks capturing the infamous Triangle. But they were too weakened by casualties and wearied by labour.

Under cover of the barrage, they had crept up right to the edge of the Pope's Nose, but the barrage of machine-gun fire directed from the Schwaben Redoubt up the hill snuffed out any hopes of holding on to the first few tenuous footholds they managed to gain. When their attack had been easily repulsed, the machine-gun crews in the Pope's Nose were able to swing their guns about to fire at point blank range on the men of the West Yorks who had penetrated the Triangle. And the German barrage, opening up within three minutes of Zero, was pounding the trenches where the troops of the second wave were waiting, with such lethal effect and with such uncanny accuracy that the 'second wave' never materialised at all. Those who were not blown sky-high by the shelling were pinned down and unable to move.

Arthur Wilson, newly commissioned, had joined the battalion in Thiepval Wood only three weeks before.

2nd Lieutenant Arthur Wilson, 1/5th Btn., West Yorkskshire Regiment, 146th Brigade, 49th Division.

We had moved forward and we got right up to the German saps, almost under the German wire, but we simply couldn't move. The shelling was so furious and our casualties were so enormous! Most of the Company Commanders were killed – there was no one to lead the men and the number of shells that fell was absolutely fantastic. We were simply blown to blazes and we couldn't do a thing. We were waiting for signals, but of course no word came back. It was a misty morning, so we could see nothing, and no runner could have got through that shelling. It was quite frightful. It was a wonder any of us escaped alive. One shell nearly took my hair off. The blast all went the other way and it killed Company Sergeant-Major Iredale. When we got out, I discovered that my right sock had been unravelled by the force of the explosion. It was completely unknitted for at least six to eight yards by the blast. It was quite extraordinary.

One message got through. It arrived at Battalion Headquarters at ten minutes past six. It had been scribbled by Lieutenant Armistead and it had taken an intrepid and lucky runner more than half an hour to cover the eight hundred yards to Battalion Headquarters. It was the first real information they received and the first they knew of what was happening beyond the thunder of the exploding barrage.

> We got part of the front wave into the enemy line. But the rest of the front wave stuck in front of the enemy wire, and then retired, leaving only a few scattered men in front line who have had to come back. I am trying to collect men into front parallel trench, but there are very few.

The few hardened survivors of the original battalion were grimly holding on. The new men, or those of them who had not been knocked out by the vicious whiplash of fire that traversed the Triangle, had indeed retired, fumbling back exhausted to huddle in small terrified groups against the low bank of the sunken road. Later, under repeated questioning, they all told the same story and could not be budged from it. They had been ordered to retire. Some of the men expressed the belief that the order must have been given by a German disguised as a British officer. It was an unlikely tale. Sadly, Captain Temple remarked that the evidence to support this claim was 'not very strong'. But none of the few remaining officers had the heart to blame the few remaining men. They had, quite simply, been asked to do the impossible.

At the pinnacle of the chain of command, opinion, less well-informed, was less sympathetic. General Gough had no hesitation in laying the blame for the failure of the attack squarely on the shoulders of the 49th Division, nor did he hesitate so to inform the Commander-in-Chief.

> *Monday, 4 September:* I visited Toutencourt and saw Gen. Gough. The failure to hold the position gained on the Ancre is due, he reported, to the 49th Division. The units of that Division did not really attack and some men did not follow their officers. The total losses of this Division are under a thousand![1] It is a Territorial Division from the West Riding of Yorkshire. I had occasion a fortnight ago to call the attention of the Army and

Extract from the diary of General Sir Douglas Haig.

[1] Even allowing for an understandable delay in the return of casualty figures, it is difficult to deduce on what information General Gough based his confident estimate of the 'total' casualties of the 49th Division. The four under-strength battalions of the 147th Brigade alone suffered more than twelve hundred casualties on the morning of 3 September and, of the 350 men of the 1/6th West Yorks. who went over the top in the first wave at the Triangle, 244 were killed or wounded. The total casualties of the Division (killed and wounded) including the shell-fire casualties of the second wave and Reserve Battalions, were approximately 3,000 – a considerable number for a division which was already under strength. Its total casualties between 1 July and 19 August had been 204 officers and 4,971 other ranks. A division, at full strength, numbered approximately twelve thousand men.

Corps Commanders (Gough and Jacobs) to the lack of smartness, and slackness of one of its Battalions in the matter of saluting when I was motoring through the village where it was billeted. I expressed my opinion that such men were too sleepy to fight well, etc. It was due to the failure of the 49th Division that the 39th (which did well and got all their objectives) had to fall back.

On the crown of the ridge the fortress of Thiepval still stood inviolable and secure. It had been touch and go. If the redoubt at Mouquet Farm had gone, the rear would have been threatened and vulnerable. But Mouquet had not fallen, even to the invincible Australians. Exhausted now, waiting for relief, the 1st Australian Division had been urged to make one final effort to take the farm. They had advanced their line, but they had not captured Mouquet. Away to their right, the troops had battered yet again into High Wood and, yet again, they had been hammered out of it. The attack at Delville Wood had resulted in a slight improvement of the line but the Germans were still strongly entrenched on its eastern edge and were fighting on. They were fighting on at Ginchy, waveringly captured, then lost at nightfall in a German counter-attack. But the village was half encircled and, a mile away, in the one real success of that day, the third of September, they had, of course, captured Guillemont.

They had not however captured Falfemont Farm and Harold Hayward believed with youthful egotism that, had he not been prevented by the Colonel from going forward with the rest of his Battalion, it might just have tipped the balance. His Battalion was the 12th Battalion, the Gloucestershire Regiment – the Bristol Battalion, which that city proudly referred to as 'Bristol's Own'.

When the Battalion had been formed in September 1914 a rash of advertisements had invited 'mercantile and professional gentlemen' to join its ranks. The 'mercantile gentlemen' had joined in large numbers. So had their clerks and the commissionaires whose prewar duties at the entrances of business premises had mainly consisted of opening doors and respectfully saluting the denizens of the commercial world who presided over the offices inside. Now the situation was reversed. Most of the commissionaires were ex-soldiers, bemedalled veterans of previous wars, and they were promptly given the rank of sergeant and entrusted with the task of instructing their erstwhile superiors in the arts of drilling and musketry.

For the first few weeks, before billeting arrangements could be made, most of the mercantile and professional gentlemen continued to live in their own homes and some were even able to continue attending their offices, unless prevented from doing so by the receipt of a polite postcard which expressed the hope that they would find it convenient to attend a drill. The drills themselves did little to lower their dignity. No khaki was available. Attired, as usual, in city suits and bowler hats the new recruits good-humouredly did their best to comply with polite requests from their former employees to 'Right wheel and left turn, if you please, sir.' The first parades were held on the artillery ground in Whiteladies road and, as they seldom lasted for more than an hour, the mercantile gentlemen had ample time in which to continue to look after their commercial interests. Unless, of course, they were courteously requested to perform guard duty.

Ten men each day were required to guard the Cumberland Basin, presumably to thwart the intentions of any German agent with villainous designs on the Bristol Docks. As this duty involved a march in the country, the gentlemen felt it appropriate to turn out in shooting-suits, Norfolk jackets and gaiters. Few of them, however, yet knew how to shoot and they harboured the secret hope that the very sight of the rifles they were privileged to carry (there were only enough of them to go round the guards and sentries) would be sufficient to terrify the enemy – should they be unfortunate enough to meet with Germans in such unlikely surroundings. The rifles were long, heavy, old fashioned and a distinct encumbrance, for the 'guard' did not travel light. They were laden with rugs, umbrellas, and picnic baskets containing wine, pickled herrings, hard-boiled eggs, cold salmon and tongue, and most hip-pockets contained the additional comfort of a brandy-flask. They looked less like a guard than like a party of country gentlemen on their way to a shoot or a picnic and the only enemy they met with in the course of their long day's vigil were groups of children who marched, jeering, behind them and occasionally, from a safe distance, favoured them with a volley of stones and, now and again, a brick.

With the move into permanent camp and later the issue of anonymous khaki uniforms, their dignity and the politeness of their respectful NCOs evaporated overnight.

The Corporals and Sergeants had not considered it necessary to show the same degree of consideration for the younger members of the Battalion. The majority were former pupils of Bristol Grammar School and had only recently left.[1] They all knew each other, hung together, treated the Army as a huge joke and introduced an element of schoolboy ragging that the Battalion could have well done without. There were pillow-fights and water-fights in the barrack-room dormitories where the beds were mere makeshift arrangements of palliasses laid on trestles and a favourite sport was to ensure a rude awakening for some unfortunate sleeper by pulling the trestle

---

[1] There was also a sizeable contingent from the Fairfield school and, like Harold Hayward, from Colston's.

smartly from beneath him so that he landed up on the floor. There was seldom any ill-feeling.

2nd Lieutenant
H. J. Hayward, MC,
No. 14314, 12th
(Bristol City) Btn.,
The Gloucestershire
Regiment, 5th
Division.

We were all firm friends. There were at least a dozen fellows I knew from school, nearly all my senior. My old form-master was our Company Commander. There were some fellows who had left the school before I went there, a few more who were prefects when I was a boy in the first form, and there were two whom had been great chums of mine, although they were both older, because we lived near each other. That was Tom Webber and Harold Howell. We stuck together like glue, even after we went to France. We were in the same section and the same platoon and we shared everything together. Life was more serious when we got to the trenches in France, of course, but we still used to rag and joke. There was one thing we got out there which was *café au lait*. It was coffee-flavoured or cocoa-flavoured condensed milk and it was the most delectable food you could get. I never saw it outside France, and it was a great treat for us. One night Tom and I were going to share a little tin of this and I was on sentry. When I got back I looked at this tin and it was empty! I said to Tom, 'What's happened to the *café au lait*?' He said, 'Well, my half was at the bottom – so I had to eat yours to get at mine.'

We nearly had a rough-house over that! But it was a joke. He'd stowed it away somewhere and there was still half a tin left. It made a wonderful hot drink. It was nectar.

Just before Guillemont the happy trio was broken up when Hayward was ordered out of the line and sent to Battalion Headquarters to act as the Colonel's runner. He was as furious as he might have been two years earlier had he been ordered to remain in the Headmaster's study while the school First Eleven played the most important cricket match of the season. Just as he might have done then, he protested to his form-master. It cut no ice. Major Beckett had been told to nominate one man from each company, he had put forward the name of his old pupil, and that was that. Half-suspecting that Beckett had seized the opportunity of keeping him out of the attack, Hayward protested to the Colonel himself. But the Colonel was adamant. Half his HQ squad had been evacuated with shell-shock. They must be replaced before the Battalion went into action. Hayward could not be spared. It was an appalling disappointment and Hayward did not make a cheerful addition to the personnel of Battalion HQ. He did not even have a sight of the battle when his comrades went over the top at noon on 2 September.

The King's Own Scottish Borderers had gone over several hours earlier, before nine in the morning. Moving forward with the French on their right, under a barrage fired by French guns, they were to capture Falfemont Farm, to knock it out and to hold it until the general attack swept forward at Zero Hour. Falfemont Farm, to the right of Guillemont, lay on the slopes of a valley hidden by the rising land. It was out of observation both from the Gloucester's HQ and from Guillemont, but the first reports were optimistic. None of the leading lines of men had returned. The assault must have been successful. The black truth was that they had not returned because all had been killed or wounded. The barrage had not materialised. Without informing the British, the French guns had been obliged to swing around to deal with a German counter-attack to the south of them and the French infantry, which should have advanced alongside the Borderers were left, like them, with no artillery support. In the Maurepas Ravine they were mown down by machine-gun fire and there they had stuck. Three hours later the Gloucesters went over the top to renew the attack.

At Battalion HQ it was a long, long day and the long night that followed was full of alarms, reports that the Germans were counter-attacking here in the Guillemont sector, waves of relief when it seemed that they had been beaten off. At dawn Colonel Archer-Shee went forward to see for himself what was happening. He took Hayward with him.

The Colonel had promised me that I could go. He said, 'I'll send you out to see how far the Battalion has gone forward. Just do your job here now and I'll let you go up to the front tomorrow.' I knew he meant when things had quietened down! We went right up to the line. It was fairly safe because we were only going to the line our boys were supposed to have occupied and there were other troops ahead of them. But all the way up, as it got lighter, we could see people lying all over the ground – I was shocked to see people in my own platoon who'd been knocked out. That was terrible!

At first, when we got to the line, we couldn't find the Battalion. There was nothing but a motley array of men in the trenches – not just people from other battalions in our Brigade, but people from other divisions I'd never even heard of. It was an awful mix up! Eventually we did find some of the boys and, by a miracle, I found my pals Tom and Harold. They were in the aid post. A shell had come over and buried Harold when they were going forward and the Company ran over him while he was down with all this earth and stuff on top of him. It was a miracle he got out! Tom Webber

2nd Lieutenant
H. J. Hayward, MC,
No. 14314, 12th
(Bristol City) Btn.,
The Gloucestershire
Regiment, 5th
Division.

was completely shell-shocked. We'd lost a lot of our NCOs and many, many officers.

There was a gap – a big gap – beyond the right of our line, and the ground was hidden, so we couldn't see anybody at all. The Colonel wanted to know who was there and what they intended to do. It was all quiet then, so he told me to run down and find out. We were standing there, quite exposed, and I had just stepped away from the Colonel and turned round when suddenly I was hit by a bullet that came from behind us, from one of the lines of trenches we'd over-run. There must have been a German sniper still holding out there and, of course, the Colonel presented a good target, standing there with his stick and his badges of rank and everything. But the sniper got me instead – right in the backside!

All the Colonel's personal interest and protection did not prevent Harry Hayward from being carried from the battlefield as a casualty. They carried him to the Colonel's own dugout where Lieutenant Fitzgerald extracted the bullet and bandaged the wound. Hayward had to wait until dark before the stretcher-bearers could carry him back to the road where a convoy of horse-drawn ambulances had managed to get up to the line. Alex Paterson was luckier. By the time Hayward was being loaded into the ambulance, Paterson was already settled in the comparative comfort of the casualty clearing station at Corbie. They must have passed within yards of each other that morning for the remnants of Paterson's company had been ordered to the rear to collect the Battalions' rations and Sergeant Paterson had been wounded leading it back to the line.

Sergeant A. K.
Paterson, DCM, MM
No. 52574, A.Coy.,
11th (S) Btn.,
The Rifle Brigade

I can hardly describe how different the ground was as we went back up through it, compared to what it had been the day before. It had been no picture then, but now there was no sign of any landmark at all, just shell-holes and mud. We had all our equipment and as well as that each one of us was carrying a full sandbag of cheese, bread, jam, whatever they were sending up. We were carrying extra ammunition in belts slung over our shoulders and we were carrying the mail up too, letters and parcels for the boys in the line. You can imagine that we didn't move very fast.

I spread the men out in single file, with five paces between each man and put Corporal Bradley with the two stretcher-bearers and stretcher in the rear, so that they could see to any casualties. When I got within waving distance of our new Headquarters – about a hundred yards away – I increased the pace and, just as I gave the order, I heard a shell coming. I could tell by the sound of it that it would drop near to my left side, so I dived into a shell-hole on my right. But I was too late. A lump of the shell penetrated my left thigh and a smaller piece went into my right hand which was holding the sandbag.

I wouldn't let the men break rank. I signalled to them to double forward and saw them all arrive safely in the Headquarters' shell-hole and then I called Corporal Bradley over and handed over my platoon roll book. During the night I had written out the new roll of A Company. It didn't take up much room.

The stretcher-bearers carried me out.

Fred White came through unhurt – but fed up.

They relieved us and took up back to the support line and told us we were going out on divisional rest. We were all formed up ready to go when who should come in but the sick, lame and lazy – those blokes who'd gone up to the Medical Officer just before we went in the line and said they'd got this and they'd got that. They made a miraculous recovery as soon as we got out! There they were, about twelve of them, looking all spick and span and smart and there *we* were, dirty and unwashed and covered with mud and looking like nothing on earth. Just as we were ready to go, my Platoon Sergeant came up and he told off five of us – 'You, you, you, you, you. You've got to stay behind and clean up the battlefield.' Well, you know what cleaning up the battlefield means? Cleaning up the battlefield means searching all the dead people and looking for all the information and identities and then burying them.

I didn't argue with the Sergeant. I just said, 'Excuse me, Sergeant, take me to Lieutenant Hannay.' That was proper Army procedure, in the line or out. Sergeant Pearce wasn't very pleased, but he took me to the officer and he said, 'This man's got a complaint.' 'What is it?' says the Officer. I told him. I said, 'We've been in this action. We've fought this action. These people there have just come out from a tidy place' – meaning the sick, lame and lazy – 'and now we've been told to go back and clean up the battlefield. *They* should go up. They're more fitter than what we are to go up!'

Lieutenant Hannay said, 'I see your point.' So we got off with it and he made them stay behind. I was popular with the platoon for that, but I wasn't so popular with the Sergeant!

Rifleman Fred White, No. R.8529, B. Coy., 10th Btn., King's Royal Rifle Corps, 59th Brigade, 20th Division.

Muddy, unshaven, exhausted but with a light tread, the victors of Guillemont went out of the line and the 56th Division went in to pursue the battle beyond the village. The Australians too went thankfully back to billets and the Canadians moved into their place. In every sector of the line divisions were reshuffled. For the next ten days the task of the Army was to pivot on Guillemont, to try to swing forward, to straighten the line to a position of advantage for the Big Push planned for 15 September.

Hopes were high, for the Army would be supported by the new Secret Weapon. The Tanks were on their way.

So were the New Zealanders.

Part 4

The Mouth of Hell

Into the mouth of hell,
Sticking it pretty well,
Slouched the six hundred.

E. A. Mackintosh,
Autumn, 1916.

Chapter 20

The evening of 5 September was fine and clear but the stiff breeze that had swept away the last of the rain clouds felt distinctly chilly to the soldiers squatting in a muddy field as they enjoyed the unaccustomed treat of an open-air cinema show at Morlancourt, fifteen kilometres from the firing line. Watching the comical misadventures of Charlie Chaplin it was possible to forget the sky beyond, flickering with the bombardment of the 'evening hate'. Even the staccato bark of the guns was masked to some extent by the sound of a tinny piano. With more goodwill than skill, a young officer was doing his best to provide a 'sound track' of appropriate music in the style of professional pianists who performed in the more civilised surroundings of picture palaces at home. Charlie Chaplin was one thing: the second half of the programme baffled the pianist, for in his limited repertoire, there was no music which could add anything to the mood and the drama of the official film of the Battle of the Somme.

It had been filmed by Geoffrey Malins, accredited to the War Office as a cinematograph photographer to capture an official record of troops in action in a major battle. He had ranged far and wide behind the front filming the troops in training, at rest and on the march. He had filmed them kneeling bareheaded on the open ground as surpliced Padres gave a final blessing on the last Sunday in June. He had filmed them moving up the line and assembling for the Big Push. When the battle started on the morning of the First of July he was placed in a hazardously exposed position in a jumping-off trench in front of Beaumont Hamel and, despite the danger, and the unnerving din, turning the handle of his hand-cranked camera at the steady two revolutions per second, he had recorded the scene with coolly professional detachment. Malins had filmed four reels before an explosion knocked the tripod from underneath the camera and very nearly knocked out the cameraman himself. Later, he had turned his lens on the wounded crowding into the aid posts, on disconsolate groups of German prisoners with their triumphant escorts and on troops returning cheerfully from the battle. The film had been shown privately to the King and Queen at Windsor Castle and now it was on show to the general public in halls and cinemas all over the country – half a dozen of them in London alone – and advertised as 'authentic, realistic pictures of Our Boys at the Front'. At the end of every showing rapturous audiences, who had queued for hours to see it, cheered and applauded until their palms ached.

The Boys who actually were at the front, viewed the film with mixed feelings. Some senior officers had doubted the wisdom of showing it at all, at least to the troops, like those at Morlancourt, who were about to take their own chance in the Battle of the Somme, but the men watched, rapt and attentive.

The celluloid soldiers marched jerkily at ease, as cheerily – to judge by their grins and inaudible mouthings – as they themselves had marched to Morlancourt. They saw them wink and laugh and salute the camera in a silent bravado of excitement as they waited to go over the top. They saw the awesome soundless swelling of the earth as the mine above Beaumont Hamel tossed half the Hawthorn Ridge into the sky and the men, who rose like phantoms from the trenches and ran like clockwork toys across the ground beyond. They saw men falling soft to the earth as a rag doll might be tossed down by a child, the gushing fountains of exploding shells, the gauze of cordite fumes that drifted lazily across the erupting earth. To the men who sat watching in the chill and the dark under the open sky it seemed like a spectral battle fought by the long-dead ghosts of soldiers uniformed in phantom grey. In all the images that flickered across the big screen in the corner of the field, there was not an echo of the fight, not a hint of the roar of the guns, the crash of explosions, the crack of rifles, the screams, the shouts, the deadly rattle of machine-guns. It was insubstantial as a dream. But for the rumble of the distant guns they might have been watching from another planet. The reality was that the cinema-goers themselves would soon be on their way to that place where the guns glowed on the thundersome horizon.

The far-off growl of the bombardment had rolled nearer with every step the New Zealanders took on the march from Amiens. By the time they reached Laviéville, just a few kilometres from Morlancourt, they could feel the vibration beneath their feet. It was 8 September. In a bid to rock the line so painfully gained by the British and French, and to thwart the big attack they were clearly preparing, the Germans had mounted a mammoth counter-attack. The line swayed, and held, but the shock-waves of the duelling guns, massed now in thousands on both sides of the line, rippled across the few miles that lay between them and the hutted camp at Laviéville as if to underline the uneasy fact that the N. Zedders were for it. It was not that they had never before heard gun-fire, but they had never before heard it on such a scale.

They had been five days on the march and on the whole it had not been unenjoyable. It was a change to get out of the trenches. It was a change to perambulate in small towns and villages where civilians kept up a semblance of normal life. They had enjoyed ogling the girls, who trailed alongside the long marching columns, fascinated by the strange appearance of the New Zealanders in their lemon-squeezer hats. There had been quaint sights to explore on rest days, wine to be sampled in *estaminets* and, finally, encamped by the River Somme at la Chaussée, a glorious bathing parade to wash away the heat and the dust and soothe swollen and blistered feet. In the 1st Canterbury Battalion Howard Kippenberger, Harry Baverstock and Jack Gee were popularly known as the Three Musketeers and commonly referred to as Kip, Bav and Gee. All three were privates and they were bosom friends.[1]

They were marching together on the last long stretch of road that led from Amiens to Albert – a full eighteen kilometres – and they were finding it hard going. By the time they had covered ten of them the Kiwis were filthy, sweating and bedraggled and there was still a long, long way to go. They were also parched and Platoon Sergeant Geordie Hudson was particular on the subject of water-bottles – so particular that he would scarcely allow his men a drink. 'You never know when your need will be *much* greater than it is now, so keep that bottle intact.' A raging thirst did not add to the delights of the march.

The long straight road between Amiens and Albert had a single bend and at it stood an imposing figure outside an equally imposing gateway. He was only a sentry, only a private like themselves but, from the stiff peak of his hat to the polished toecaps of his boots, his burnished, immaculate turnout was the very antithesis of their own. Despite the splendour of their recently acquired lemon-squeezer hats, the New Zealanders felt like a bunch of grimy hobos. 'Look boys! A soldier!' It was Kip who called out as they passed – and he was only half joking.

The sentry was not only every inch a soldier but every inch a Guardsman. The place was Querrieu and he was on guard outside the château where General Rawlinson presided over 4th Army Headquarters and where, even now, the finishing touches were being put to the plans for the next big effort on 15 September. This time it would not, must not, fail. This time even partial success would not be good enough. This time they would smash the German line and break through, at last, to Bapaume and beyond. Like the New Zealanders, the cavalry was already moving towards the line and the time had surely come, after so many disappointments, when

---

[1] 'Kip', however, was at the start of an illustrious military career and eventually became Major-General Sir Howard Kippenberger and Second-in-Command of the New Zealand Forces in the Second World War.

they would at last come into their own and dash triumphantly through the German lines to exploit the advance, to finish the job. It only needed the infantry to punch the first hole and, with the help of the new Secret Weapon, the infantry could scarcely fail.

There were fewer than sixty tanks, to be sure, and far fewer than the Commander-in-Chief had desired, but there were enough to scare the wits out of the Germans. The tank was the ace in the British hand, but there was one small anxiety. The Germans still held two trump cards on the front between Delville Wood and Guillemont and, at all costs, they must be forced to relinquish them before the battle for the break-through began.

By some feat of tenacity, which even the British Staff were reluctantly forced to admire, the Germans still clung on to part of Delville Wood. They still held Ginchy village to the right of it. Worst of all, they still held the Quadrilateral. Nothing, it seemed, would push them out of it and, until they were pushed out, the troops could barely budge beyond Guillemont.

They wanted to go up the hill. It was such a short distance – a mere ten minutes brisk stroll to the woods that lay so tantalisingly close to the village on either side of the road that led to Combles hidden in the dip beyond. The maps proclaimed them to be Leuze Wood on the right and Bouleaux Wood on the left. With natural logic they became, in the language of the Tommies, 'Lousy' and 'Bollocks' and as they stumbled and fumbled and fought and died in attempt after attempt to capture the woods the names seemed more and more to be appropriate.

It was the 56th Division, regrouped, reinforced, rested and refreshed after their ordeal at Gommecourt who were, for a second time, burning out their strength in the furnace of Lousy Wood and it was the Quadrilateral that thwarted their every effort. To the right of Guillemont village the 56th had managed to fight forward in the shelter of the valley to capture part of the wood, to drive the Germans out of their deep dugouts and to cling obstinately to one corner, but unless they could advance from Guillemont itself, straight up the slope of the hill, they could do no more. The Quadrilateral, away to the left, dominated the road and everything that tried to move along it.

This strongpoint was a complex of entrenchments built round part of the old railway cutting. It was furnished with fortifications of iron and concrete, stalwart enough to defy an earthquake and skilfully sited to command a field of fire which, in every direction, was absolute.[1]

---

[1] Almost seventy years later they still stand and even explosives have done no more than tilt them.

Linked by a strongly held trench to another strongpoint (the Triangle) on the Ginchy Ridge which dominated the village of Ginchy beyond, the Quadrilateral was the king-pin and the key to the solid second line of the Germans' defences, built as an impregnable insurance three miles behind the first. Their front line had long been shattered. The Germans were resolved to hold on to the second. The British were equally determined to dislodge them. If, on 15 September, they were still in possession of the Quadrilateral it would imperil the whole attack. Ginchy was taken on 9 September. The Guards moved in to secure the village and, in the scant week that remained before the new offensive, to have one more go at the Quadrilateral.

Two miles away, on the evening of the same day, Arthur Agius found himself in command of his Battalion among the bloody stumps of Lousy Wood. Every other officer had been killed or wounded. He noted rather sadly that, after the day's fighting, there was precious little left of the Battalion to command.

It was as well that Agius had plenty to do. It kept his mind occupied and the responsibility of holding the Battalion together helped him to hold himself together too. His sojourn behind the lines had cured him of his 'nerves' after Gommecourt but now he was shocked to notice the old familiar symptoms of 'shakiness'. He hoped to God that this time he could hang on. Being busy helped. The saddest and most dispiriting of the manifold duties of command were the letters which had to be written – and written as soon as possible – to the relatives of the people who had been killed. Agius sat in the newly captured German dugout and, by the light of a candle that guttered and sank in its evil-smelling, airless depths, penned letter after letter in a hand that showed a disturbing propensity to shake.

> Dear Mr and Mrs O'Dell, It is my very sad duty to have to tell you that your son Oliver. . . . Dear Mrs Scarlett, I am so very sorry. . . . Dear Mr and Mrs Starling, By now you will have received official notification. . . .

They were painfully difficult letters to write but there was a formula which eased the process and which Agius, in common with a thousand other officers engaged on the same sad task, fervently hoped would ease the hearts of sorrowing relatives.

> . . . always so cheerful. He will be greatly missed . . . much loved by his men who would have followed him anywhere . . . one of our best officers . . . a real loss to the battalion . . . genuinely missed . . . although he had not been with the battalion for long . . . loyal,

reliable and trustworthy . . . the men adored him . . . wise beyond
his years . . . hope that it will be at least some comfort to you to
know . . . he died bravely, doing his duty . . . was shot through the
head and died instantaneously . . . immediately became unconscious . . . killed outright by a bullet through the heart . . . could
have felt no pain . . . assure you that he did not suffer. . . . Deepest
sympathy. . . . Deepest sympathy. . . . Deepest sympathy.

It was kinder that way. The aim of every man who wrote such a letter
was to preserve the illusion of heroic death, of a clean fight, of noble
warriors struck down in battle by a bullet which flew straight and true
to extinguish a brave life in the execution of some desperate advance
or noble act. The ugly truth would be too hard to bear. Few of the
bodies that littered the battlefield lay in the classic attitude of the
Fallen Warrior. Few bore the single disfiguring mark of a neat bullet
wound. Many had not even been killed 'in action' as people at Home
could have understood the term. The vast majority had been tossed,
mutilated, dismembered, decapitated by monstrous splinters of
shells. Some were sliced apart by machine-gun fire. Some, like
Harold Scarlett, caught in the epicentre of an explosion, had been
scattered to the four winds. It was just two months since Scarlett had
joined the Battalion in the wake of the Gommecourt disaster, fresh
from England and newly married. How, Agius asked himself, could
you tell a young wife of four months that her husband's body had
simply been blown out of existence? Agius wrote on . . . *died doing his
duty and was buried where he fell.* . . . In a sense, it was true. Even as he
wrote he could hear, barely a mile away, the awful clamour of the
battle bursting in the night. With every breath, with every stroke of
his pen, with every ear-splitting explosion, more men were falling
wounded and dying in the struggle for the Quadrilateral and already,
in preparation for the big breakthrough on 15 September, the troops
were moving closer to the line.

The Canterbury Battalion had marched on Sunday morning from
Laviéville to bivouac on the hill above Fricourt and 'bivouac' meant
bedding down and finding such shelter as they could manufacture by
their own efforts. Even the succession of draughty barns and
shell-torn attics, which were a good deal too airy by half, seemed, in
retrospect, like luxury to the Three Musketeers. There was nothing
for it but to dig a man-sized rectangle on the sloping hillside, line it
with a waterproof sheet and, with an overcoat masquerading as a
blanket, to settle down to uneasy slumber and to try not to dwell on
the close resemblance of the 'bivouac' to a grave. To cap it all it
rained. Nevertheless, it had been an exciting day.

As the boys marched past Bécordel on the Fricourt road, the New

Zealanders, who had moved up ahead of them, were lining the road to cheer them on, and one particular shout directed at Bav came from four pals from his schooldays, Jackson, Ricketts, Biss and Hickmott. Rupert Hickmott had been the idol of Christchurch High School. He was the school's top cricketer – a skilful batsman, a deadly googly bowler and his fielding was an inspiration. It was no surprise to any of his schoolmates that he was chosen to play for New Zealand and, for three years before the war, the school had basked in reflected glory. Now, like the rest of them, Hickmott was in khaki and in France, and a new generation of schoolboys was basking in a glow of patriotism. No less than 786 Old Boys were serving in the forces and, since the entire roll of pupils numbered only 390, the school considered that this was not a bad record. Now that all the New Zealanders were assembled together, Baverstock kept bumping into old friends. Having dug his gloomy bivouac he went visiting and then, with Kip and Gee, indulged in a little sight-seeing.

It was an unforgettable sight. On the other side of the valley was the totally wrecked village of Fricourt. As far as the eye could see there were shattered forests, the mutilated skeletons of the trees. Down below us there were several nine-inch long-barrelled guns and on the opposite slope between Fricourt and Mametz Wood was a long line of six-inch Howitzers about thirty yards apart and, up near the front line, the eighteen-pounders were barking away. The nine-inch monsters just below our bivouacs erupted from time to time in groups of four and the detonation was so terrific that it hurt horribly. Without thinking I stood just a yard away from one of them. There was a sudden rush of hot air and then concussion, so loud that you actually couldn't hear it. That sounds paradoxical, but it is quite true. I caught just a fleeting glimpse of the shell tearing through space.

Private H. Baverstock, No. 11608, 1st Canterbury Btn., New Zealand Division.

The same night, we were ordered to go on a road-repairing expedition to just behind the front line. We wandered off with shovels and got as far as the high ground beyond Caterpillar Valley, not far behind where the Aucklands (the Dinks) had gone into the line on the 9th. I hate to say this but, as we had no officers with us, we didn't do a tap of work. The sights we saw were far too tremendous for that.

It was a panorama you could never hope to see again. The sky was deep opalescent blue and it was continuously being stabbed by spurts of flame, just like lightning. The din was diabolic and the devil must have been grinning. All that inferno was right up his street, because it was like hell let loose. Overhead we could just hear the *boom, boom, boom* of huge shells lumbering over to the

German back-areas. They were so big and huge that they seemed to take an unconscionable time and occasionally we could see a glare spreading out as they exploded far off in the distance. We had to run the gauntlet of the big guns in Mametz as we went back to our bivouacs.

The Reserve Brigades of some six Divisions were packed in a vast gypsylike encampment across the slopes of the ridge beyond Fricourt and Mametz and, as they awaited orders to move up to relieve their comrades in the front line, they led a gypsylike existence, sleeping in holes in the ground and, with water strictly rationed, washing infrequently, if at all. Only the Guards managed to conduct themselves as if they were still quartered at Pirbright or Caterham. They were disciplined and immaculate. They kept themselves apart, posted sentries round the limits of their exclusive area and dared any disreputable Tommy to put so much as a toe within it.

Lance-Corporal Len Lovell, No. 18692, A Coy., King's Own Yorkshire Light Infantry.

We were lying next to the Guards and you couldn't help admiring them. They were in exactly the same conditions as we were. It had rained on them just the same as it had on us. We were all in the open air, but we were all scruffy and dirty and they were clean and tidy. We didn't know how they did it! Their Quarter Guard was spick and span. Their sentry was on his beat, marching up and down, saluting officers and presenting arms as if they were all still at home in barracks. What discipline! It was marvellous!

Lance-Corporal Charles Frost, MM, No. 17256, 1st Btn., The Leicestershire Regiment.

I only joined up two years under age in March 1915 but I was drafted to the 1st Leicesters after they'd had a lot of casualties and, of course, being a Regular Battalion, a bit of their glory rubbed off on us. We thought we were a cut above the rest of Kitchener's mob, but we were nothing to the Guards. We saw a lot of them, because we were in the same Army Corps, and they were often up with us. We used to think they were looked after a damned sight better than we were. Nothing was too good for the Guards! The things they got from home! Well, the officers of the Guards were nearly all moneyed people and their women organised a lot of things for the Guardsmen. They even had a chip van right there, behind Fricourt. They'd got an old caravan frying chips for them! You could smell them all over the place. The smell was all *we* got. That was my biggest worry in the Army – I never got enough to eat and, being only seventeen or eighteen, I was growing all the time.

Private John L. Bouch, No. 1176, 1st Btn., The Coldstream Guards.

I enlisted in the Coldstream Guards at the end of August 1914. You'd never believe the training and discipline we went through at the Guards Depot at Caterham. We were subjected to a volume of abuse and scorn which is difficult to imagine. I found out swear words I'd never heard before. I found out a combination of swear words of such degree and magnitude that weren't imaginable! They called us these things in front of officers and nobody said a word.

We were run until we were breathless and then we had to run again simply because we couldn't do a complicated piece of drill as quick as they wanted us to. 'On the left, form SQUAD!' When you found that the man next door had two right feet instead of a left and a right and he went the wrong way, the Drill Sergeant would shout, 'You bloody idiot! Double up the parade ground!' And up we would all have to go, up the parade ground and back again, up again and back again until he shouted, 'Have you had enough, you buggers?' The Drill Sergeant had a voice that carried fifty miles! 'You're in the Guards, remember!' he used to shout. 'This is *not* a regiment of the line. You are supposed to be the people to guard the Sovereign, God help him!'

All our officers were lords, or nearly so. The Honourable Charles Knowles was our Company Commander. Lord Hugh Kennedy was a Lieutenant in charge of Number 12 Platoon. Viscount Holmesdale was another Lieutenant in our Company. I was a Private. We were worlds apart. Even the distinction between Private and non-commissioned officers was very, very marked. In fact a private couldn't speak to an NCO without standing to attention. At the barracks at Caterham, we even had to stand to attention to speak to an old soldier who was in charge of the barrack rooms – and he was just a private like ourselves!

I was Captain Morrison's servant. He was a multi-millionaire and he used to pay for a lot of the stuff that came to the Officers' Mess. Before we went to France in 1915 I had to go to Fortnum and Mason's and arrange for what you might call tuck boxes to be sent out to the Battalion regularly. Then I had to go to Berry's, the wine merchants, and place an order with them – a bottle of 1900 port to be sent to us every three days and cases of whisky and brandy. They used to arrive marked with a red cross. Medical comforts!

By the time we went down to the Somme Captain Morrison had left the Battalion, but he never cancelled the order and the stuff kept on coming. It used to arrive in batches and sometimes we'd have as many as a dozen boxes from Fortnum and Mason's arriving at the same time. They were boxes of tinned stuff, mostly, like galantine of chicken, soups, puddings, tins of fruit, tins of grouse and pheasant, ham – everything you could think of for the Officers' Mess. We used to have that much stuff that we couldn't

Private William Jackman, No. 2604675, 3rd and 4th Btn., The Grenadier Guards.

cart it about with us, so we had to make dumps here and there. Often we didn't go back to the same place, so there must have been some farmhouses who did very well out of us!

After Captain Morrison left to go back to England, Lord Henry Seymour, who was our Commanding Officer, asked me to go into the Officers' Mess, on the catering staff. That suited me! It was a good job with plenty of perks. We were living like lords and I wasn't anxiously looking for promotion, believe me!

When the battalion went up the line on 9 September I went up with Battalion Headquarters to look after the officers. We had a cook when we were out at rest, but he didn't come with us into the line. I used to take up soup cubes and dried eggs and make scrambled eggs for the Colonel and the officers at Battalion HQ and before we went up I made up four sandbags, one for each company to take into the forward line to feed the Company officers. They couldn't do any cooking there, so they were filled with tinned stuff and a bottle of whisky, a bottle of brandy and one of port.

Battalion Headquarters was in a shell-hole – a huge shell-hole. You could have put a bus in it! Of course we were a bit to the rear of the companies and that saved us, although when they started throwing shells and stuff over you had to take what came the same as the rest.

Jackman was better off by far than the Grenadier Guardsmen of the four companies in the front line. It was hardly a line at all. The trenches were so broken and so shattered that in places they had all but disappeared and where they did exist they were littered with the dead of the 47th Brigade whom the Guards were relieving. The relief took a long time. In the grizzly shambles of the ground to the south-east of Ginchy, the Guards had had difficulty in finding the positions so neatly marked on the trench maps. They had been on the move since dusk, but the relief was completed just sixteen minutes before the sun rose beyond the German line to reveal the full havoc and destruction around the Quadrilateral. There was no rest for the Grenadiers after their sleepless night. If the line was to be held, let alone advanced, it would need the efforts of every man to improve it. The Guardsmen slogged at the job all day and they worked on for most of the night. For once, they were cursing the fine weather. For five days it had been warm and summerlike. The night was clear and starry. The moon was not quite full, but it was almost as bright as day and every inadvertent movement brought swift retribution from enemy machine-gunners.

Next night, 11 September, the tanks began their slow grinding journey towards the battle. With no lights of their own they needed the moon to show them the way. They had been parked well back, closely guarded, and shrouded in tarpaulin covers so vast that imagination could barely conceive the nature and the dreadfulness of whatever mechanical mammoth might be skulking underneath. They looked so much like hump-back monsters that the troops, agog with rumour and gossip, had begun to call them 'Mastodons'. The Army, hoping that any such rumours as might reach the Germans would be scotched by the supposition that they were portable water tanks for the benefit of the troops in the line, called them 'tanks'. The Admiralty – under whose aegis they had first been developed – called them 'land-ships'. After two years of almost static warfare, of fruitless effort and endeavour, of vulnerable flesh perishing against unyielding iron and concrete, after two months and more of calculating the bitter cost of every painfully captured yard of ground on the Somme, the Staff were calling them a Godsend. Their hopes were high. The trials had been impressive. There was hardly an obstacle the tanks could not run over as easily as a child might propel a wooden toy, step by step, up a flight of stairs. They could uproot trees, over-run trenches, crush barbed wire entanglements and, given enough of them, surely they could crush the enemy too.

The Army had unfortunately not been given enough of them and the mammoth engines of the fifty prototypes they did receive were already fast degenerating through the wear and tear of the very training exercises, trials and tests which, ironically, were essential to their success. There had been neither enough time nor enough tanks to train the infantry to work with them in new techniques of attack. There had been little enough time to train the embryo tank crews to handle them.

A tank weighed twenty-eight tons. It took one hour and one gallon of petrol to travel half a mile. Ten had been kept in reserve and now, in the light of the full moon, the roads were shaking and vibrating under the weight of forty-two tanks as they went clanking to their assembly positions a mile or two behind the front line between Fricourt and Bray. The soldiers who saw them looming out of the night like immense black whales could hardly believe their eyes.

The tank crews were elated to be on the move at last, but the excitement of some of their Commanders was tinged with unease. They had been training for barely three months. Their instructions for the battle were complicated. Closeted with the Divisional Staff Officers they had spent hours studying maps and aerial photographs of the routes their tanks would take when the battle started. They had studied the Order of Battle and the timetables of each Corps and Division and, finally, each Commander had drawn up his own map, worked out the compass bearings from point to point, the estimated time of his arrival at each place and then readjusted his calculations to fit in with timing of the infantry. They had been bombarded by an avalanche of directions, instructions, advice and dire warnings in such profusion that there had not been enough written copies to go round. It had been almost impossible to memorise them all. They were ordered, furthermore, that their painfully prepared maps must be similarly imprinted on their minds. They were not to be allowed to carry them into action. It was hardly surprising, as the tanks lumbered towards their first engagement, that many brows were furrowed.

Certain Staff Officers at GHQ were worried too. They doubted the advisability of using the tanks at all. If two hundred had been available it might have been a different matter, but could a mere forty-two, spread over the fifteen kilometres of the attack, possibly succeed in breaking the line wide open and ushering the British Army through the gap? It was a moot point. It had been argued, discussed and gone over again and again. There were those who wished to wait until the tanks were available in sufficient numbers to guarantee success. There were those who were tempted to try the few forerunners out as an experiment but were nonetheless worried that, by doing so, they would lose the vital element of surprise which in a future massed assault might easily bowl the Germans over. And there were those who, like the Commander-in-Chief, felt that, whatever the risks, the opportunity must be seized to break the deadlock before autumn turned to winter. It would be a gamble but it was their only chance and overall confidence was high. This time there was a good deal more than the hope of success – there was near-certainty.

The guns struck up the overture to the battle on the morning of 12 September and this time they were ranging uncompromisingly on Bapaume. On the 13th, GHQ sent out a ringing call to arms. It was addressed to all ranks of the Fourth and Reserve Armies and appealed to them for 'bold and vigorous action'. It pointed out that the British Infantry outnumbered the Germans by four to one, that the Allies had far more guns and almost total supremacy in the air. It spoke of the cavalry massed to exploit the gains of the infantry. It hinted at the mysterious Secret Weapon which *may well produce great moral and material effects*. It pointed out the losses and hardships suffered by the enemy, the deterioration of his morale, the *'confusion and disorganisation'* in his ranks. It assured the troops that there was little depth or strength left in the enemy's defences, that his reserves were weak and *'composed entirely of units which have already suffered defeat'*.

It boomed encouragement:

Under such conditions risks may be taken with advantage which would be unwise if the circumstances were less favourable to us.

The assault must be pushed home with the greatest vigour, boldness, and resolution, and success must be followed up without hesitation or delay to the utmost limits of the power of endurance of the troops.

The bombardment redoubled. All day shells thundered on the Quadrilateral and on the last uncaptured corner of Delville Wood. The Guards edged forward in front of Ginchy and straightened their line. On their right the 6th Division pushed forward to the Ginchy–Morval road but stopped short in the withering face of the Quadrilateral itself.

That night it poured with rain. Just as he had been a day or two earlier in bivouacs above Fricourt, Len Lovell, in the 6th King's Own Yorkshire Light Infantry, was occupying a position adjacent to the Guards, or at least his Brigade was immediately to the left of theirs. Lovell himself was not aware of being adjacent to anyone, with the exception of Bobby Pearce and a handful of A Company's Bombers. They had been sent forward from the ragged linked-up shell-holes which served the 6th King's Own Yorkshire Light Infantry as a trenchline, to see if, by some miracle, the Germans on the edge of the wood had survived the pounding of the day's bombardment or if, as was fervently hoped, they had had the good sense to retire. In Delville Wood hardly one of the skeleton tree trunks stood more than two feet high. Many were broken off so low that only a few treacherous splinters spiked from their jagged roots in the path of the Bombers crawling belly-down in the pitch-black, feeling ahead for obstacles, striving impossibly for silence, stifling curses when unseen talons of broken timber caught and tore at their hands and clothing, stopping for long moments to listen as they drew near the edge of the wood where the Germans had last been seen. They were experienced raiders. They were used to it and, unlike the Guards, they were handier with bombs than with bullets.

Bobby Pearce had recently proved himself to be just a bit too handy with bombs, or rather, with an unexploded trench-mortar shell he dragged back from one of their patrols in No Man's Land and whose innards – being of a mechanical turn of mind – he was anxious to inspect. It was unfortunate that he accidentally dropped the nose-cap on the floor of the Bombers' billet. Five sleeping men received a rude awakening plus painful, if convenient, Blighty wounds in their feet. In the bedlam that followed the explosion the coke brazier was knocked over and the billet burnt down. As Section NCO Len Lovell received a severe reprimand. Bobby Pearce received a nasty head wound and, following his recovery, a Court-Martial. He had rejoined the Battalion on the march down to the Somme and now, creeping forward through Delville Wood, Lovell was glad of it.

Even before the embellishment of the ugly new scar he now bore on his forehead, Bobby Pearce had a face that only a mother could love. He could neither read nor write. It was Lovell who wrote his letters home and read out, with difficulty, the infrequent, near-illegible replies. Pearce was a rough diamond and an old soldier. He was entitled to wear the campaign medal of the South African War, but he scorned it as a 'bare-arsed medal'. That war had ended before Bobby had got nearer the front than Gibraltar and he did not agree with the opinion of the Army that he qualified for the statutory decoration. Pearce was a hard swearer and a hard drinker. Lovell had covered up for him, had got him out of trouble a dozen times but there was no man he would rather have had at his own shoulder when there was trouble ahead.

Corporal Len Lovell, No. 18692, 6th Btn., King's Own Yorkshire Light Infantry.

When we got to within a few yards of what we thought was Jerry's position, we lay there for a long time waiting for a lull in the shelling. All we had to do was see if we could hear them and then creep back and report that they were there. There was no question of making an attack, or anything like that. It seemed like hours before there was a pause in the terrible noise and, when it came, lying there right under the German wire, we could hear them moving about, even talking. That was all we had to know, so I signalled to my nearest man to pass the word to retire. We crept back the way we'd come, keeping low and as quiet as we could. When we were just a few yards from our own position – which was just linked up shell-holes with a few sandbags here and there as a kind of parapet – one of the men jumped up to dash the last few yards to his own shell-hole. At that very moment, there was a break in the clouds and a blink of moon came out. The Jerries must have been suspicious that something was up and looking out for any movement because, instantly, a machine-gun opened fire and the man fell. We got back into the trench, reported to our Bombing Officer and then, as I looked around the party, I realised that we'd lost Bobby Pearce.

Two of us crawled over the parapet, back to where we had seen the body fall and dragged him in. Bobby was completely dead. A bullet had struck him at the back of the head and the whole top of it had gone. He had been my father figure – a much older man than me, who really had looked after me like a father although I was his Section NCO. I felt really terrible.

Before it got light we buried him just a few yards away and stuck a rifle in the ground, bayonet downwards, to mark the spot. The shelling had started up again and, when we went across the following morning to attack Hop and Ale Alley, I noticed that the place where the grave had been was one enormous shell-hole.

Dawn broke shortly after the Bombers had scraped between the tree stumps and buried Bobby in the shallow grave, the rain went off and later in the morning a watery sun did its best to dry out the soldiers bivouacking on the hillsides, waiting for the move. It was the 14 September and the wait was almost over. They were issued with bombs and extra ammunition, gathered their kit together, enjoyed a last hot meal and prepared to move up the line. Mail had come up for the New Zealanders and Harry Baverstock was suffering from an embarrassment of riches. He received an accumulated batch of more than twenty letters and no less than four parcels. There were four tins of pipe tobacco, four tins of condensed milk, a mountain of chocolate, a pile of books, a three-month supply of razor blades, sweets, soap, and enough home-knitted woollen goods to start a respectable small business. The best he could do was to put some sweets and chocolate in his pocket, shove a useful looking woollen cap into his light haversack, and stuff the rest of the largesse, as best he could, into his already bulging pack before leaving it, as instructed, at the battalion dump. He never saw it again.

Shortly after seven o'clock, when the Brigade marched off in the gathering dusk, there was a lull in the shelling. At a quarter to eight, as they were moving past the rubble of Mametz village, the guns opened up behind them in such an intensity of fire that the ears of every man rang. The road to Mametz Wood flashed in the necklace of light that ribboned into the distance from Death Valley just below, where the guns, standing wheel to wheel, were pouring fire towards the German lines. It was the beginning of the great bombardment that was paving the way for tanks, infantry and cavalry. Together, in the morning, they would make the breakthrough.

As the New Zealanders struck across country to their assembly position in the wood, they could see the gunners, working flat out. It was a chilly evening but, sweating with their labour, many had discarded tunics and shirts as well. They looked like demons, bare torsos glowing red as the shells left the muzzles and disappearing into the shadows as the guns recoiled. It seemed to the New Zealanders, half-deafened by the noise, half-suffocated by the fumes, half-mesmerised by the sight, that they were passing through hell itself.

In the evil depths of Mametz Wood Bav, Kip and Gee settled

down to pass the night in an old German dugout. The luck of the draw had dictated that their half of the New Zealand Brigade should remain in reserve. The others, who would go across in the morning with the first wave, moved on up the line and into the trenches to the left of Delville Wood. They were facing the Switch Line. It had been the objective of the 7th Rifle Brigade when Ted Gale had gone over the top more than three weeks before and they were back again, for the renewal of the attack. This time they were in Delville Wood itself and Ted Gale was having an unpleasant time for he had mislaid most of his platoon. They were part of the draft of two hundred new men sent to make up the Battalion after the slaughter at Orchard Trench. It was their first time in the line. In the gruesome depths of Delville Wood, with its scattered dead, the remnants of mangled trees clawing grotesquely in the moonlight, the screaming shells, the all-pervading stench, the sickening dread of tomorrow's dawn, it would not have astonished Gale if they had panicked and run. But eventually he rounded them up. They had gone souveniring. Between them they had gathered a fine collection of German revolvers, buttons and badges and a fortunate few, scouring through the ghoulish litter of corpses, had been rewarded with the most prized of trophies – a German helmet.

Unabashed by Gale's fury as he hounded them into the shell-holes where the Battalion was waiting for the jump-off, they were passing them round for less-fortunate scavengers to admire.

Chapter 21

After the early morning mist had cleared it was good flying weather, clear and cold in the upper air where the wind, blowing straight from the north, whistled and twanged through the wires of the aeroplanes, toy-like in the sky, and straight into the goggled faces of the men peering anxiously over the sides of the open cockpits. The goggles were a distinct impediment to observation, for they were flying high above the battle. To venture lower would be to risk a nasty encounter with one of the high-trajectory shells that filled the sky, tearing through it with the speed and sound of an express train. Even the most prudent of pilots could not escape the heart-bumping moments when his eggshell aircraft, swooping down for a closer look, sank, yawing in a rush of turbulence as a 'heavy' passed close beneath its belly, ripping the air apart and leaving a vacuum in its wake. The thrumming of the wind, the howling high-flying shells, the clatter of the aeroplane's own engine shut out the uproar of the battle on the ground below where harmless puffs of smoke flagged the progress of the bombardment.

Between the criss-crossing maze of trenches that divided the grey morass into a jigsaw of crazy pieces, matchstick men bobbed and scurried like ants through the haze of the battle and a million specks of light, a million split-second flashes of fire, flickered in the mist like the shimmering of a host of fireflies. It looked from the air just as such actions had looked a thousand times before. And just as they had done a thousand times before – or so it seemed to them – Corps Commanders sweated with the strain of waiting for the wireless messages that would bring the hoped-for news of progress or weary tidings of failure.

The troops went over the top at twenty-past six in the morning and two nerve-racking hours later a message was wirelessed from the aircraft observing for 3rd Corps. It was worth waiting for.

TANK SEEN IN MAIN STREET OF FLERS GOING ON WITH LARGE NUMBERS OF TROOPS FOLLOWING IT.

It was the best news of the whole battle. It was more. It was the best news of the entire war.

In the euphoria of the moment it hardly mattered to General Pulteney at 3rd Corps Headquarters that on his own front of Martinpuich and High Wood things were not going quite so spectacularly well, that it was 15th Corps on their left which had made the breakthrough and that it was to 15th Corps Headquarters that the message should have gone. What *did* matter was that in a single leap the Army was in Flers. Two miles beyond High Wood. Two miles beyond Delville.

General Pulteney passed the signal on to 3rd Corps who flashed it on to 4th Army Headquarters at Querrieu. By ten-fifteen it had reached the delighted ears of Sir Douglas Haig who gave permission for the signal to be passed verbatim to the Press. By early evening it had reached London. The presses in Fleet Street began to roll and before ten o'clock late editions of the evening newspapers were on sale with the glorious news blazoned in banner headlines.

A TANK IS DRIVING DOWN THE MAIN STREET OF
FLERS WITH THE BRITISH ARMY CHEERING BEHIND

Someone along the way had taken the trouble to polish the prose a little. It was only a slight and, under the circumstances, a very human exaggeration. For once it was good news. But it was not quite as good as it seemed.

Only twenty-five tanks of the forty-two had succeeded in going forward from the start-lines and, of those twenty-five, the hulks of seventeen were lying destroyed, damaged, broken down or irretrievably ditched on the battlefield. The performance of the tanks had been disappointing but their effect had been enormous. They had terrorised the Germans. More important, they had put heart into the infantry and, by the very fact of their presence, propelled the troops forward with such a thrust of optimism that they had felt themselves to be invincible. It was their morale that had broken the line and it had started to rise on the eve of the battle with their first sight of the tanks.

Some soldiers on their way to the line had even managed to hitch a lift and, as Billy Banks and Roland Otley remarked – or rather roared to each other above the unearthly clatter of the tank – it was not unlike riding on a hay-wain. This time last year, at harvest-time in England, most of the boys who were now in the 21st Battalion of The King's Royal Rifle Corps had been doing exactly that, for they were the Yeoman Rifles. It was the Earl of Feversham who had the idea of raising a battalion of farmers' sons and country lads from the north of England but, by the time he had obtained official approval, arranged his own transfer from the Yorkshire Hussars and enlisted young hopefuls of his acquaintance as fledgling officers – young

Anthony Eden fresh from Eton was one of them – it was already September 1915. So many lads of military age were already in the Army that, although the most remote farms and villages were scoured for recuits and although there were accommodating Recruiting Sergeants who needed little persuading to sign up farm-lads whose tender years were belied by a hefty physique, there had not been quite enough 'Yeomen' to make up a full battalion. They had come in dribs and drabs and it was not until their numbers had been swelled by a draft of recruits of less exclusive origin that they had started training in earnest. And that was months later.

They had come to the front in May, to the quiet, still bucolic surroundings of 'Plugstreet' Wood and one young farmer, standing sentry for the first time in the line, had neatly summed up the Battalion's collective attitude to the war. An officer on his accustomed round stopped by the fire-step.

'Well, Sentry,' he enquired, 'do you see anything?'

'Aye,' replied the Sentry. 'I see a bloody good field of hay going to waste!'

This saying had tickled the Battalion and like its first 'battle' was always good for a laugh. It had happened while they were training on Lord Feversham's estate, Duncombe Park at Helmsley in Yorkshire, under the beneficent eye of Lord Feversham himself, who was struck by the happy idea that the Battalion might practise advancing in open order against a herd of deer which, fortuitously, he wished to move to another part of the estate. The deer were not keen to go. They were not encouraged by the sight of a hundred or so men advancing to the attack! They stood their ground and then turned and charged the Yeoman in a counter-attack, so purposeful that there was no question of dignified 'retirement'. It had been a total rout.

Moving up to Delville Wood under the shrieking bombardment intended to deafen the ears of the enemy to the cacophonous progress of the tanks, the Yeoman Rifles were hoping for better luck in the morning. They were to be supported by the tanks of D Battalion.

At the very head of the long column of machines crawling towards the line, the leading tank – officially known as D1 – was to have the distinction of being the first tank in history to go into battle. It was to cross the front line on a special mission one hour and five minutes before Zero. Len Lovell and the other Bombers of A Company were to go with it, for the 'special mission' was to break the grip of the Germans' last tenuous hold on the edge of Delville Wood and to push them out of Hop Alley and Ale Trench before the start of the main assault.

The noise of a passing tank was deafening. Inside, it was ear-splitting. Even a full-pitched bellow had no chance of being heard above the beat of the mammoth engine, 105 horsepower, the clank and slap of the caterpillar tracks, the crash of the giant gears, the grinding of brakes so powerful that it took all the strength of the brakesman to operate. At least he benefited from a little light from the narrow slit in the up-front 'cab' where he crouched behind the driver and the officer in charge. The gearsmen were less fortunate. Low down in the middle of the tank it was dark even in daylight. It was hot and it was airless, and on the long haul up, instead of circulating fresh air, the fans were showing a nasty tendency to pick up heavy petrol fumes belching from the exhaust of the vehicle in front and to send them billowing through the tank. Before they had progressed a quarter of the way, the crews were gasping for air, choking and spluttering as they would later choke and splutter in the fumes of smoke bombs and poison gas.

Of the eight men squeezed into the claustrophobic gloom, the gearsmen were the worst off. They had to have their wits about them, ears pressed close to the sides of the sponsons, alert for orders tapped out by the driver on the cover of the engine, and woe betide them if they failed to pick them up. The gunners' place was in the sponsons themselves. They had a little light, a little air, and just sufficient field of vision to operate the guns that were mounted in the two vast protuberances which stuck out on either side of the tank.[1] They weighed a ton apiece and every man in every tank crew had cause to curse them. With the sponsons fitted, the tanks had been too wide to pass through the tunnels on the French railway system. There had been nothing for it but to take them off and to put them back again at the end of the journey. Their muscles were still aching.

Corporal A. E. Lee, MM, No. 32198, A Btn., Heavy Section, Machine Gun Corps (later Tank Corps).

We joined up with our tanks at Yvrench, a small village near Abbeville, and then came the job of bolting on the sponsons which carried the guns on each side of the tank. They were carried on small trolleys and they had to be manhandled into position, the sponsons lifted off the trolley and manoeuvred into position until the bolt holes in tank and sponson coincided exactly. Then the bolts were inserted and tightened. It sounds easy, and so it was – in theory! But, have you ever tried to lift a ton of metal into a position where not one but every pair of bolt holes must exactly coincide? If the fit was not absolutely perfect, even to one-

---

[1] The 'male' tank carried two six-pounder cannon, the 'female' tank four Vickers machine-guns.

sixteenth of an inch out, the bolts wouldn't fit. Sometimes the first bolt did go in but, perhaps because the sponson had warped slightly, none of the others would! Then it was a case of using drifts, levers and brute force! But it was done eventually.

Nick Lee, like every other man in A Company, was bitterly disappointed to be held back in reserve while D and C Company were even now on their way to the line and the glory of the tanks' first action. The crew of D1, on the other hand, arriving at the eastern edge of Delville Wood to lead the infantry in its preliminary action against Hop Alley and Ale Trench, were disconcerted to discover that they were quite alone. Of the three tanks which should have been at the rendezvous, only D1 had made it. At a quarter-past five it left its starting point on the Longueval–Ginchy Road and with machine-guns firing, with black clouds of smoke snorting from its exhaust, with a noise that sounded as if all the furies of hell had been let loose, it lumbered down the edge of Delville Wood lurching, dipping and rearing its mountainous bulk above the German trenches. For a full half-minute the Germans were paralysed with shock. Then they began to run.

The Bombers of the 6th King's Own Yorkshire Light Infantry waited as near as they dared to the edge of the wood. It was a good ten minutes before the tank reached a point opposite their position, changed direction, circled to the right and began to blunder forward up Hop Trench. Smartly and on schedule, the Bombers jumped up and went forward behind it.

It was marvellous. That tank went on, rolling and bobbing and swaying in and out of shell-holes, climbing over trees as easy as kiss your hand! We were awed! We were delighted that it was ours. Up to now Jerry had supplied all the surprises. Now it was his turn to be surprised!

The tank waddled on with its guns blazing and we could see Jerry popping up and down, not knowing what to do, whether to stay or to run. We Bombers were sheltering behind the tank, peering round and anxious to let Jerry have our bombs. But we had no need of them. The Jerries waited until our tank was only a few yards away and then fled – or hoped to! The tank just shot them down and the machine-gun post, the gun itself, the dead and wounded who hadn't been able to run, just disappeared. The tank went right over them. We would have danced for joy if it had been possible out there. It seemed so easy! Hop Trench was 'kaput' and in a very few minutes Ale Alley got the same treatment. We were elated!

Lance-Corporal Len Lovell, No. 18692, A Coy., 6th Btn., King's Own Yorkshire Light Infantry.

A Company Bombers were having a thoroughly good time. They were more than a little bit sorry to leave their glorious private victory and to rejoin the Battalion for the main attack. They got back just in time to line up in Delville Wood and just in time to miss the German bombardment which started up in retaliation. The tank was not so fortunate. A shell caught it fair and square and D1, the first tank across, became the Tanks' first battle casualty.

But Hop and Ale which for so long had dominated the eastern edge of Delville Wood were, as Lovell had gloated, 'kaput' and the way had been cleared for the troops. Over at the Quadrilateral, in a similar operation, things had gone badly wrong.

They had planned to send three tanks in to subdue the Quadrilateral twenty minutes before the troops went over at Zero. One tank broke its tail on the way up. Another developed engine trouble. The third appeared but, unlike the solitary tank which so dramatically subdued the Germans' resistance at Delville Wood, it made a tragic error. Lurching along beside what its crew took to be the Germans' front-line trench, they sprayed it with machine-gun fire. The trench was packed with soldiers. The kill was enormous. But it was a British assembly trench and the soldiers were men of the 9th Norfolks waiting to go over the top. It was Captain Crosse who put a stop to that. He leapt out of the trench and rushed up to the tank whose guns were still blazing. It was difficult to make himself heard above its pandemonium, but furious gesticulation was enough. The tank swung away and was last seen turning to the north, moving parallel to Straight Trench. Possibly it did a little damage. Straight Trench *was* the German front line running between the Triangle and the Quadrilateral. But on the Quadrilateral itself not a shot had fallen. The tank moved off leaving it untouched and inviolable in its wake. When the infantry attacked it, the Germans had no difficulty in holding out.

But they were perhaps unnerved. In spite of their losses before the battle even started, the 1st Leicesters and the 9th Norfolks succeeded in rushing Straight Trench and rushed on over the crest beyond. And there they stuck in front of a belt of barbed wire, so formidable, so wide and so deadly that it looked to the astonished troops as if no single shell of the long preliminary bombardment had fallen within a mile of it. They lay all day in front of the wire, waiting for orders, for reinforcements, for the tanks to come up to pave the way for a fresh attack, and as they lay there they were shelled. They could not understand why no British guns were retaliating on their front. But the reason was simple. They were lying in a 'lane' in the barrage. The tanks should have been forging ahead. The artillery had been ordered to leave wide gaps in the supporting barrage rather than run the risk of destroying them or holding up their triumphal progress. But, on the 6th Division Front, no tanks came.

If the Guards Division had waited for their tanks to appear they would never have advanced at all. They had been allotted no less than ten of them, for their task was the hardest of all. They were to make straight for Lesboeufs and Morval – but the Triangle, twin fortress to the Quadrilateral, stood slap in their path. Three of the tanks were to help them subdue it. But, when Zero came, the Guards were on their own. And on their own they advanced.

We manned the parapets at Zero Hour waiting to go over and waiting for the tank. We heard the chunk, chunk, chunk, chunk, chunk, chunk, chunk. Then silence. The wretched tank never came. There was split-second timing. We couldn't wait for it, so we had to go over the top. We got cut to pieces. Eventually the tank got going and went over past us. The Germans ran for their lives – couldn't make out what was firing at them. The tank did what it was supposed to have done, but too late! We lost hundreds and hundreds of men. Well, what was left of our three battalions of Coldstreams, didn't know what to do. We were all over the place in shell-holes and bits of trenchline, anywhere there was cover. Then Colonel Campbell of the 3rd Battalion Coldstreams got up on the trench and he'd got a hunting horn. He stood right up there in full view and he blew the hunting horn and got us together. He stood on top of the trench. The Germans was firing everything at us! But they say God was in the trenches. If ever God *was* in the trenches He was there then. Colonel Campbell won the Victoria Cross. He was only yards away from me. I saw that VC won. If ever a man deserved it, that man was Colonel Campbell.

Private Charles Coles, No. 12245, 4 Platoon, 1st Co., 1st Btn., Coldstream Guards.

The Guards had lost direction. Confused by the creeping barrage (which was actually intended for the adjacent 14th Division) they had strayed to their left and come under enfilade attack from Pint Trench. It was to knock out this danger that Colonel Campbell had rallied the scattered troops.

They were firing and slinging these bombs at us. We had to knock them out and we didn't know where we were really. You're firing at one and firing at another as you run forward and, what with getting on and getting a Lewis-gun Section up to deal with them, you didn't think of anything else. We made a mistake there, because we went off slightly to the left, following this group of Germans. We took prisoners. A lot of them threw up their hands

Private John Bouch, No. 11776, 1st Btn., Coldstream Guards.

and came forward and the rest of them started to run back and we
followed them, rather to the left, when the main attack had gone to
the right – and we followed them a long way.

The right flank of the Grenadier Guards attacking the Triangle
alone and unsupported were not worried that they were not in touch
with the Coldstreams who should have been advancing ahead of
them. They assumed that, having captured their objective, the
Coldstreams had pressed on and that all the Grenadiers would have
to do was to occupy and consolidate the captured position. In fact the
Grenadiers were advancing into a gap in the line. The Germans
were still in possession of the 'captured' strongpoint.

But, by eleven o'clock, the Triangle had been subdued. The
Guards paid a high price for it. Of the officers and men who had
gone into action, two-thirds were killed or wounded or missing.

Some of the 'missing' who had wandered to their left were still
trespassing in the sector of the 14th Division whose fortunes too had
been mixed.

Lance-Corporal
Len Lovell, No.
18692, A Coy., 6th
Btn., King's Own
Yorkshire Light
Infantry.

We Bombers moved off with the first line and we got to within ten
or fifteen yards of Jerry's position. I had a Mills bomb ready in my
hand. I pulled the pin out and I was holding down the lever ready
to throw it when a Jerry seemed just to pop up out of a hole and let
fly. I was struck in the left forearm below the elbow and it spun me
round like a top. I fell into a shell-hole with two other fellows. One
of them had half his left ear gone and he was drenched in blood,
and he was yelling and screaming, hanging on to his ear with blood
pouring through his fingers. The other chap had been hit in the
right arm. By some miracle I was still clutching my bomb in my
right hand – without the pin of course. My big problem was how to
get rid of the bomb. My hand and fingers were getting stiff. I
couldn't hold on to it for much longer and if I let go of the lever it
would explode right away. Besides we knew we must get away
quick before Jerry's barrage began to fall behind us to keep our
reserves from coming up. I took the risk of standing up to make
sure that there was no one else in holes behind us. Then I waved
at my two chums to keep low and threw the bomb away into
another shell-hole, praying for the best.

We shed our equipment, and took a drink of water out of our
bottles. You could hardly make yourself heard above the din but I
yelled to the other two that it was time we were off – or else! We
hopped in and out of shell-craters as best we could and after a lot
of effort we managed to get to the dressing station at Bernafay
Wood corner. We thought we should be about the first. But there

were hundreds there before us. We joined the queue and there were so many of us that when it came to my turn to reach the doctor there were no splints left: He had to make do with corrugated cardboard and a sling.

It was some hours before Ted Gale reached the same dressing station. His wound was worse than Lovell's and it took a long, long time to walk, to stagger and even, for part of the way, to crawl the best part of two miles to the dressing station at Bernafay Wood. He was losing blood and was half-fainting before he had gone half-way. When he saw the tank parked by the roadside Ted wondered, in his light-headed state, if he might already be delirious. The crew was standing in the roadway and he recognised – or thought he did – an old chum from Chichester. He hadn't seen George Hopkins since their schooldays; he was hardly certain if he was seeing him now, but he took a chance and hailed him with a yell that emerged as a croak. George came running and caught Ted just as he passed out. When he came to he was lying on a stretcher outside the dressing station. There was no sign of the tank. He was still not quite sure that it had not been a dream. But there was nothing dreamlike about the tank he had seen earlier in the morning as his battalion lay waiting to go over the top in the second wave.

It was one of three that should have led the advance. One had broken down on the way. Another was late. Only D3 arrived – but it was enough.

The whole Brigade, that's between three and four thousand men, went over on part of the front that would normally have been a one battalion front – so you can imagine how crowded we were. Our job was to take the second line, so we were lying back a bit from the trenches, among the stumps in Delville Wood, ready to go forward. I was keeping a close eye on all this new lot in my platoon, because they were going across for the first time.

Just before Zero Hour we heard this damned racket, and I remember saying, 'What the hell is this?' Then these tanks appeared, one on our front and one a bit away from us. We were all absolutely flabbergasted. We didn't know what to think. We didn't know what they were because we hadn't been told anything about them. It was an amazing sight. It crossed my mind about the old Duke of Wellington's remarks about the Battle of Waterloo. He said, 'I don't know. My troops scare me, I don't know what the hell they're going to do to the French.' They scared Jerry all right! The tanks scared the Jerries more than what we did!

They came up right in front of us and swung round and went

Corporal E. Gale, No. 3774, D Co., 7th Btn., The Rifle Brigade, 41st Brigade, 14th Division.

straight for the German line. The barbed wire entanglements had been pretty well smashed by our artillery but the tanks just rolled over what remained of them and smashed them all to pieces. They scared the guts out of the Germans. They bolted like rabbits. We saw them! Our tank went straight over the German first-line trench and straight on and the boys just had to walk across behind it and occupy the front line. It was easy.

It was so easy that the second wave went over just ten minutes after the first, got caught up with the fighting in Pint Trench and, in their enthusiasm, were carried forward to the Switch Line by the momentum of the first wave. The Switch Line, which had loomed so large and so sinister in all the attacks of the last two months, was subdued with comparative ease. And there, according to the battle plan, they should have waited until twenty-past seven before moving on to the second objective at Gap Trench. No orders in the world – no shelling, no machine-gun fire, no casualties, no risk, no battle-plan – could compete with the heady thrill of the dash forward. The remnants of the first wave advanced together with the remnants of the second. They lost the tank and they lost Ted Gale almost simultaneously. The tank ground to a halt before Gap Trench and almost at the same moment Gale was hit.

Corporal E. Gale, No. 3774, D Coy., 7th Btn., The Rifle Brigade, 41st Brigade, 14th Division.

There was another Corporal alongside of me. I grabbed hold of him and I said, 'I've stopped one!' I felt it go through me, into my shoulder, and the feeling was just like somebody jabbing a needle or a pin into your hand. Just a short sharp dig. No pain really. I knew it was a Blighty one – and I was thankful! I can remember what I thought before I passed out. I felt that faintness coming over me and, as I began to fall down, I thought, 'Oh, good! I'm on the way home.'

The rest of the battalion were on the way to Gap Trench in a hurly burly of troops which had become hopelessly mixed up in the excitement and confusion of the advance. For Burton Eccles, one of the new draft, it was the first time over the top.

Rifleman Burton Eccles, No. 203694, 7th Btn., The Rifle Brigade, 41st Brigade, 14th Division.

We'd only been with the battalion for a matter of days. I was in a draft of King's Royal Rifle Corps but they called us out in the middle of the night, changed our shoulder badges and put us in the 7th Battalion, The Rifle Brigade. I had my first drink of rum that morning, before we went over. I'd never tasted spirits in my life! I was ready for anything after that.

The bombardment was terrible and, by the time we got over the top, the machine-gun bullets were simply racing at us. You'd wonder how anybody got through it! I had my clothing torn and something hit my tin hat – but the very worst thing was that I had a shovel on my back and a bullet hit the shovel. You never heard such a clang and a row as it made. It scared the life out of me!

I didn't see any Germans at all until the third line of trenches. I must have been looking a lot more fierce than I felt, because out of the trench came about twelve big Germans. I thought, 'Here goes! This is it!' And then they all put their hands up! I thought, 'Thank God for that!' We didn't need to give them any guard to take them back – we just waved them through. As they were running back towards our line one of our chaps turned and he fired at them. I was shocked. I stopped and I yelled at him, 'You dirty dog!' He yelled back, 'We were told not to take prisoners!'

We got into this trench and there wasn't really room for us, there were so many milling about. The trench was really badly knocked about, full of Germans, wounded and dead, and our own chaps as well. You couldn't move. And we stood there while the Germans counter-attacked from further on. We beat them off. Later we went on again.

We had to go through a perfect hail of stuff, branches and bits of tree trunks were flying about in all directions and our chaps were falling all the time. We had to go forward in short bursts from one shell-hole to another. I lost touch with my party in the smoke and, at one point, I found that the fellow in front whom I was following was actually not moving on because he was dead. He had died in a kneeling position.

Of my draft of twenty-five, only ten of us got out and of my own five pals who'd all stuck together, I was the only one to answer the roll call. I never saw anything of them after we started. In an advance over so much ground, in such terrible fire, it is impossible to keep in touch with one's pals.

Perhaps remembering their innocent curiosity of the night before and the jaunt which had so infuriated Ted Gale, Eccles later wrote home, 'I could have got heaps of souvenirs, but I only wanted one. That was myself!' He might also have had added that, in any event, he had been rather too busy to collect any.

The 14th Division was advancing across the open country that lay between Lesboeufs and Flers. On their left the 41st Division was advancing on the village of Flers itself.

Afterwards, when the name of the battle had become synonymous with the capture of Flers and Courcelette, when it had been forgotten or only dimly remembered that the tanks had been intended to lead the infantry far beyond, it seemed a signal honour that this youngest and most inexperienced of Divisions had been chosen to attack Flers – and a signal achievement that they had captured it. The 41st had been given ten tanks to help them. Seven had trundled up to the start line, but the troops, lying well out in No Man's Land, were up and away and ahead of them. They went so fast that the tanks had no chance of keeping up. They went so far that they ran into their own barrage and so enthusiastically that the Germans in the first line of trenches were overwhelmed almost before they realised that the attack had begun. And the tanks rumbling up behind bowled them forward to the second line and into the fight for Switch Trench.

The Yeoman Rifles, with the exception of Billy Banks, took off in the first wave. Billy did not see them go. He was oblivious to the tanks, although they must have rumbled past within feet of the shell-hole where he lay. He was oblivious to the victory. He had not even heard the whistle blow at Zero. His last recollection was of waiting in the advanced position to go over and of the whistle of a shell that seemed to be making straight for him.

Rifleman W. Banks, No. 12021, 21st Btn., King's Royal Rifle Corps, 41st Division.

It was a long time before I woke up and when I did it was ever so quiet. Oh, I could hear the guns and the sound of fighting in the distance, but there wasn't a sound near me and there wasn't anybody in sight either. I wondered where my pals were. I climbed up out of the shell-hole, looked around and I still couldn't see anybody. I felt myself all over and there wasn't a scratch on me, so I thought I'd better follow on. I went Over the Top by myself!

I kept looking around and, after a bit, I saw a group of men about half a mile away and I thought, 'That'll be the lads.' So I set off to catch up with them and I'd gone no distance when a machine-gun opened up and I got one in the left arm. I looked at it and I thought, 'That's nothing.' So I carried on, and I hadn't gone ten steps when I got hit in the *other* arm. That was it!

Banks never did succeed in catching up with the lads nor in completing his one-man advance on Flers. Fortunately his assistance was not required. D16 was already making its triumphal progress down the main street and D6, D9 and D17 were smashing through a hornet's nest of strongpoints on the eastern edge of the village and putting the Germans to flight. They were the only tanks on the Divisional Front which were still in action. The others lay ditched in the shell-holes along the line of the advance. One wreck, foundered just two hundred yards from the British line, was at least serving some sort of purpose. It had been pressed into service as a makeshift dressing station and the wounded who could hobble or crawl were crouched in the shelter of its battered bulk. Sergeant Norman Carmichael was there with a number of his men, for it was his Number 10 Platoon, in the vanguard of the Yeoman Rifles, which had taken the first shock of the attack and suffered the first casualties.

Lieutenant Benton and myself took the platoon across. We were the first to go in C Company. I think our Captain gave the order to advance a little bit before the time because we'd been trained that the closer you kept to the creeping barrage the safer you were. But we overdid it. We walked into it and it has to be said that there were a lot of shorts. The artillery was very good but they weren't all that perfect and they couldn't guarantee to put a curtain in a straight line that you could keep behind.

I went down very early and I saw my officer going on just in front of me. He was brandishing his revolver and shouting, 'Come on, Number Ten!' And he just went down. He got a machine-gun bullet right through the head. The Germans had got up by then and my platoon was literally put out of action in a very short time. The last I saw of them there were about half-a-dozen going through the smoke climbing up this ridge to get into the German trenches and I was left lying there. It was a gorgeous summer's day and, after the rest of the Battalion had gone through, I was able to crawl about. I put a bandage round my leg and crept about going to the rest of my lads in the platoon that were wounded. Some of them were shouting. They used to make horrible sounds when they were in pain, when they were wounded and some were wounded pretty badly. I went round to as many as I could, just to try and cheer them up and then I went in and sheltered behind a tank that had broken down trying to get up this ridge. It stopped there all day and we collected as many of the walking wounded as we could. It was doubly safe, behind the ridge and behind the tank.

It was a long time before the Germans got the range and started shelling. When they did, it was a horrible sight. The shells were falling on Delville Wood and it had been fought for over and over again, so it was full of dead bodies and they were being tossed up by the explosions. In a strange sort of way it was fascinating to watch these bodies rising into the air above the tree stumps and circulating almost in slow motion and coming down again. Horrible, but fascinating. It seemed so strange to be lying there on that lovely warm summer's day watching these bodies going up and down.

Sergeant Norman Carmichael, No. 10 Platoon, C Coy., 21st Btn., King's Royal Rifle Corps, 41st Division.

Beyond Delville Wood, the New Zealanders too had leapt forward ahead of schedule without waiting for the snail-crawling tanks to lead their advance. They too had suffered casualties from their own bombardment but they had kept going, spurred on by the sight of some two hundred Germans running for their lives. They were bellowing and cheering as they went. Disdaining the tanks, lumbering up painfully slowly behind them, they took the Switch Line with the bayonet. They took it so quickly that Harry Baverstock, asleep in his rabbit-warren in Mametz Wood, was roused by '... fellows rushing around yelling that the Green Line had been taken by the Dinks'. It was just ten minutes to seven and the attack had been underway for exactly half an hour.

Looking over the parados of the captured trench the New Zealanders could see, on their right, the ruined village of Flers tucked into its shallow valley. They could see the troops and the tanks making steadily towards it. And now that they had a chance to look around, they could see how thin they were in numbers. When they realised the full measure of New Zealand casualties, they sent a message back urging the Reserve Battalion to prepare to take over the line.

At High Wood, on the 47th Divisional Front, the tanks had been a positive hindrance. One of them had even been responsible for a fair number of the New Zealand casualties. It strayed out of the wood, was confused by the lie of the line, unsure of its direction. It opened fire on what it took to be enemy troops. In fact it was firing directly at the New Zealanders as they advanced with the 7th Royal Fusiliers on their left and just behind.

Of course the tanks should never have been ordered into High Wood at all and so the Commander of the 47th Division had told GHQ in the frankest of terms. In the opinion of General Sir Charles Barter, even a child could have seen that the pitted, fought-over ground, the upturned trees, the stockade of jagged stumps, the morass of craters and shell-holes lying lip to lip, were insurmountable obstacles to any vehicle, regardless of its might, regardless of the brilliance of its trials over open country. He had not succeeded in convincing the powers-that-be. They patiently pointed out that the British and German lines lay too close to each other in High Wood for the artillery to bombard and crush the enemy defences. The tanks must do the job. The powers-that-be had not seen for themselves the conditions in High Wood. The General had. Let the tanks go round the perimeter of the wood, he suggested, and the wood itself could then be crushed as easily as a walnut in the jaws of a nutcracker. The General had been overruled, but he had been right. Only one of the tanks had been able to move forward through the wood and, before long, it had stuck. Its crew fought on with the infantry, and the fighting was hand-to-hand.

But, beyond High Wood, the tanks were ranging towards Martin-puich, across the tangle of trenches that had so formidably defended it, followed by the triumphant 50th Division. Soon they were in the outskirts of the village, prisoners were streaming back and the demoralised German line began to crack.

In High Wood the Tommies lay low while trench-mortars poured a short-range barrage into the Switch Line. The bombing parties, creeping forward in its aftermath, found little opposition. By one o'clock, the wood had fallen. It was two months to the day since the three Brigadiers had walked towards it through fields of standing corn and in those two months High Wood had cost the lives of several thousand men.

Just as they had been waiting two months before, the cavalry was massed behind the line, impatient for the order to dash through to Bapaume. Again the order never came. But the German line had been broken. Like the New Zealanders four kilometres away, the Canadians had swept ahead well in advance of their tanks, and swept right into Courcelette. A tank had driven 'up the main street of Flers with the British Army cheering behind'. The British Army had undoubtedly advanced – and further in a few hours than in the previous ten weeks. But they had not advanced quite far enough. The cavalry would not be required to exploit the breakthrough. For the moment the advance had stuck.

It had stuck on the far side of Flers. It had stuck in front of Gueudecourt and in front of Lesboeufs. It had stuck at the Quadri-lateral. It had stuck beyond Lousy Wood at the foot of the road that led into Combles. And more than half the tanks which had boosted the infantry on it way had stuck as well, or been wrecked by enemy fire. Most divisions were reduced to half their strength long before the day ended. Most battalions had lost their colonels. Some had lost every single officer.

The 7th Battalion, The Rifle Brigade, were holding five hundred yards of Gap Trench with a modest force of five officers, one warrant officer, four sergeants and no more than one hundred and fifty riflemen. They were uncomfortably aware that, if the Germans decided to counter-attack, they would stand little chance of beating them off. The best they could do was to set up a Lewis-gun in a forward post and reinforce the gun-team with a sergeant and a few riflemen to lend moral support. Burt Eccles was one of the party. The men were exhausted and dazed by the day's fighting. They had had little sleep the night before and another sleepless night lay ahead. They set off up a long narrow trench which, until that morning, had been manned by Germans. The Germans were still there in heaps of contorted bodies that smothered the floor of the trench. Eccles hesitated and stopped. The Sergeant prodded him roughly from behind. 'Get on!' he said. 'What's the matter?' Eccles stood, paralysed. 'I don't like treading on their faces.' The Sergeant had no time for such niceties. 'Never mind their bloody faces! MOVE!' Eccles moved, through the sweet stench of blood, wobbling as the bodies yielded softly under his feet, fighting the impulse to vomit. It was the worst moment of the day.

Captain Brown had established what passed for Battalion Headquarters in 'a well-furnished Boche cubby-hole' in Gap Trench. It contained a welcome supply of food. There was rye bread, dried figs, prunes, dates, dried meat, mineral water, lump sugar and cheese. There was not a great deal, but there was plenty to go round what was left of the Battalion.

The Yeoman Rifles were considerably fewer than this time last night when they had been marching to the line with the tanks. Now they were out in the fields beyond Flers and, at the head of a reconnoitering party, Lord Feversham had gone farthest of all. His body still lay in the uncut corn. Billy Banks had been found by stretcher-bearers. Others had got back under their own steam.

When the shelling became too hot, when a battery of guns had moved forward and opened up disconcertingly close to them, when it was only a matter of time before the German guns would register on such a tempting target, Sergeant Carmichael had left the shelter of the tank and made for safety. Nelson Lawson and Geoff Hutchison went with him. Together they crawled back to the British wire and pulled stakes from the entanglements to serve as makeshift crutches. They could never have made it across the moonscape surface of Delville Wood itself, so they worked their way round it and hit on a half-constructed highway of planks and a Pioneer Battalion working flat out to extend it up to the new line. It made the going easier. They must have passed within yards of the New Zealand reinforcements, who were on their way through Carlton Trench to the front.

Now, the ground where their comrades had gone over cheering in the morning was strewn with hideous evidence of the fight. The bodies of four New Zealand soldiers lay staring from one shell-hole. Baverstock's section faltered and the Sergeant urged them on. 'Come on, never mind them. They've only stopped for a rest!' There were a lot of 'resting' bodies about and Baverstock had a black premonition that the bodies of Hickmott, Jackson and Biss were probably among them. He was right. And he was also right in his conviction that they too would be 'for it' in the morning.[1]

At dusk it began to rain. Several miles in the rear the disappointed cavalry turned their horses' heads for home. If all had gone according to plan, they should have galloped through the gap many hours ago, past Gueudecourt and Lesboeufs, across the lower ground beyond and by now might have been ranged along the Transloy ridges from Sailly-Saillisel to Bapaume. No trenches there! No barbed wire, few emplacements, nothing to prevent swift-moving patrols from dashing through the night to raid Divisional and even Corps Headquarters to demoralise the enemy's generals much as the tanks had demoralised his infantry that morning.

If all had gone according to plan the victorious tanks would now be sitting behind the new line, waiting for morning and daylight to swing to the north. Then, with the British Army cheering behind, they would have rolled up the German line as they might roll up a carpet laid over their path to Bapaume. But half the tanks were knocked out – and the advance had halted.

The night was kind to the Germans. Rain-clouds gathered low in the sky, glowing red above the guns and concealing the shrinking moon. The Germans were thankful for that. They needed the dark. The Transloy ridges were alive with troops, with guns, with wagons, with supplies, rushing forward to support the sleepless weakened regiments clinging to their beleaguered line. There was no sleep for the German Generals nor for their Staff. In their Headquarters' châteaux, which should even now be surrounded, lights burned until dawn and the German Staff who, according to plan, ought to have been quailing under the lances of the cavalry, attempted to make sense of the situation, tried to unravel the riddle of the new 'secret weapon' from incoherent front-line reports, pondered, conferred and planned counter-attacks for tomorrow. At all costs they must force the British to give up ground. At all costs they must capture a tank.

They had, as yet, no clear idea of their losses, except that they must be huge. And they were right. Their dead littered the battle-field and, trotting disconsolately through the drizzle to their billets, the British cavalrymen were overtaking long columns of bemused German prisoners plodding with their escorts to the cages.

---

[1] Harry Jackson survived the war, but the other two had indeed been killed on 15 September.

Chapter 22

There was no shortage of prisoners after the fighting of 15 September. There had been a disturbing shortage after the First of July. Even where the troops had successfully advanced and where, consequently, large numbers of captives might have been expected, the cages that had been prepared received the merest trickle of Prisoners-of-War. They were full enough now but, even so, in the ten weeks since the start of the campaign, an idea had grown up on both sides of the line that the British infantry would give no quarter and would take no prisoners and that, furthermore, they were acting under direct orders.

This idea was assiduously fostered by the German Staff as a useful means of stiffening the resistance of their front-line infantry. The British staff, equally anxious to foster the offensive spirit with tales of German atrocities, would have vehemently denied it. The British sense of justice and fair play was renowned throughout the world. It was the Germans who, as all the world was equally aware, brutally hounded innocent civilians, cut off children's hands, bayoneted babies, shot – and even crucified – prisoners. It was the Germans (albeit the descendants of Schubert and Schiller and Göethe) who had first launched upon the unsuspecting Tommies the infamous evils of poison gas and liquid fire. Was it conceivable that the heirs of Nelson, of Wellington, of Clive could descend to such depths of brutality as to shoot enemies who desired to surrender? All the rules of 'honest warfare' forbade it.

But in the minds of many Tommies the conviction that they were directed to take no prisoners had taken a curious hold and it was rooted in an order which had been issued from GHQ on 28 June 1916 – on the eve of the Battle of the Somme.

1. All ranks must be on their guard against the various ruses at which the enemy has shown himself to be an adept, especially *the use of British words of command* such as 'Retire', etc.

2. The German machine-gun is carried on a sledge, and the Germans sometimes throw a blanket over the gun. This makes the sledge and gun resemble a stretcher.

3. It is the duty of all ranks to continue to use their weapons against the enemy's fighting troops, unless and until it is beyond all doubt that those have not only ceased all resistance but that, whether through having voluntarily thrown down their weapons or otherwise, they have definitely and finally abandoned all hope or intention of resisting further. In the case of apparent surrender, it lies with the enemy to prove his intention beyond the possibility of misunderstanding, before the surrender can be accepted as genuine.[1]

It was signed by General Kiggell, Chief of the General Staff. It was sent out to every corps, every division, every brigade, every battalion of British troops on the Western Front and, through colonels and company commanders, to every platoon officer to read and pass on, for it was further instructed that the warning *'should be communicated verbally to all ranks before taking part in an assault'*. The order had never been rescinded and its message, though disguised, was unequivocal. Interpretations inevitably varied in the course of 'verbal communication' by several thousand platoon officers, but there was no doubt that to many soldiers of the infantry the message had come across loud and clear.

Prisoners were a nuisance. Fighting troops had to be spared from the battle to escort them back. Prisoners consumed supplies as well as manpower. 'The more Fritz eats the less there will be for you', was a potent argument. But, an even more powerful argument, as the infantry was rapidly working out for itself, was that brutality to prisoners, failure to give Fritz the benefit of the doubt *in the case of apparent surrender*, if practised on too wide a scale, might result in similar treatment being meted out by the Germans to British soldiers who were forced to surrender. Privately, individually, the Tommies made up their own minds and acted according to circumstance, to character and to conscience. After the advances of 15 September the Prisoner-of-War cages were well populated. They were guarded by Corps Troops of non-combatant units and, in contrast to the slog of trench digging and road building, looking after German prisoners was a sinecure.

The first thing you did if you got hold of a Jerry was to see what you could get off him – if he'd got a watch or anything like that. Most of our chaps had a load of Mark notes on them that weren't worth the paper they were printed on. All I was after was cap badges. I tried to get some watches but that was no good. None of the

Private W. G. Bell, No. 4640, 9th Btn., Army Cyclist Corps.

[1] Army Order Number W,19.A.16. O.A. 104.

scruffy ones that came into our Prisoner-of-War camp had any
that were worth having.

There was a lot of talk about Zeppelin raids and the Jerries
bombing London and killing a lot of civilians and, just at that time,
we had a Jerry airman who'd been brought down. He was handed
over to us and one of my mates interrogated him. He tried to find
out whether he'd been over, dropping bombs. He said, 'If he's
been over *there*, I'll shoot him! He'll never get away!'

He would have done too! Life meant nothing to you. Life was in
jeopardy and when you'd got a load of Jerries like that on your
hands, all stinking to high heaven, you hadn't much sympathy for
them with their *Kamerad* and all this cringing business. It brutal-
ises you, war does. You don't find that you've got much sympathy.
All you're looking after is your own skin all the time. Head down.

Attitudes were hardening at home as well as in France. The casualty
lists had burgeoned horribly since July, taking up more and more
columns of the daily newspapers, casting a shadow across the
summer and a blight over almost every family in the land. Now came
the stories of other pathetic events – of homes wrecked by German
bombs, of women, children, pet animals and caged birds wounded
or killed by 'Hun raiders'.

And then, on 3 September, a raiding Zeppelin was shot down by
Lieutenant Leefe Robinson of the Royal Flying Corps. He was
acclaimed as a hero and, rightly, in the opinion of Londoners,
awarded the Victoria Cross. They had flocked to Potters Bar to gloat
over the burnt-out wreck and a brisk market sprang up in souvenirs.
Everyone wanted a bit of the Zeppelin and everyone was prepared to
pay. At the Polytechnic jumble sale, held on 17 September in aid of
comforts for the 'Poly Boys' serving in the forces, the 'Zepp
Remnant Corner' was the success of the afternoon. It was presided
over by Miss Morel who had spared no effort in collecting, begging,
borrowing and even advertising for bits of Zeppelin with which to
astound the public who had braved a day of teeming rain to attend. It
cost a penny to pass behind a screen to inspect the relics and, as an
added bonus, to be regaled by Miss Morel with thrilling stories,
graphically related, on the origin of each item. Miss Budgeon and
Miss Ross, presiding over the refreshment stall, Mrs Gravelin on
Old Clothes, Miss Whitewright in charge of Fancy Goods, Miss
Ashby and Miss Bowen well ahead of the season with Christmas
cards and calendars, Miss Mitchell and Mrs Bangert persuasively
selling rubbish under the title of Penny Odds and Ends and even
Miss Cooper, whose Lucky Fish Pond Dip attracted many clients,
had lean takings compared to the receipts of the Zepp Remnant

Stall. But no one minded. Stall holders and buyers alike had done their bit and raised no less than seventeen pounds. It was estimated with satisfaction that this sum would provide enough khaki wool to enable the knitting committee to provide socks for nearly three hundred 'Poly Boys'.

Like many other organisations and institutions the 'Poly' looked after its own. Since Quintin Hogg had founded the Polytechnic Young Men's Christian Institute, no one was absolutely certain how many boys had passed through its Lower School and gone on to higher education in either the Commercial or the Technical Secondary Department. But they did know that, by September 1916, no less than two thousand six hundred and forty-five Old Boys were serving with the forces. There were probably many more who had not thought of letting them know.

The Polytechnic took a particular interest in boys who had served in the Institute's Cadet Corps and graduated to the Rangers – officially the 12th Londons, but referred to proprietorially as 'The Poly Regiment' – now fighting with the 56th Division in Lousy Wood. Many other 'Poly Boys' in the 47th London Division had helped to make the final thrust that captured High Wood. The September fighting had taken a high toll and, in October, the task of compiling the monthly 'Poly Roll of Honour' was unusually onerous. There were no less than four pages of photographs and obituaries, headed by a verse which was sincerely intended to be of comfort to the bereaved relatives of the boys who had died.

> Remember what he was, with thankful heart,
> The bright, the brave, the tender, and the true.
> Remember where he is – from sin apart,
> Present with God – yet not estranged from you.
> But never doubt that love, and love alone,
> Removed thy loved one from this trial scene,
> Nor idly dream, since he to God has gone,
> Of what, had he been left, he might have been.

But the currency of such high sentiments had tended somewhat to devalue since the start of the Big Push. There was a growing hint of disillusionment, of doubt, of questioning, not the Cause, but the Execution of the war. It was summed up by Ethel Bath in the letter she wrote in reply to condolences on her shattering news from France.

> It is a small comfort to know he gave his life in a successful attack. His Captain wrote that the success was entirely due to the magnificent way the men went forward led by their officers. He

also said that of the five officers from the 10th only one was left. . . .
I am very proud of my boy but at the same time it grieves me
dreadfully to think those boys are given such a small chance to
show their grit. You will understand what I mean when I tell you
he was only out 16 days in all, and he was attached to the
Middlesex Regt on Friday 6th, sent into the trenches the same
afternoon and attacked on the Saturday at 2.30 in the afternoon,
when he was killed. It all seems too quick to give them a chance.

She signed it 'Ethel Bath'. She had hardly had time to get used to the
unfamiliar surname. Reg died in Lousy Wood just three weeks to the
hour since they were married and, in Lousy Wood itself, where the
weary 56th Division was still in the line, letters much like Ethel's
were arriving by every mail that came up with the rations from the
transport lines. There were several for Arthur Agius. One came
from Florence Scarlett and Agius read it in a filthy dugout, not much
further advanced than the one in which he had penned his own sad
letter to her.

> 305, Thorold Road,
> Ilford.

Dear Captain Agius,
    I wish to take this opportunity of thanking you for your kind
letter of sympathy, and for the few details you were able to give me
concerning my dear husband's death. The sad news was a terrible
shock to me, and, up till now, I have felt too ill to write to you,
although I have been eager to do so.
    If it is not taking too great an advantage of your kindness, will
you please let me know whether, at the time my dear one fell, there
were any personal possessions on him that could be sent to me. I
know there was nothing of real value, but I think you will
understand that any little thing no matter what it is will become
one of my most cherished possessions.
    It was a great relief to know that dear Harold did not suffer any
pain, although what would I not give to have had just one last
message from him. We have been married such a short time (only
five months) and I cannot realise that he has gone – never to see
him again. The last time we were together he was so happy and
well and eager to do his level best for his Country at all cost. This
horrible war is dealing some cruel blows, and one is apt to grow
hardened to the Casualty List until someone very dear is taken.
There is scarcely a home, but what the occupants have some great
trouble to bear, and sometimes I think, knowing this, helps us to
bear our grief more bravely.

Will you please also tell me, if possible, where my husband was struck. I feel I would like to know. After the war I hope to be able to visit his last resting-place and, in that case, I suppose I should have no difficulty in distinguishing it.[1]

Once again thanking you for your kindness in writing to me. With every good wish for your safe and speedy return to England.

Yours very sincerely,
Florence E. Scarlett.

Florence Scarlett and Ethel Bath had experienced, between them, just eight days of married life. The letter from Mrs Scarlett worried Agius. The same post had brought a letter from his fiancée, Dolly, full of excited plans for their own wedding and enclosing one of the invitations, hot from the printers. More than a hundred had already gone out to friends and relatives:

Madame Noel
announces the marriage of her younger daughter
Evelyn ('Dolly')
to
Captain Arthur J. Agius
1/3rd London Regiment
Which will take place on his next leave from the Front
at St. Dominic's Priory, Haverstock Hill.
(The exact date will be announced later.)

Agius wondered gloomily if he was being fair to Dolly. He also wondered what the 'exact date' would be. He was 'sweating on leave' but, until another officer came to take over command of the Battalion, there was no hope of getting it.

Leave had been stopped at the beginning of the Somme Offensive. Now it had started again. Filthy, lousy, encrusted with the mud and sometimes with the blood of the trenches, the men poured off the leave trains into seven days of delight. To the families who waited, the long casualty lists, the knowledge of those other *families in the land who have some great trouble to bear* made it all the more poignant and eagerly awaited. Joe Murray got leave on 18 September. His train arrived at Newcastle at the unearthly hour of twenty-past three in the morning. There were four frustrating hours to pass before the

---

[1] Harold Scarlett has no known grave. He is commemorated on the Thiepval Memorial to the missing and his name (one of some 73,000) appears on Pier 9, near the top of Face D.

local train left for the mining village of Lintz Green and he put in the first of them by trying to get rid of at least the top layer of the dirt that encrusted his uniform and his body. With the limited facilities available in the station's 'Wash and Brush Up', he made little impression on what seemed to be half the filth of France. At half-past four he set off across the high-level bridge to Gateshead and knocked at his Aunt Maggie's door.

Able Bodied Seaman Joseph Murray, No. TZ276, Hood Btn., The 63rd (Royal Naval) Division.

I said, 'I'm not even going to sit down. I'm as lousy as a cuckoo.' Uncle Bill said, 'Sit down, lad. Bugger the lice. Sit down!' Right off, I got a cup of tea and Aunt Maggie got the frying pan on and I tucked into a good breakfast. First meal in England! My, it was good!

I wanted to send a telegram because I didn't want to give my mother a shock just walking in. So Aunt Maggie and Uncle Bill walked me round to the Post Office as soon as it opened, which was ten minutes before the train went. It took half an hour on the train and then a two-mile walk which took about another half-hour to get home. I didn't mind that, because I didn't want to get home before my telegram. The quickest way was to walk along the track that the colliery trucks used to get down to the main line, and of course in France I'd been walking on railway tracks for months. So I'm walking up the colliery railway and I see somebody waving from the bridge. I thought, 'It's our Mum!'

Apparently the telegram came to our local Post Office and, of course, the Post Mistress knew everybody in the village. She said to the postman, 'Dobson, I've got a telegram here for Mrs Murray.' He said, 'Oh no!' She said, 'No, no. It's good news. Joe's got leave.' So the postman got on his bike and he delivered the telegram before he did his round.

Well! She put the kettle on the fire to boil and then she was off – a pair of slippers on, no shawl, no nothing – straight out of the front door and across the cricket field to meet me. When she got to this bridge, she daren't go any further, in case I was coming by the road. So she waited there and I saw her up on the bridge. I waved and I ran down the embankment and she ran down the bridge and she just collapsed on the wet grass. I had to lean down to give her a hug and a kiss. She didn't faint, but she couldn't walk. All she could do was sit there greetin', sitting on the wet grass. I had to carry her home across the fields, into the cottage and into the kitchen, full of steam from the boiling kettle.

I had a cup of tea but I wouldn't sit down. I said, 'Look, Mum, I'm very lousy. I'm going to have a bath.' There was a big rain barrel in the back yard and Mum used to do the washing in there with a big poss stick to agitate the water. So, we got the water boiled again and took it out to the yard, put in some carbolic crystals and I got stripped off and got into the barrel. And she went off to get me some clean clothes. All the neighbours were there, all shouting 'Hello' over our back wall and, 'Welcome home, Joe,' and all that sort of thing. Well, I had my wash and then I had to get out of the rain barrel with all these folk there and I was naked of course. I thought I'd lost all my modesty in France, but I didn't like to stand there drying myself, so I ran in with just a wet towel round my waist and went in front of the fire and Mum dried me – just like she'd done when I used to come home from the pit as a little lad.

A soldier's seven days leave started officially the moment he arrived at the main-line station nearest his home destination. Before the new ruling, travelling had taken up hours and even days of the precious seven days leave and it had been commonplace for soldiers, whose homes were in the Hebrides or the far north of Scotland, to arrive home just in time to turn around and set off on the journey back.

For soldiers, like the Colonial troops, who had no homes to go to, London was the Mecca. Many had new-found relatives to visit; many more were at a loose end. From the moment they arrived at Victoria Station, London received them with open arms. There was the YMCA All-Welcome Hut where pretty girl volunteers dished out tea, sandwiches and smiles. There was Paddy's Bar, thick with troops and thick with the smoke of pipes and Woodbines, where from early morning until late at night blasée barmaids pulled endless pints of beer, shrugged off the advances of Tommies who had not seen a girl for months, and prospered on tips from the lavish Aussies. They never bothered to pick up copper coins in their change and were known throughout London as 'the Silver Kings'.

The YMCA was well aware of the temptations of the big city to healthy young men, long deprived of feminine society, and organised leave hostels where a bed could be had for ninepence and a square meal for the same price. They set up canteens, rest and recreation huts where a soldier could enjoy the luxury of a comfortable armchair, a game of draughts or billiards, as many cups of tea as he could consume and the society of pleasant young women of unimpeachable character. At the Shakespeare Hut for New Zealand troops, there were more than two hundred such volunteers, working in shifts, because the ever-vigilant authorities had concluded that a frequent turnover of smiling faces behind the tea urns was the best insurance against the indiscretions and unsuitable attachments that were almost inevitable in the highly charged atmosphere of wartime. They set up Leave Enquiry Bureaux where kindly advisers would arrange accommodation, suggest a sight-seeing programme or persuade soldiers to join one of their own free tours around London, to Hampton Court or to the Zoo.

The YMCA extended its vigilance to soldiers who disdained such innocent pleasures, and set up night patrols to scour the back streets of Soho and the West End. They were groups of well-meaning volunteers of mature years, 'doing their bit' in work of . . . *a delicate personal nature requiring the utmost tact to separate men from women of known disreputable character.*

Most of the boys were content to goggle at the sights by day and to retire at night to their ninepenny beds, whistling or humming whatever song had been the highlight of their evening at the theatre.

In the theatres and music halls the emphasis was on light entertainment, and every performance was packed out. Few soldiers returned to the front without being able to boast of having seen at least four shows in his seven days London leave. There was *Ye Gods*, advertised as 'a scream', at the Aldwych. The beautiful Alice Delysia was starring in *Pell Mell* at the Ambassadors. A. E. Matthews toyed sentimentally with Moya Mannering in *Peg O' My Heart* at the Globe. There was *Chu Chin Chow* at His Majesty's, naughty Teddy Gerard in *Bric Brac* at the Palace and, best of all, among a score of other reviews and musicals, George Robey and Violet Loraine at the Alhambra in *The Bing Boys are Here*. Their famous duet was the success of the summer:

> *If you were the only girl in the world*
> *And I were the only boy,*
> *Nothing else would matter in this world today,*
> *If we could go on loving in the same old way.*
> *A Garden of Eden, just made for two,*
> *With nothing to mar our joy,*
> *I would say such wonderful things to you,*
> *There would be such wonderful things to do,*
> *If you were the only girl in the world,*
> *and I were the only boy.*

The Palm Court Orchestra played it at teatime at the Waldorf, errand boys whistled it as they teetered along on bicycles, and they played it every afternoon at Madame Vacani's Dancing School at her famous tea dances. The young lady teachers and the more mature and accomplished of their pupils danced impeccably and mooned just a little in the arms of soulful young officers with nowhere else to go. It was romantic, it was exciting, it was quite respectable and it was well worth the five shillings admission. The charge was fixed high enough to discourage lower ranks from indulging in this genteel entertainment and there was no escaping the eagle eye of Madame Vacani herself. She supervised every dance, played the gracious hostess and introduced the officers to partners who were strictly forbidden, on pain of instant dismissal, to accept any invitation other than to dance. But her eagle eye did not extend beyond the premises of her exclusive school. There was privacy on the dance floor, the music was sentimental, the girls were delightful, the officers were returning soon to France, to an indeterminate and possibly brief future. It was not difficult to persuade the discreet dancing partner of the afternoon to be the charming theatre companion of the evening. They all had a wonderful time.

But there was another side to leave and it was a side that most soldiers dreaded. Since he had been away there was hardly a man who had not lost a comrade, hardly an officer who had not lost a colleague. Relatives at home were avid for visits, for news, for information, for any tiny detail of comfort that would assuage the pain of mourning. It cast a blight over even the most joyous of leaves.

When I was safe in hospital, out of that hell of France, I scarcely knew how to adjust to decent society after living like an animal for so long. The only thing that kept worrying me was my promise to go and tell Bobby's people about his end. I dreaded the thought of them asking where he was buried. How could you tell a mother he was blown to pieces? We'd buried him all right, a few yards behind our position in the wood, with a rifle plunged into the earth to mark the grave and his tin hat on top of it. But by the next morning it had entirely disappeared.

Bobby was well in his forties, so his mother was not young. He was separated from his wife – he'd only ever mentioned her to me to rail at her and they had no children. But she was there that day, the day I went to see his mother.

All I could tell them was that he was buried in Delville Wood.

Lance-Corporal Len Lovell, No. 18692, 6th King's Own Yorkshire Light Infantry, 14th Division.

My pal George McCarthy had been killed on 4 June the year before when we were in Gallipoli, and this was my first leave. I had to go to the next village to see his father. He lived in the Aged Miners' Cottages. It was difficult talking to him. I said, 'Look, I didn't see him killed but we *did* bury him.' We didn't, of course, because we couldn't! But he was a Catholic and I knew it would be important to his father so I said, 'He had a good Christian burial I can assure you of that!'

Able Bodied Seaman Joseph Murray, No. TZ276, Hood Btn., The 63rd (Royal Naval) Division.

Next day I had to go and see another pal's parents. That was
even worse. It was another mining family and the father had got
his leg broken and he had a permanent limp, so things weren't so
good for them. You're paid by the jobs and if you're not fit you
don't get any work – and no pay either. Their boy was an old
school pal of mine. All the time I sat there talking to the father, his
Mum didn't say much and I could sense that she was uneasy. I
wasn't in the house ten minutes when the postman knocked at the
door with a telegram to say that the other son had been killed in
France.

What can a bloke do then? What kind of man from the war,
home on leave, goes into a house to make condolences with a
fellow's family and a telegram comes to say that the other one's
killed?

It spoiled my leave. I felt I could see it on everyone's faces like as
if they were saying, 'How come you've come home and *he* hasn't?'

I was sorry I came home on leave. I didn't enjoy it. It's funny,
but I wished I hadn't gone. You couldn't get these things out of
your mind.

On the whole, Joe Murray was not sorry when his leave came to an
end on 25 September. When the night-train from Edinburgh drew
into Newcastle it was already filled with troops returning to the front,
but Murray squeezed into an over-crowded carriage and sat on his
pack on the floor. There was no question of sleep and the talk was all
of Zeppelins. Two had been shot down the night before and
newspapers bought to while away the journey were full of dramatic
accounts. There was a certain excitement in travelling by night
through blacked-out England. With the stepping-up of the air raids
a new theory had taken hold in the imaginations of authorities, so
sensitive about 'showing a light' that smokers striking matches in the
street were being prosecuted and fined. It was now believed that
plumes of sparks from the funnels of the engines of express trains
were guiding the raiders through England.

Whatever guided them, they had arrived in force the night before
last and dropped bombs that killed forty civilians and injured a
hundred and twenty-six, including four soldiers who were on leave in
London. But this time the Zeppelins had not got away with it.

Since the raids had started more than a year earlier, a considerable
number of troops had been kept back from the front to stiffen the
Home Defences, badly though men were needed in France. Searchlights and gun batteries were set up on the east coast, around the
outskirts of important cities and at strategic points in the cities

themselves. It had never occurred to Frank Mayhew that his peacetime training as an electrical engineer would lead him to a position in an open field at Cuffley.

Our main job was to keep the searchlights in good order – because Zeppelin raids weren't at all frequent. There was always the possibility, but as a rule weather conditions were so abnormal that the Zeppelins couldn't operate. When the alarm came I was lucky enough to be the operator and to pick up the Zeppelin. It's an extraordinary sight! A Zeppelin in a searchlight beam looks just like a goldfish in a bowl and one could follow it quite easily. The gun was a thirteen-pounder mounted on a three-ton Daimler lorry and it could fire to about sixty degrees. After that, the angle would be so steep that the recoil would have knocked the bottom of the lorry out. On this particular occasion, after holding the Zeppelin for a few minutes, the gun fired four or five rounds and then the angle got too steep for further gunfire so we were out of action and we had to shut down.

Sapper F. L. Mayhew, No. 2259, London Electrical Engineers, Royal Engineers (TF).

To 'shut down' we used to use a copper lid to cover up the beams, but the lamps remained lit under it and a little later the guns thought they should be in action again, so we opened out. Quite by chance I'd sort of mentally followed the Zeppelin and, when we opened out, I was able to pick it up straight-away. But we scored no hits and we had to pass the target on to some other lights.

It had been a very peaceful day and we were all in bed – except for the people with late passes or the people who'd taken a night off without them. Suddenly there was a whirring noise overhead and we all rushed out and stood looking up and watching. We could see the silhouette up in the sky – a huge cigar-shaped thing caught in a searchlight. Presently we heard the noise of one of our own aeroplanes coming along behind it and the tracer bullets went from the aeroplane to the Zeppelin and the Zeppelin burst into flames and began to fall. It was so huge that it looked as though it was just about half a mile or a mile away.

Trooper Charles Williams, MM, No. 1598, 1st Btn., Royal Buckinghamshire Hussars.

Some of the fellows rushed in and put on their boots and trousers and started off to see it. There were dozens of them jumping over the fence but most of us stayed behind watching the flare and it was such a blaze that we could even hear the crackling noise from it. While we were watching, the bugles started to sound the alarm and the order to saddle up and get going to where the Zeppelin had come down. We were saddled up and trotting off in no time and, as we went we passed a lot of the boys who were making for the Zepp on foot and we yelled at them that they were wanted and they had to rush off back to the camp to get saddled up and follow us in.

We were to put a guard round the Zeppelin. It had actually fallen some distance away, outside a village just before you get into Billericay. It was much further away than we thought but when we got there it was still burning and it burnt well into the early hours of the morning. What a sight it was! What a sight!

It was a sight that everyone wanted to see. By three o'clock in the morning the road to the farm where the Zeppelin had crashed was jammed with motor-cars, bicycles, pony traps, donkey carts and hundreds of pedestrians who had risen from their beds and walked several miles to gawp, to gaze, to exclaim and to get as near as they could to the wreck. The soldiers, standing guard with bayonets fixed, kept them well back. By dawn there were thousands of people craning their necks from the steep banks of the lane. Some had even climbed trees to get a better look. The wreckage was spread over hundreds of yards and shortly after dawn Bert Williams was one of the party detailed to clear up the area around the smouldering wreckage.

Trooper Charles Williams, No. 1598, 1st Btn., Royal Buckinghamshire Hussars.

The worst bit was gathering up the crew. The ground was very soft where they fell and when we picked them up there were indentations in the soft soil of the shape of their bodies, arms, legs, everything – a mould of the bodies really.[1] We carried them to the farmhouse. We picked up wicker chairs, loaves of German bread and bits of burnt silk and pieces of aluminium – all sorts of stuff. It kept us in beer for months! Everybody wanted souvenirs and, when the officers weren't looking, we were selling them to the crowd for half a crown and two bob a time. It was a good morning. Special trains came down with London sightseers and they were all begging us to get souvenirs for them, so those that weren't actually on guard duty were able to get inside the guard-line without the officers noticing and bring out pieces of burnt silk and broken aluminium, to flog it to the Cockneys. You nipped in, got a piece, tucked it up your tunic and then broke it up into small pieces and sold it for about two bob a time. Sergeant Chiltern was in charge of us and he turned a blind eye. Major Francis was in command, but we easily dodged him.

We did two hours guard at a time and the field kitchen even

[1] The remains of the crew were buried on 27 September in Great Burstead Churchyard. The officiating clergyman felt it appropriate to change the words of the Burial Service from 'our brothers here departed', to 'these men here departed'.

cooked our Sunday dinner for us there. We had beef, roast potatoes and Yorkshire pudding. Some of the sightseers were envious! Some of them said, 'Your dinner smells good, Tommy!' They were starving. They'd been there for hours and hours, some of them, and all day more were arriving. It had been seen for thirty miles around and those that hadn't seen it for themselves had heard about it. It was a fantastic thing – so huge you wouldn't believe it. The wreckage stretched across two fields.

At five o'clock in the afternoon the troopers were relieved and rode back to camp. A fair quantity of Zeppelin wreckage went with them. It turned out to be an excellent investment.

The blacksmiths and the shoeing smiths, like Bert Williams, made the largest profits. As tradesmen they were quick to see the possibilities of exploiting this unexpected windfall and soon they were spending all their time off-duty – and a good deal of on-duty time too – in the Battalion forge, zealously engaged in the manufacture of souvenirs. The light aluminium was easily melted down to make crosses and medallions. As a finishing touch, Trooper Charlie Curtis, whose father worked as a typesetter on the *Daily Mirror*, obligingly got hold of some type. Business flourished. The boys raised their prices and began to take orders for identification discs and bracelets bearing the appropriate name and number and to embellish rings and medallions with the words: *Zeppelin Souvenir. Billericay. 24th September, 1916* stamped into the metal. They hammered it very thin so that it went a long way and they were rich for months.

The 24th had also been an exciting night at West Mersea where the crew of a Zeppelin had, with some difficulty, been captured alive. It was the crew, rather than the captors, who had experienced the difficulty. They hammered on the door of a nearby farmer who was still in such a state of shock at the sight of the monster Zeppelin descending almost in his farmyard that he was too terrified to open up. When the Germans tired of knocking and threw stones at his bedroom window, accidentally breaking it in their anxiety to surrender, it merely reinforced the farmer in his opinion that the beastly Huns were bent on some fresh atrocity. His relief was considerable when he heard them march off towards the village, though he was not reassured by the sound of a salvo of shots as they emptied their pistols towards the sky before tossing them into the undergrowth at the side of the lane. But the prisoners gave no trouble. They allowed themselves to be escorted to the Police Station and accepted cups of tea while awaiting the arrival of a military escort. The Commander, in excellent English, asked politely to be escorted to the Post Office

The October Fighting

The Butte de Warlencourt and the land beyond le Sars where the fighting came to a standstill at the end of the Battle of the Somme in November 1916.

The valley behind Beaumont Hamel and the slopes to the right above it where the boys of the Glasgow Tramways Battalion were cut off in Frankfurt Trench and fought a private battle of their own after the Battle of the Somme officially ended and all attempts to rescue them had to be given up.

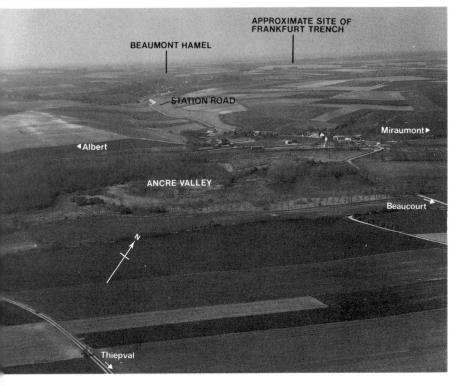

The British and German lines on either side of the present-day Newfoundland Park where the trenches (which are chalk-marks beyond it) have been preserved by the Canadian Government as a memorial to the men of the Newfoundland Regiment who died here. Y-Ravine runs just behind the slope on the right and past the foot of the trees in the park.

The valley behind Beaumont Hamel (Station Road) with the Thiepval Ridge to the east, which for obvious reasons had to go before Beaumont Hamel could be captured. The old deep dugouts, so joyfully explored by the boys of the 13th Rifle Brigade after they had helped the Royal Naval Division to capture the valley and many gun positions, can still be seen in the lee of the bush-covered bank in the foreground.

The 'fortress' village of Beaumont Hamel sheltered in the cleft of its valley. The German front line ran across the slopes of the rising ground on either side. The white chalk-marks in front of the copse on the left mark the perimeter of their outpost wired defences, but the ditch-like vestiges of trench running towards the village in the middle foreground was dug, after its capture, as a British communication trench. Munich and Frankfurt trenches were on the left of the rising ground behind the village.

Station Road, running from Beaumont Hamel village to Beaucourt station, which was the 'Green Line' captured by the Royal Naval Division supported by the 13th Battalion, The Rifle Brigade, on 13th November. The terrain has been long ago returned to farmland but the rugged vestiges of dugouts, trenches and gun positions show how formidably it was fortified.

Advanced First Army.
Second Army.
Third Army.
Fourth Army.
----

3.   June 29

Platoon Comdrs.

*Please read to your platoons
and initial when you've done so*
Capt Lloyd for no 8
Lieut Henri   7
"   Lidiard   6
"   Thomas   5

O.A.104.

The following warning should be communicated
verbally to all ranks before taking part in an assault:-

1.   All ranks must be on their guard against the
various ruses at which the enemy has shown himself to
be an adept, especially the use of British words of command,
such as "Retire", etc.

2.   The German machine gun is carried on a sledge, and
the Germans sometimes throw a blanket over the gun. This
makes the sledge and gun resemble a stretcher.

3.   It is the duty of all ranks to continue to use
their weapons against the enemy's fighting troops, unless
and until it is beyond all doubt that these have not only
ceased all resistance, but that, whether through having
voluntarily thrown down their weapons or otherwise, they
have definitely and finally abandoned all hope or intention
of resisting further. In the case of apparent surrender,
it lies with the enemy to prove his intention beyond the
possibility of misunderstanding, before the surrender can
be accepted as genuine.

G.H.Q.,   Sgd/ L.E. KIGGELL, Lieut-General,

26.6.16.   Chief of the General Staff.

167th Inf. Bde.   - 2 -
168th Inf. Bde.
169th Inf. Bde.

Herewith 25 copies to provide for a distribution
of one per company.

The importance of the above instructions must be
impressed on all ranks.

Hdqrs. 56th Divn.   Lieut. Colonel,
28th June, 1916.   General Staff.

Left: All that remains of old Beaumont Hamel village is a single pane of stained glass depicting the head of the Virgin Mary. In 1916 a German officer picked it out of the rubble of the old church and took it back to Germany as a souvenir. In 1978 he returned it to the village and it was incorporated into a window of the 'new' church (rebuilt in 1922).

Right: This photograph was found by a British solder in the wallet of a dead German.

Opposite: The Order issued from G.H.Q. on the eve of the First of July which was later denied to be an instruction to 'take no prisoners'.

Left, below and opposite: The letter Captain Agius received from Harold Scarlett's widow Florence (*see page 292*).

305, Thorold Rd
Ilford.
Oct 3rd /16.

Dear Capt. Agius —

I wish to take this opportunity of thanking you for your kind letter of sympathy, and for the few details you were **able** to give me concerning my dear husband's death. The sad news was a terrible shock to me, and, up till now, I have felt too ill to write to you, although I have been eager to do so.

If it is not taking too great an advantage of your kindness will you please let me know whether at the time my dear one fell, there were any personal possessions on him that could be sent to me. I know there was ... of real value but, I think you ... understand that ... little ... matter what ... my most

cherished possessions.

It was a great relief to know that dear Harold did not suffer any pain, although what would I not give to have had just one last message from him. We have been married such a short time (only five months) and I cannot realize that he has gone — never to see him again. The last time we were together he was so happy and well, and eager to do his level best for his country at all cost. This horrible War is dealing some cruel blows, and one is apt to grow hardened to the casualty list until someone very dear is taken. There is scarcely a home, but what the occupants have some great trouble to bear, and sometimes I think, knowing this, helps us to bear our grief more bravely.

Will you please also tell

me if possible, where my husband was struck. I feel I would like to know. After the War, I hope to be able to visit his last resting-place, and in that case, I suppose I should have no difficulty in distinguishing it.

Once again thanking you for your kindness in writing to me. With every good wish for your safe and speedy return to England.

Yours very sincerely,

Florence E. Scarlett

Below: 'Fond Love to my Dear Boy'. Such postcards were more popular with the senders than with the recipients.

FOR KING & COUNTRY,

WITH FOND LOVE TO MY DEAR BOY.

DEAR BOY I'D LOVE TO FEEL YOUR ARMS
ENFOLD ME IN EMBRACE,
TO HEAR AGAIN THE LOVING VOICE
NO OTHER CAN REPLACE;
I MISS YOU SO AND OH I WISH
YOUR LIPS TO MINE COULD CLING,
BUT, DEAR, I FEEL RIGHT PROUD TO KNOW
YOU'RE FIGHTING FOR YOUR KING.

584.S.   COPYRIGHT.   M. WATKINSON.

BEAGLES'
POSTCARDS.

Above left: The New Recruits: Joe Hoyles (*standing*), Fred Lyons and Sid Birkett, photographed the day they joined up.
Above right: The Seasoned Warriors. Len Lovell at home on convalescent leave.
Below left: George Roy Bealing, MM 6th Wilts. 19th Div. 1914-18.
Below right: Tom Easton of the Tyneside Scottish in 1914.

in order to telephone the Dutch Embassy in London who would let his wife know that he was safe. Reporters had quickly arrived on the scene and the next day's newspapers made much of this piece of cheek – typical, they insinuated, of 'Hun arrogance'.

2 MORE ZEPPELINS DOWN, trumpeted the *Daily Mail* in inch-high letters. The *Continental Daily Mail* copied the headlines plus four pages of coverage and carried the news to France.

Three weeks after his experience at Thiepval with the West Yorks on 3 September, Arthur Wilson was at the Base in hospital and he was having a painful time. He had been wounded by a chance shell and wounded in an awkward place. Now the pleasure of being in a real bed, the relief of being in hospital and out of the line, was offset by considerable discomfort. His stomach was distended, his bladder was bursting and he could do nothing about it. It was hell. That morning Sister had come down the ward with a catheter in her hand and a purposeful look in her eye. 'Just another hour!' Wilson begged. Sister relented. 'One hour then, Mr Wilson, and then we really must use the catheter.' Ten minutes had ticked past when the newspapers arrived. Heedless of the dignity that hospital protocol dictated should prevail in an officers' ward, a VAD burst through the door shrieking, 'Two Zeppelins shot down last night!' Wilson's bed was nearest. She brandished the newspaper under his nose and he grabbed it. As he read, he became aware of a warm, moist sensation which had nothing to do with excitement, and it went on and on and on. The nurses roared with laughter, produced clean pyjamas, changed the sheets without complaint and teased him without mercy. After a few days the joke began to wear thin. Every nurse who presented him with a bottle or a bedpan felt obliged to remark encouragingly, 'Two Zeppelins brought down, Mr Wilson!'

It was not the only good news. The same edition of the *Daily Mail* reported that Morval and Lesboeufs had been captured. Next day, eighty-eight days after the first attempt, they would at last conquer Thiepval.

Chapter 23

The Germans fought to the death for Thiepval – for every inch of
trench dug deep through the pulverised rubble, for every strongpoint hidden in the old vaults and cellars, for every gallery and
dugout burrowed into the chalk. One by one they were overwhelmed. When night fell the few who were left were still fighting to
retain a last foothold in the north-western corner of Thiepval village.
The British infantry paused, drew breath and attacked again in the
morning. Before the sun rose through the thick autumn mist,
Thiepval was finally captured.

The Germans had been in possession for exactly two years. It was
27 September and, on just such a morning, through just such a mist,
two years ago to the day, Boromée Vaquette drove his cows for the
last time up the narrow road from Authuille to their pasture on the
hump of the ridge above and never came back. It was two years since
the villagers of Thiepval had peeped warily through neat cottage
windows as German horsemen clattered through the village. Two
years since German officers took up their quarters in its spacious
château and, dining at a table heavy with the Comtesse de Bréda's
china and silver, planned the disposition of their forces who, even as
their officers savoured the old Count's best wine, were digging
trenches across the meadows of Thiepval Ridge. Now nothing was
left. Not a blade of grass. Not a tree. Not a bird. The roads and tracks
had all but disappeared. Here and there on the site of the old village a
line of brick-dust staining the cratered earth between the trenches
hinted at a long-vanished row of cottages. The twisted fragment of a
weather-vane, a few chips of brick marked the church; a scattering of
jagged grey stones was all that remained of the château and, as far as
the eye could see, the churned-up land was covered with the grey
humped bodies of British and German dead.

In a terrible travesty of that other harvest-time two years and many
lives ago, they looked like haycocks through the morning mist.

In the eighty-nine days since Thiepval had been first attacked, it was
Kitchener's Army which had borne the brunt of the fighting on the
Somme and it was not surprising that certain people in high places
were beginning to question the rate at which the Empire was eating

into the capital of its young manhood. In 1914 – in four months' fighting – there had been 90,000 casualties of whom more than 50,000 were killed or missing. That had put paid to the old Regular Army. In 1915, with its dreadful chronology of disaster – Neuve Chapelle, Aubers Ridge, Festubert, Ypres, Loos – the toll of casualties had mounted to 285,000, of whom 92,000 were killed or missing. That had put paid to most of the Reservists and Territorials and it needed no statistician to work out that the Somme Campaign was well on the way to putting paid to Kitchener's Army. Already, between July and September, more than 90,000 men had been killed and the medical records showed that 228,632 others had been sent, badly wounded, to the Base – just 4,000 fewer in three months than in the first sixteen months of the entire war.

For four months now the hotly-debated Military Service Act had been in force. By early next year the first batch of conscripts would be trained and ready for active service. How were they to be used? Among politicians high talk of 'victory' and 'breakthrough' began to give way to mutterings of 'attrition' and to doubts that the High Command of the Army should continue to be given a free hand to prosecute the war on the nation's behalf entirely as they saw fit and to dispose with such profligacy of its young men. It was an over-simplified view but, in some quarters, it was strongly felt – particularly among the cabal within the Cabinet itself which was now actively canvassing peace. Lloyd George was not among them. He had been a champion of conscription but he was not immune to doubt and, now that he was Secretary of State for War, he saw it as a duty to inform himself on matters which were believed by some to lie outside his province.

During the first half of September, Lloyd George had made an extended visit to France on what Haig described as 'a huge joy ride'. Haig looked askance at Lloyd George's untidy dress – the flowing, undisciplined locks, the long shapeless overcoat, the battered trilby hat, the artistic disarray of his floppy ties. He disapproved of Lloyd George's propensity for changing plans at the last minute, sneered at his willingness to be convivial with newspapermen and photographers, and was censorious about his unpunctuality. The Secretary of State spent a mere two days as Haig's guest at GHQ. He had spent five times as long as the guest of the French Army, talking his way along the French Front from Verdun to the Somme – and he had talked a little too much. Lloyd George liked talking to people. Since the start of the Somme Campaign he had gone out of his way to meet officers and men home on leave from the front and to sound out their opinions. But it was one thing to quiz the fighting men; it was quite another to invite General Foch to express his opinion of the performance of British Generals as a whole and of the Commander-in-Chief in particular, and to hint, moreover, that his own confidence in their ability was far from complete. As a high-ranking officer in the French Army, Foch was no stranger to interference by politicians. He was shocked at such a breach of protocol, discreetly replied that he 'had had no means of forming an opinion', and took the first opportunity of repeating this conversation to Sir Douglas Haig. Despite his disapproval of Lloyd George, Haig was genuinely astounded '. . . that a British minister could have been so ungentlemanly as to go to a foreigner and put such questions regarding his own subordinates'.

The Commander-in-Chief was rightly aggrieved, but his own ingrained gentlemanliness and phlegm, and a strong awareness of the importance of 'pulling together', decided him that the whole affair was best ignored. He had more than enough on his plate. Besides, even if they had not achieved the hoped-for breakthrough, the Army's achievements during the latter half of September had been considerable. On the 15th they had crushed the enemy's formidable second line. On the 18th they had captured the Quadrilateral. A week later they had secured Lesboeufs, Morval, Gueudecourt, and one last valley lay between them and the Transloy ridges that snaked round to Bapaume. The Germans had been forced to loosen their grip and retire from Combles. Now the bastion of Thiepval village had crumbled in the face of the British assault, and Mouquet Farm with it.

But although the Germans had been shrugged from the shoulder of the Thiepval Ridge they still held the crest, and the crest was crowned with formidable defences – Schwaben Redoubt, with Stuff Redoubt to the east of it and Zollern Redoubt between that and the Albert–Bapaume Road. The Canadians had pushed well up the road, beyond Courcelette. They were within sight of le Sars and they were almost halfway to Bapaume. It had taken the Army almost three months to get this far and the autumn was well advanced. They must make one last effort to gain the redoubts, to conquer the whole of the Thiepval Ridge with all its advantages of observation, to link up the line that ran along the high ground through Morval and Lesboeufs, through Gueudecourt and Martinpuich to Courcelette on the other side of the Albert–Bapaume road. The September weather had been mixed and could be expected to worsen at any moment. Before it did, there was one last chance – and it was almost a gamble – that they could make the breakthrough. The Commander-in-Chief was convinced that the enemy was almost at his last gasp, that his casualties had been enormous, that his reserves were few, that his morale was quite possibly about to crack.

Along the straggling line of advance between Thiepval Wood and the Albert–Bapaume road the situation was confused and the Signallers were having the worst of it. General Gough, in command of the attack, heard disturbingly conflicting reports and often, by the time a runner had managed to get back through the bombardment with news of an advance made or an objective captured, the fortunes of the troops had been reversed by a German counterattack. Shells damaged signal lines as soon as they were laid and it was up to the Signallers to mend them and to carry the line forward over the captured ground. Eric Rossiter was not aware that he was performing a personal service for General Gough. He only knew that he was somewhere in the chaos of the thundering battle, that Mouquet Farm was behind him, that Hessian Trench was somewhere out in front and that somehow the cable had to be got up to it. Not far to his left the fighting sounded disconcertingly close, for the 11th Division, also acting under General Gough's instructions, was trying to 'clear up the situation' at Stuff Redoubt. They would finally clear it up on 14 October.

Until that moment I'd always considered myself to be a lucky soldier. I'd been at the Signals Headquarters at Ypres the year before, so I'd missed that horrible business when the Germans attacked with gas and the Canadians had to cover up. I'd been in and out of the line on the Somme and never got a scratch. I nearly got it another time at Ypres when the Germans blew a mine right underneath us. We lost seventeen guys, but I wasn't touched. Then we came down to the Somme and this was my second stint in the front line. We'd been out on so-called rest, on fatigues all the time carrying sandbags of rations and supplies up to Pozières and, even then, I'd had a lucky escape just the week before. We were going up in single file in a carrying party and there was a fellow in front of me carrying a sandbag of Mills bombs. A pin in one of the bombs must have worked loose, because suddenly the whole lot went up. It killed and wounded a lot of men. I was only seven or eight yards back, but I never got a scratch.

That night, I suddenly had the feeling that my luck was going to run out. It was the toughest job I'd had. My pal, Jimmy Leaken, and I had to lay a line up from Battalion Headquarters to Hessian Trench. We only had a single Company there, so we didn't have much of a hold on it and it was touch and go if the guys could hang on. We tried to keep in the communication trench as far as we could go but it was so blown in by shellfire that we had to get out in the open. Imagine laying these goddam wires in the daylight,

Corporal Eric Rossiter, MM, 7th Canadian Infantry Battalion.

diving from shell-hole to shell-hole and dashing out when the coast seemed to be a bit clear. I was shaking, absolutely.

We made a dash and jumped into one shell-hole and there were five Canadians lying dead there. Jesus! It gave me a fright. Something flashed into my mind that I'd completely forgotten about. I had an uncle who'd dabbled in palmistry and years ago he'd read my hand. He said, 'You're going to get killed before you're twenty years old.' It never hit me till then. There I was, lying there in that shell-hole with those five dead Canadians and I thought, 'Jesus! I've only got four days to go!' It was no comforting thought.

Beyond the Canadians, across the Albert–Bapaume road, Ernest Deighton, now recovered from his wounds and his ordeal at the Leipzig Redoubt on the First of July, was back with the 8th King's Own Yorkshire Light Infantry, but he hardly recognised it as the same Battalion. Most of the new men were not even Yorkshiremen. There were Northumberlands, there were men from the Durham Light Infantry, there were some from the King's Royal Rifle Corps and there was even a bunch of Scots of the Argyll and Sutherland Highlanders. He looked in vain for familiar faces but, like familiar landmarks, there were few to be seen. To crown the confusion the Brigade was no longer apprenticed to the 8th Division but back again with the 23rd and occupying a newly-captured trench on the far side of Martinpuich. An abandoned tank was inextricably ditched half in, half out of the trench, blocking it so effectively that some unfortunates whose positions were on the other side had been obliged to leave the trench and run the gauntlet of the skyline in order to reach them.

Corporal Bernard Minnitt, MC, MM, 11th Btn., The Nottinghamshire and Derbyshire Regiment (The Sherwood Foresters), 70th Brigade, 23rd Division.

It was one of the best trenches imaginable – well buttressed, with fine solid fire-steps and beautifully clean deep dugouts. It was pretty evident that the enemy had panicked and left in a hurry and it was probably the tank coming over the hilltop just a few yards away that had put the breeze up them. They could have taken their time if they'd known that the tank's engine was about to give out! There was no sign of any troops in the trench, though it made a sharp turn and appeared to wind away to our right, so we weren't sure if we were alone. To be on the safe side, Lieutenant Lacey strolled up to me and said quite casually, 'Come on, Corporal, let's go for a walk.' I picked up my rifle and we went off down that trench as if we were going for a walk along a promenade. We walked what seemed like half a mile and saw nothing and heard nothing – for which yours truly was really grateful!

Late in the evening I was told to take a fighting patrol of twenty men and go with Lieutenant Benton of B Company on another exploration down the trench. This time we were to go further and try to make contact with another division who someone had a half idea was occupying the same trench about a mile away. I was at the front of the party with my rifle loaded and very cautiously I kept climbing up on the fire-step and looking over the top. I'd taken my bayonet off, because it was very awkward in getting round the trench corners. I pushed the safety catch of my rifle forward and stopped every time we came to the corner of a bay and looked round very carefully before going on to the next. Then a Very light burst just as I was looking round the corner ahead – and there was a face looking back at the other end of the bay!

Lieutenant Benton was just at my back and he whispered, 'Challenge them.' So I said, 'Halt! Who goes there?' There was no reply. I tried again, 'Halt! Who goes there?' Still no reply. Then one of the men behind shouted, 'If you fellows don't reply we'll throw this bloody bomb among you!' Someone shouted back, 'We're the 5th Northants.' What a relief! I walked on round the corner and met this chap halfway along the traverse. It was too dark to tell from the shape of his tin hat if he was English or German but the gleam of his bayonet was at the high port position, above my head and I had my loaded rifle pointed towards him, so it seemed all right. Then a very windy voice behind me shouted, 'Look out, Corporal. They're Boches! The 5th Battalion's a training battalion!'

Then things started happening. The man facing me took a step backwards to bring his bayonet down six inches from my stomach. I knocked it away just as he fired and I heard someone behind me fall with a groan. I fired back, went down on one knee to make a smaller target and reloaded just as a Very light showed up the trench. There was no one in front of me. They had backed round the corner and, when I looked behind me, my 'fighting patrol' had disappeared except for the man who had been hit. He was groaning on the ground and I knew I couldn't move him without help. I dodged back two or three bays, thinking the patrol had moved back for shelter, when someone came jumping over the top of the trench from the direction of the enemy and he shouted, 'Is that you, Corporal?' He was just in time to stop me from shooting him! I said, 'Come and give me a hand. Someone's hurt. Where are the others?' He said, 'They all skedaddled so fast that they knocked the rifle out of my hands and broke my thumb. I can't lift anything.'

We had to leave the wounded man and go back for help. When we got to our sector there was great excitement. The patrol had come rushing in and told the Colonel that we'd run into a crowd of Germans, Lieutenant Benton and Corporal Minnitt were killed and Private Green was missing. They were standing by for an attack when we got there! Dawn was breaking by the time I got back with a stretcher-party to the wounded man. It was Lieutenant Benton and by then he was dead.

It was an awful business – a complete shambles. I was very upset about it and I made it my business to get hold of three men of the patrol we'd clashed with. They were from the 12th Durhams, in our own Brigade, but they hardly knew who they were themselves. They'd joined the Battalion with a new draft a few days before and the man who was out in front as number one bayonet man was on his first patrol and scared stiff. When we'd challenged them everything had gone out of his head but the title of his training battalion in England. He was very down in the mouth over the death of Lieutenant Benton. I told him not to blame himself. It was the fortune of war.

When daylight came, we could see that during the night an assembly trench had been dug at right angles to our old position. It was directly facing the Germans' line where they were dug in in the village of le Sars and our job was to shift them out of it. About half-past twelve we got orders to pack up and move into the assembly trench and keep our heads well down until Zero.

Ernest Deighton was one of the two hundred men who had dug the assembly trench in the night and now he too was crouched in it waiting with the first wave of the 8th King's Own Yorkshire Light Infantry for Zero. Unlike most of the Battalion, Deighton's platoon had lunched after a fashion. A shell exploding in the ragged field behind had fortuitously dug up some potatoes and showered them into the trench along with a fountain of earth. Hardly troubling to clean them, the boys had eaten them like savages. Now, as they waited for the off, the raw potatoes lay heavy on Deighton's stomach. He still had vivid memories of the nightmare of July and the long solitary wait in his sniper's post in No Man's Land. He was now a Lewis-gunner. Charging into a fight with a heavy machine-gun on your shoulder was no joke but at least the course at the Machine-Gun School had kept him out of the line for a while. For Minnitt waiting fifty yards away, it would be the first time over the top.

Corporal Bernard Minnitt, MC, MM, 11th Btn., The Nottinghamshire and Derbyshire

My position was on the extreme right, next to Lieutenant Coates from Nottingham. As we were on the top of the slope, we could see all the men of the Battalion and they were all looking in our direction for the signal to go. It was a bright sunny day and the whole outlook seemed unreal to me. Suddenly, with one movement, all the bayonets flashed in the sun as the men fixed them on their rifles. Mr Coates' watch showed ten seconds to go, then five, four, three, two, one – then up went his arm and the Battalion went over the top like one man and off at the double into No Man's Land. I was so fascinated at the sight of it all that I suddenly came to my senses and realised that I was still standing there and Lieutenant Coates was thirty yards in front of me. I pulled myself together and jumped over and, just as I did, it seeemed as if all hell was suddenly let loose. Every Gunner behind us must have had their fingers itching to fire and thousands of shells started screaming over our heads, firing the creeping barrage and four hundred yards away Jerry's trenches disappeared in smoke and explosions.

I came to a large shell-hole with half a dozen of our fellows in it, scared stiff and sheltering. I ordered them out and rushed on, making sure they came with me, and we came to the one gap in the enemy's barbed wire that seemed to have been broken by our shell-fire. We doubled through it and fanned out again and went on to the German trench. We started taking prisoners right away, and we could see other Germans hopping it, back to their next trench. We'd been given four minutes to get to the first trench, two minutes to clear it and then to move on to number two, but the Germans were obviously so surprised and stunned by our barrage that we jumped the first trench and went straight on to the next and started to clear that and dig ourselves in. We were so far ahead of ourselves that the barrage hadn't lifted past the last trench. Unfortunately we had to put up with being shelled by some of our own missiles before it did lift.

My objective was Destremont Farm, just this side of le Sars. We had to pass to the right of it, but I never got any distance! I went over with my whole Lewis-gun section – eight trained gunners and eight reserves, because I was learning them the job. They were carrying extra ammunition and the idea was that if I got hit they would take over the gun. But we all got hit. I lost the lot! The shell hit us all.

We'd just got set up in a shell-hole and I'd started firing the gun when this shell came, and I don't know if it was ours or theirs. That was the last I knew. When I come round I was still in the same position but all I could see was part of the Lewis-gun butt against my face on the side of the shell-hole. Where the rest of the Lewis-gun had gone, I don't know, and there was no sign of any of my section either. I never saw any of them again.

Regiment (The Sherwood Foresters), 70th Brigade, 23rd Division.

Private Ernest Deighton, No. 25884, 8th Btn., King's Own Yorkshire Light Infantry.

I don't know how long I was knocked out cold. They were still banging away when I came round and my leg was all anyhow and covered with blood. I took my puttee off the other leg and grabbed the shattered one and straightened it and wrapped my puttee round it. Then I pushed in my entrenching tool and turned it round like a tourniquet to stop it bleeding and I reckon that's what saved my life. Then I started to crawl back to the trench the best road I could. It was dark by then, so I couldn't see much and I fell into the trench all anyhow and my legs fell in after me. The stretcher-bearers picked me up straight away and put me on a stretcher and they shoved me for shelter underneath this knocked-out-tank that was half over our trench and I stopped there till they were able to carry me down, right the way through to the dressing station under the ruins of the church at Contalmaison. It was a hell of a journey and I was in agony, for the numbness had worn off. My knee was shattered and my whole leg was burning. But I knew I was on my way to Blighty. I'd a fair idea I was on my way out of the war.

But Deighton's Battalion had managed to join hands with the Canadians north of Destremont Farm across the Bapaume road. The Brigade as a whole had taken the first three lines of trenches, but they had not managed to get into le Sars. Later that night the boys were relieved. It had started to rain and the Germans, well aware that troops would be on the move, bombarded the tracks with tear-gas. The new drafts, who now outnumbered the old hands in most battalions, were not familiar with the soft plopping of the gas shells and, by the time the order was passed to don gas helmets, most had received a generous dose. Rain beating on the outside of their goggles and eyes streaming within, did not add joy to the journey.

It rained hard for the next four days. The mud, which had been bad enough after the changeable weather of September, turned to mire. The broken land, raked and cratered by a thousand bombardments, trampled by regiments of feet, scarred and rutted by a million wheels creaking under heavy loads of ammunition and supplies, cut to its chalky bone by the thunderous passage of countless guns, mashed to a porridge by the monstrous weight of the tanks, now sank beneath the lashing rain into a viscous swamp. It engulfed every landmark, every duckboard track, every gun site; it engulfed the bodies of the dead and sucked at the bodies of the living as if to engulf them too. The trenches crumbled and dissolved into runnels of liquid mud that streamed into dugouts and rose in the trenches to the depth of a man's thigh.

Mud. A hundred years earlier, Napoleon's Army, floundering in its glutinous grip, had called it 'the sixth element'. Now, on the Somme, every relief resembled the Retreat from Moscow. Now it took two days to travel from reserve lines to the front through a succession of miserable staging posts, miscalled camps, where the troops could shiver for an hour or two beneath flapping tarpaulins before shouldering mud-encrusted rifles and sloshing on through the waste. Every battalion on the move left the smell of sodden khaki in its wake. Even the metalled roads – the arteries of the battlefield, the lifelines of supply – were coated with a layer of mud two inches deep, despite the efforts of an army of Pioneers, equipped with heavy brooms and scrapers, to keep them clear. Lorries skidded and gave up the ghost; waggons floundered and sank; for hours at a time traffic ground to a halt and even when it managed to keep going, found no feature or landmark to guide it.

A convoy started out on the Somme with the hope of a quiet trip, but each one was an adventure. My job was to take up the battalion stores – food and, most important, water. By October the conditions had got so bad that we could get nowhere near the line with a limber and so the ration parties from the Battalion had to come down further and further to meet us and carry the stuff back in sandbags. We made the sandbags up at the transport lines – so many to each Company, and the water we poured into old petrol cans. That was an awkward load to carry. The men hated it. It was a terrible job struggling back through the muck with a heavy petrol can of water in each hand and your rifle over your shoulder and the mud two or three feet thick.

On this particular night the battalion rendezvous was at Ginchy. I knew the ration party would be waiting and I knew I was late but I simply couldn't find it in the dusk and the mist. Then, out of the dark, in the flash of the guns I saw a battalion straggling along – a big bunch of soldiers all looking exactly the same in tin hats and capes, and I stopped the limber and shouted, 'Hey! Where's Ginchy, can you tell me?' A Sergeant stopped and came over to me. He said, 'Do you see those two bricks? Well, that's Ginchy!'

Corporal J. Pincombe, No. 40045, 1st Btn., Queen's Westminster Rifles, 56th Division.

Sometimes the supplies never came up at all – especially if you weren't attached to a big unit, as we weren't. A guide met us and took us to our positions in a cemetery and, when we got there, there were as many dead on top of the ground as underneath it. We were supposed to be relieving a four-gun platoon and there was just one gun and five men out of a platoon of thirty-odd left. There was no

Sergeant George Butler, 12th Machine Gun Co., 4th Division.

shelter anywhere, only shell-holes. The people we were relieving were glad to be off. They just said, 'There's the front. Fritz attacks with machine-gun fire night and morning.'

It had taken us a long time to get up to the line at Lesboeufs. We walked all the way, through thousands and thousands of shell-holes, rim to rim. Every time you put a foot forward you sank, and you were sinking into a mass of dead as well as mud, because there weren't enough people to collect the bodies in.

We had nothing to eat for three days – no food! Of course, all the time we were under shellfire and that's why they couldn't get the supplies up. We lost three guns and more than a dozen men. Eventually my gun was the only one left. I sent the rest of the fellows off, crawling round the dead looking for food and water and ammunition off dead machine-gun teams. What with this collecting ammunition and running from one shell-hole and one body to another one, we lost a devil of a lot more men, but we collected the best part of seven or eight thousand rounds of ammunition off the dead.

We were in a devil of a state by the time we got to the fifth night. We were starving, nothing to drink or any damned thing and lying there in all the slush in that cemetery. So I thought it out. I decided that we'd fire all the ammunition we had into No Man's Land. We couldn't see the Germans. You could see odd parties when the flares went up, that was all. But we fired off all these guns – I was practically buried in empties when we'd finished. When I'd fired off the last round I said to my men, 'Pick up your kit. We're off out.' I knew I could be shot for it, but I couldn't see the sense in staying. We waded back through the mud and eventually we hit the duckboard track. We'd only gone down it about two hundred yards when we met a party coming up. It was our relief! There was an officer with them, but he said nothing. He probably thought I'd got the order from elsewhere, but I knew myself I was cutting things a bit thin.

Private J. L. Bouch, No. 11776, 1st Btn., Coldstream Guards.

We set off. A ghastly night. We followed this line, everybody carrying something and we fell and floundered. There was a fellow who had come to join us and he was a baker and he was a strong man. He could do fifty press ups on his thumbs because he had very strong hands with kneading the dough – a fair, tall chap, very strong. His name was Howarth and we called him Snowball because of his white hair. He went down in the mud. He says, 'It's no good, I can't get up. I can't get up, leave me, leave me here,' and I went to him and I got hold of him. I said, 'I'll kick your bloody guts out if you don't get up,' and he got up and off we went. We came to a sunken road, narrow and fairly steep at the sides. It had been raining and we slithered down to the bottom without any bother. Then we had to get up the other side. Do you think we could get up? No matter how we clawed we just kept slipping back. I threw my can of water up first of all and my rifle and I scrambled and scraped and dug my way up this bank and eventually I managed to get to the top and pulled the others up and we went across to this post that we were relieving.

You couldn't imagine such a shambles. It was a machine-gun post. They would be a machine-gun detachment and possibly twenty men, and it was a round emplacement and it was a shambles of mud and old equipment and rubbish. You couldn't sit down. You sank in the mud. I don't think there would be three rifles that would have fired because you see we'd gone in and out the mud, and down in the mud and some had got it in the barrel and others had all their mechanism covered in mud. Anyhow, the amazing thing was that the following morning in front of us we could see fairly open ground sloping down and no sign of the Germans at all. We'd no rations. I think the only thing we'd got was this can of water, because the rations that we were carrying had gone into the mud. We were a hundred per cent miserable. We had a Sergeant named Dukes and, after a couple of days of this, he said, 'I'm going back to tell them we've got to be relieved,' and he went back and they sent a relief for us and out we went.

When we came out of the line, I didn't appear to be walking on my feet at all. I was walking on my knees. We went into some rest huts and took off our boots and clothing and you were given a ration of tea and rum and you went to sleep like a log and, when I woke up in the morning, my feet were just like huge bladders of lard with the toes sticking out at the top, no feeling at all. Trench feet. No excuse for it. You weren't supposed to have it but, there it was, you got it. All of us had it.

On our second night on the Somme the stretcher-bearers were called out and marched off in pitchy darkness, through mud and pouring rain, blindly following an officer. How he found his way is a marvel to me for, even if there had been any landmarks, it would have been impossible to find them on such a night. After about an hour, we struck a surfaced road which made the marching, if anything, more difficult. We were split up and forced through narrow passages between the waggons, up to our eyes in mud. The only objects we could see in the blackness were the roadway filled with traffic and the flashing of the guns nearby. The officer had to ask the way and then we set off again – not on the road, but

Private Arthur Hales, No. 302, 2nd/2nd London Field Ambulance.

across a trackless main of mud, down a slope. It was almost impossible to stand upright. Most of us did it on our hands and knees. All over the place were dumps of stretchers, ammunition boxes, shell cases and so on. We stopped at one heap of stretchers and were told that this was our 'station'. They said we could rest for a while before starting our stretcher-bearing stint. We were so dog-tired that we dropped on to the soaking stretchers to try to sleep for a while and forget our misery. Very soon we had to rouse when some stretcher cases arrived from some unknown place in the dark. Our job was to carry them over the sea of mud back to the road and the waggons. It took so long that it was dawn before we completed even the first journey.

Trooper Reg Lloyd, No. 1035, Cheshire Yeomanry (attached to 8th Btn., South Lancashire Regiment, 25th Division).

They were short of troops and no cavalry were wanted by then, so they dismounted us. It was a terrible come-down. To be turned into infantrymen, was like being pole-axed. Of course, we weren't very good at walking at the best of times, never mind in those conditions. We'd just arrived in France and they gave us a couple of weeks' infantry training at the Bull Ring until we were ready for the slaughterhouse. We went up to relieve the Canadians. We'd never seen anything like it. Going up through this area it was just as if an earthquake had been there. It was all mud and I was frightened to death. Eventually we came to a noticeboard. That's all. Just a noticeboard in among a bit of rubble. And the noticeboard said *Pozières*. That was all there was! Just a noticeboard that said *Pozières* to tell us where we were.

Gunner George Worsley, No. 690452, 2nd West Lancashire Brigade, Royal Field Artillery, 55th Division.

We'd moved the gun lines forward and the Headquarters, just behind the gun-line, were set up in some old deep German dugouts and the Germans started firing over gas shells. When a gas shell comes over it makes the same noise as a light shell but, instead of a bang, there's just a plop, although the impact moves the earth. You say, 'Thank goodness, that's a dud!' We got about five of these before we realised that they weren't duds. I said, 'Good Lord, our luck can't be as good as this! All these dud shells!' A couple more came and then we smelled the gas and put our gas masks on. The Germans simply saturated us with gas shells – they reckoned later there must have been more than twenty thousand, trying to knock the gun-lines out and knock out the reserves coming up. We had those gas masks on for twenty-four hours. You can't describe how uncomfortable they are, because they make you feel as if you're choking. There's a grip that holds your nose tightly and you have to breathe through the mouth, through a tube you hold between clenched teeth. Your mouth and throat get unbearably dry.

The telephone lines were down in all the other dugouts so, after twenty-four hours of this, the Colonel came to my telephone to get through to General Headquarters fifteen miles behind. When he asked to speak to the General, some young cub at the other end, said, 'I'm afraid you can't speak to the General. He's dining.' Well, the Colonel absolutely howled down the phone. He said, 'Do you realise, young man, that it's only by the grace of God I'm speaking to you now? Get me the General at once!' So, after quite a while, the General came to the phone and the Colonel said, 'We've had our masks on for twenty-four hours. We can't live here any longer. What must we do?' Well, the General gave him orders to abandon the area. The whole Brigade moved out and that full brigade of guns was left untended for forty-eight hours.

Two of us were ordered to stay to keep the telephone line open and I was unfortunately one of them. What a night that was! The dugout was about ten feet under the ground and we took turns sleeping on the floor. In the early hours of the morning, it was my turn to keep watch. Shells were coming over steadily and it was freezing cold in there, with just a tiny dim light. This other chap was snoring on the floor and I looked at the dugout entrance and I noticed for the first time that there were five gas cylinders dumped at it. I knew that, if one of those shells hit one of those cylinders, we'd absolutely had it.

I'd had a long time in the line with just a few days out and my nerves weren't too good. I never felt so alone in my life sitting in that dim dugout and the shells falling all round and the sky flashing and those five gas cylinders just outside the door. By and by I heard a voice and it seemed to be coming from a long way away. It was calling my name – 'George Worsley'. Then a long pause, and then, 'George Worsley. George Worsley.' I was absolutely terrified. I was too terrified to answer. I thought I was having a hallucination. So I kept mum. Next day, when the Brigade moved back to the guns, I discovered that it was one of the chaps who'd been trying to find me. They'd sent him back up with a message. He didn't know which dugout I was in so he was going along the lot, dodging the shells and calling my name all over the place. Down in the dugout, his voice sounded so faint and ghostly that I thought my hour had come!

October stormed towards the end of the month. On days when the rain moved out, winter moved in. Hard night frosts laid a crackle of ice across the swamps and in the morning the troops pitched forward to the attack through frozen mud. The fighting went on. The redoubts fell. The Germans were driven from the crest of Thiepval Ridge. Le Sars was captured.

The month ended in a spate of torrential downpours and thunderstorms so violent that they even out-thundered the guns.

Arthur Agius trudged thankfully out of the line, hitched a lift to Amiens and caught the leave train from the railhead to Boulogne. It was a stormy crossing, but the sun shone on his wedding day, though a blustery wind swept the bride's veil into a tangle that was hard to undo. Agius looked exceedingly smart in a dapper new uniform specially purchased for the occasion. Everyone agreed that it was a wonderful wedding. There was time for a three-day honeymoon in Eastbourne before the bridegroom returned to France to rejoin his Battalion in the trackless swamps in front of Gueudecourt and Lesboeufs, facing the Germans on the Transloy ridges across the valley.

Wallowing in the mud of the front line Fritz was as cold, as miserable, as muddy and despairing as any Tommy. But he suffered less from shortage of ammunition; he was better provisioned; his supplies had a better chance of getting through. Unlike their unfortunate counterparts, German soldiers were not obliged to struggle over six exhausting miles of battered desolation to reach the firing line. There was shelter close behind them. There were usable roads that ran right up to communication trenches, and a network of light-gauge railways to ease the transport of troops and supplies.

But Sir Douglas Haig was right in deducing that the Germans were shaken by the wearing fighting of the past months. He was right in his belief that they were over-stretched and that they were rethinking their position – but they were not thinking of surrender. They were planning to shorten their line.

Three days before the fall of Thiepval, with infinite secrecy, the Germans had put their plans in hand, and miles behind the front, from Arras to the Somme, even as the British Command was planning the next series of attacks that would bring them closer to Bapaume, German engineers were reconnoitering fresh ground and plotting positions of tactical advantage. Early in November they began to draw up blue-prints for a new line of defence – a line so strong, so formidable and so impregnable that, by comparison, their citadel on the Somme had been as fragile as a child's toy fort. In honour of the Wagnerian hero of German victories they code-named it 'The Siegfried Line'. When it was completed they would retire to it. For the winter they would stand where they were, ready to do battle if the British chose to fight the German Army as well as the elements. In the spring, if need be, they could toss them Bapaume, as they might toss a bone to a snarling dog.

Chapter 24

It was 11 November and the boys of the 13th Battalion, The Rifle Brigade, were back on the Somme and none too pleased to exchange the 'cushy' trenches at Calonne for the bleak chill of canvas huts in the muddy environs of Puchevillers. At Calonne the British line ran through the abandoned houses of the village and, although they were something of a shambles, the cellars at least were habitable. Furnished with household goods salvaged from the wreckage of the upper storeys, they made luxurious dugouts. In one section of the line, a soldier could literally step down from the fire-step into a front parlour, complete with sofa, table and chairs, and Joe Hoyles, sent with four others to man an observation post, was delighted to find that some previous occupant had had the foresight to purloin real beds to furnish the cellar beneath it. It was sufficient of an event to warrant a place in his diary: 'I've had the pleasure of laying on something soft for the first time out here!'

By contrast Puchevillers was unanimously voted the most filthy and desolate spot in France, and there they had spent a miserable week, in miserable weather, rehearsing yet again for battle, and that afternoon they had lost the Colonel. Prideaux-Brune had been playing full-back for the Officers against the Other Ranks in a game of rugby organised 'to keep the lads amused' when he was tackled and brought down by Corporal Percy Eaton. It was generally felt that Eaton might have chosen a more convenient time than the eve of a battle to break the Commanding Officer's collar bone.

Joe Hoyles, Tommy Bennett and two other sergeants had pulled rank and had succeeded in getting a canvas hut to themselves. It was freezing cold but, with the help of a little rum purloined from the communal jar, they were managing to pass the evening enjoyably. They fancied themselves as singers and Tommy Bennett of the Welsh contingent undeniably had a fine tenor voice. He sang the harmony for an old favourite.

> *Just a song at twilight when the lights are low*
> *And the flickering shadows softly come and go.*
> *Though your hearts be weary, sad the day and long,*
> *Still to us at twilight comes love's old song,*
> *Comes love's old, sweet song.*

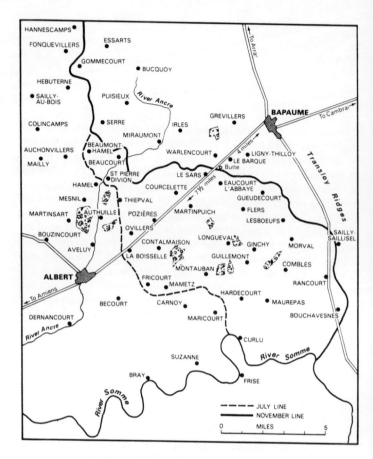

The Line at the end of the fighting in November

Under the circumstances, the choice was, to say the least, unusual. But who cared?

The 13th Battalion was temporarily attached to the 63rd Division, now encamped in similarly nasty conditions in the shelter of the Mesnil Ridge as they waited to move up the line. It was more than two years since they had fought at Antwerp in a vain attempt to staunch the flow of the German Army through Belgium; they had spent most of 1915 fighting the Turks in Gallipoli and for eight months now they had been in action in France. In spite of this imposing military record, the men of the 63rd Division did not regard themselves as soldiers. Their Division was the Royal Naval Division and no amount of rifle toting, nor even the indignity of the khaki uniforms and tin hats which the Army now insisted on their wearing, would make them into anything but sailors. Those officers who had gone forward to reconnoitre up the flooded valley of the Ancre saw the irony behind the Army's decision to put the Naval Division in to attack it. It was unfortunate that they had not gone so far as to supply them with boats.

They were a mixed bunch of pre-war naval reservists from seaports round the coast of Britain who had been mildly surprised, when King and Country called them up before even the Army was mobilised, that the mighty British Navy had insufficient ships for them to man and that they had been transmogrified into land-lubber forces of the British Army instead. But God help the British Army if it tried to deprive them of their jealously guarded naval traditions. God help the War Office pundit who suggested changing commanders into colonels, petty officers into sergeants, able seamen into privates, or who suggested, in order to fit in with the Army's arithmetical calculations, that battalions should give up such ringing titles as Howe, Hood, Drake, Nelson, Anson, in exchange for mere numbers. Altogether the Royal Naval Division considered itself to be something special and a cut above mere soldiers with their kow-towing khaki discipline. Their own disciplinary structure, they were happy to say, was as free and easy as their *esprit de corps* was strong. They had recently fallen foul of their new Divisional General who had been sent to replace their own Commander, General Paris, whose leg had been severed by a shell. General Paris was of the well-publicised opinion that 'man for man and officer for officer the Naval Division is incomparably better than nine-tenths of the divisions in France'. His successor, none other than General Shute, did not share this opinion and the antipathy was mutual. The qualities of discipline and leadership, which had so excited Alex Paterson's admiration when he had guided the General into No Man's Land in front of Guillemont, were not appreciated by the Royal Naval Division.

General Shute had no time for the Royal Naval Division and we had no time for him. The first thing he did was to insist that all NCOs should wear army rank on one sleeve as well as their naval rank on the other. They loathed that!

Another bee in his bonnet was Salvage. Actually that's what got Hall out of trouble. This chap had gone into a dugout and left his rifle leaning against the wall. Naturally his rifle was absolutely filthy, because we didn't go in a great deal for spit and polish in our Division. Along came Shute and spotted this dirty old rifle and picked it up, bellowing what a disgrace it was and demanding to

Sub-Lieutenant Jeremy Bentham, Hood Btn., Royal Naval Division.

know who it belonged to. Of course it was Hall's! But he had great presence of mind and, knowing how keen Shute was about salvage, he said, quick as a flash, that it was one he had picked up in No Man's Land the night before! Shute was pleased as punch and said, 'Well done!' We enjoyed a good laugh over that.

Sub-Lieutenant William Marlow, MC (RNVR), Howe Btn., Royal Naval Division

Shute was a proper Army bloke. He never really liked this naval tradition stuff and when he took over he came and inspected us. We'd only just gone into the line in the Souchez Sector and we'd taken it over from the Portuguese. Of course, it was in a bloody mess, but we hadn't had time to clear it up or anything. Well, Shute was furious. He went back and wrote an absolute stinker about the disgusting state of our trenches and really created a most awful fuss. Alan Herbert was an officer in the Royal Naval Division – A. P. Herbert, who later became very well known as a writer. He wrote a poem about this episode, well it was a song really, and it started off in the wardroom and then it went right down through all the ranks. It was absolutely filthy!

> *The General inspecting the trenches*
> *exclaimed with a horrified shout,*
> *'I refuse to command a Division*
> *Which leaves its excreta about.'*
>
> *But nobody took any notice*
> *No one was prepared to refute,*
> *That the presence of shit was congenial*
> *Compared with the presence of Shute.*
>
> *And certain responsible critics*
> *Made haste to reply to his words*
> *Observing that his Staff advisers*
> *Consisted entirely of turds.*
>
> *For shit may be shot at odd corners*
> *And paper supplied there to suit,*
> *But a shit would be shot without mourners*
> *If somebody shot that shit Shute.*

That song didn't just go through the whole of the Royal Naval Division – it went through the whole of the Army!

But it was the sailors who sang it with particular relish. They sang it to the tune of *Wrap me up in my tarpaulin jacket* and thought it the last word in wit. Small groups of them were singing it now, under their breath, in defiance of the rule of silence as they made their way by various routes across the face of the Mesnil Ridge to assemble behind the line. The assaulting Battalions of the Division had been split up into small parties. Although the Thiepval Ridge, rearing up across the valley, was now in British hands, it was bright moonlight and who knew what unfriendly eyes were marking their passage?

Across the valley, across the heights beyond, across the Albert–Bapaume road where the 50th Division was in the line, Lieutenant Cecil Slack was far from happy about the full moon. Earlier in the day he had received an order which was unequivocal and also, in his opinion, bordered on insanity.

SECRET
TO: O.C. 'C' COMPANY

A series of strong posts is to be formed in advance (75 yards) of our front line tonight. Your Company will have to furnish them and make them. I shall require four posts of an Officer (or good N.C.O.) and 12 men each to go forward at dusk and dig themselves into strongposts by improving shell holes. These posts will work under your supervision and will be provided with a day's rations before dawn.
You had better come and see me at 3 p.m. re above.

W.T.W.

Slack was only too pleased to visit the Commanding Officer in his dugout. He knew that the order had come from Brigade. He also knew that it was suicide, and he challenged the Colonel accordingly.
'Does the General realise that there will be a full moon tonight, sir?'
There was a long pause before the Colonel replied. Then he looked Slack straight in the eye.
'The General is a very able soldier.'

A lot of these brainwaves were from people who didn't know what it was like to be in No Man's Land in broad daylight – and broad moonlight is as good as broad daylight. The idea was that, if the Germans made an attack – and they were expecting them to make an attack – there would be a post here, and a post there, to break it up. The Germans were supposed not to know that those four posts were there but you can see 150 yards in broad moonlight and it was a beautifully clear night. You could see everything. You could see your breath going up in front of you in steam. To go out in those conditions was utter suicide, but the General had ordered it, so that was that.

Captain C. S. Slack, MC. 1/4 Btn., East Yorkshire Regiment, 150 Brigade, 50th Division

I picked up my first party. As soon as we got out through our own wire the bullets came. A man was killed next to me. We crawled from shell-hole to shell-hole and somehow or other we got to what I thought was a suitable shell-hole to be strengthened. I left my first party there in charge of a corporal and came back to take another party out. I was supposed to take them out seventy yards – and that would be about halfway across No Man's Land – but I didn't. I took them out maybe sixty yards. Then I went back and took the third party out and I had decided by then that I wasn't going to take them out so far. Another man was killed and all the time bullets were crashing round us. The Germans could see us as plain as daylight! Why more of us weren't hit I don't know, because we were being shot at all the time.

Another man was killed at the third post. I crawled back for the fourth party and, this time, I went out twenty yards and stopped.

They were in the line in front of the village of le Sars. It was a month since it had been captured but they had got no further. Just beyond the village the road to Bapaume ran down a gentle slope and, at the foot, where the land flattened out, a long mound of white chalk glistened in the moonlight, dominating the countryside like some cold evil eye. It was not surprising that the soldiers holding the line in front of le Sars were edgy, for the Germans had made a strongpoint of the Butte de Warlencourt. From its rearward slope it looked across to Eaucourt-l'Abbaye – once a farm on the site of an old abbey, now an outpost in the wasteland, captured at the cost of many lives. The Butte also overlooked the country road that once had ambled past on its way to Gueudecourt. It was held now by the Australians, back in the line and fighting for the Maze, the Gird lines, Grassy Lane. Despite their legendary toughness, the Aussies were suffering more acutely than anyone else from the damp and the mud and the chill of the bitter weather.

But the weather had changed with the full moon and, just as the Army Commanders had hoped, it had changed for the better. General Gough's Reserve Army – which, since 30 October, had been redesignated The Fifth Army – stood poised, ready for a battle which, with the season so far advanced, the Germans would scarcely be expecting. On 21 October the cavalry had moved back to winter billets. Shivering in the front line the infantry wished that they could do the same.

The heights of the Thiepval Ridge had been captured but deep in the sharp-cut valley, protected by their tenure of the high land across the river, the Germans still clung fast to St Pierre Divion and Grandcourt on its banks. They still held Beaucourt. They still held

Beaumont Hamel and they still held Serre. They had settled down for the winter. One short sharp surprise knock now, when it was least expected, might easily accomplish great things.

Sir Douglas Haig had another reason for wishing to gamble on a late offensive. He had made it clear to General Gough, through his Chief of Staff, General Kiggell, that it should be mounted entirely at the General's own discretion; that, if the weather and conditions weighed unfavourably against the likelihood of success, he need not commit his Army and he was perfectly entitled to cancel the operation. But the weather had cleared up. It had not rained since the 8th. The 12 November dawned unseasonably bright and sunny. It was a perfect autumn day. The air was clear and the cold changed from bone-stiffening chill to a brisk, invigorating freshness that lifted the spirits. It had also, to some extent, dried out the ground. It was a fine day for a ride but the necessity for speedy action forced General Haig to travel by motor car to General Gough's headquarters at Toutencourt. He was anxious to have a private word.

The Commander-in-Chief did not retract the message which his Chief of Staff had passed to General Gough the previous day. General Gough still had a free hand. The final decision was still his. But Haig made it quite clear that the capture of Beaumont Hamel would be useful to him. Three days hence, on the 15 November, he would be conferring at Chantilly with the High Command of the French Army, and at that meeting future strategy would be decided. The French were cock-a-hoop. At long last the tide had turned at Verdun. On 24 October the French Army had recaptured its mighty forts and, if the Germans were not precisely on the run, the initiative had passed decisively to the French. But they could not afford to relax. The enemy must be kept occupied here in the west to prevent him from switching any of his manpower to reinforce his position at Verdun and consequently Marshal Joffre was pressing the British to continue their attacks.

But Haig was worried about his own manpower. The main purpose of the Chantilly Conference was to agree on joint plans for a Spring Offensive. The British Army had informed the Government that it would require 350,000 men as reinforcements. Even if they got them all (which, on past performance, seemed unlikely) Haig was uneasy and doubtful if such a number of new recruits could be trained to full fighting-pitch before he was forced to commit them alongside the French in the spring.

He chatted about these matters to General Gough. It was obvious to both men that Beaumont Hamel, if it could be easily captured, would serve to keep the French quiet and would undoubtedly act in the British interest at the Chantilly Conference. One daring thrust, now that the weather was on their side, might achieve much.

It was a fine night, cloudless and frosty as the troops assembled for the assault. Between Serre and the Ancre they were waiting in precisely the same positions as on the eve of 1 July. Only the season had changed. Two thousand men of the Royal Naval Division were lying on the open ground in the trenches and ruins of the village of Hamel where Joe Murray's billet for the night was a groove of mud between two flooded shell-holes. The water quivered slightly with the vibration of the bombardment and, when it momentarily paused, they could hear steady firing from the German line, like the crackle of twigs in a bonfire, and the fire-cracking explosions of hand-grenades thrown haphazardly into the waterlogged mud in front of their wire. The Germans were uneasy. A major attack at this time of year seemed out of the question but, nevertheless, they had no doubt that something was afoot. The troops, lying out in the dank chill of the November night, dared not reply for fear of bringing the full force of the German artillery down on their tight-packed position.

The Hood Battalion was right down in the valley of the River Ancre – now less of a river than a lake of mud that seeped across the low ground to the foot of Thiepval ridge. Towards midnight haze gathered in the valley and thickened as it spread towards the slopes. The chill deepened. Soon the troops waiting for the assault were enveloped in rolling mist. In Hood Battalion, the Commanding Officer, Lieutenant-Commander Freyberg, taking advantage of its concealing folds, began to move among the lines of his battalion, stopping with a word of encouragement whenever a muffled cough suggested that men were awake. Spirits were not high. The previous evening the officers of B Company had organised a macabre sweepstake. They each wrote a personal cheque for five pounds payable 'to Bearer' and left them, with their kit, in charge of the Quartermaster. Those who survived tomorrow would cash the cheques of those who did not, and share the jackpot.

The 3rd Division was waiting to attack at Serre just as the Pals had waited four months and a half before. The line of attack would be the same, but there were two differences. This time the troops would have twice the number of guns to support them; and this time the ground was a quagmire of oozing mud that stretched back beyond the gun lines one thousand yards behind. The guns had been heaved up on to solid platforms of pit props to keep them from sinking into the swamp and, in the line, the troops crouched and shivered and

tried to sleep to the murmur and thud of the pumps that were
keeping the trenches comparatively clear of water.

In the White City in front of Beaumont Hamel they had been
double-pumping for weeks now to keep the tunnels and trenches
reasonably dry. The old tunnels had been refurbished; new ones had
been dug; another mine had been laid and they would explode it at
Zero under the old crater on the Hawthorn Ridge, for the Germans
had re-fortified the redoubt that protected Beaumont Hamel in the
cleft of the valley behind. Beaumont Hamel was the main objective –
the prize of the battle, and the 51st Highland Division was ordered to
take it. They were known to be 'bonny fighters'. They frequently
practised by fighting each other. No one recalled the origins of the
feud between the 6th and the 8th Battalions of the Argyll and
Sutherland Highlanders but, after several *estaminets* had been
wrecked in the course of wild rumpuses for which the Army was
obliged to foot the bill, it had been generally recognised that, when
the Division was out at rest, those in charge of the billeting
arrangements of the three Brigades would be well advised to make
sure that the 6th and the 8th Argylls were separated by a considerable distance. The 8th Argylls, who came from Argyllshire itself,
were largely Gaelic speaking, and sneered at the idea that the 6th,
who hailed from Paisley in Renfrewshire, should pass as Highlanders at all. Furthermore, the 8th Argylls considered the 6th to be
undeservedly spoilt. Bell's, a local tobacco company, sent out a
weekly present of twenty cigarettes per man, and they were vastly
superior to the ration of issue cigarettes which came the way of the
8th Argylls. Local football clubs also sent cigarettes and supplied
sports kit and equipment. The 6th Argylls never lacked whisky and
the Paisley thread manufacturers, J. & P. Coates, who regarded the
Battalion as their own, plied the men with comforts. The last straw
was when the same firm, in the kindness of its heart, presented every
officer with a breast-plate and every man with a heart-shaped mirror
of polished steel to place in his breast-pocket as insurance against
German bullets. The fact that the 8th Argylls taunted the 6th in
Gaelic simply added fuel to the fire. None of the Paisley boys spoke a
word of anything but English, but they found no difficulty in
understanding the insulting tone of the Highlanders' remarks.
  Matters had improved very slightly after the 6th Argylls came out
of the Labyrinth in front of Arras with so many casualties that they
were reinforced mainly by Englishmen, made into a Pioneer Battalion and transfered to another Division. Although Sergeant 'Wul-
lie' Stevenson was an original member of the 6th Argylls (and of the
Auldhouse football team which had joined up en masse), as a

machine-gunner he had not suffered the indignity of being reduced with the rest of the battalion to navvying. Now, in preparation for the battle, he checked and rechecked the four guns of his section and filled his water-bottle with rum against the exigencies of the day ahead. His orders were to make straight for Y Ravine.

The fog thickened. At 5.45 when the bombardment crashed out it was still black night. In order to keep the Germans guessing precisely where the attack would come, the guns opened up from Serre in the north to Lesboeufs in the south and the soldiers holding the muddy draggle of line in front of Lesboeufs and Gueudecourt stood up and cheered as the shells screamed over their heads to crash on the Transloy ridges, in an excess of pleasure that, for once, someone else was going over the top. Astride the Ancre, up the Beaumont Hamel valley, into the slough in front of Serre, the 5th Army went forward through thick swirling fog and were swallowed up.

Sergeant William Stevenson, DCM, MM, No. 3113, 6th Btn., Argyle & Sutherland Hdrs., 51st (Highland) Division.

We came straight out of the White City. They put us in the tunnel the night before and in the morning they blew the top off it and the infantry went straight over. The machine-gunners and trench-mortar parties were the last to get out – right near the German lines. The bodies of our boys who'd gone over on 1 July were still lying there between the lines and the stink would have knocked you down. You can believe me or believe me not, but we got right into the German trenches – and there was nobody there! They were all still in their dugouts, because we shelled and knocked hell out of each other every morning and night with shell-fire anyway, and they just thought it was the usual thing and never even bothered to get out of their shelters. They never expected an attack in that weather.

I thought the place was very quiet and I said to Lance-Corporal Hopkins – he was an English boy, a Cockney – I said, 'Come on, Hoppy. You come on with me here. I don't like this!' We went away along the trench, a great wide trench and, as we went along, I heard voices and we listened and Hoppy says, 'They're Germans! I'll tell them to come up.' Well it took a bit of coaxing! They were down in the dugout and there were about twenty to thirty steps, but up they came eventually and all the boys gathered round to see what was going on. We took seventeen prisoners! I sent my batman, wee Hope, an Edinburgh fellow, away back with them to Headquarters. 'March the whole lot back,' I said to him. Lance-Corporal Robertson and myself went in the dugout and, the silliest thing was that there were one or two openings to it. The Germans could easily have got out of them.

We went along and searched and we got all their ammunition and their rifles and revolvers and other souvenirs (later we sold them to the transport boys and the ASC boys at the back!) and then we went up to the top of the hill and Y Ravine was down in front of us. They had this tunnel right along it and there was even electric light in the damned place. There were wire beds for the men to sleep in and everything you could think of. They had machine-gun emplacements and they had concrete emplacements and the tunnel was all linked up to them. No wonder our boys couldn't get into the front-line trenches in July! Beaumont Hamel was really a fortified place and they just couldn't take it.

I believe in other sectors they got it pretty badly but where we were our boys just went sailing through and we followed.

Stevenson was right in thinking that in other sectors things had not gone so well. On the left of Beaumont Hamel another battalion of Argylls lost half their force in their advance towards the same orchards, against the same machine-guns which had mown down the Hampshires on 1 July. On the right, the Seaforths floundered and groped through the fog searching for gaps in the wire. In front of Serre the infantry waded through mud, so deep, so heavy, so clinging that more than half of them were bogged down before they had got halfway to the German trenches. Only small groups of exhausted men ever succeeded in reaching them and, when they did, their rifles were so useless, so clogged with mud, that they were easy prey.

Slogging up the river valley, splaying out over the slopes of the Beaumont Hamel spur, Hood and Hawke Battalions, leading the advance of the Royal Naval Division, had also run into trouble. To be more precise they had run past it. Just over the brow, the Germans had well-concealed strongpoints and unsuspected defensive positions and they were not marked on the trench maps for the very good reason that no one knew they were there.

. . . It was very misty, a really wet mist. It wasn't a Scotch mist, it was a double Scotch mist, nasty, wet and claggy. As soon as the barrage opened the sky turned red – just like the ironworks at home across the Derwent valley. When they were drawing their furnaces you'd get a red glow, and that was the picture I saw looking back over the lines at our own barrage. The whole sky was lit up and you could *feel* the shells. You could actually feel the damned things going over your head like a wind in the fog.

Able Bodied Seaman Joseph Murray, No. TZ.276, Hood Battalion, 63rd (Royal Naval) Division.

There were twelve or thirteen rows of barbed wire in front of the first trench and when the bombardment goes into that, it's supposed to cut it, but it doesn't destroy the wire, it builds it into a bloody heap with gaps in it here and there and, when the enemy's alive and awake to the idea that you're coming, they've got their machine-guns trained on these gaps – therefore you get slaughtered. But we got through it – some of us anyhow! There didn't seem to be many of our chaps about as we pressed forward and entered his second line. The Drakes and the Nelsons got all mixed up and, on our left, they were all banging and crashing about and there was terrible fire coming from this redoubt. It was a square of trenches lined with men manning machine-guns – probably a hundred men in it – and it wasn't even touched by the artillery. How they missed that, Lord only knows! We had terrible casualties. When we got to the second line there were hardly any of us about. We were supposed to rest there for forty minutes and the next lot were supposed to go through us and take the Green Line – which was the station road. But they'd had such casualties that hardly any of them turned up, so instead of us resting there, we had to go on and *we* had to capture the Green Line. It was Freyberg who got us together and led us on, and there were all too few of us, believe me. But we went on and we captured the Green Line although there was nobody on our left at all by then. . . .

Sub-Lieutenant Jeremy Bentham, B Coy., Hood Btn., 63rd (Royal Naval) Division.

I had two men with me, two runners to take messages back to Battalion HQ, and my Petty Officer who was to take command of my platoon if I fell. We advanced quite steadily and went on to the Jerry front line and I found myself firing my revolver at anyone I saw emerging from the dugouts. There were plenty of them coming out and running! Unfortunately our 18-pounder guns had got so hot that their shells started falling short and one exploded quite near. The next thing I knew was that I was on the ground with all the chaps who were with me. I had been hit in my left thigh and couldn't walk or even hop. So there we lay while other men jumped over us on their way to catch up with the chaps who were still going forward. I did my best to try and bandage my leg – it was bleeding profusely – and the other men were doing the same, except for one who'd been killed. There was nothing I could do but wait for our surgeon, McCracken. He came along eventually and he bandaged us up as best he could under this terrible shellfire. He was laughing. I'll always remember him laughing as he poured iodine into my wound. 'This will stop you giggling in church!' he said. We settled down to wait for the stretcher-bearers but it was a long time before they came. We were there all day. There were hundreds of us lying there wounded.

I hadn't been going half an hour when I was hit in the right wrist. It was my batman who saved me – Molly Milburn. His nickname was Molly. The trouble was that my wound had severed the main artery and I could easily have bled to death. Well, I don't even know how little Molly found me in the fog, but he did and he put a tourniquet on and stopped the flowing of the blood. I was right out for the count. Then he left me and had to go on, naturally. He was a good soldier.

The next thing I knew was that there was a whole load of German prisoners being brought down with two or three blokes guarding them and the Battalion had struck unlucky because we'd struck strongposts that the guns hadn't obliterated. As these prisoners were coming back they were actually being picked off by chaps firing from these strongposts. Germans! They were probably going for the half-a-dozen British who were guarding them, walking on the outside of the lines of prisoners and I remember shouting at them, 'You bloody fools! Get inside of them!' Simple, isn't it? That's what they did – went in the middle of the prisoners and, of course, the Jerries stopped firing. They picked me up on the way past and carried me back the same way – surrounded by German prisoners. When they dumped me at the aid post, there were scores of blokes in there all with terrible wounds, and the quack, old Dr McCracken, said to me, 'Do you think you can make your own way down the line?' I said, 'Too bloody true I can!' So off I went again with the Jerry prisoners and they helped me down to the field dressing station and from there I went to the casualty clearing station.

Our gun positions were in Aveluy Wood and I had my signal lines running down this steep communication trench they called Jacob's Ladder. I had to send up a signaller, name of Waugh, not a lot of brains but a big strapping lad, and he had to go up and extend the line as we went forward and he needed two spools of wire of a hundred yards each. I said, 'Look here, two spools are a bit hefty for you to carry up there on your own.' So I got hold of this other chap, Ernest Reevie, a pal of mine from South Shields (we called him Paddy) to go with him. Eighteen-pounder shells come in a case of four with a steel rod going through the middle to keep them in place, so I got hold of two of these rods and put the two reels on them so they could carry them on their shoulders and sent them off up this road on the north side of the Ancre towards where the Division was attacking. Well, of course we didn't know really what was happening up front, and Waugh and Paddy had gone no distance when suddenly they saw hordes and hordes of

Sub-Lieutenant William Marlow, MC, Howe Btn., 63rd (Royal Naval) Division.

Bombardier William J. Muir, No. 751367, D 317 Bty., 63rd (Royal Naval) Division Field Artillery.

Germans coming down the road. There were no guards with them, and the lads were quite unarmed, except for these steel rods and two reels of wire. They didn't think they could fight hundreds of Germans with steel rods and they didn't stop to notice that the Germans were unarmed as well! Well, they were just about to dive into a dugout at the side of the road and hope for the best when one of the Germans shouted at them and managed to make himself understood. He wanted to know the way to the prisoners' cage! So Paddy and Waugh just pointed to the rear, and very thankful they were when the Jerries went straight on and didn't bother them.

They must have been about the first lot to be captured, but we saw hundreds that day coming past our positions and we didn't see a single guard with them! I noticed that happening more than once, though. You start a line of prisoners and they all go marching down following each other. The guards can't catch up with them half the time!

By nine o'clock when the fragments of the Royal Naval Division had fought through to the third German line they estimated with amazement, and with a fair degree of accuracy, that the prisoners outnumbered the attackers.

As soon as the line gave way on the Hawthorn Ridge and in front of Beaumont Hamel itself, the geographical accident which had guaranteed its safety now set the seal on its defeat, and the Germans were forced back between the high banks of the valley behind the village. There was nowhere else for them to go. They were waiting there in thousands before the astonished eyes of Lieutenant-Commander Freyberg as he breasted the hill at the head of his tiny force. It was an encouraging sight.

After that it was only a matter of time. By four o'clock the Scots were well established in Beaumont Hamel. They had captured two Battalion Headquarters and, in addition to quantities of maps and papers which British Intelligence would doubtless be glad to receive, they were delighted to find a good supply of canteen stores, a large stock of bottled mineral water and a handsome piano. They also found several sacks of mail from Germany and spared a sympathetic thought for Jerry, trudging towards the Prisoner-of-War cages without the consolation of letters from home.

In the deep-tunnelled dugouts below Y Ravine the stench and the cries were terrible. Tiers of wire bunks were stacked with wounded, terrified by the sight of mud-encrusted Jocks appearing, with bayonets fixed and rifles at the ready, ahead of the stretcher parties.

But these Germans were past giving trouble. While the medical teams got on with the job, their escorts began to explore. They were like children in a toyshop. There was Schnapps, there was brandy, there was wine, there was food, there were cigars and, best of all, there was dry clothing.

'Hey, Jimmy,' shouted one Highlander, ecstatic at the discovery of a packing case full of dry socks. 'This is no' a dugout. It's a shop!'

They could hardly get their boots off quick enough. The dugout was littered with souvenirs and they were theirs for the taking, but, for the moment, dry socks were the most coveted of all the spoils of war.

In the elation of achievement it was easy for the troops, now taking possession of the captured ground, to overlook the fact that they had won a pyrrhic victory. By four o'clock it was dark and new accumulations of fog, thick with the fumes of battle, clammy with damp, rolled up from the river to spread a chill blanket across the bodies of the wounded who still lay on the open ground. There was no hope now that they would be rescued before morning and, for many, little hope that they would survive through the icy November night.

Just as it had done on the sunny evening of the First of July, and just as it had done with haunting regularity in the intervening months, the spectre of partial success laid a dead hand on the decisions of the Command. Partial success, which invariably left the Germans holding certain positions of advantage (from which, with a little more effort, they could surely be evicted) had led to a weary cycle of more 'partial successes'. They were better than total failure, but shabby substitutes for total victory. If General Gough's Army had only partially succeeded in pushing the Germans back, it was axiomatic that the Germans had partially succeeded in stemming the British advance.

There had been stark failure at Serre. A swift advance on the Redan Ridge had soon been forced back when other divisions failed to come forward, and the early advantage was lost. The Germans had been pushed out of St Pierre Divion across the Ancre, but Beaucourt village, further along the river valley, was still unsecured. Thousands of prisoners had been captured, but at a cost of casualties too numerous to calculate. The line had been broken at Beaumont Hamel but the thinned-out ranks of troops who had won through were holding a weak line. If it were not secured, if they did not push on, winter would find them trapped in the valley with the enemy firmly entrenched halfway up the high ground with Munich and Frankfurt trenches guarding the heights.

Sergeant W. J.
Hoyles, MM, No.
3237, 13th (S) Btn.,
The Rifle Brigade,
37th Division.

We had to pass across a valley to get to this high hill where the battle was going to go on next morning. We should have dodged across, of course, and gone up in the shelter of the other bank but the Colonel was gone, and we were led by the Second-in-Command. He wasn't one of the original officers – well, we hardly had any of the original officers left – and he was no damned good, this man. He led us in open order right across the valley, across a huge open space, and the Boche were shelling us. We lost no end of men! Freddie Lyon, my great chum, got hit almost right away. I shoved him and some other chaps into a shell-hole on the hillside and I'd hardly turned away when another shell came over and dropped right into it. They were all killed, bar Freddie.

Then I had to find my Battalion and it was pitch dark. Everyone was all mixed up, and the hill itself was nothing but shell-holes and water. Eventually, by a miracle, I stumbled across a bit of a captured trench and this officer chap, this Major who was in command, was in it and he looked up at me and he says, 'Where have you been to?' I said, 'Down there, shifting the wounded – and there are plenty of them! You left us all out in the open. You didn't go far enough!' I didn't care what I said to him, I was so wild. I was shouting at him above the noise, and it was bedlam! He never spoke, so I shouted at him again. I said, 'Where's my Company? Where's A Company?' And he never answered. He was a wash-out.

I left him and a bit further on I came to a shell-hole and there crouched into it was a Sergeant-Major and two other Sergeants I knew. The extraordinary thing was that I knew these fellows were going to die – and they knew it too. You get that instinct. I said, 'What's the orders? What's happening?' They didn't know. They just looked back at me, absolutely blank. They knew they weren't going to come back.

By the time I got my section up to the top of the hill we were being enfiladed by machine-gun fire. We were crouching in a shell-hole, a very shallow one, waiting to go on and this burst of machine-gun fire took the tops of their heads straight off. I lost the whole of my section – every single man! I got it in the lung, and that was the end for me. The whole thing was an absolute muck-up.

Sergeant C. M.
Williams, MM, No.
54556, 13th (S) Btn.,
The Rifle Brigade.

I was in charge of the Battalion Machine-Gunners, and we'd lost a tremendous lot of men in the shelling before we even reached the Green Line where we had to jump off from. But it wasn't until after we'd taken the first German line and a lot of prisoners who gave up without much trouble, that our left flank came under heavy sniper fire and machine-gun fire, because the Battalion to the left of us hadn't got forward. I was in a shell-hole with three of my machine-gunners and I shouted to the men who were round about to drop down and take cover. Rather than dropping where they were, three riflemen made a dash for a shell-hole further away, where there were some other chaps, and, just as they got alongside our position, they were caught in a burst of fire and they literally fell in on top of us. All dead. All killed outright.

Sergeant Johnson collected some bombers and detoured and crawled round the back of the Germans who were firing at us and smashed them out. We went on again and managed to capture another few yards of ground, but again we came into enfilade fire on our left, because the battalion to the left of us was still held up. It was all terrible confusion. We didn't know where anyone was the whole day long, so all we could do was to stop where we were and do the best we could. When dusk fell I collected Corporal Bissell and five other machine-gunners and we crawled out thirty yards or so and dug a position in line with the German sniper position, but beside an old German dugout that gave them a bit of cover and protection. There was terrible firing going on and Very lights started going up. When I'd seen the boys settled, I crawled off again, making for the trench I thought I'd come from, and I hadn't gone a dozen yards before I saw a German in it. It was a German trench I was crawling into! And it wasn't a dozen yards from the machine-gun post we'd just set up. Heaven knows how we'd missed them on the way forward! I crawled backwards, very cautiously indeed, and got back to the boys to warn them.

When I moved off again I didn't know where I was! I knew full well that I'd lost my direction, but I just kept on going, trusting to luck and lying close to the ground when the flares went up and when there were bursts of machine-gun fire. They were spraying the ground practically all the time, but I kept on moving to my right and eventually I struck our line – or rather, the place where most of the boys were! I crawled back again at daybreak and the Germans had gone out of the post I'd stumbled across. Later we were relieved and by morning we were back where we'd started, on the Green Line.

It was the second time in the space of ninety-five days that the Battalion had lost almost half its fighting strength – three hundred and twelve casualties, of whom ninety-three were dead.

Looking around them at the protective belts of wire, the gun positions sheltered by steep banks, the warren of deep dry dugouts, the survivors marvelled that the Green Line in the valley had ever been captured at all. Even now the dugouts had not been entirely cleared of Germans but those who remained, waiting to be marched back as prisoners, were in no mood to cause any difficulty. Nevertheless, a few of the boys, observing Sergeant-Major 'Rainbow' Oliver sitting on the top-step of a dugout occupied by thirty surly Germans, rather admired his nerve. He was unarmed, he was reading a letter from home, and he had every appearance of being completely relaxed. He explained kindly that he had not had time to digest his correspondence before going into action.

Charlie Williams' machine-gunners had 'captured' a Westphalian ham. It was covered with green mould but they had easily scraped that off. Now they were frying thick rashers in a mess-tin lid and pronouncing it a jolly sight better than bully beef. Through the mist the rattle of continued fighting reached towards them from the high ground across the valley.

It was the morning of 15 November and they were conscious of having done well. They had advanced the line halfway up the ridge and D Company on the left had got as far as the edge of Munich Trench. On the right they had taken Beaucourt Trench and linked up with the Royal Naval Division. Lieutenant-Commander Freyberg had rallied a conglomerate force of men and led them, against the odds, to capture Beaucourt village.[1]

The outcome of the gamble had been limited success and less than General Gough had hoped for. But the capture of St Pierre Divion, of Beaucourt and of Beaumont Hamel were three trump cards. The previous evening Gough had had the gratification of placing them in the hand of his Commander-in-Chief and that morning Haig laid them on the table at the opening session of the Chantilly Conference where they had the desired effect of mollifying the French. He played them again next day at the Paris Conference of the Anglo–French Governments and they even trumped Lloyd George. He had come prepared, with all the powers of his formidable rhetoric, to plead the case for shifting the main arena of the battle away from the atrophy of the Western Front and, even after the Prime Minister had insisted on his deleting the most virulent and inflammatory passages of Lloyd George's prepared speech, it had promised to be a lively meeting. Now all was changed. The Conference, which had set out to curb the powers of the Military, unanimously accepted the conclusions which the Military Commanders had reached at Chantilly and endorsed their plans for the continuance of the war in the spring. A few had doubts. Lord Lansdowne was already mentally

---

[1] A feat for which Lieutenant-Commander Freyberg was awarded the Victoria Cross.

composing the memorandum which, on his return to London, he would circulate to the Cabinet. *Are we to continue until we have killed ALL our young men?* But, for the moment, all was accord.

But although, from his own point of view, the outcome of the Conferences had been highly satisfactory, Sir Douglas Haig was not without qualms and he had already sent a message to General Gough clearly stating that he did not wish him to continue with any large-scale attacks during his own absence. Gough was perturbed. His Army had hardly had a fair crack of the whip. The omens were good. He was assured that all ranks were fighting fit and eager to go on. They had captured Beaumont Hamel. They had captured Beaucourt. But the Germans were still dug in on the hump of high ground between them, still holding out in the high redoubts at Munich and Frankfurt trenches. With just a little more effort, one last push, his Army could gain the heights.

Against his better judgement the Commander-in-Chief allowed himself to be persuaded.

General Gough was delighted and put the matter in hand right away.

Part 5

Friends Are Good on the Day of Battle

Translation of the Gaelic inscription on the 51st. Highland Division Memorial which looks across to Beaumont Hamel.

Chapter 25

The scrag-end of the Glasgow Boys Brigade Battalion – officially the 16th Highland Light Infantry – paraded by companies in a gale-swept field at Mailly Maillet, but the sight was too awful for words and, shortly before General Gough arrived to inspect them, Colonel Kyle ordered the ranks to close up. They were still a sorry sight. Three days earlier, on the heights above Beaumont Hamel, they had advanced through the first snow-storm of the winter to fight the last action of the Battle of the Somme. The Battalion could claim to have been in at the kill. A handful of the originals who had escaped annihilation at Leipzig Redoubt on the first of July could also claim to have been in at the beginning.

General Gough addressed the men with kindly words. He thanked them for their efforts in the battle. It had been a considerable achievement to capture Munich Trench and it was no reflection on their courage and endurance that a counter-attack by a vastly superior force had pushed them out again. They might rest assured that, by their deeds, they had added fresh laurels to the name of the Highland Light Infantry.

The men gave three apathetic cheers. General Gough stood stiffly saluting as they marched off, then he turned to Colonel Kyle.

'What were your casualties?' he asked.

Even after two roll-calls the Colonel was unable to answer with precision. There might yet be stragglers. In the early hours of the 18th they had gone into the attack on Munich and Frankfurt trenches with twenty-one officers and six hundred and fifty other ranks. Eight officers had returned. At the last count 390 men had been killed, wounded, or were missing.

In the afternoon of the same day an urgent signal from Divisional Headquarters brought Colonel Kyle the astonishing news that ninety of his casualties were not 'missing' at all. They had been trapped by the German counter-attack and were lying low, marooned in Frankfurt Trench some distance behind the recaptured German line. At roughly the same time this interesting information also came to the notice of the Germans and, almost as routine, anticipating little trouble, they sent a sergeant and a small armed party down the communication trench to take the

Highlanders prisoner. The handful of men who returned reported that half of their number had been killed or captured by the British who had blocked and fortified a stretch of Frankfurt Trench, that they seemed determined to fight and that, to all appearances, they were armed to the teeth.

They were not armed to the teeth. All they had, apart from a length of battered trench and two captured dugouts, were their rifles, four Lewis-guns and a reasonable supply of ammunition, most of it retrieved from the scattered bodies of dead soldiers. They also had the fixed intention of defending their position until the next successful attack brought comrades to the rescue.

But it was 21 November. The Battle of the Somme was over and the long campaign had fizzled out in the failure of Saturday's attempt to seize the heights. Three days had passed. It was Tuesday now and, until winter loosened its grip, there would be no more attacks on Frankfurt Trench. Except, of course, by the Germans, faced with the galling necessity of attacking a part of their own line where a small isolated British force was still, unaccountably, holding out.

They held out until Sunday.

Tuesday evening. In the German front line there is an outbreak of heavy fighting, a frenzy of rapid fire and explosions. Hopes soar in Frankfurt Trench. At midnight the fighting dies down. They listen on for a long time. Eventually there is silence.

By Wednesday, there is no food left. A reconnoitering aeroplane pinpoints the Highlanders' position and flashes an ambiguous message which causes excited speculation. Did it read *Coming tonight* or *Come in tonight*? No one can be sure. They wait, on the *qui vive*. The British do not come – but the Germans do. The Highlanders fight them off. Two men are killed and half a dozen more are wounded. At night they hear another British raid on the front line. The Germans repulse it.

On Thursday, a short-range hurricane bombardment smashes part of the parapet. Explosions in the morass around the trench break up the snow-filled shell-holes. The precious supply of clear water left by the melting snow trickles away and soaks into the mud. A force of German infantry attacks in the wake of the bombardment. The Lewis-gunners guess that they have accounted for at least a dozen. The surviving Germans retire. The Highlanders repair their parapet. There are now more than fifty wounded in the foetid dugout. The last candle has guttered out and they lie there in the dark. Later three men crawl through the freezing slush to search the bodies of the dead Germans. They retrieve their water-bottles. There is another raid on the German line, but no breakthrough.

On Friday, the Germans attack again at close quarters, but without success. Company Sergeant-Major George Lee is hit. He is a foreman in the Glasgow Corporation Roads Department and has taken the lead for the past five days. The bullet strikes him in the head and he slumps across the parapet. As they lift him down he opens his eyes once, and says, 'No surrender, boys.' Then he dies. Some of the wounded have died too, but in the dark of the dugout they cannot tell how many. The night is quiet.[1] Two men crawl to within arm's length of the Germans in Munich Trench in search of water.

On Saturday, a small party of Germans approaches behind a captured British soldier who carries a large white flag and a message from a German Colonel. *Surrender quietly and you will be well-treated. Otherwise you may take what is coming to you.* The Highlanders are given an hour to decide. They ponder, take a vote, and decide to send no reply. After dark they search for water and return with a small quantity which is brackish and polluted. A few are driven to drink it. The night is quiet.

On Sunday, the able-bodied men take stock of their remaining ammunition. There is a single drum of bullets for four Lewis-guns and one Lewis-gunner left alive. They load spare rifles and place them in readiness round the crumbling mud walls of the trench. They spot a continuous line of German helmets moving down the communication trenches and brace themselves for an attack.

The Germans had surrounded the position and they attacked it simultaneously from all sides. The fifteen able-bodied men defending it were easily overwhelmed. Of the original ninety, some thirty badly wounded men were still alive. The rest were dead.

In a mood of understandable pique the Germans ordered the survivors to clear the dugouts of bodies and then, with the dregs of their strength, to carry the wounded back to the transport lines on the other side of the hill. Then they marched them to Brigade Headquarters for interrogation. Starving, filthy, frozen, exhausted and on the verge of collapse, they stumbled to attention in front of a German Major. An interpreter was present. Long years later, Private Dick Manson remained convinced that there was a touch of admiration in his glance as he translated the Major's words.

'Is *this* what has held the Brigade up for a week? Who are you and where have you come from?'

They replied with name, rank and number. They were too weary

---

[1] After three seperate raids which incurred 300 casualties the Army had reluctantly called off the rescue.

to say more. But they might have answered that they had come, by a
roundabout route, from Glasgow. That they were a representative
cross-section of their Battalion – shipping clerks, errand-boys,
stevedores, railway porters, grocers' assistants, postmen. That they
were, in short, fifteen soldiers of Kitchener's Army.

Bibliography

Author's Note

Index

Bibliography

Military Operations France and Belgium, 1914, Vols 1–2, compiled by Brigadier-General Sir James E. Edmonds (Macmillan & Co., 1925)

Military Operations France and Belgium, 1915, Vols 1–2, compiled by Brigadier-General Sir James E. Edmonds (Macmillan & Co. Ltd., 1928)

Military Operations France and Belgium, 1916, Vols. 1–2, compiled by Brigadier-General Sir James E. Edmonds (Macmillan & Co. Ltd., 1932)

Medical Services General History, Vol. 3, Major General Sir W. G. MacPherson, KCMG, CB, LLd (His Majesty's Stationery Office, 1924)

The Guards Division in the Great War, 1915–1918, Cuthbert Headlam, DSO (John Murray, 1924)

The Story of the 55th (West Lancashire) Division, The Rev. J. O. Coop, DSO, TD, MA (*Liverpool Daily Post* Printers, 1919)

The Eighth Division in War, 1914–1918, Lieutenant-Colonel J. H. Boraston, CB, CBE., and Captain Cyril E. C. Bax (The Medici Society Ltd., 1926)

The History of the Rifle Brigade in the War of 1914–1918, Vol. 1, Reginald Berkeley, MC (The Rifle Brigade Club Ltd., 1927)

The History of the Rifle Brigade in the War of 1914–1918, Vol. 2, William W. Seymour (The Rifle Brigade Club Ltd., 1936)

The 47th (London) Division 1914–1919, edited by Alan H. Maude (Amalgamated Press, 1922)

The West Yorkshire Regiment in the War, 1914–1918, Vol. 1, Everard Wyrall (Bodley Head)

The 56th Division (1st London Territorial Division), Major C. H. Dudley Ward, DSO, MC (John Murray, 1921)

The Worcestershire Regiment, Captain H. FitzM. Stacke, MC (G. T. Cheshire & Sons Ltd., 1928)

The New Zealand Division, 1916–1919, Colonel H. Stewart, CMG, DSO, MC (Whitcombe & Tombs Ltd., Auckland, 1921)

The Cambridgeshires, 1914 to 1919, Brigadier-General E. Riddell, CMG, DSO, and Colonel M. C. Clayton, DSO, DL (Bowes & Bowes, 1934)

The Royal Naval Division, Douglas Jerrold (Hutchinson & Co. Ltd., 1927)

The Story of the Tyneside Scottish, Brigadier-General Trevor Ternan, CB, CMG, DSO (The Northumberland Press, 1918)

The History of the 13th Battalion A.I.F., Thomas A. White (Tyrrells Ltd., Sydney, 1924)

Forward With The 5th, A. W. Keown (The Speciality Press Pty. Ltd., Melbourne, 1921)

The History of the 15th Battalion, The Highland Light Infantry (15th Highland Light Infantry Association, John M'Callum & Co., 1924)

The History of the 16th Battalion, The Highland Light Infantry, edited by
Thomas Chalmers (John M'Callum & Co., 1930)

The 17th Highland Light Infantry, John W. Arthur & Ion S. Munro (David J.
Clarke, 1920)

History of the 11th Battalion, The Queen's, Captain E. W. J. Neave, MC (The
Brixton 'Free Press', 1931)

With The Tenth Essex in France, Lieutenant-Colonel T. M. Banks, DSO,
MC, and Captain R. A. Chell, DSO, MC (Burt & Sons, 1921)

The 11th Royal Warwicks in France 1915–1916, Brevet Colonel C. S. Collison,
DSO (Cornish Brothers Ltd., 1928)

The 15th Battalion, Royal Warwickshire Regiment in the Great War, Major C.
A. Bill (Cornish Brothers Ltd., 1932)

For the Duration, The Story of the 13th Battalion, The Rifle Brigade, D. H.
Rowlands (Simpkin Marshall Ltd., 1932)

The 4th Battalion, The King's Own and The Great War, Lieutenant-Colonel
W. F. A. Wadham and Captain J. Crossley (privately published, 1920)

History of the 6th Battalion West Yorkshire Regiment, Vol. 1 (1/6th Battalion),
Captain E. V. Tempest, DSO, MC (Percy Lund, Humphries & Co.
Ltd., 1921)

The Sherwood Foresters in the Great War 1914–1918 (the 2nd/8th Battalion)
Lieutenant-Colonel W. C. Oates, DSO (J. & H. Bell Ltd., 1920)

History and Memoir of The 33rd Battalion Machine-gun Corps, by members of
the Battalion (privately published, 1919)

A Record of D.245 Battery 1914–1919, Sergeant A. E. Gee, MM, and Corporal
A. E. Shaw (privately published, 1932)

British Regiments 1914–'18, Brigadier E. A. James, OBE, TD (Samson
Books)

History of the First World War, B. H. Liddell Hart (Cassell Ltd., 1970)

My War Memories 1914-1918, General Ludendorff, Vol. 1 (Hutchinson &
Co. Ltd., 1936)

Sir Douglas Haig's Despatches, edited by Lieutenant-Colonel J. H. Boraston,
CB, OBE (J. M. Dent & Sons Ltd., 1919)

The Private Papers of Douglas Haig 1914–1919, edited by Robert Blake (Eyre &
Spottiswoode, 1952)

Sir Douglas Haig's Command 1915–1918, G. A. B. Dewar (Constable, 1922)

The Man I Knew, The Countess Haig (The Moray Press, 1936)

Twenty-Five Years with Earl Haig, Sergeant T. Secrett, MM (Jarrolds, 1929)

Haig, Duff Cooper (Faber & Faber Ltd., 1935)

Field-Marshal Earl Haig, Brigadiér-General John Charteris, CMG, DSO,
MP (Cassell Ltd., 1929)

Le Maréchal Haig à Montreuil-Sur-Mer, Raymond Wable (privately published by the author, 1968)

Goughie, Anthony Farrar-Hockley (Hart-Davis, MacGibbon Ltd., 1975)

The War Memoirs of David Lloyd George (Odham's Press Ltd., 1934)

Tempestuous Journey, Lloyd George, His Life and Times, Frank Owen (Hutchinson & Co. Ltd., 1954)

The Press and the General Staff, Neville Lytton (W. Collins, Sons & Co. Ltd.,
1920)

Now It Can Be Told, Philip Gibbs (Harper and Brothers, Publishers, 1920)

The Pageant of the Years, Philip Gibbs (William Heinemann Ltd., 1946)

World War 1914–1918, edited by Sir John Hammerton (The Amalgamated Press Ltd., 1924)

Twenty Years After, Vols. 1–3. edited by Major-General Sir Ernest Swinton, KBE, CB (George Newnes Ltd., 1938)

The Rifle Brigade Chronicle for 1918, compiled and edited by Colonel Willoughby Verner (John Bale, Sons & Danielsson Ltd., 1919)

Unwilling Passenger, Arthur Osburn (Faber & Faber Ltd., 1932)

Twelve Days, Sidney Rogerson (Arthur Barker Ltd.)

Courage Past, Alex Aiken (privately published by the author)

War Letters to a Wife, France and Flanders 1915–1919, Rowland Feilding (The Medici Society Ltd., 1929)

Transport and Sport in the Great War Period, Captain A. O. Temple Clarke (privately published by the author, 1938)

Machine-gunner 1914–1918, compiled and edited by C. E. Crutchley (Bailey Brothers & Swinfen Ltd., 1975)

A Padre in France, George A. Birmingham (Hodder & Stoughton Ltd.)

Frank Maxwell, VC, by his wife (John Murray, 1921)

By-Ways on Service, Notes from an Australian Journal, Hector Dinning (Constable & Co. Ltd., 1918)

Behind the Lines, Colonel W. N. Nicholson, CMG, DSO (Johathan Cape Ltd., 1939)

Extracts from an Officer's Diary 1914–1918, Lieutenant-Colonel Harrison Jodston, DSO (Geo. Falkner & Sons, 1919)

Happy Odyssey, Sir Adrian Carton de Wiart, VC (Jonathan Cape Ltd., 1950)

A Private in the Guards, Stephen Graham (William Heinemann Ltd., 1928)

Our War, James Milroy McQueen (privately published by the author, 1921)

Treasure Trove of Memories, Hector Macdonald (privately published by the author)

German Spies at Bay, Sidney Theodore Felstead (Hutchinson & Co. Ltd., 1920)

Open House in Flanders, Baroness Ernest de la Grange (John Murray Ltd., 1929)

Quand Montreuil Était sur Mer, Jean Leroy (Quentovic)

GHQ. Montreuil-Sur-Mer, G.S.O. (Philip Allen & Co., 1920)

A Pilgrim in Picardy, B. S. Townrowe (Chapman & Hall Ltd., 1927).

With the British on the Somme, W. Beach Thomas (Methuen & Co. Ltd., 1917)

England in France, Sidney R. Jones (Constable & Co. Ltd., 1919)

Le Temps des Guerres 1914–1939, Gerard Boutet (Editions De Noel, 1981)

L'Hécatombe Sacrée de la Flandre Française 1914–1918, (Imprimerie Desclée, Lille, 1921)

An Der Somme. Erinnerungen der 12 Infanterie-Division an die Stellungskampfe und Schlacht an der Somme Oktober bis November 1916, Verlagsbuchhandlung (Berlin, Ferd. Dümmlers, 1918)

Author's Note

I wish to acknowledge my debt to all of the
following, without whose valuable assistance this book
could never have been written.

Captain A. J. J. P. Agius, MC, 1st/3rd (City of London) Battalion, London Regiment (Royal Fusiliers) (TF).

Acting Corporal E. J. Albrow, 7th (S) Battalion, Norfolk Regiment.

Private J. W. Alderson, 4th Battalion, Grenadier Guards.

Private F. J. Alhquist, 2nd/20th (County of London) Battalion, London Regiment (Blackheath and Woolwich).

Gunner H. J. Allen, Royal Siege Artillery.

Lance-Corporal J. F. E. Alpe, 13th (S) Battalion, The Rifle Brigade.

Corporal F. Arnold, 21st (S) Battalion (Yeoman Rifles), King's Royal Rifle Corps.

Private C. D. Ashby, 4th Battalion, Duke of Cambridge's Own (Middlesex Regiment).

Captain A. L. Ashwell, DSO, 8th Battalion (Nottinghamshire and Derbyshire Regiment) Sherwood Foresters (TF).

Lieutenant F. Bailey, 3rd Battalion, Royal Scots.

Lance-Corporal S. F. Bailey, 1st Life Guards.

Staff Sergeant W. W. Bain, 15th (S) Battalion, (1st London Welsh), Royal Welsh Fusiliers.

Sergeant F. Baker, TD, 1st/5th Battalion, Lincolnshire Regiment (TF).

Rifleman J. Baker, 13th (S) Battalion, The Rifle Brigade.

Private L. M. Baldwin, MM, 8th (S) Battalion, East Surrey Regiment.

Signaller H. J. Bale, 308 Brigade, Royal Field Artillery; 242 Brigade, Royal Field Artillery.

Gunner W. Ballard, D Battery, 290 Brigade, Royal Field Artillery.

Corporal W. Banks, 21st (S) Battalion (Yeoman Rifles), King's Royal Rifle Corps.

Sergeant F. J. Bantock, Royal Regiment of Artillery.

Private W. J. Barfoot, 11th (S) Battalion, Queen's (Royal West Surrey) Regiment.

Rifleman G. W. Barker, 21st (S) Battalion (Yeoman Rifles), King's Royal Rifle Corps.

Rifleman G. Barnes, MM, 13th Battalion, The Rifle Brigade.

Corporal G. Barnes, 8th Battalion, Oxford & Buckinghamshire Light Infantry.

Private W. S. Barnett, 8th Battalion (City of London), London Regiment. Post Office Rifles (TF).

Sergeant A. A. Barron, 16th (S) Battalion, King's Royal Rifle Corps.

Trooper G. O. Barson, Household Battalion, 2nd Life Guards.

Private P. J. Batchelor, D. Squadron, Queen's Own Oxfordshire Hussars.

Sergeant H. Bartlett, 115th Brigade, Royal Field Artillery.

Private F. H. Bastable, 7th (S) Battalion, Queen's Own (Royal West Kent Regiment).

Private H. S. Baverstock, 12th Battalion, 1st Canterbury Regiment, New Zealand Division.

Lieutenant F. W. Beadle, 156 Brigade, Royal Field Artillery.

Lance-Corporal G. R. Bealing, MM, Duke of Edinburgh's 2nd Battalion (Wiltshire Regiment).

Corporal J. Beament, MM, 16th (S) Battalion, King's Royal Rifle Corps.

Sergeant S. V. Bearup, 21st (S) Battalion (Yeoman Rifles), King's Royal Rifle Corps.

Rifleman S. Bell, 21st (S) Battalion (Yeoman Rifles), King's Royal Rifle Corps.

Private W. G. Bell, MM, Army Cyclist Corps.

Private J. R. Bennett, 22nd Battalion, Australian Imperial Forces.

Private J. Bennett, 15th (County of London) Battalion, London Regiment (Prince of Wales' Own, Civil Service Rifles) (TF).

Lance-Corporal T. A. Bennett, 7th (S) Battalion, The Rifle Brigade.

Sub-Lieutenant J. H. Bentham, Hood Battalion, Royal Naval Division.

Private H. W. Bickerstaff, MM, 19th Battalion, Canadian Expeditionary Force.

Private W. A. Billingham, 25th Battalion, Machine Gun Corps.

Private F. W. Bindley, 2nd Battalion, Honourable Artillery Company.

Private T. Bingham, 12th (S) Battalion, York and Lancaster Regiment.

Rifleman H. Blackburn, Croix de Guerre, 21st (S) Battalion (Yeoman Rifles), King's Royal Rifle Corps.

Sergeant-Major J. F. Blackemore, MM, 2nd Canterbury Infantry Battalion, New Zealand Division.

Private H. Blankley, 5th Battalion, Northumberland Fusiliers (TF).

Gunner R. Bletcher, 280 Siege Battery, Royal Garrison Artillery.

Rifleman T. S. Bond, 11th (S) Battalion, The Rifle Brigade.

Private G. Boss, 1st/8th (City of London Battalion), London Regiment (Post Office Rifles).

Lance-Sergeant J. L. Bouch, 1st Battalion, Coldstream Guards.

Rifleman W. Bowhill, 13th (S) Battalion, The Rifle Brigade.

Rifleman A. E. Boyland, 13th (S) Battalion, The Rifle Brigade.

Corporal T. Bracey, MM, 9th (S) Battalion, Royal Fusiliers (City of London Regiment).

Major W. J. Brockman, DSO, 15th (S) Battalion, Lancashire Fusiliers (1st Salford).

2nd Lieutenant H. Brooks, 6th Battalion, Tank Corps.

Lance-Bombardier J. H. Bromwich, 138th Heavy Battery, Royal Garrison Artillery.

Private A. B. Brown, 21st (County of London), London Regiment (1st Surrey Rifles) (TF).

Private H. R. Brown, 2nd Battalion, Royal Marine Light Infantry.

Sergeant J. Brown, MM, 16th (S) Battalion, King's Royal Rifle Corps.

Corporal A. T. A. Browne, MM (TD), 20th (S) Battalion, Royal Fusiliers (City of London Regiment).

Sergeant J. Bryant, MM, 8th Battalion, Australian Imperial Forces.

Corporal A. W. Buckingham, 70th Company Motor Transport, Army Service Corps.

Rifleman A. E. Burroughs, 7th (S) Battalion, King's Royal Rifle Corps.

Gunner Charles E. Burrows, 104 Battery, 22nd Brigade, Royal Field Artillery.

Sergeant G. Butler, 12th Machine Gun Company, 4th Division.

Lieutenant S. A. V. Butler, 3rd Battalion, King's Own (Yorkshire Light Infantry).

Private F. Burbeck, 2nd Battalion, Oxfordshire and Buckinghamshire Light Infantry.

Private W. H. Callow, 15th (S)

Battalion, Royal Welsh Fusiliers (1st London Welsh).

Rifleman T. E. Cantlon, 18th and 21st Battalions (Yeoman Rifles), King's Royal Rifle Corps.

Corporal C. G. Capel, 1st Battalion, Oxfordshire and Buckinghamshire Light Infantry.

Rifleman N. Carmichael, 21st (S) Battalion (Yeoman Rifles), King's Royal Rifle Corps.

Rifleman C. Carter, 5th (City of London) Battalion, London Regiment, (London Rifle Brigade) (TF).

Private W. F. R. Carter, 7th (S) and 9th (S) Battalions, Leicestershire Regiment.

Private E. S. Cecil, 2nd Battalion, Hampshire Regiment.

Captain Leonard Chamberlen, MC, 13th (S) Battalion, The Rifle Brigade.

Private W. Chambers, 1st Battalion, (Nottinghamshire and Derbyshire Regiment), Sherwood Foresters.

Rifleman A. L. Chapman, 21st (S) Battalion (Yeoman Rifles), King's Royal Rifle Corps.

Rifleman S. F. Charrington, 13th (S) Battalion, The Rifle Brigade.

Private H. M. Chaundy, MC, Motor Transport, Army Service Corps (later Lieutenant).

Pioneer G. T. H. Cheeseman, 7th Signal Troop, 3rd Cavalry Division, Royal Engineers (Signal Service).

Colonel R. A. Chell, DSO, MC, 10th (S) Battalion, Essex Regiment.

Corporal R. T. Chiffey, 33rd Division, Royal Engineers (Signal Service).

Private J. J. Christie, 8th (S) Battalion, Gordon Highlanders.

Private Percy Clark, 5th Battalion, Cheshire Regiment (TF).

Acting Lance-Corporal F. B. J. Cleary, 1st/5th (City of London) Battalion, London Regiment (London Rifle Brigade) (TF).

Private J. Clements, Royal Marine Light Infantry.

Sergeant H. B. Coates, 14th (County of London) Battalion, London Regiment, (London Scottish) (TF).

Sergeant F. H. Cobb, 18th (S) Battalion, King's Royal Rifle Corps.

Company Sergeant-Major W. J. Coggins, DCM, 1st/4th Battalion, Oxfordshire and Buckinghamshire Light Infantry (TF).

Rifleman W. F. Coldrick, 13th (S) Battalion, The Rifle Brigade.

Corporal C. F. Cole, 2nd/21st (County of London) Battalion, London Regiment (1st Surrey Rifles) (TF).

Sapper A. E. Comer, 1st Field Company, Royal Engineers.

Corporal W. E. Cook, Royal Engineers.

Corporal F. H. Corduker, 21st (S) Battalion (Yeoman Rifles), King's Royal Rifle Corps.

Rifleman A. W. C. Corkett, 11th (S) Battalion, The Rifle Brigade.

Trooper J. Cowling, 18th Hussars.

Lieutenant T. C. Cresswell, MC, Hood Battalion, Royal Naval Division.

Gunner A. E. Crook, J. Battery, Royal Horse Artillery.

Sergeant J. T. Cross, 13th (S) Battalion, The Rifle Brigade.

Private R. T. Crowe, 2nd Battalion, The Highland Light Infantry.

Private Frederick Darby, DCM, 10th (S) Battalion, Worcestershire Regiment.

Sergeant William Darlington, 18th (S) Battalion, Manchester Regiment.

Corporal L. A. Darnell, 11th Battalion, Sussex Regiment.

Sergeant E. J. Davidson, MM, Royal Engineers.

Corporal J. W. Davies, 18th Field Ambulance, Royal Army Medical Corps.

Private J. Dearman, 266th Field Company, Royal Engineers.

Private E. Deighton, 8th (S) Battalion, King's Own Yorkshire Light Infantry.

Private J. W. Dicker, 13th (S) Battalion, The Rifle Brigade.

Sergeant R. Dickson, MM, 3rd Battalion, Grenadier Guards.

Corporal H. Diffey, 15th (S) Battalion (1st London Welsh), Royal Welsh Fusiliers.

Corporal A. W. Dunbar, 236 Brigade, Royal Field Artillery.

Sergeant-Pilot G. F. Duncan, Royal Flying Corps.

Captain F. E. Dunsmuir, MC, 17th (S) Battalion, Highland Light Infantry.

Private J. C. Dwelly, 4th Battalion, Grenadier Guards.

Sergeant H. J. Dykes, Tank Corps.

Private Tom Easton, 21st Battalion, Northumberland Fusiliers, (2nd Tyneside Scottish).

Rifleman B. F. Eccles, 7th (S) Battalion, The Rifle Brigade.

Sergeant S. E. Elford, New Zealand Rifle Brigade.

Gunner A. E. Ellingford, MM, 28th Brigade, Royal Field Artillery.

Private C. H. U. Embery, 1st/16th (County of London) Battalion, London Regiment (Queen's Westminster Rifles) (TF).

Lance-Corporal G. England, 3rd Battalion, Grenadier Guards.

Acting Lieutenant-Colonel R. E. England, Croix de Guerre, 13th (S) Battalion (Miners and Pioneers), The King's Own (Yorkshire Light Infantry).

Driver W. Everett, Army Service Corps.

Private V. E. Fagence, 11th (S) Battalion, Queen's (Royal West Surrey Regiment).

Private B. Farrer, Royal Army Medical Corps.

Corporal Signaller H. E. W. Fayerbrother, DCM, 291st Brigade, Royal Field Artillery, 58th Division.

Private B. Felstead, 15th (S) Battalion (1st London Welsh), Royal Welsh Fusiliers.

Private A. W. Fenn, 2nd Battalion, The Suffolk Regiment.

Private W. S. Fisher, 1st Hertfordshire Yeomanry.

Lance-Corporal W. G. Fleet, 7th (S) Battalion, Bedfordshire Regiment.

Corporal O. S. Flowers, Motor Transport Section, Army Service Corps.

Corporal R. A. Ford, 35th Divisional Ammunition Column, 157 Brigade, Royal Field Artillery.

Lance-Corporal H. Forrest, 9th (Dunbartonshire) Battalion, Princess Louise's (Argyll and Sutherland Highlanders) (TF).

Lieutenant-Commander J. C. Forster, Hood Battalion, Royal Naval Division.

Private A. B. Foster, Queen's Own Oxfordshire Hussars.

Private E. Foster, 3rd Battalion, Durham Light Infantry.

Gunner F. Foster, Royal Field Artillery.

Corporal J. Francis, 1st Battalion, Duke of Cambridge's Own (Middlesex) Regiment.

Sapper G. A. Franklin, No. 2 Section, 57th Division, Royal Engineers Signal Company.

Lance-Corporal C. Frost, MM, 1st Battalion, Leicestershire Regiment.

Brigadier R. E. Fryer, OBE, 62 Field Company, Royal Engineers.

Acting-Corporal E. Gale, 1st Battalion and 7th (S) Battalion, The Rifle Brigade.

2nd Lieutenant G. Garnett-Clarke, MC, Royal Field Artillery.

Driver C. Garrard, D. Battery, 87th Brigade, Royal Field Artillery.

Lieutenant P. H. Gates, 2nd Battalion, Lincolnshire Regiment.

Private J. R. Glenn, 12th (S) Battalion, York and Lancaster Regiment (Sheffield Pals).

Captain A. L. Goring, MC, 6th (S) Battalion, Alexandra, Princess of Wales' Own (Yorkshire Regiment).

Private J. Hain, 9th (S) Battalion, Royal Irish Fusiliers.

Private A. Hales, 2/2nd London Field Ambulance, Royal Army Medical Corps (TF).

Private H. Hall, 12th (S) Battalion, York and Lancaster Regiment (Sheffield Pals).

Corporal P. A. Hall, 2nd/4th Battalion, Gloucestershire Regiment (TF).

Corporal W. B. Hand, 1st/7th Battalion (Worcestershire Regiment).

Lieutenant-Colonel P. W. Hargreaves, MC, 3rd Battalion, Worcestershire Regiment.

Corporal H. J. Hart, 9th (S) Battalion, Royal Fusiliers.

Petty Officer H. Hart, Royal Naval Air Service.

Acting Lance-Corporal A. V. Hartland, 2nd/5th Battalion, South Staffordshire Regiment.

Lieutenant R. M. Hawkins, MC, 11th (S) Battalion, Royal Fusiliers.

Private W. Hay, 9th Battalion (Highlanders), Royal Scots (Lothian Regiment).

Private H. J. Haynes, 2nd/6th Battalion, Royal Warwickshire Regiment (TF).

A/B. J. Haynes, Anson Battalion, Royal Naval Division.

Captain E. W. Hayward, DCM, MM, D Battalion (Heavy Branch Machine Gun Corps) (Tanks).

Lieutenant H. J. Hayward, MC, 12th Battalion, Gloucestershire Regiment (Bristol's Own).

Private F. Haywood, 15th (County of London) Battalion (Prince of Wales' Own) Civil Service Rifles (TF).

Brigadier T. E. H. Helby, 59th Siege Battery, Royal Garrison Artillery.

A/B. E. Henderson, Drake Battalion, Royal Naval Division.

Brigade Trumpeter J. Henderson, 1st Northumberland Brigade, Royal Field Artillery.

2nd Lieutenant G. C. Henry, 2nd Battalion, King's Own Yorkshire Light Infantry.

Lance-Corporal A. C. Hill, Army Service Corps.

Private A. J. Hill, 15th Battalion, Royal Welsh Fusiliers.

Rifleman A. Hill, 2nd/9th Battalion, Queen Victoria's Rifles (London Regiment).

Signaller L. Hill, 16th Battalion, Cheshire Regiment.

Fitter R. Hill, Croix de Guerre, Royal Horse and Royal Field Artillery.

Sergeant T. S. Hogg, 12th (S) Battalion, York and Lancaster Regiment (Sheffield Pals).

Sergeant H. A. Horne, Lincolnshire Regiment.

Corporal J. Hoyles, MM, 13th (S) Battalion, The Rifle Brigade.

Corporal R. Hudson, MC, London Regiment (Queen's Westminster Rifles) (TF); (later Lieutenant).

Lance-Corporal W. R. Hudson, 13th (S) Battalion, The Rifle Brigade.

Private G. H. Huggins, Queen's Own Oxfordshire Hussars.

Colonel N. H. Huttenbach, DSO, OBE, MC, Royal Artillery.

Private F. Ibbotson, 14th Battalion (1st Birmingham City), Royal Warwickshire Regiment.

Private H. H. Innis, 7th Battalion, Northumberland Fusiliers.

Private R. Ison, 9th (S) Battalion, The Rifle Brigade.

Private W. Jackman, 4th Battalion, Grenadier Guards.

Rifleman H. A. Jago, 13th (S) Battalion, The Rifle Brigade.

Private J. H. James, 2nd/7th Battalion, Manchester Regiment (TF).

Private A. J. Jamieson, 11th Battalion, Royal Scots.

Private H. N. Jeary, 1st Battalion, Queen's (Royal West Surrey Regiment).

2nd Lieutenant A. B. Jeffries, 2nd Battalion, Royal Berkshire Regiment.

Corporal F. F. Johnson, A/70 Brigade, 15th (Scottish) Division, Royal Field Artillery.

Lance-Corporal R. G. Johnson, 58th London Signal Company, Royal Engineers.

Private I. A. T. Jones, 2nd Battalion, Royal Welsh Fusiliers.

Lieutenant F. Jones, MC, Tank Corps.

Private S. H. E. Kemp, 14th (County of London) Battalion, London Regiment (London Scottish) (TF).

Private E. C. Kimber, 2nd, 3rd and 4th Battalions, Grenadier Guards.

Sergeant G. W. Kimble, Queen's Own Oxfordshire Hussars.

Lieutenant P. T. King, 2nd/5th Battalion, East Lancashire Regiment.

Lance-Corporal G. Labdon, Machine Gun Corps.

Rifleman H. R. Langley, 16th (S) Battalion, King's Royal Rifle Corps.

Rifleman S. E. Lawrence, 13th (S) Battalion, The Rifle Brigade.

Sub-Lieutenant T. M. Lawrie, CBE, TD, 63rd Royal Naval Division.

Lieutenant-Colonel W. F. Lean, DSO, Croix de Guerre, 3rd Battalion, West Yorkshire Regiment.

Corporal C. A. Lee, 3rd Battalion, The Rifle Brigade.

Corporal A. E. Lee, MM, 'A' Battalion, Heavy Branch, Machine Gun Corps (Tanks).

Lance-Corporal T. C. Levell, MM, 9th (S) Battalion, Norfolk Regiment.

Sergeant W. E. H. Levy, MM, 'D' Battalion, Heavy Branch, Machine Gun Corps (Tanks).

Sergeant E. Lincoln, 13th (County of London) Battalion, London Regiment.

Rifleman H. E. Lister, MM, 12th (S) Battalion, The Rifle Brigade.

Corporal C. W. Lloyd, 13th (S) Battalion, The Rifle Brigade.

Lieutenant R. Lloyd, Royal Horse Artillery.

Corporal L. Longhurst, 16th (County of London), London Regiment (TF).

Private L. Lovell, 6th (S) Battalion, King's Own (Yorkshire Light Infantry).

Corporal J. V. Lowe, 10th (S) Battalion, Cameronians (Scottish Rifles).

Private C. H. Luffman, 7th (S) Battalion, King's (Shropshire Light Infantry).

Gunner W. Lugg, MM, 83rd Brigade, Royal Field Artillery.

Private C. Lunn, 2nd/3rd HCFA, Royal Army Medical Corps.

Warrant Officer W. J. Lush, Royal Garrison Artillery.

Colonel R. Macleod, DSO, MC, Royal Field Artillery (then Captain attached Royal Flying Corps).

Private J. Makin, Medical Unit, Royal Marine Light Infantry.

Gunner Maltby, MM, 29th Brigade, Royal Field Artillery.

Lieutenant F. Mansfield, 8th Siege Battery, Royal Garrison Artillery.

Lance-Corporal H. E. Marden, 13th (S) Battalion, Royal Sussex Regiment.

Sub-Lieutenant W. Marlow, MC, Howe Battalion, 63rd Royal Naval Division

Private H. Marshall, 9th (S) Battalion, Royal Fusiliers (City of London Regiment).

General Sir James Marshall-Cornwall, KCB, CBE, DSO, MC, Royal Artillery (attached GHQ) (then Captain).

Private M. A. Martino, 149th Brigade, Royal Field Artillery.

Corporal P. Mason, 9th (S) Battalion, Prince of Wales' Own (West Yorkshire Regiment).

Private A. W. Maycock, 13th (S) Battalion (4th Hull), East Yorkshire Regiment.

Corporal F. L. Mayhew, Royal Engineers (London Electrical Engineers).

Private N. Mellor, 4th Battalion, Bedfordshire Regiment.

Gunner D. N. Meneaud-Lissenburg, Royal Horse Artillery.

Lieutenant G. F. Middle, Royal Engineers Wireless Section.

Trooper F. W. Miller, 1st Battalion, Hertfordshire Regiment.

Private H. R. Milson, 2nd Battalion, Royal Welsh Fusiliers.

Corporal B. A. Minnitt, MM, MC, 11th Battalion, Sherwood Foresters (Nottinghamshire and Derbyshire Regiment) (later Lieutenant).

Sergeant J. H. Mitchell, A. Battery, 1st Canadian Motor Machine Gun Brigade.

Rifleman E. G. Morgan, 13th (S) Battalion, The Rifle Brigade.

Lieutenant S. G. Morgan, 2nd Battalion, South Staffordshire Regiment.

Private W. Morgan, 10th/11th (S) Battalion, Highland Light Infantry.

Sergeant L. Morris, Royal Army Medical Corps.

Private W. M. Morriss, 12th Battalion, Canterbury Regiment, New Zealand Expeditionary Force.

Bombardier W. J. Muir, D 317 Battery, Royal Field Artillery, 63rd Royal Naval Division.

Private H. Munday, 5th Battalion, Oxfordshire and Buckinghamshire Light Infantry.

Able Bodied Seaman Joseph Murray, Hood Battalion, Royal Naval Division.

Captain J. Y. Murray, 1st Battalion, Essex Regiment.

Private W. Myatt, 8th Battalion, Tank Corps.

Sergeant J. A. Myers, DCM, 16th (S) Battalion, West Yorkshire Regiment (Bradford Pals).

Gunner J. W. Naylor, Royal Artillery.

Rifleman J. J. Newman, 13th (S) Battalion, The Rifle Brigade.

Private C. J. Nicholls, C Company, Heavy Branch, Machine Gun Corps (Tanks).

Rifleman E. C. Nicholson, MC 21st (S) Battalion (Yeoman Rifles), King's Royal Rifle Corps (later 2nd Lieutenant).

Private O. Nielsen, 25th Battalion, Australian Imperial Force.

Private W. H. Nixon, DCM, 2nd Battalion, Cheshire Regiment.

Sergeant M. J. O'Connor, MM (and Bar), 13th (S) Battalion, The Rifle Brigade.

Act. RSM L. M. Odell, MM, 1st Canterbury Battalion, New Zealand Expeditionary Force.

Lance-Corporal E. R. Organ, Queen's Own Oxfordshire Hussars.

Corporal R. W. Otley, 21st (S) Battalion (Yeoman Rifles), King's Royal Rifle Corps.

Corporal H. Oxley, 23rd Battalion, Middlesex Regiment.

Brigadier E. K. Page, MC, 130 Battery, Royal Field Artillery (then Lieutenant).

Corporal A. D. Pankhurst, 56th Division, Royal Field Artillery.

Lance-Corporal G. W. Parker, MM, 2nd (City of London) London Regiment (Royal Fusiliers) (TF).

Private R. Parker, 12th (S) Battalion, York and Lancaster Regiment (Sheffield Pals).

Sergeant A. K. Paterson, DCM, MM, 11th (S) Battalion, The Rifle Brigade.

Private A. Paterson, 7th Battalion,

Argyll and Sutherland Highlanders (TF).

Lieutenant J. R. Patten, 20th (Light) Division, Royal Field Artillery.

Private W. Pattenden, 2/6th Battalion, Prince of Wales (North Staffordshire Regiment) (TF).

Rifleman E. Pearce, 16th (S) Battalion, King's Royal Rifle Corps (Church Lads Brigade).

The Reverend L. T. Pearson, Chaplain.

Corporal J. Pickard, MM, 78th Winnipeg Grenadiers, Canadian Expeditionary Force.

Rifleman J. A. Pincombe, 16th (County of London) Battalion, London Regiment (Queen's Westminster Rifles) (TF).

Sergeant G. E. Pople, MM and Bar, 8th (S) Battalion, King's (Shropshire Light Infantry).

Rifleman W. T. Poucher, 21st (S) Battalion (Yeoman Rifles) King's Royal Rifle Corps.

Rifleman E. T. Pretty, 9th (S) Battalion, The Rifle Brigade.

Lieutenant B. B. Rackham, MC and Bar, Hawke Battalion, Royal Naval Division.

Corporal A. C. Razzell, 8th (S) Battalion, Royal Fusiliers (City of London Regiment).

Private J. A. Reed, New Zealand Light Railway Engineers.

Private W. G. Reynolds, 4th Battalion, Duke of Cambridge's Own (Middlesex Regiment).

Corporal W. Richards, 1st/8th Battalion, Royal Warwickshire Regiment.

Captain N. Ries, 13th (S) Battalion, The Rifle Brigade.

Acting Corporal J. W. H. Rippin, 7th Battalion, Essex Regiment.

Sergeant F. H. Robbins, 13th (S) Battalion, The Rifle Brigade.

Lance-Corporal F. Robinson, DCM, 8th (S) Battalion, York and Lancaster Regiment.

Rifleman B. Robson, 21st (S) Battalion (Yeoman Rifles), King's Royal Rifle Corps.

Private G. Roden, 22nd (County of London) Battalion, London Regiment (The Queen's) (TF).

Regimental Sergeant-Major A. Roffey, DCM and Bar, 7th (S)

Battalion, Queen's Own (Royal West Kent Regiment).

Private F. Rogers, 11th (S) Battalion, Royal Sussex Regiment (1st South Down).

Private R. K. Rolfe, 26th (S) Battalion (Bankers), Royal Fusiliers.

Private H. B. Rose, 1st Battalion, Trench Artillery, 151st Field Artillery, 42nd (Rainbow) Division. U.S. Army.

Rifleman W. T. Rowe, MM, 13th (S) Battalion, The Rifle Brigade.

Rifleman C. P. J. Ruck, 3rd/2nd Battalion, The London Rifle Brigade.

Private E. W. Russell, 5th Canadian Battalion (Western Cavalry), Canadian Expeditionary Force.

Captain F. C. Russell, 22nd Battalion, Australian Imperial Forces.

Private A. Ryland, 13th (S) Battalion, The Rifle Brigade.

Major R. F. J. Sanders, TD, 16th Heavy Battery, Royal Garrison Artillery.

Rifleman H. F. Saunders, 16th (S) Battalion, King's Royal Rifle Corps.

Rifleman F. Saville, 21st (S) Battalion (Yeoman Rifles), King's Royal Rifle Corps (Church Lads Brigade).

Gunner W. Sayers, 1st/3rd London Regiment, Royal Fusiliers (TF) Tank Corps.

Rifleman A. T. Sears, 11th (S) Battalion, The Rifle Brigade.

Corporal W. H. Shaw, 9th (S) Battalion, Royal Welsh Fusiliers.

Rifleman H. V. Shawyer, 13th (S) Battalion, The Rifle Brigade.

Rifleman C. W. Shepherd, 13th (S) Battalion, The Rifle Brigade.

Rifleman J. Shrimpton, 13th (S) Battalion, The Rifle Brigade.

Signaller A. V. Simpson, 2nd/6th Battalion, Duke of Wellington's (West Riding Regiment).

Private J. Simpson, 2nd Battalion, Grenadier Guards.

Sergeant J. Skuce, 2nd Battalion, Irish Guards.

Captain C. M. Slack, MC and Bar, 1st/4th Battalion, East Yorkshire Regiment (TF) (then Lieutenant).

Private H. J. Smith, 9th (S) Battalion (Northumberland Hussars Yeomanry), Northumberland Fusiliers.

Corporal H. W. Smith, MM, 13th (S) Battalion, The Rifle Brigade.

Rifleman R. W. Smith, 13th (S) Battalion, The Rifle Brigade.

Corporal R. Smith, 21st (S) Battalion (Yeoman Rifles), King's Royal Rifle Corps.

Warrant Officer S. A. Smith, 11th (S) Battalion, The Rifle Brigade.

Rifleman E. G. Snell, 5th (City of London) Battalion, London Regiment (London Rifle Brigade) (TF).

Corporal A. E. Somerset, 3rd Battalion, Grenadier Guards.

Corporal R. G. Spearman, 19th Heavy Battery, Royal Field Artillery, Royal Garrison Artillery.

Corporal T. A. Spencer, MM, Royal Scots Fusiliers; 108 Machine Gun Company, Machine Gun Corps.

Rifleman C. Spilsbury, 11th (S) Battalion, The Rifle Brigade.

Private F. G. Staite, MM and Bar, 1st/8th Battalion, Worcestershire Regiment (TF).

Private C. S. Stevens, 1st Battalion, Leicestershire Regiment.

Acting Sergeant-Major W. O. Stevenson, DCM, MM, 6th (Renfrewshire) Battalion, Argyll and Sutherland Highlanders.

Bombardier B. O. Stokes, 3rd Brigade, New Zealand Field Artillery.

Private W. T. Stokes, 2nd/4th Battalion, Royal Berkshire Regiment (TF).

Corporal H. L. Stride, 13th (S) Battalion, The Rifle Brigade.

Private G. C. Stubbs, Royal Army Medical Corps, 12th Field Ambulance, 4th Division.

2nd Lieutenant J. A. Talbot, 10th (S) Battalion, The Rifle Brigade.

Reverend E. Tanner, MC and Bar, Chaplain 4th Class, 2nd Battalion, Worcestershire Regiment.

Corporal J. H. Tansley, 9th (S) Battalion, York and Lancaster Regiment.

Corporal R. Tate, 3rd Battalion, Tank Corps.

Private W. Tate, 4th Battalion (Pioneers), Coldstream Guards.

Private W. R. Thomas, 14th (S) Battalion, Royal Welsh Fusiliers.

Major A. G. C. Thompson, Royal Army Medical Corps.

Corporal R. E. Thompson, 13th (S) Battalion, The Rifle Brigade.

Rifleman A. E. Thorne, MBE, 13th (S) Battalion, The Rifle Brigade.

Lance-Corporal C. Tomlinson, King's Own (Liverpool Regiment).

Corporal F. C. Toogood, 3rd Wellington Battalion, 4th New Zealand Brigade.

Private J. F. Tucker, 1st/13th (County of London) (Princess Louise's Kensington Battalion), London Regiment (TF).

Corporal J. Turnbull, 8th (S) Battalion, King's Own Yorkshire Light Infantry.

Corporal W. B. Turnbull, 12th (S) Battalion, The Rifle Brigade.

Private H. Turner, 50th Divisional Machine Gun Corps.

Lance-Corporal Bugler W. S. Turner, 15th Battalion, Highland Light Infantry (City of Glasgow Corporation Tramways Battalion).

Private J. E. Tyson, 3rd Battalion, King's Own (Royal Lancaster Regiment).

Sergeant F. G. Udall, MM and two Bars, 4th Battalion, London Regiment (Royal Fusiliers) (TF).

Corporal F. G. Vail, MD, Machine Gun Corps.

Private A. Vanpraagh, 253 Tunnelling Company, Royal Engineers.

Corporal E. C. Vickery, 13th (S) Battalion (Forest of Dean) (Pioneers), Gloucestershire Regiment.

Major E. H. Wade, MC and Bar, South Staffordshire Regiment, Machine Gun Corps.

Able-Seaman J. A. Wade, D Company, Hawke Battalion, 63rd Royal Naval Division.

Worker C. H. Wagstaff (now Mrs Brereton), No. 26178, Womens Auxiliary Army Corps.

Company Quartermaster-Sergeant J. Wainwright, 5th Battalion, Machine Gun Corps.

Private A. E. Walker, 4th Battalion, Northumberland Fusiliers.

Sapper F. E. Waldron, 30th Division, Signals, Royal Engineers.

Sergeant R. Walker, 126 Machine Gun Corps, 42nd Division.

Corporal J. Wallace, Oxfordshire and Buckinghamshire Light Infantry.

Sergeant A. B. Walsh, Royal Engineers.

Trooper H. P. Ward, Queen's Own Oxfordshire Hussars and Machine Gun Corps.

Sergeant W. Ward, MM, 2nd Battalion, Grenadier Guards.

Lance-Corporal D. A. M. Watson, 9th, 12th and 11th Battalions, Royal Scots.

Private F. Watts, 4th Battalion, North Staffordshire Regiment.

Private H. W. H. Watts, 2nd Battalion, Queen's (Royal West Surrey Regiment).

Acting-Corporal R. Weeber, 13th (S) Battalion, The Rifle Brigade.

Private A. E. West, Duke of Cambridge's Own (Middlesex Regiment).

Sergeant F. Wheatcroft, Machine Gun Corps.

Rifleman F. C. White, 10th (S) Battalion, King's Royal Rifle Corps.

Private W. E. White, Oxfordshire and Buckinghamshire Light Infantry.

Lance-Corporal A. J. Whitehouse, MM, Lancashire Fusiliers.

Corporal J. E. H. Whittaker, 21st (S) Battalion (Yeoman Rifles), King's Royal Rifle Corps.

Private E. Wickens, 12th (S) Battalion, Duke of Cambridge's Own (Middlesex Regiment).

Sergeant A. E. Wiffen, 9th Battalion, Essex Regiment.

Corporal H. G. Wild, Royal Flying Corps.

2nd Lieutenant M. C. Wilkinson, 25th Battalion, Royal Welsh Fusiliers.

Trooper C. H. Williams, MM, Royal Buckinghamshire Hussars (TF).

Corporal E. G. Williams, 19th Battalion, King's (Liverpool Regiment).

Gunner G. A. Williams, MM and Bar, 232 Brigade, Royal Field Artillery.

Gunner H. G. R. Williams, 5th Battalion, London Regiment (London Rifle Brigade).

Rifleman/CQMS H. Willis, 21st (S) Battalion (Yeoman Rifles), King's Royal Rifle Corps.

Lieutenant A. G. Wilson, MC, 1st/5th Battalion, Prince of Wales' Own (West Yorkshire Regiment) (TF).

Private C. A. Wilson, MM, 1st Battalion, Grenadier Guards.

Lance-Sergeant G. E. Winterbourne, 16th (County of London) Battalion, London Regiment (Queen's Westminster Rifles) (TF).

Lieutenant T. H. Witherow, 8th (S) Battalion (East Belfast), Royal Irish Rifles.

Acting-Corporal L. Wolfe, MM, 6th Battalion, King's Own Scottish Borderers.

Sergeant A. Wolfman, A Company, A Battalion, Heavy Branch Machine Gun Corps (Tanks).

Private C. T. Wood, Royal Army Medical Corps.

Corporal H. C. Wood, MM, East Surrey Regiment and Royal Flying Corps.

Lance-Corporal J. D. Woodside, 16th (S) Battalion, Highland Light Infantry.

Private F. Woolley, 2nd/4th Battalion, South Lancashire Regiment.

Private J. H. Worker, 1st Battalion, Scots Guards.

Rifleman W. J. Worrell, 12th (S) Battalion, The Rifle Brigade.

Gunner G. Worsley, 276 Brigade, Royal Field Artillery.

Lance-Corporal G. Worth, 6th Battalion, Prince of Wales' Own (North Staffordshire Regiment) (TF).

Gunner E. C. Wright, 62nd Brigade, Royal Field Artillery.

Lance-Corporal F. Wright, Royal Warwickshire Regiment.

Corporal G. Wright, Machine Gun Corps.

Platoon Sergeant G. S. W. Yarnall, 14th Battalion, London Regiment (London Scottish).

Corporal J. H. Yeoman, 21st (S) Battalion (Yeoman Rifles), King's Royal Rifle Corps.

Corporal R. Zealley, 18th (S) Battalion (1st Public Schools) Royal Fusiliers, City of London Regiment.

Index

Abbeville, 180
Acklom, Major, 74, 75, 86, 94
Adams, Rifleman, 23
Agius, Arthur, 30, 32–3, 55, 66–7, 196–7, 259–60, 292–3, 318
Ainger, Mr, 199, 200
Albert, 7, 78, 105–6, 108, 111, 126, 257
Ale trench, 269, 273, 275, 276
Alexandra, Queen, 210
Amiens, 8, 78–81, 257
Anzac, 112, 158–66, 167–72, 246
Archer-Shee, Colonel, 249
Argyll and Sutherland Highlanders, 308, 327, 329
Armistead, Lieutenant, 244–5
Army School of Instruction, 21
Army Service Corps, 185–7
Arras, 33, 38
Artillery Observation Post, 61
Artists' Rifles, 210
Aubers ridge, 30, 161–3
Australian Divisions, 112, 158–66, 167–77, 246, 252, 324
Australian Division, 1st, 171, 172, 176, 246
Australian Division, 2nd, 171, 176
Australian Division, 5th, 161
Authuille, 6, 8, 36, 64
Authuille Wood, 72
Auxi-le-Château, 21–2, 24–6, 196
Aveluy, 7
Aveluy Wood, 7, 49, 63, 243, 331

Bailleul, 168

Baird, Brigadier General, 138, 145, 146
Balfourier, General, 132–3
Banks, Billy, 272, 282, 286
Bapaume, 3, 35, 257, 318
Barker, Sir Charles, 284
Barrington, Sir Eric, 23
Barton, Pipe-Sergeant, 17
Barton-Smith, Charles, 142
Basin Wood, 69
Bath, Ethel, 291–2, 293
Bath, Reg, 292
Baverstock, Harry, 257, 261–2, 269, 284, 286–7
Bavincourt, 88–9
Bazentin, 138, 207
Bazentin Le Grand, 133
Bazentin Le Petit, 133, 138, 141, 156
Bazentin ridge, 171
Bazentin Wood, 157
Beadle, Fred, 137–9
Bealing, Roy, 95–7, 100–1, 205
Beament, Jack, 140, 141–4, 147–50, 153, 154
Beament, Stanley, 154–5
Beaucourt, 7, 36, 324, 336, 337
Beaucourt Trench, 336
Beaumont Hamel, 35–7, 57, 70, 71, 110, 255, 325–33, 337, 341
Beauquesne, 39, 40, 41
Beaurepaire, 38
Bécordel, 260
Bécourt, 167
Bécourt Château, 75
Bell, Frank, 25

Bell, W. G., 289–90
Bennett, Tommy, 319
Bentham, Jeremy, 321–2, 330
Benton, Lieutenant, 283, 309–10
Bernafay Wood, 116, 278–9
Bienvillers, 107
Birdwood, General, 159, 177
Birkett, Sid, 25
Biss, 261, 287
Bissell, Corporal, 335
'Black Buttoned Bastards', 27
Boisselle, la, 36, 37, 60, 73, 74, 75,
    82, 86, 95, 97–102, 109, 110, 112,
    117, 170, 205
Bottomley, Horatio, 173
Bouch, John, 277–8, 314–5
Bouleaux Wood, 258
Bouzincourt, 41, 63
Bradley, Corporal, 250, 251
Bréda, Comtesse de, 8
Bréda, Monsieur le Compte de,
    7–8
Bresle, 93, 103, 126
Brown, Captain, 286
Brown, Jack, 139, 140–3, 144,
    146–50, 153
Burrows, Charles E., 45
Burrows, Lieutenant, 56
Butler, George, 313–14
Butler, Harry, 71
Butte de Warlencourt, 324
Buxton, Mr & Mrs, 143

Calonne, 319
Cameron, General, 60
Cameron, Jack, 89
Campbell, Colonel, 277
Canadian Divisions, 285, 306
Canterbury Battalion, 257, 260–2
Cantlon, T., 83–4
Carmichael, Norman, 283, 286
Casino Point, 60
Chantilly Conference, 12, 13, 325–6,
    336
Chapman, Harry, 143
Chaulnes, 8
Chell, Robert, 60, 76

Chiltern, Sergeant, 300
Chinese Labour Corps, 190–3
Church Lads Brigade, 139–43,
    146–50, 151–2, 155, 203–5
Churchill, Winston, 211–12
Clegg, Bill, 62
Coates, Harry, 55–6, 67–8
Coates, Lieutenant, 310–11
Cochrane Alley, 210, 211
Coldstream Guards, 262–3, 277–8,
    314–15
Coles, Charles, 277
Combles, 306
Comer, A. E., 175
Contalmaison, 114, 117–19, 123, 165,
    207, 312
Contay, 177
Cooban, Major, 147
Corbie, 6, 250
Courcelette, 281, 285, 306
Crease, Fred, 106
Crécy, 191, 196
Cross, Jack, 22–3, 106, 108, 113, 119,
    122–3, 124
Crosse, Captain, 276
Croucher, Sergeant-Major, 124
Cuffley, 299
Cunliffe, Sir Foster, 107, 108,
    124–5
Cunnington, Clem, 72, 73
Curtis, Charlie, 301

Darby, Fred, 98
Darling, Dick, 113
Daynes, Sid, 92
Deccan Horse, 137
Deighton, Ernest, 59, 72–3, 84,
    93–5, 308, 310, 311–12
Delve, Professor, 196
Delville Wood, 76, 133, 134, 139, 151,
    167, 171, 207, 214, 224, 225, 227,
    246, 258, 267, 268, 270, 273,
    275–6, 279, 283
Denham, 142, 143
Destremont Farm, 311–12
Dillsen, Telly, 88–90
Divisional Artillery, 7th, 45

Division, 3rd, 134, 154, 326
Division, 4th, 35
Division, 6th, 267, 277
Division, 7th, 133, 134, 135, 138, 145
Division, 8th, 27, 308
Division, 11th, 307
Division, 14th, 277, 278, 281
Division, 16th, 240
Division, 18th, 60, 232
Division, 19th, 94, 102, 109
Division, 21st, 27, 136, 138
Division, 23rd, 118, 120, 121, 308
Division, 25th, 118, 120, 121
Division, 29th, 35
Division, 30th, 61
Division, 31st, 34–5, 58, 159
Division, 32nd, 49
Division, 33rd, 136, 138, 145, 225, 227
Division, 34th, 16–17, 60, 87, 103, 109, 113, 155
Division, 36th, 58, 242
Division, 37th, 21, 30, 88, 90, 103–4
Division, 38th, 118
Division, 39th, 242, 246
Division, 41st, 281–2
Division, 46th, 30, 32, 34, 66
Division, 47th, 284, 291
Division, 48th, 56, 171, 172, 175–6
Division, 49th, 242, 245–6
Division, 50th, 285, 323
Division, 51st, 156–7, 181, 189, 327
Division, 55th, 207, 208
Division, 56th, 30, 31–4, 55, 56, 196, 251, 258, 291
Division, 61st, 161, 163, 164–6, 173
Division, 63rd, 320
Dixon, 226
Dragoon Guards, 7th, 137
Dukes, Sergeant, 315
Duncan, Reverend Mr, 40, 85, 173
Durham Light Infantry, 308, 310
Dwelly, Jim, 185–7

East Surrey Regiment, 15
Easton, Joe, 112

Easton, Tom, 27, 28, 74–5, 86, 94–5, 102, 112
Eaton, Percy, 23–4, 127, 319
Eaucourt-L'Abbaye, 324
Eccles, Burton, 280–1, 285–6
Eden, Sir Anthony, 273
Elliott, Lieutenant-Colonel, 134
Elphinstone, Colonel, 74
England, George, 182
Esher, Lord, 131–2
Essex Regiment, 60, 76
Estrées, 3
Evans, Gomer, 113
Eversmann, Freiwilliger, 42, 49, 59, 71

Fairfax, Colonel, 61
Falfemont, Farm, 246, 249
Falkenhayn, General von, 224
Fayolles, General, 208
Festubert, 4, 30
Feversham, Earl of, 272, 273, 286
Fitzgerald, Lieutenant, 250
Fitzgibbon, Lieutenant, 119, 125
Flers, 151, 271, 281–2, 284, 285
Flowers, O. W., 213–17
Foch, General, 222, 305–6
Fonquevillers, 32
Fowler, J. S., 169
Francis, Major, 300
Frankfurt Trench, 337, 341–4
Freyberg, Lieutenant-Commander, 326, 332, 336
Fricourt, 36, 37, 86, 136, 140, 156, 167, 260, 261, 262, 267
Fricourt Salient, 60, 76
Frise, 38
Fromelles, 161–6, 170, 173, 177
Frost, Charles, 262

Gaffney, Maggie, 183, 184
Gale, Ted, 224–7, 270, 279–80
Gallipoli, 35, 158–9
Gap Trench, 280, 285–6
Gee, Jack, 257, 261, 269

George V, King of Great Britain, 210–12, 220–2, 255

Gibbs, General, 195

Gibbs, Philip, 80

Ginchy, 207, 208, 246, 258, 259, 313

Glasgow Boys Brigade Battalion, 341–4

Glasgow Highlanders, 138, 146

Glasgow Tramways Battalion, 183

Glavieux, Rose, 9

Gloucestershire Regiment, 246–50

Goat Redoubt, 36

Gommecourt, 24, 31, 32–4, 35, 55, 56, 66, 71, 85, 180, 195

Gommecourt Park, 32

Gordon, Colonel, 24

Gordon, Edward, 21

Gordon, Major, 176

Gough, General, 86, 109, 112, 166, 176, 245, 307, 325, 336, 337, 341

Grandcourt, 7, 63, 324

Grenadier Guards, 15, 186–7, 263–4, 278

Grenfell, Lord, 152

Guards Division, 262–4, 267, 277–8

Gueudecourt, 285, 306, 328

Guillemont, 167, 205, 207–11, 214, 228, 237–40, 249–52, 258, 321

Gwynne, Bishop, 85

Haig, Sir Douglas, 13, 18, 29, 34, 38–40, 70, 79, 85–6, 111–12, 133, 135, 163, 166, 172–3, 176–7, 178, 200, 201–2, 208, 210–12, 220–2, 228–9, 245, 272, 305–6, 318, 325, 336–7

Hales, Arthur, 315–16

Hall, 321–2

Hall, Jack, 226, 227

Hamel, 7

Hannay, Lieutenant, 251

Hannescamps, 91–3, 107

Hawthorn Ridge, 36, 58, 70, 256, 327, 332

Hay, Bill, 157

Hayward, Harry, 246, 248, 249–50

Hébuterne, 31, 55, 66

Heniker, Major, 74

Herbert, A. P., 322

Hessian Trench, 307

Hickmott, Rupert, 261, 287

Higginson, General, 76

High Wood, 134–9, 140–1, 144, 145–51, 152, 156–7, 167, 171, 203–5, 207, 224, 225, 227, 246, 272, 284–5, 291

Highland Light Infantry, 94

Highland Light Infantry, 4th, 181

Highland Light Infantry, 15th, 71–2, 183

Highland Light Infantry, 16th, 341–4

Highland Light Infantry, 17th, 59

Hogg, Quintin, 291

Holford, Sergeant, 122

Holmesdale, Viscount, 263

Hop Alley, 269, 273, 275, 276

Hope, 328

Hopkins, George, 279

Hopkins, Lance-Corporal, 328

Hornshaw, Lieutenant, 64, 65

La Houssaye, 27

Howarth, Snowball, 314

Howell, Harold, 248, 249

Hoyles, Joe, 25–6, 90–1, 93, 109, 112–13, 118, 119, 122, 125, 319, 334

Hudson, Geordie, 257

Humbercourt, 88–90

Hunter, Captain, 72

Hunter-Weston, Sir Aylmer, 70

Hutchinson, Geoff, 286

Illife, George, 147

Indian Cavalry, 135

Indian Labour Corps, 189

Ingouville-Williams, General, 109, 112, 155

Iredale, Sergeant-Major, 244

Jackman, William, 263–4

Jackson, Arnold Strode, 23

Jackson, Harry, 261, 287

Jennings, Lieutenant, 98, 100, 101–2
Joffre, Marshal, 208, 221–2, 325
Johnson, Sergeant, 335
Jolly, Tom, 121
Jones, Duggie, 23

Kain, James, 193–4
Keene, Sergeant Major, 126
Kennedy, Lord Hugh, 263
Kiggell, General, 20, 37, 289, 325
King, Herbert, 150
King's Liverpool Regiment, 61, 210
King's Own Scottish Borderers, 249
King's Own Yorkshire Light Infantry, 59, 62, 267, 268–9, 275, 278–9, 308, 310
King's Royal Rifle Corps, 139–43, 146–50, 152, 155, 203–5, 234–6, 238–9, 272, 280, 282–3
Kippenberger, Howard, 257, 261, 269
Kitchener, Lord, 15, 16, 17, 18
Knotman, Jack, 22
Knowles, Charles, 263
Kyle, Colonel, 341

Lacey, Lieutenant, 308
La Chaussée, 257
Laney, 119, 122
Lansdowne, Lord, 337
Laviéville, 256, 260
Lawson, Nelson, 286
Leaken, Jimmy, 307
Lee, A. E., 274–5
Lee, George, 343
Lefroy, Captain, 96, 97
Leicester Regiment, 262, 276
Leipzig Redoubt, 59, 71, 84, 111, 207, 223, 227, 240
Leipzig Salient, 111
Le Petit, Commandant, 61
Le Sars, 312, 318, 324
Lesboeufs, 277, 281, 285, 303, 306, 328

Leuze (Lousy) Wood, 258, 259, 285, 291, 292
Lincolnshire Regiment, 17
Lissenburg, Dudley, 58
Lloyd, Reg, 316
Lloyd George, David, 305–6, 336
Loch, General, 55–6, 59, 68
London Regiment, 30, 55
Long Valley, 94
Longueval, 133, 134, 135, 138, 139
Loos, 4, 10, 30
Love, Corporal, 174
Lovell, Len, 62, 262, 267–9, 273, 275, 278–9, 297
Lowe, Ernie, 23
Lucas, Corporal, 21–2
Lucas, Private, 95, 96
Lyle, Lieutenant-Colonel, 74
Lyon, Fred, 25, 125, 334

McCarthy, George, 297
McCracken, Dr, 330, 331
McFarlen, Major, 71
McGrath, Ed, 118, 119, 124
Mackintosh, E. A., 1, 129, 253
McNeil Smith, Lieutenant, 74
Mailly Maillet, 341
Malcolm, Neill, 176
Malins, Geoffrey, 255
Mametz, 36, 86, 213
Mametz Wood, 114, 116, 117–18, 133, 155, 207, 261, 262, 269, 284
Manson, Dick, 343
Marlow, William, 322, 331
Marshall, Captain, 94
Marshall-Cornwall, General Sir James, 45–8
Martinpuich, 146, 151, 171, 224, 272, 285, 308
Mash Valley, 171, 175
Maurepas Ravine, 249
Mayhew, Frank, 299
Mellor, Norman, 191–2
Mesnil Ridge, 7, 61, 241, 320
Middle, George, 167–71, 174, 175, 176
Middlesex Labour Company, 190

Milburn, Molly, 331
Millencourt, 102, 103, 112
Minnitt, Bernard, 308–11
Monckton, Walter, 92, 112–13, 124
Monro, Géneral, 161, 163–4
Mons, 224–5
Montauban, 36, 37, 60, 76, 86, 116
Montgomery, Major-General, 132–3
Montreuil, 38–40, 190, 192–3, 210
Morel, Miss, 290
Moricourt, 8
Morlancourt, 135, 255–6
Morrison, Captain, 263–4
Morval, 277, 303, 306
Mouquet Farm, 222, 227, 240, 241, 246, 306
Moxham brothers, 96–7
Muir, William J., 331–2
Munich Trench, 337, 341
Murray, Joe, 293–5, 297–8, 326
Murrell, George, 24, 118–19, 120, 123, 124
Murrell, Ted, 124
Myers, Jimmy, 56, 83

Nab Valley, 59, 72
Neame, Philip, 55–6, 67, 68
Neuve Chapelle, 10, 30, 55
Neven, Major, 74
New Zealand Divisions, 356–7, 260–2, 269–70, 284, 286
New Zealands Division, 4th, 171
Nicholson, Archie, 25
Norfolk Regiment, 276
Northcliffe, Lord, 172–3
Nothard, Bill, 23, 24

Oakham, 25
Oliver, Rainbow, 336
Ollersch, Drummer, 42
Orchard, Trench, 224, 270
Otley, Roland, 272
Ovillers, 36, 60, 73, 84, 86, 109, 111–12, 117, 170

Page, Kenneth, 48
Paisley Dump, 64
Pals, 34–5, 56–7, 58, 69, 159
Paris, General, 321
Parker, Reg, 57, 69
Parker, Willie, 56–7, 69–70
Parratt, Bill, 97
Paterson, Alex, 228–31, 237–8, 239–40, 250–1, 321
Pearce, Bobby, 267–9, 297
Pearce, Sergeant, 251
Pendant Copse, 71
Phipps, Rifleman, 23
Pincombe, J., 313
Pint Trench, 277, 280
Poincaré, President, 132, 222
Poly Boys, 290–1
Potter, General, 134
Pozières, 7, 86, 111–12, 117, 118, 121, 123, 157, 166, 167, 171–7, 207, 240, 241, 307, 316
Pretor-Pinney, Colonel, 21, 104, 109, 113, 118, 120, 121, 124, 126
Prideaux-Brune, Colonel, 126, 319
Puchevillers, 40, 319
Puisieux, 32
Pulteney, Sir William, 112, 272

Quadrilateral, 258–9, 267, 276, 306
Queen Victoria's Rifles, 180
Queen's Regiment, 138
Queen's Westminster Rifles, 181, 195
Querrieu, 257, 272

Rawlinson, Sir Henry, 85–6, 111, 133, 135, 257
Redan Ridge, 36, 57, 58, 70, 333
Redman, Johnny, 148, 149
Reevie, Ernest, 331
Régiment d'Infanterie, 153rd, 61
Reid, Captain, 95
Reilly, Major, 208
Repington, Tim, 173
Reviere, Captain, 122, 124